Don't Die in Bed
The Brief, Intense Life of Richard Halliburton

Richard Halliburton
Courtesy Rhodes College

Don't Die in Bed

The Brief, Intense Life of Richard Halliburton

Chapters on Paul Mooney, Moye Stephens, Elly Beinhorn,
& Pancho Barnes

John Harlan Alt

Quincunx Press

Library of Congress Cataloging-in-Publication data

Alt, John Harlan.
   Don't die in bed : the brief , intense life of Richard Halliburton / John
Harlan Alt.
   p. cm.
   ISBN-13: 978-0-9886232-0-0
   ISBN-10: 098862320X
   From title page: "chapters on Paul Mooney, Moye Stephens, Elly
Beinhorn & Pancho Barnes"
   Includes index.
1. Halliburton, Richard, 1900-1939. 2. Travelers --United States --
Biography. 3. Voyages and travels. 4. Adventure and adventurers. 5. Mooney,
Paul, 1904-1939. 6. Stephens, Moye W., 1906-1995. 7. Beinhorn, Elly, 1907-
2007. 8. Barnes, Pancho (Lowe, Florence), 1901- 1975. I. Title.

G226.H3 A48 2013
910.4 --dc23

BISAC: Biography & Autobiography / Adventurers & Explorers

British Library cataloguing data are available

First Edition 2013

Quincunx Press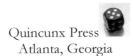
Atlanta, Georgia

To my wife, Judy, for being there and to my daughter, Jen, who discovered Richard Halliburton for me.

Richard Halliburton in Khevsur Armor,
Caucasus Mountains, Soviet Union, 1935.
Like Medieval Knights the Khevsuretis
kept this armor into the 20th Century.
Legend has them as Crusaders lost on the way back
to Europe from the Holy Land

Contents

Richard Halliburton, 1937

ACKNOWLEDGMENTS

In all projects there is an official beginning, although there is always something unofficial, happening before the project itself. In my case, thanks begin with my daughter, Jen, who bought a book about Richard Halliburton, which I read. In the same vein, I should acknowledge Halliburton himself for the life he lived and wrote about, without which I could not have traveled with him in spirit. As I read his works, I found in them a person who deserved pubic attention. He has been too long neglected. A book was in order. My purpose set, I must say that Bill Short was a big help. Barret Library's Coordinator of Public Services at Rhodes College, Bill gave me access to the Halliburton archives, and they provided insight as well as information on the man himself. Bill was always helpful and went out of his way to show me valuable material. He did more than cooperate, driving me past the Halliburton house in Memphis and locating information on Elly Beinhorn in the Rhodes archives, as well as screening *India Speaks* and an amateur movie of *Sea Dragon* and its crew in Kowloon. As to another source in writing this book, I had a stroke of luck with the friendly cooperation of Moye Stephens' son. His son volunteered material that I had not asked for—that I did not even know existed. From his fathers' unpublished manuscript I gained deep appreciation of the era in which Moye and Richard lived as well as great admiration for Stephens' himself. So impressed was I with this pioneer aviator that I almost wrote my book about two people, Richard and Moye, for Stephens both witnessed and participated in early aviation. As only one instance, he was flight instructor for Howard Hughes. A book on both men, though, would have lost focus. That said, the information on Moye was valuable. His letters to his parents provided important material for the flight of Halliburton and Stephens across continents in the open-cockpit biplane Flying Carpet. Again, then, my thanks to Bill and Moye's son, who truly were instrumental. Although she provided no tools, my wife, Judy, insured a mental ambience that made this book possible. While I spent long hours bent over research and writing, sometimes frustrated, her companionship, understanding, and support enabled me to continue. Not only that, I want to thank her for her proofreading and common sense with critical comments. She read my typescript and often trod on my authorial pride but her recommendations and insights promoted needed improvements.

Richard & Ibn Saud,
first monarch of Saudi Arabia

Richard & Foreign Legionnaires,
Colomb Bechar, Algeria

Dad, you hit the wrong target when you write that you wish I were at Princeton living "in the even tenor of my way." I hate that expression and as far as I am able I intend to avoid that condition. When impulse and spontaneity fail to make my "way" as uneven as possible then I shall sit up nights inventing means of making life as conglomerate and vivid as possible. Those who live in the even tenor of their way simply exist until death ends their monotonous tranquility. No, there's going to be no even tenor with me. The more uneven it is the happier I shall be. And when my time comes to die, I'll be able to die happy, for I will have done and seen and heard and experienced all the joy, pain, thrills—every emotion that any human ever had—and I'll be especially happy if I am spared a stupid, common death in bed. (In Richard Halliburton's letter to his father from Paris, December 5, 1919.)

Shouldn't we leave that sort of thing to Mr. Halliburton? (Actor George Sanders on a risky action in *Mr. Moto's Last Warning*, a 1939 film noir with John Carradine and starring Peter Lorre.)

All of man's misfortune comes from one thing, which is not knowing how to sit quietly in a room. (Blaise Pascal, *Pensées.*)

The movie starring Richard

Mary Grimes Hutchison
("Ammudder")

Wesley Junior, twelve

Richard, Nelle, Wesley Jr

Nelle (Nellie) Halliburton

Wesley Halliburton
Courtesy Rhodes College

Richard & monkey Niño

Paul Mooney
Courtesy Rhodes College

Hangover House

Hangover House
Courtesy Rhodes College

Giving Prince Ghazi, later King of Iraq, his first airplane ride.
Seen are two Royal Air Force planes escorting Flying Carpet.
Gunners in the escorts have machine guns trained on Flying Carpet
in case her crew tries to abduct the Crown Prince.

Front row, first on left, Richard Halliburton at Princeton.
Front row, second on left, James Penfield "Shorty" Seiberling.

CHARACTERS

Richard Halliburton
Wesley Halliburton
Nelle Halliburton
Wesley Halliburton Junior
Mary G. Hutchison ("Ammudder")
Ainsworth
William Alexander
Frances Bailey
Pancho Barnes
Elly Beinhorn
Malcolm Boylan
David Laurence Chambers
T.R. Coward
Pyotr Ermakov
William Feakins
Harry Franck
Walter Futter
Irvine "Mike" Hockaday
Captain Charles Jokstad
Fat Kau
Edward L. Keyes
John Henry Leh
Paul McGrath
Paul Mooney
John R. Potter
David Russell
Moye Stephens
James Penfield Seiberling
Walter Gaines Swanson
Gordon E. Torrey
John Welch
White Ranee of Sarawak
Père Yakouba

Sea Dragon

Richard in typical legs-spread pose,
standing on ancient column

Bell lifted on Halliburton Tower, Rhodes College
during construction
Courtesy Rhodes College

INTRODUCTION

I had not heard of Richard Halliburton until one day when my daughter and I were browsing in a used bookstore. She noticed an old book, its blue bleached by the sun, and about some man long forgotten. She picked it up, leafed through it, and showed it to me. We were both curious about it, a bit worn, a bit quaint, and of a bygone era. She bought it, brought it home, and tucked it away to read when she had the leisure. I paid no further attention to it until one evening after she moved to New York City I opened it to discover a remarkable life and personality. The book was *Richard Halliburton: His Story of His Life Adventure*, letters edited by Wesley Halliburton, the father. I found in it the fickleness of time—that somebody famous in his day became forgotten and this in itself was not surprising but the man's life was. Perhaps I should speak of his lives, for he lived enough for ten men. I wanted to know more about this extraordinary person and began searching for his books. I found and bought all of them and, reading them, discovered a sensibility both cursed and blessed with an acute awareness of life's passing. Cursed, in that he felt constrained by a world of unimaginative plodders who measured their days with coffee spoons; blessed, in that his will, drive, and appetite for life allowed him to experience what few can. His life could make a novel, yet he shaped it as poetry. It was his kind of poetry, far from books, close to life as he wanted it.

I came around to the idea of a book on him because his was a gargantuan appetite for life and he is now forgotten. He was a larger public figure than Amelia Earhart, both of the same era. Amelia quickly came into public attention and then vanished, leaving the world to wonder about her fate. Richard endured for almost two decades. Although his public longevity was far longer than hers in their lifetimes, her name has lived beyond his. They both have in common that each disappeared in the Pacific, one in an airplane, the other in a Chinese junk. Unlike Halliburton, she was not forgotten because, in part, the mystery of her disappearance remained fueled by the hope of finding crash remains. With Halliburton there was no chance of finding the boat at the bottom of the ocean. The Earhart legend endures because the public does not know what happened to her. There was no doubt what happened to him and so there was no mystery. End of story.

Earhart's life is noteworthy but Halliburton's is remarkable and because of that I confess a motive for this book—to renew interest in him and his works. He has been neglected too long. The question became, How to restore interest in him and present him to a modern public? The answer appears as his wildly improbable life. It offers adventures and a worldview that should have wide interest. The problem was that he saw and did so much in his brief span that this book cannot include it all. Instead, it does provide some incidents in order to whet the reader's appetite for what it omits. My challenge was to know what to include and what to leave out. He had so many facets to his life, personality, travels, and adventures, that more than one volume would be necessary to cover them all. For this book, I concentrate on a few of his travels and adventures while providing biographical and historical background as well as insight into his personality. To foster an appreciation of what he saw and did, I provide backstories in some instances—including the Matterhorn, the Romanov Assassination, and Halsey's Typhoon. I had tough decisions to make on what to leave out. Although Halliburton attracts interest for his romantic relationship with Paul Mooney, and although I do include Mooney, Paul has been well-covered and the relationship did not need another book on it. For the same reason, little mention is made herein to movie star Ramón Novarro, also a romantic companion. I instead kept in mind the catholicity of Halliburton's appeal. With his adventurous and passionate life, Richard spoke to everybody in his books. He had a wide message and a wider scope. For him, life was to be lived to its fullest, and the world offered broad avenues for exploration. That was his belief and this book focuses on it.

In terms of his passionate intensity, he reminds me of Henry David Thoreau, who wrote,

> My life has been the poem
> I would have writ,
> But I could not both live and utter it.

Richard wanted his life to be a poem in the making.

An instance of how he struck those in his own time appeared on April 13, 1938, when the *Review* of Niagara Falls printed an article on his lecture at St. Patrick's Hall on Victoria Avenue. The reviewer described him as "the embodiment of the spirit of youth today" and noted there was "almost a capacity house." Richard's talk, in which he related some of his adventures, was found to be "breathtaking" and "outstanding in thrills" as well as "grim and stark in every detail." Just as he lived his life, Halliburton spoke with great enthusiasm. The reviewer was fortunate to hear Richard, for this was among the last of his personal appearances. In fact, Halliburton had less than a year to live. But what a life he led.

He seized the day and began his adult life with a passion for new and strange scenes. A brief catalog of places would be these. The Pyramid of Cheops. Calcutta. Delhi. Rwalpindi. Srinagar. Ladakh. Rangoon. Bangkok. Phnom Penh. Angkor Wat. Java. Bali. Peking. The Khyber Pass. The Great Wall of China. Siberia and Vladivostok. Japan and Mount Fuji. The places do not begin to describe his experiences and itinerary but he traveled to them all, not in a jet liner, but afoot or on horseback, or as ship stowaway and at a time when many of Richard's countrymen could only identify on a map Canada to the north and Mexico to the south. His appetite rarely abated.

In his early career he believed he offered his public a different way of looking at the world. He presented his own experiences as testimony of how life can be lived so long as people break the chains that bind them to normal points of view. He reached out to people with his books and although they were written for various readers, he especially identified with boys and girls who read them, for he saw them as still innocent, not captive to the world's grayness. "Youth is everything," he said, believing that time is the fire in which we burn and in the fires of spring he must burn with a gem-like flame.

Seize the day, yes. He believed in it but was not a hedonist because he believed in goals and hard work. At Princeton, Richard was not out of touch with the reality awaiting so many people—nine to five office walls, a product of the slow, grinding glacier of history, the Industrial Revolution. Not that, he said. Not for him. He clearly assessed his strengths and sought to put them in service to a different vocation, travel-adventure writing. In past centuries, vocation implied a call by God to one's purpose in life and Richard's faith was that he had to find real meaning in his life and, as he came to understand it, he believed his purpose was to experience the beauty and intensity of life. Somehow, it would serve him as a business and it would serve his readers, for in his twenties he wanted them to see as he did. They, too, could throw off the imaginary shackles that bound them to their lives.

That said, I regard him both as a remarkable human being and as a man limited by his time and place to a certain worldview. He saw the potential and beauty of life on the one hand. On the other, in his early adulthood he did not see that powerful feelings could be powerfully diverting. For that reason, this book is informed by a tension. What I mean is this. There is the Richard who moved through the world with a passion to explore and experience it. He was not diminished by hardships, by illness, or by threats to his life. He recovered from near-disasters and went on. Then there is the Richard traveling through a world grown increasingly dangerous and evil. While his focus was on the shortness of life, other lives were shortened by the growing menace of fascism and communism. Only as he grew older did his romantic readiness become tempered by politics, war, and modern history. The names of regiments, the types of bombs, and the number of dead or wounded were facts that did not viscerally engage the youthful Halliburton.

His critics found his style too breezy, his enthusiasms too rosy, his youth too obnoxious. I understand why they felt that, but I take him for what he was—a man with an immense gusto for life and, in his youth, a desire to share his sense of excitement, beauty, and adventure with his readers. His prose and worldview were not assumed just for style; they expressed who he was, and that view enabled him to break free where few dared. On the other hand, his were the defects of his successes. That which enabled also obscured. In early adulthood he saw the world as a grand and glorious place without paying much attention to impending fascism and other evils looming in dark clouds on the horizon of the later Twentieth Century.

On the one hand, I marvel at the life he dared to live. On the other, I see what, in his early years, he sometimes did not. Because of this tension, I set him against his times and point out what he might not have noticed in his adventures. In doing so, I offer vignettes of history, a vantage that provides a way to understand him in a larger context. He was a child at the dawn of the Twentieth Century, with the First World War becoming prelude to the Second and he was typically American in that he saw the world changing for the better. He came of age during the Roaring Twenties. He felt lucky to be part of the "ultra-modern generation," as he put it. His last decade occurred against the backdrop of nations stockpiling tanks and warplanes while awaiting the march of boots across beleaguered lands. Within this historical background, Richard Halliburton lived with his character, will power, and energy. He read the newspapers, listened to the radio, and was clever enough to understand what was coming and it had eventual affect on him. Its effect shows in his later books. He had eyewitness encounters with history. Among them, he interviewed Lenin's widow as well as an assassin of Czar Nicholas II and family. To render the significance of these encounters I provide background material for the events—this also for setting Richard against his times.

In his thirties, he wrote about the disaster of the Soviet system and, had he lived, his historical vision would have continued to expand. Despite his desire to make a poem out of his life, the times worked their way into his awareness and this is the way history happens to all of us. We look back on wars and presidents and take supermarkets and shopping malls for granted, yet they did not occur because somebody waved a magic wand. Our lives, like Halliburton's, are history's products. Halliburton fit his life into historical context when he called his the "ultra-modern generation" but that was early on. The Twentieth Century happened to him and he accepted its flappers, speakeasies, and Jazz bands. It was how the world was. The 1920s wore into the stock market's Black Tuesday of October 1929 and in that year another young man, Walter Lippmann, wrote grimly about "the acids of modernity" in his *A Preface to Morals.* At thirty-five Richard had come to accept that poetry is one thing, reality another.

To understand him, Richard must be read as a product of his time and place. He was a creature of Memphis, Tennessee at the dawn of the century and of his parents' values, just as he was shaped by an America that failed to understand its own privileged position in the world. His tone to his readers suggests itself to us today as sometimes rather insensitive regarding what has been called the Third World—but he shared the commonly-held view that people of the Western world offered an instructive relationship to those in poorer nations. For that reason, to paint him in broad strokes would be a mistake. Wherever he went, in whatever remote corner, he was ever sympathetic and friendly, especially to children, whom he saw as without guile, just as he would like to have the world.

Halliburton lived outside history in the sense that he knew he was not a mover and shaker of great events. He understand that history was not made to record his deeds and he actually expected to be remembered, if at all, in a modest way. He grew up among friends and family in Memphis. He lived in California. He died at sea. An unpresuming man, he realized that, statistically speaking, he was no different from anybody else. He was keenly aware that he was among billions of people who have come and gone through this world. Like them, he preferred sunlit days. He would avoid the darker niches if possible. As a young man, Richard sought only sunshine. As he aged, he accepted clouds of grey as facts of life, but he resolutely resisted letting them color his intensity and they only piqued his keen appreciation of time's passing.

In Halliburton's early books the reader finds a youthful enthusiasm, one that critics called naïve, even gushy, but Richard believed in his style and he was, if anything, honest—he meant what he said. Better put, he believed in the meaning behind what he said. His life had to be true to his vision of it. If he did not understate, it was because he wanted the reader to feel the same enthusiasm, the same keen high he had felt at the moment described. He tried to convey with his style but the style pales against his life. With his tenacity, courage, and appetite for living, the man behind the style was very real indeed and he is the one to whom I seek to draw attention in this book. Halliburton's life remains a testimony to a worldview absorbed into Richard's own flesh and bones. His capacity to enjoy life was immense and his joie de vivre made friends for him wherever he went.

The book carries his parents as major themes in his life because they were. This is revealed by his unceasing letters home to them, from boyhood to his last days in Hong Kong. Wesley and Nelle saw him through parental eyes—doting mom and dad toward loyal son—and, indeed, he was loyal with his unwavering responses to them through his letters. Of course, there was another Richard Halliburton unknown to them but this man is also unknown to us except through the people he chose as friends or romantic companions in a life he led far from Memphis and its mores. The romantic-companion aspects to his life have been covered by others, especially by Gerry Max in his fine work largely based on the documents and memory of William Alexander, while elsewhere the coverage is speculative. The speculation was fed because accounts and documents are not so much in abundance as are his letters home, which give the letters their role in this book.

He inherited a strong work ethic from his parents and writing became his business just as real estate was his father's. Once decided on it, he became determined to succeed despite repeated disappointments, rejections, and setbacks. Part of his message was to live with courage and determination. In trying to sell his first book, he met repeated disappointments and rejections but he had in him a will that would not accept defeat. Not only did he sell the book but it became a huge success followed by other books on places where his restless feet next took him. In his mid-twenties, he became rich and famous but did not forget that success is a bitch goddess, fickle and easy to turn on him. His rites at her altar mark his life and it can be argued that he should have seen her as a false idol. That is a counterpoint to his ambition.

Still, his was quite a vision, not just because of its clarity but because his belief in life's possibilities enabled his will and energy. Many youths have felt the same stirrings, the same desire to break free, and he did. In this, he was like Jack London, who also died young after writing works such as *The Call of the Wild*. Long ago, I visited the Valley of the Moon. With rolling slopes of fine vineyards, the Valley is close to California's Napa Valley. At Jack London's ranch I browsed through the writing den where London wrote his later books. From the museum near the site I picked up this, which was London's manifesto, and was also Richard's, although Halliburton had never read it.

I would rather be ashes than dust!
I would rather that my spark should burn out
in a brilliant blaze than it should be stifled by dry-rot.
I would rather be a superb meteor, every atom
of me in magnificent glow, than a sleepy and permanent planet.
The function of man is to live, not to exist.
I shall not waste my days trying to prolong them.

Call Richard crazy if you want but in this he was crazy in a way only few are. The Book of Job tells us "Naked came I from my mother's womb, and naked will I depart." Richard Halliburton's craziness was that early-on he saw this very clearly and it shaped his life.

Pyotr Ermakov, Romanov assassin, c. 1919.
He wrote on back of photo:
"I am standing on the grave of the Czar."

BOOK ONE

Richard atop Popocatépetl, Central Mexico, 1928

THE TIMES & HIS FAMILY

Live! Live the wonderful life that is in you. Be afraid of nothing. There is such a little time. The pulse of joy that beats in us at twenty . . . becomes sluggish.
Richard Halliburton

Levee, steam boat, & cotton bales, Memphis, 1900

THE BEGINNING

Richard's father, Wesley, described his son to the press as "an ordinary human being with light hair, blue eyes, light complexion, five feet nine inches tall, weighs about 140 pounds. He has the general appearance of a lounge lizard and also the manner." Wesley was proud of his strikingly handsome, auburn-haired son but wanted reporters to see Richard as a real person and not somebody they hyped into mythic proportions. His father wanted Richard to be seen like other youths and threw a catch-phrase, "lounge lizard," to reporters—meaning a young man who liked flappers and speakeasies. In fact, Richard was different. He had little use for flappers and speakeasies because his feet would not let him rest in the United States during Prohibition, sending him far from Memphis or even New York and Chicago. He had a hunger for intense life, although as a boy he was diagnosed with tachycardia, abnormally fast heart beat. Despite this youthful infirmity, he became a man with stamina and energy. Wesley could have described his son as having an inner fire, a passion that few possess but that did not make good daily-news copy.

Halliburton experienced the world through his body and this body-knowledge affected his life. At sixteen in his senior year at Lawrenceville he wrote his parents that no preacher should preach unless he could "see the colors in the setting sun, feel a power in the pathless woods." The vibrancy of everyday things became what he believed in.

Poet Rupert Brooke was Richard's hero because Richard found in Brooke a passion, an urgency, for experience, and in this he met a kindred spirit. Two years before he died in World War I, Brooke wrote to Miss Catherine Nesbitt about "the tearing hunger to do and do things." He said, "I want to walk a 1000 miles, and write a 1000 plays, and sing a 1000 poems, and kiss a 1000 girls." Richard also burned with a fever to see it all, experience it all. Brooke had died young and Halliburton's hunger was to live while young because he did not know when he would die.

Richard Halliburton was the popular icon of an era, the handsome, debonair Princeton man, the admirer of Rupert Brooke and Lord Byron. He found adventure and exotic lands while others worked for the dollar. He fulfilled his dream and his fame spread. Today, his books are still found in libraries—pages brown and tattered, perhaps—but they remain on shelves. At one time they sold very well, providing income allowing him to follow his heart.

Five words summarize what he reacted against. To his father's letter hoping that he return to Princeton and live in the "even tenor of his way," he replied in 1919, "I hate that expression and as far as I am able I intend to avoid that condition."

This was not an idle response. As he put it, "When impulse and spontaneity fail to make my way as uneven as possible then I shall sit up nights inventing means of making life as conglomerate and vivid as possible."

To parents he loved and cared for, he was saying farewell to their values, the values of Memphis. He had lived his boyhood in a sleepy town next the Mississippi, had watched the Twentieth Century explode at places like the Somme, blasting out bomb craters, with doughboys going over the top into the machine guns and mustard gas of No Man's Land. In the next decade, he saw the Jazz Age born with its scorn of the older generation and their staid sense of duty. His, he said, was "the ultra-modern generation."

He not only rebuked his father, but he rebuked Memphis when he wrote, "So, Dad, I'm afraid your wish will come to naught, for my way is to be ever changing, but always swift, acute and leaping from peak to peak instead of following the rest of the herd, shackled in conventionalities, along the monotonous narrow path in the valley. The dead have reached perfection when it comes to even tenor!" He was nineteen at the time, and for many teenagers such declarations can be dismissed as adolescent arrogance not yet confronted with hard reality but for Halliburton a fierce determination lay behind the words.

Despite his opinion toward their conventional ways, in his adventures he remained devoted to his parents. Letters home were always considerate of their feelings, trying to sooth them against worry. Of their fears about his Pacific voyage from Hong Kong to San Francisco, he tried to assure his father: "Dad, if I could talk to you about the junk trip, I'm sure you would lose all hesitation over it." In 1921, after visiting the Taj Mahal, one of the most profound experiences of his young life, his letter home said he was in Agra with his notes, but in Memphis with his heart. Four years before his death he wrote from Athens, still the loving son, saying of his pieces for the

Memphis *Commercial-Appeal*, "All my Sunday stories are letters to you. As I write each one I begin it mentally with 'Dear Family'." Although his visits home were brief after graduation from Princeton, he wrote his parents regularly.

In his early career, his parents were somehow deeply entwined in his ambition. When a youth, he had returned to the states after roughing-it around the world and he had a book to sell about his adventures. He walked New York City sidewalks seeking a publisher to launch his career. Editor after editor rejected his manuscript. Discouraged, he wrote home, "Dad, I get such stimulation and gratification from your letters," and added, "We'll get there yet, you and Mother and I. Who and what can resist our united determination!" In 1933, while far away in Hollywood, starring in the movie *India Speaks*, he asked them of the new Memphis house, which he would rarely sleep in, "So you think we'll be in it by February 1st?" The last year of his life, he thought of them while on the other side of the world in Hong Kong, soon to voyage 9,000 miles across the Pacific in a 75-foot junk. He tried to reassure them, "Think of it as wonderful sport, and not as something hazardous and foolish. I embrace you all and will give my sweet mother an extra hug on her birthday. You know how much I love you."

For all his loyalty, his parents belonged to a generation wholly different and this, Richard thought, was why he was so unlike them. Halliburton's was the generation of the Roaring Twenties, the Jazz Age. It was an era of prohibition, of speak-easies and bathtub gin. At the Cotton Club in Harlem, white youth went to hear Duke Ellington, Louis Armstrong, Cab Calloway, and Fats Waller. It was an age irreverent toward history and tradition. A silly song could make the Father of the Country into a hip character in the War of Independence.

> Washington at Valley Forge
> Bitter cold but up spoke George
> Said vo-doe-de-o, vo-doe-de-o, doe
> Crazy words, crazy tune
> All that George could croon and swoon
> Was vo-doe-de-o, vo-doe-de-o, doe

Girls' hemlines went up while their necklines went down. As they rode to football games couples pulled out a hip flask and canoodled in rumble seats. Young men and women did the Charleston. In speak-easies women for the first time could publicly drink whiskey while sitting next men. The Charleston gave way to the Black Bottom and youth took to it as the new dance rage, just as irreverent as the others.

> Now I'm gonna show y'all my black bottom

They stay to see that dance
Wait until you see me do my big black bottom
I'll put you in a trance

There was no defeat in any of this. In this era of new possibilities, Richard wrote of his travels and adventures. You too can do this, Richard said to his readers, if only you cast off the shackles you think bind you. You can visit Dyak headhunters. You can trek across the Himalayas, sail the Moluccan Strait, and climb Fujiyama. Just free yourself with an imagination of the possible.

This was an American message and the myth of capitalism turned on its head. Money? Who needs it? If you dream, your imagination will sustain you. Travel, Americans. You don't need much. It doesn't take great wealth. I, Richard Halliburton, did it on little. So can you. Dream, that's all. Dream and let it become reality.

For the generations who read him, he opened eyes. He took them to Africa, still called the Dark Continent because largely unexplored, a great question mark. Like that continent, most of the world was terra incognita to Americans. Reading his pages, they climbed the frigid air of Mount Everest in an open-cockpit biplane. They sailed the Indian Ocean on a tramp steamer. They spent the night at the Taj Mahal, visited Timbuktu, and marched across the Sahara with the French Foreign Legion. They visited a leper colony on a Greek island, or lived with convicts on Devil's Island. Here was a world beyond Omaha and Poughkeepsie and Cleveland.

He changed with his travels just as he changed with his generation but something in him never changed. He had a debt of gratitude to Memphis, had he thought about it. He believed in respect and common decency. Wherever he traveled, people found him sympathetic to them. He was horrified by the plight of the average Soviet citizen. He respected Bedouin customs in Sudan and Morocco. He had great kindness for children, letting them ride on his elephant as he traced Hannibal's march across the Alps. He even played with them, rich or poor, much to the amusement of their parents. He was solicitous of others' feelings. He sent money to help his parents build their new Memphis house. People regarded him as considerate, helpful, and appreciative. In the plain sense of old-fashioned words, he was a decent man.

His taste for travel and adventure was shaped by stories read to him as a child. He read adventure books with these among them: *Stories of Adventure the World Over*; *On Board a Pirate Junk*; *Life at a Frontier Fort*; *Bill Fasset and His Last Moose*; *Getting Away From Gibraltar*; and *A Race for Life*. He had many others with similar themes.

Unaware of the Second Law of Thermodynamics, that through entropy things lose energy, Richard nonetheless knew the principle intuitively, as we do. While still an adolescent, he was keenly aware of Time's Arrow, that life flows only one direction, from birth to death, and this awareness shaped him into a kind of Peter Pan who admired childhood and youth. He became concerned that things wear out, and knew he would. The wearing-out is a basic law of physics, impartial within the universe, equally applicable to Earth's sun as well as the human body. Like most of us, he would rather have had nothing to do with this wearing-out but there is no arguing against entropy and the Second Law of Thermodynamics.

There was a Peter Pan in him that looked at the door adults held open and Peter did not like what was on the other side. This view of Richard was held by Earle Halliburton, a distant relative whose company figured prominently as a major contractor in the American occupation of Iraq. (U.S. Vice President Dick Cheney was once Halliburton chief executive officer.) As a man, Richard occasionally visited Erle's California estate and played with his young children. They were fascinated with his stories and delighted in his games. Observing Richard with them, Erle believed that Richard didn't like children as adults do. He liked them because a part of him was a child.

The adult world held something the youth did not want. * Toward the end of *New Worlds to Conquer* he writes, "My childhood profited from every comfort and advantage, but as I grew older it became apparent to my father who had planned for me the life of a gentleman that I was of a restless and rebellious nature and not likely to follow his wishes." His tongue is in his cheek when he claims that he "was called Richard after the town's chief patriarch whose life had been so distinguished for wisdom and prudence it was hoped that I in receiving his name might also receive his virtues." He drips with irony and had no desire to live in Memphis, certainly not as a town patriarch.

Richard met novelist Kathleen Norris after he became famous and she often invited him to her California ranch in Saratoga, south of San Francisco. Some of her novels were made into movies starring Mary Pickford. Her husband was novelist Charles Norris, author of *Salt* and brother of California novelist Frank Norris, who wrote *McTeague* as well as *The Octopus*. Richard spent most of his time with the children, hers and her

---

* In *New Worlds to Conquer* he strolled the streets of Buenos Aires as an organ grinder with a monkey, Niño. While he played music on the organ, the monkey held out a hat for the pesos Richard needed to continue his journey. The monkey's name is itself revealing as it means boy-child in Spanish. Halliburton says that Niño had no malice in his own heart and that the monkey was trusting of others, seeing the world and its creatures as good, generous. In early adulthood, he saw Niño and the generosity of Buenos Aireans as the way he wanted to see the world—without evil, without scheming design and with a spontaneously giving spirit.

visitors, such as those of poet William Rose Benet, husband of poet Elinor Wylie and brother of novelist Stephen Vincent Benet ("The Devil and Daniel Webster," and *John Brown's Body*). William was a founder of *The Saturday Review of Literature*.*

The kids roamed the countryside with Richard as their leader. Richard masterminded the construction of a tree house in the crotch of an oak some twenty feet above ground. "You'll fall and break your necks," Kathleen Norris said. More than once she told Richard, "You're like a little boy." One day Richard proposed to the older kids that they go with him on a trip around the world.

They went to Kathleen Norris for consent. She asked the children, "Who'll take care of you?"

Richard replied, "I will."

She responded, "I know, but who'll take care of you?"

She had observed him with the children and saw that he could lose himself with them. Yet, here was also the man who carefully planned projects, who shaped goals, and who took his responsibilities seriously.

When he was on the lecture circuit, a woman introduced him in terms so extravagant that she embarrassed him. He had traveled the globe, had adventures few even dreamed about, she said, and when she was done, he leaned forward from the lectern and smiled at his audience. "I'm none of those things," he said. "I'm just a little boy playing Indian."

Richard Halliburton found in children something he missed in adults—a sense of wonder, something he had in abundance. In *New Worlds to Conquer*, he opens his "Monkey Business" chapter by watching a little girl's eyes brighten as he told her about his monkey in Buenos Aires. It cheered him to look at her and her smile was like a burst of sunshine. "To hear her sing makes me happy for the day."

There was no lingering in childhood. The way was forward whether he liked it or not. Time's Arrow had no other direction. When he was five, Oklahoma became a state. When he was six, on Bloody Sunday two hundred thousand workers marched on the Winter Palace in St. Petersburg and several hundred were killed. He was born in 1900 "in a small city

---

* In *While Rome Burns* (1934) Alexander Woolcott describes Kathleen Norris' ranch. "When I think of it, I hear the click of croquet balls on a greensward fitted with electric projectors so that mere nightfall shall not cut short the delightful animosities of that game. I hear old Nevin tunes [Ethelbert Nevin?] coming faintly through the redwood trees. I hear the gong which warns the swimmers in the pool that luncheon is ready—luncheon served in a sequoia grove, with Mrs. Norris brandishing a huge wooden spoon over the salad bowl, while two youngsters spear the chickens from the pot. . . . I see the unpretentious house and the row of guest cabins along the leafy ravine." Woolcott ends with "nowhere in my wanderings around the world have I come upon any home which seemed so crowded with laughter and good works and loving-kindness."

situated in the state of Tennessee." Youth is everything, he said, and as it turned out, he did not have to grow old. In 1939 he was lost in the middle of a vast Pacific nowhere. In a sense, he escaped having his life fixed by coordinates as it had been in Tennessee. Maybe he would have thought of it as a minor triumph.

TURN OF THE CENTURY

The year Richard became seven, 1907, was like any other year. It had births and deaths, successes and tragedies, loves won and lost, and most beyond our comprehension but some of its events and facts can be listed. In 1907 a speaker at the International Aeronautical Congress stated that flying machines had no commercial or military future. The average life expectancy was forty-seven years. Eight percent of homes had a telephone and a three-minute call from Denver to New York cost eleven dollars. Fourteen percent of homes had a bathtub. Instead, families heated water over a stove then took turns bathing with the same water. Women washed their hair once a month with either egg yolk or borax. If you did not live in a city, you went outside to a privy and had no toilet paper on a roll, for that was not invented until 1907 and was not marketed until later. The average wage in the United States was twenty-two cents an hour. Ninety percent of all doctors had no college education but instead attended medical schools, many of which were deemed substandard by both the press and the government. Ninety-four percent of the population had not graduated high school. Over ninety-five percent of all births took place at home. There were only one hundred forty-four miles of paved roads and two hundred thirty reported murders in all of the United States. Las Vegas, Nevada had a population of thirty. Iowa, Alabama, Mississippi, and Tennessee were each more heavily populated than remote California, ranking twenty-first with its 1.4 million.

He was born on January 9, 1900, in Brownsville, Tennessee. In *New Worlds to Conquer*, Richard writes, "I was born in the early part of the present century," adding that he came "of good family," his "ancestors having migrated to that state from England six generations previously." Actually, the ancestor, David Halliburton, was born in Edinburgh, Scotland and settled in North Carolina, where he died in 1767.

Attention to detail was never Richard's strength. Indeed, he could take poetic license to enhance his narrative. In *Seven League Boots*, he writes about John the Baptist and says of the story, "No doubt I learned it from the huge and somewhat lurid picture-Bible that was a cornerstone of my grandparents' house." He never knew them. All his grandparents had died before he was born.

He moved with his family to Memphis in 1906. It was a different place then, one that we today would find hard to imagine but imagine we must, because Memphis shaped Halliburton. To understand the man we must know something of his origins.

When Richard and his family moved to the city, Memphis had not been thrust into the larger world. Cotton was still king. The city had changed, for the better if you were white, by very little if you were black. The population had grown to slightly over its 1900 level of one hundred two thousand. "Steam boat a'comin'" was still shouted from the levee. River commerce remained very important. Merchants prospered. Affluent suburbs grew. Jim Crow laws were strictly enforced. As called then, "negro" men and women, boys and girls, stepped off wooden sidewalks for approaching whites. Restrooms separated the public into white gentlemen and white ladies with a third, single room for "colored." W.C. Handy's blues was listened to as jungle music, a phenomenon of primitive people— entrancing, driving, but certainly not respectable.

The Mississippi was still Mark Twain's river, the avenue of commerce and culture, the highway of a nation. It was yet Abraham Lincoln's Father of Waters going down to the sea when Halliburton was a boy. Its dominance was not to fade until Detroit and Henry Ford and the Model T brought the need for paved roads. In Halliburton's childhood the river brought prosperity to its burghers and so bestowed an Edwardian mien on Memphis. The city's gentry built their houses for passersby to admire as they strolled on sidewalks, ladies under parasols, men under Homburgs, people greeting one another on Sunday afternoons.

Mark Twain recalled his boyhood on the Mississippi's banks, only a half century before. "After all these years I can picture that old time to myself now, just as it was then: the white town drowsing in the sunshine of a summer's morning; the streets empty, or pretty nearly so; one or two clerks sitting in front of the Water Street stores, with their splint-bottomed chairs tilted back against the wall, chins on breasts, hats slouched over their faces, asleep." Then a "negro drayman, famous for his quick eye and prodigious voice, lifts up the cry, 'S-t-e-a-m-boat a-comin'!'" and "the town drunkard stirs, the clerks wake up, a furious clatter of drays follows, every house and store pours out a human contribution, and all in a twinkling the dead town is alive and moving." Twain writes that "after ten more minutes the town is dead again, and the town drunkard asleep by the skids once more."

12

By 1907 Memphis was not a sleepy hamlet waiting for a steamboat but instead was a busy river town. It had been defined by the river and was the commercial hub for Mississippi Delta traffic.

Mindful of its heroes, in the town center Memphis had a bust of Andrew Jackson, absurdly dignified with a Roman toga. In an October 1874 issue of *Scribner's Monthly*, Edward Smith King admiringly noted that "Jackson frowns upon the tame squirrels frisking" around him in the "exquisite little park, filled with delicate foliage" while watching the animals "climbing on the visitor's shoulders and exploring his pockets for chestnuts." Jackson offered a fitting reminder to citizens of their Southern heritage and for this they had paid tax dollars to build his monument. Some readers must have grunted in reading that squirrels crawled into pockets while others granted King this small rhetorical flourish.

In 1908 the city had sixty white-only churches. Of these, nine were Baptist, six Catholic, seven Cumberland Presbyterian, eight Presbyterian, twelve Methodist Episcopal, eight Episcopal, three miscellaneous, and one each of Congregational, Christian Science and Lutheran. The count specified three "churches" as Hebrew among the sixty. "Colored" churches were not included in the 1908 count.

Its hospitals were four: the Presbyterian Home Hospital; the United States Marine Hospital; St. Joseph's Hospital; and City Hospital.

The asylums and homes were twelve: Church Home Orphan Asylum, Foundling Home; Home for Incurables; Leah Orphan Asylum; Mary Galloway Home for Aged Women; Memphis Day Nursery and Half Orphanage; Memphis Home for Aged Men; Memphis Home for Friendless Women; Poor and Insane Asylum; Refuge Home; St. Peter's Orphan Asylum; and the Anne Brinkley Home. Social Security, Medicare, and states-aid did not exist. People fallen on hard times had nowhere else to go. They swallowed their pride, knocked on these doors, and were thankful for some Christian charity. This, in the days when expectations to act Christian were high. Franklin Delano Roosevelt's Social Security was implemented much later, in 1935.

The city had eighteen men's clubs and two for women, both in the same building.

It had eleven fire engine companies and three hook-and-ladder companies.

It had seventeen public schools for whites from grammar to high school, with eleven for colored and without separate classes for grade level in the colored schools. Of academies and parochial schools it had twenty-one. Its higher education institutions consisted of two medical colleges.

Memphis had six theaters, including the Bijou, where the Cinematograph was demonstrated in 1897. The first Memphis theater with electric lights was The Lyceum, where Maud Adams, Lillie Langtry, Anna Held, and George M. Cohan starred on its stage. But serious, respectable people had better uses of their time. Those who succumbed to such entertainment hoped that neighbors did not notice them buying tickets to a nickelodeon or a stage play. They preferred being seen on Sunday morning when they sat on hard wooden pews and listened to church sermons.

Mississippi steamboats and railroad trains were large in public consciousness. Roads were unpaved as well as bumpy, and traveling long distances by horse and buggy was only for the sturdy and non-arthritic. When people thought about travel, they pictured the river or the railroad. In 1908 Memphis had seven steamboat lines: Arkansas River Packet Company; Lee Line; Little Rock and Memphis; Memphis and Arkansas; West Memphis Ferry; West Memphis Packet; and Planters Packet Company. The city had five railroad depots: Illinois Central; Iron Mountain and Cotton Belt; New Union; Union; and Jackson Mound.

The City of Memphis Hack and Cab Ordinance prescribed that hackney coach drivers be paid fifty cents per passenger and another fifty cents per trunk if the horse carriage transported people from a Mississippi steamboat or railroad platform to any hotel within the city limits of 1899.

It had a mass transit system. The Memphis Street Railway Company ran from car barns at the Southeast corner of Beale Street to various parts of the city, allowing one transfer when a full fare was paid.

Memphis had another side to it.

On Beale Street, it had female boarding houses, a term used to dignify whorehouses. While jazz bands played in honky-tonks, the prostitutes led customers into their cribs, so-called. As the man followed, a child played with a porcelain doll or toy shay, watching the stranger and her mother disappear behind a curtain drawn over the bed. The child's next-day meal was thereby provided for.

When Richard was nine, W.C. Handy arrived on Beale Street with his band, Knights of Pythias, and played a strange, new music called the blues, something respectable citizens with manicured lawns had never heard. Handy had learned its universal power when playing for white audiences. They shouted, "Play some of your own music" and his band did. The negro music had a drive and a rhythm that gradually drew crowds to Beale Street.

Out on the sidewalks, white people heard pulsing, rhythmic sounds coming through walls, a trumpet, a clarinet, a piano, and they went inside, lured by something wholly unlike Stephen Foster's sweet, nostalgic tunes. They found no "Way Down Upon The Sewanee River" here. The music seemed to have no respect for them and what they believed in but they liked it.

For mayoral candidate Ed Crump, Handy wrote a song that became

"Memphis Blues," and was used in the political campaign.

> Mr. Crump won't allow no easy-riders here,
> Mr. Crump won't allow no easy-riders here,
> I don't care what Mr. Crump won't allow,
> I'm gonna barrelhouse anyhow.
> Mr. Crump can go and catch hisself some air.

Crump was elected, probably not because of Handy's song.

A few years later, 1914, Handy published his famous "St. Louis Blues," also unrespectable and ungrammatical with its "my gal done left me."

Today, Memphis has a well-kept and dignified park in honor of Handy and maintained by tax dollars, the budget for it written grammatically.

But in 1909 the well-to-do would never frequent Beale Street to abandon themselves to its lustful, foot-stomping syncopations. They considered it the tom-tom beat of the jungles, the primitive, passionate, orgasmic, in-your-face response to their own sweet, gentle Stephen Foster.

As Memphis slept, the Twentieth Century arrived. In 1906, thirty-two years after Edward Smith King's *Scribner's* article, Teddy Roosevelt was president. U.S. population was about 85.5 million.

Dark clouds soon gathered over the globe, boding the 1914 assassination of Archduke Ferdinand in Sarajevo and World War I. In 1917 the Bolsheviks stormed the Winter Palace in St. Petersburg. In 1933 Adolph Hitler was elected Reich Chancellor of Germany. In 1935 Mussolini attacked Ethiopia. In 1937 the Imperial Japanese Army invaded Chinese Manchuria. In 1939 the German wermacht defeated the Polish army.

In 1900, the year Richard Halliburton was born, all that was part of things to come. Lights had just gone out on the Nineteenth Century with the Twentieth in swaddling clothes. Memphis and the United States were turned inward, isolationist to the core, and away from the corrupt Old World. The guns of August 1914 had not boomed and the doughboys of 1917 had not been sent to No Man's Land.

In 1917 both Memphis and America would watch their young men drafted into the army. In 1900, on a sunny day with warm breeze blowing from the Mississippi, nobody would have believed it.

BIG CHIEF

In 1958, long after Richard had died, long after newspapers and magazines stopped writing about Richard Halliburton, and after his mother, Nelle, passed on, a frail old man with white, bushy eyebrows sat alone in his Memphis house at 2275 Court Avenue in Memphis. Wesley, Richard's father, looked through his window at the street. Leaving his house, with his cane he strolled under shade trees that lined the sidewalks of his neighborhood. He tipped his hat to ladies, nodded at gentlemen, and after a stroll went back to his home. He opened his son's books, leafed through the pages, thumbed through old news clippings about Richard. He looked at their wedding portrait. He and Nelle gazed at the camera and saw the bright future ahead. He picked up a photograph of Richard's brother, Wesley Junior, so young, so much promise, gone all those years.

The year before, the Russians had beaten America into space, hurling Sputnik aloft, arousing the United States into a national debate about poor public education in science. Gyrating his hips, Elvis Presley rock n' rolled teen-age girls into swoons and finally was allowed on prudish Ed Sullivan's variety show. As a white boy, he played a large role in making black music popular. W.C. Handy's Memphis music would soon find worldwide acceptance.

Wesley didn't listen to Elvis. He read about the rock n' roll phenomenon in his study, had looked through his windows out upon the cars and pedestrians but, like the world, they were passing him by. While teenaged girls swooned over Elvis, he watched shadows creep onto the streets and over his life. It was all behind. Hormones and rock stars, they weren't new. This was only a generation thinking it was modern. Richard had called his own peers "the modern generation." Wesley had thought the same about his college days at Vanderbilt. No, this was not a new day, only another one.

That year, James Cortese, a Memphis *Commercial-Appeal* editor, called on the eighty-seven-year-old man. When Cortese showed up at his door to discuss a series of articles the father might write on his long-dead son, Wesley asked him inside and pulled a fifth of Scotch off a shelf and then a fifth of bourbon, telling Cortese to name his poison. Cortese didn't care and just took bourbon on the rocks. For Cortese, Wesley was the connection to a bygone era. For the old man, Cortese was somebody who belonged to the world he watched through the window.

Born in 1921, Cortese read Richard's *The Royal Road to Romance* the summer he was nineteen. Like so many of his generation, he became an avid reader of all Halliburton's books. Years later, he discovered a connection to his boyhood idol. Here was the father, still devoted to stories about the son. Seeing the old man was lonely, himself interested in the story, Cortese became an evening caller. Cortese stopped by once or twice a week and they became good friends. Sipping bourbon together, Wesley named him Bigg Jimm. Cortese called the old man Big Chief.

One evening, Big Chief sat, his arm on his desk, gazing down at his glass. After discussing Richard's fame, Bigg Jimm said of Richard, "Sorta the Elvis Presley of his day, eh?"

The old man looked up from under thick eyebrows. "Richard wasn't involved in all that hoop-la surrounding Elvis Presley."

He went on "Don't ever compare them. Richard was poetry and literature and the arts, not all that bang-bang Presley hoop-la stuff." People thought Presley was something modern but Wesley saw it differently. Elvis did not offer a new day, just another one.

The old man dropped his head and fell back into his thoughts.

He was filled with the past as street lights blinked on, casting a glow on the carpet. He looked at his friend and reminisced. They were all gone, his wife and two sons. He said that he missed his Nelle and added, "I have no Nelle, no Richard, no Wesley." He paused. "All my friends are dead. I can't see to read and I can't hear. I'm no good any more."

Cortese tells us that on another evening the old man was quite matter of fact when he said, "I have lived this long," and he "marked off with his hands about three feet along the edge of his desk" then added "I have perhaps this long to live." With that remark "he measured off a quarter inch with his fingers."

Their friendship lasted about a quarter inch more until Wesley Halliburton died in 1965 at ninety-five.

Wesley is now a name on a gravestone. He and those he loved have faded from memory. Images of his era get rendered as sepia in a Hollywood movie, telling us we are supposed to think of it as bygone, quaint. With its traffic congestion and its Five O' Clock Action News,

Memphis is too busy to remember the riverboats and the cotton bales.

So very much is experienced in a life yet we can only describe it. We cannot have the memories evoked by the morning breeze Wesley once felt on his cheeks, or an evening when he tasted apple pie just as Nelle told him she was pregnant with their first child. We don't know the name of the first girl whose kiss thrilled his lips. What we have left are a few facts but we cannot know the life he breathed into them.

Born in 1870, he graduated Vanderbilt University in 1891 with a degree in Civil Engineering, a rather practical course of study, and one designed to earn a living in the world as he found it. Named after John Wesley, the founder of Methodism, both Wesley and his father, John Wesley, had proper Methodist names although Wesley and his wife Nelle attended Presbyterian services. Still, the name implied Christian character. Husband and wife were observant Christians and maybe religious.

On June 24, 1891 *The DeWitt Gazette* of his home town, DeWitt, Arkansas, stated that Wesley Halliburton "graduated from the Vanderbilt University on the 17th, with the highest honors, receiving the Founders Medal for having received the highest grades in his class during his four years at the University. The Founders Medal in Engineering is considered the highest medal bestowed upon any of the students since it requires more hard work and harder study to get it. It is of pure gold and valued at $50." Wesley had been busy and had even designed a bridge while at university. In Nashville a newspaper noted that a bridge at the foot of Broad Street "is the conception of Messrs. Halliburton and Dyer, who have been students at Vanderbilt for the past four years." With an eye for the practical world of buildings and bridges, Wesley was determined to lay the foundation of a career.

Bridges were solid spans above water and anchored in earth. You left solid ground and always you returned to it. This was a metaphor of his life. Getting across rivers smoothly and easily, that was important. No rafting or boating adventures downstream to the wide sea. You stayed home and raised a family. Children were Wesley's bridge to the future.

His son had no interest in a career so practical. Adventure, yes; engineering, no. Richard's worldview was enabled by the education and comfort his father provided him and in his letters the son expresses his gratitude. The father's worldview helped shape the boy, both in what he rejected and in what he assimilated.

Wesley's father died when he was two and he moved with his mother from near Brownsville, Tennessee to DeWitt, Arkansas. His story has him at the age of two on a farm on the frontier of Arkansas. His first school was small and made of logs with split logs to sit on, where he "learned to spell 'dog' and 'cat' and 'pig' and 'hen' and learned that two and two made four." As he grew, his story recalls him galloping on his mustang over the plains to distant horizons. It invokes, in his own words, "a wild, free and open life," with something in these memories that crept into Richard's own outlook.

We imagine the boy Richard listening to the father's tales of a pony running across a plain as far as the eye could see. There it was. The burst of freedom, wind in the face, a distant horizon, and sheer delight in being young, with the world new. Here is more than a touch of the son but with its dirt farming, log cabin school, and tragedies it also holds hardships Richard's boyhood never knew. Then sorrow came.

His mother, Juliet, died when he was thirteen. One day in September 1883 Wesley received a message at his school in Covington, Tennessee. He read that she was gravely ill and he was to hurry home. Rivers were the highways then. The steamboat, he recalled "was the only means of transportation." It took the boy "down the Mississippi, then up the Arkansas and White Rivers, and by Wagon to DeWitt in Arkansas."

"When I arrived," he said, "it was too late: my mother had been buried a week."

An orphan, the boy, with his two brothers, was given a court-appointed guardian, W.E. Cappell. This was the knock of fate and it would change his life. He was lucky. Here, though, would be no joy in riding a mustang on an Arkansas plain.

Cappell was not a hardscrabble farmer but a man of parts in a small town about sixty-five miles northeast of Memphis—Durhamville, Tennessee, today not even a dot on a map. Wesley might not have known it at first, but he had a promising future and a kind protector. At fourteen he was enrolled in a Fayetteville, Arkansas preparatory school. This prep school was a harbinger of what he could now expect from life.

While Wesley was at the school, some school chums decided to take a trip to New Orleans and he asked Cappell for permission to go. In what followed we assume he told this tale to Richard, who took it to style his own adventure when he ran away from home. The difference is that Richard went to New Orleans but did not stop there.

In the father's story a certain élan was passed on to the son. It is a tale of youthful folly and fun, of being spunky and getting away with something. The spirit of the story crept into the way Richard regarded life.

Wesley wrote Cappell that he wanted to go with his pals but his guardian replied, "Too young." As an indicator of their good relationship, the boy was not afraid to write Cappell again, saying he "wanted to make the trip more than anything." Cappell relented and sent money although the other boys had departed.

In New Orleans he did not find his pals after a week of looking and still had a wonderful time, alone in the Big Easy in 1884 at age fourteen, rather unlikely today. The final day of his adventure, he spent his last dollar on hot dogs and the merry-go-round. He would grow out of this impulsiveness. Richard did not. Wesley clutched his train ticket in his pocket knowing it would get him only through the coming stretch of the journey and not the stretch from Corinth, Mississippi. After that, he had a problem.

Next day, the train stopped in Corinth for twenty minutes and the boy's stomach growled but he had no money. Watching the passengers get off at the depot to buy grits, pickles, hog's feet, and pies from the station cafeteria, he decided to wait for his chance. The boarding whistle sounded, smoke snorted from the stacks, wheels slowly turned and still he waited. At the last moment, he lunged for a pie on the counter. He legged it for the moving train, feet pumping "like crazy."

Once back on the train, Wesley munched on his pie, dreading his encounter with the conductor. Moving through each car, asking ticket please, the man finally came upon Wesley. He asked the boy where he was headed and Wesley said to Fayetteville, Arkansas.

No money, huh?

No, sir.

Fayetteville was a long way off for a boy with no money. After further questioning, the conductor learned that Wesley's older brother Garland lived in Jackson, Tennessee. He put him off there. Garland insured that he got safely home.

Richard must have heard this story many times as a child. He must have laughed at his father's race for the train with a pie in his hand. His father rode without a ticket. In Halliburton's books the reader finds a pride in being able to get away with things, to put one over on petty officials. He stole free rides on the trains of India. He took forbidden photographs of Gibraltar.

After Wesley graduated Vanderbilt, he took a job at sixty dollars a month as an engineer in Phoenixville, Pennsylvania at the Phoenix Bridge and Iron Company. "I couldn't take it," he told Cortese, "sitting at that desk all day and sometimes all night. It drove me crazy." He probably told Richard how he grew tired of looking through office windows. His next step became part of family lore.

He had inherited a farm, rather run-down, but nonetheless his, and it must have inhabited his imagination as a place where he could feel the breeze on his cheeks and the sun on his forehead as he sweated, working for himself and his own future rather than as a drudge in a dark office. Over time, the farm took on a life of its own in his mind, and he probably caught himself thinking of it when he should have been examining blueprints. He could see himself in its fields, behind a plow, harvesting crops.

He chucked it all and moved to the farm in Tennessee—to Brownsville, Haywood County, Tennessee, the place he left as a boy when moving to Arkansas with his widowed mother.

Wesley's reason for the move—greater freedom—was not lost on Richard.

Wesley got up each morning to fresh air and outdoor labor. He never looked back on the office in Pennsylvania. He had come home.

He pioneered in the use of clover and peas to build top soil, regarded as an eccentric innovation, earning him the nickname, "the pea crank of Forked Deer," a nearby river. One day he was no longer seen as a crank but as far-sighted when the Tennessee State Agricultural College invited him to join its faculty. No, he said. For him, it might as well be Pennsylvania. The classroom was one more office and this rejection was something Richard heard about.

He branched out into business. The Memphis city directory of 1923 reveals a listing for "Halliburton and Moore, Farm Timber and Cut Over Land. Dr. D.T. Porter Building. 10 N. Main St." His business office remains to this day. It is number seven of the Porter Building in downtown Memphis. Completed in 1895, the Porter Building was the tallest building south of St. Louis. At the time, skeptics believed it was too tall to withstand strong winds and would blow over in a storm. People paid a dime to ride elevators to its top; many were so frightened they took the stairs back down.

His office was only a place to hang his hat, a place to do business, then to travel to land he bought as he developed his farm real estate business. It was a future and a hope. It promised a comfortable living for him and his family, a good education for his boys and fine prospects for their future. Wesley moved through his years with an even tenor, feeling the wearing grind of daily demands but taking pride and pleasure in his wife and sons as well as the life his work made possible for them. Year in, year out, as he ate ham and eggs and read the newspaper before going to work he could see that the world's troubles remained as he grew older. Each day became another one.

Big Chief and Bigg Jimm sipped their whiskeys those evenings at 2275 Court Avenue and the old man talked long about the past and about his once famous son. He told Cortese that although Richard had been lost at sea for many years he was still very proud of him. "People think I don't want to talk about Richard," he said. "I do. I glory in it. If it wasn't for Richard, nobody would know me." He poured another shot of bourbon into Cortese's glass.

One night, he looked at Cortese. "I miss my Nellie," he said softly. The house was still as cars passed by—as somewhere in the night a radio played

"Blue Suede Shoes" and "You Ain't Nothin' but a Hound Dog." Big Chief finally said, "I have no Nellie now. I have no Wesley, no Richard. I have nobody. And when I die it will be the end of my line of the Halliburton's."

At his Memphis grave in Forest Hill Cemetery Midtown stand four Roman columns on a triple-tiered plinth. They are next a stone in the earth. On the stone is engraved *Wesley Halliburton, 1870-1965*. Two stones rest next his, one reading *Nelle N. Halliburton, 1869-1955*, the other *Wesley Halliburton Jr., 1903-1918*. The fourth stone in the earth reads *Richard Halliburton, 1900-1939, Lost at Sea*.

The Court Avenue house stands today under shade trees as people go about their business in Memphis. On their morning run, joggers listen to music through ear buds. Out on East Parkway, the rush hour begins with drivers thinking about asking the boss for a raise, or spending more time with the kids, or they listen to the latest news out of Washington, DC. The sun will set, with people homeward bound and next day it will rise again. Wesley might have said it is not a new day, only another one.

NELLIE

Nellie is her name of record although as a woman she dropped the diminutive ending and became Nelle. She was born March 11, 1869 in Paris, Tennessee, her father John W. Nance, her Mother Amanda, neé Blythe. The 1910 Tennessee census for Memphis lists her as Nellie. With her husband, Wesley, and sons, Richard and Wesley Junior, the same census lists two people probably household servants—Hafford Porter, twenty-two, and Cato Walker, twenty-five. Mary Grimes Hutchison, or "Ammudder," Richards' surrogate grandmother, is also listed. Little is known of Nellie's parents, John and Amanda and, indeed, little is known of her background.

In the 1880 census for Paris, Henry County, Tennessee, she is also found as Nellie. Her last name Nance, she is eleven years old and a schoolgirl with her father and mother both born in Tennessee. They are not listed as heads of the household. Instead, she is in the house of C.B. and Love Crutchfield, fifty-two and forty-two respectively. The document reveals an Amanda Nance age fifty-five. Nelle's father does not appear. That year's census has a John Woods Nance in Brazos, Texas. Crutchfield's was a large household, comprised of eighteen people, some of them probably negro servants. With so many people in the household it would seem that Crutchfield was well off but he was not. He is listed as a clerk in a store. The residence was probably a boarding house where Nellie's mother paid for room and board. This indicates she came from a background not wealthy.

Richard and his brother, Wesley Junior, must have heard often how their parents met. The first chance encounter of Wesley and Nellie was probably part of family legend. Perhaps the boys listened to their father explain that one Sunday afternoon he passed Nellie Nance, then a fetching twenty-something, and turned to glance at her, with parasol and bustled skirt. Perhaps he told them, "Right then and there, I decided I'd marry that girl some day."

Perhaps.

Fact is, they were married in Tennessee in the Brownsville Methodist Church on July 19, 1898. On that date, about a year and half before turn of the century, they did not know she would have another fifty-seven years of life until 1955 or that he would follow her in ten years after seeing the opening salvoes of the Civil Rights movement. They did not know that one of their boys would die before adulthood and that the other would leave them without grandchildren in their middle age. In family legend they could reconstruct the past but were helpless before the future.

Richard's parents were not apolitical. Because of their state's past, throughout their lives they remained staunch Democrats, a political allegiance held by Southerners since Reconstruction and Carpet Baggers. They had little confidence in Republican Warren G. Harding. This was confirmed by the Teapot Dome Scandal and publication of a book, *The President's Daughter*, by Nan Britton, who accused Harding of fathering her illegitimate child. They had even less confidence in Calvin Coolidge. They passed their views to Richard. In 1933, when lecturing in Chattanooga, he wrote home that, to cheer up the Southern audience, the announcer told them President Coolidge, a Republican, had just died. Speaking before a wide assembly the announcer was confident of no mixed response in the hall. In *The Glorious Adventure*, Richard wrote that his companion Roderick Crane was always berating Halliburton's "Democratic partisanship."

He shared their politics, although Nelle took on social responsibilities. Lecturing before a women's club in New York, Richard told the club president that his mother was "president of the biggest club in the South." The middle-aged Nelle Halliburton was local president in the Nineteenth Century Club, an organization continuing in the United States today despite its dated title. A notable in Memphis society of her day, Nelle was President of the Club's Memphis chapter, although to many of its modern members her name is buried deep in a dusty list of past presidents. Before, during, and after Nelle Halliburton's presidency, members tackled many issues: needy mothers and children; public sanitation; health; education; employment; labor conditions. The Club ladies got women hired, including a police matron for female prisoners in the city jail and a female sanitary inspector at the Board of Health. They saw to the formation of the Shelby County Anti-Tuberculosis Society and a new city hospital. They played an important role in bringing higher education to Memphis in the form of the West Tennessee State Normal School, now the University of Memphis. They initiated a municipal clean government campaign, calling attention to violations of the liquor laws and widespread gambling and prostitution. They demanded the ouster of corrupt officeholders. During Nelle's presidency the membership rose, reaching fourteen hundred members in

1926.

Under her leadership, the Club sold the old building and in 1925 bought a Union Avenue building, once a wealthy burgher's home and still Club headquarters today. In this regard, her name and her role are found in the 1932 *New York Times*. The *Times* informed readers about the sale of the previous building and that the Club "sold the pool and building under the presidency of Mrs. Wesley Halliburton when it was decided to move further east, to the site of the old Le Master home on Union."

Her sense of civic affairs did not rub off on Richard, probably because he saw it as duty, something of even tenor. Richard shouldered individual responsibility; he learned it from both parents and not as something passive but as proactive. He was determined to make a success of his life. His mother accepted leadership roles. His father was an entrepreneur.

Together with Wesley Senior, she gave him an appreciation for social standing. Richard enjoyed his celebrity and the entrée it offered to dinners with the rich and famous—at least in his early years. Nelle did not shun recognition within Memphis society. Because of her son's celebrity, in 1930 she was named Most Distinguished Mother by the Memphis Cooperative Club. He was a popular writer, his books on best-seller lists. His books meant high regard among her lady friends and she received a good deal of publicity in the Memphis press, where she advised other mothers, "Give your best to the child." Her child became a man in absentia, who rarely came home for long, so she took solace in his success.

He gained from both her and Wesley a view of the world that had to do with bloodlines. Like her husband, she was a creature of her epoch and had an interest in ancestry, claiming to trace it to Huguenots on her father's side as well as to Scotch soldiers and adventurers on her mother's. She believed the Nance's went back to Nantes, France. In 1921, while visiting France, Richard spent a night in Nantes. To his mother he wrote, "If it's true the Nances come from Nantes, I'm among the spirit of my ancestors. *Nance*, though, can also be followed to a Cornish origin, *nuns*, meaning *valley*. A definitive answer must be left to genealogists, for the English Channel, after all, is not that wide, and allowed a free exchange of people in either direction. Anglo-Saxon as well as French surnames can be found in either place, Cornwall and Normandy." He is saying to her, You might be right mother and then again you might be wrong.

Theirs was a time just after 19th Century Frenchman Hippolyte Taine, who claimed that nationalities had racial characteristics transmitted in a manner that can be described as vaguely Darwinian. Taine defined race as the innate and hereditary dispositions a nation's people bring into the world. His meaning lingers in our modern clichés, which offer the French as rational, the English as practical, or a nation of shopkeepers, as Karl

Marx described them. Taine's perspective was widely held by the public and people were of good stock or they were not, both racially and socially. This view helped Rudyard Kipling arrive at his "White man's burden" in an epoch when nations of the West saw their responsibility as "civilizing" undeveloped countries.

Nellie had an influence on Richard that was aesthetic, this as distinct from Wesley as practical—civil engineer and businessman. She was artistic, bringing to her son a sensibility for beauty in painting, music, and poetry. Richard was left to sort-out the two temperaments as he found them in himself. She graduated spring of 1894 from the Cincinnati College of Music, now part of the University of Cincinnati. That fall she became head of the music department at a female college in Brownsville, Tennessee, where she met Wesley. She introduced Richard and his brother to the objects of her sensibilities, although she might have had less effect on Wesley Junior. Between the boys, Wesley Junior played baseball outdoors with his pals while Richard liked the indoors. "Richard had a violin," Wesley Senior told Cortese, "and he fiddled on that damn thing until I had to take it away from him and send him outside to play." Her influence would last. In London, Paris, New York, or other cities, Richard sought out symphonies, operas, and ballets to attend. His letters home regularly describe his opinion of the music and the dance, revealing a developed aesthetic sense.

On quiet evenings the young couple sat by the fire as a baby grew in Nelle. Three years after Richard, Wesley Junior arrived. He grew into a boy different from his brother. Wesley Junior liked competitive sports such as baseball, while Richard preferred riding alone on Roxie, his horse, or romping with his mongrel dog, Teddy, or playing his violin in the house. Wesley was a robust boy among robust boys and liked their comradeship. Richard liked the companionship of his father. Black and white photographs show Wesley with the same light hair as his brother's. They reveal family resemblance, although Richard's forehead was higher. When twelve, Wesley had a portrait taken of himself, dressed in suit, tie, and starched collar, a young gentleman with hands folded together, and sent it to Richard, away at Lawrenceville Academy in New Jersey. A fine looking boy, Wesley must have thought he had the bright future ahead of him. He did not live long.

By November 1917, Wesley was ailing. It burst into profound illness. Wesley's condition was not unusual in those times, when so many fell prey to unknown diseases. In the Halliburton accounts, it is alternately termed as heart trouble or rheumatic fever. The parents took their son from his school in Lawrenceville, which he attended in Richard's footsteps, and returned with him to Memphis. Richard hurried home from Princeton for the Christmas holidays and was in Memphis when Wesley died. His father was holding Wesley at the time. To James Cortese, Wesley described his boy's last moments.

"I was sitting, holding him on my lap, it seemed the only way he could be comfortable, sitting up. And as we sat there he died. I called to Nelle and Richard, 'Wesley's gone!' "

The death of Wesley cast a pall over the family and each coped in his or her own way. Wesley Senior grieved inwardly in his usual stoic manner. Nelle found herself in the depths of something she couldn't comprehend.

In it, she reveals a deep need that made claims on filial devotion. In a letter to Richard she remembered her sons as boys at home, where she was comforted by their presence. After Wesley Junior's death, she fell into a depression that demanded reassurance from Richard. He had to reach into the depths of her sorrow lovingly to sooth her fear that he did not always hold her near in his thoughts.

After the funeral, he returned to Princeton and she wrote to tell him he could get on with his life while her pain was too deep for that. Tomorrow he could "get to work" while she "will have only reminders and recollections." Her pain was inconsolable and she told him it was. He was free to live while she was stuck in the past. He could let Wesley slip from memory while she could not. She compares her condition to his and in the comparison implies her dark state, which he cannot begin to understand. She wants him to know of her black mood in order that he be reminded of her as he goes through his own days. The suggestion here is of a kind of emotional blackmail in which she made Richard responsible for realizing her condition and sympathizing with her, although it was perhaps not consciously intended as such. From Princeton on January 9, 1918 Richard writes her as the comforting son, "I'm miles away in body but, like Wes, in spirit I, too, am with you in the sitting room upstairs."

Before Wesley's death, in September, she had written Richard, about him and his brother. "My Darling—you can never know how lonesome this old house is without you and Wesley." She tells him that she wanders in their rooms and looks at their "straw hats, for instance, and nearly die." She was separated from them, finding it difficult to accept the fact of her separation.

When Richard went back to Princeton he was what they had left. His brother's death left him with a feeling of responsibility toward his parents. He wrote consolingly to Nellie, "What is left of our family is more of a unit than ever." Wherever he traveled on the globe he said in his letters that he was with them. His letters always sought to please despite any danger he was in.

Emotionally, she might have held him too close. As a consequence, Richard tried to reassure her of his devotion on the one hand, while on the other he kept his distance by writing or calling and only occasionally visiting.

Like his mother, Richard also could make nothing of Wesley's death, except to realize that you never know when you are going to die and it helped shape the rest of his life.

On May 31, 1921, he wrote to Nelle. In this letter, three years have passed since the death in the family, yet Nelle apparently is still depressed. His own mood reflects the season, happy, sunny, and he uses the season to try to lift her spirits because the 31st was also his brother's birthday. Of the day, he asks his "Dear Mudder" if it isn't "splendid that Wesley's birthday comes at such a beautiful season of the year?"

We gain the sense that he is writing for his mother as much as for himself. He seems to be reaching to lift her out of a deep mood into a fresh perspective. He seems to be saying to her, after all, three years have passed. Life must go on. His words are tactful. "It is a great consolation to have today a day of flowers and sunshine and happiness, rather than cold, gray weather." He refers to the winter of Wesley Junior's death. He continues, " Year by year we drift farther away from the time when he was such a vital part of our family, when it was impossible to contemplate the four of us being ever any more or any less, but the succeeding years can never dim the memory of him as he was at fifteen. He will still be so when we are old. He would have been nineteen today, almost grown and moulded. We can remember him always only as a fine-looking curly-haired youth. I always think about you, Mother, on May thirty-first and love you more that day."

He then reminds her to pull herself together. "Well, I do not believe he would have us despond because he is dead, but he would have us love his memory." This letter shows he cared about her, and understood reciprocal feelings in her.

We know her mainly through Richard's letters home. One in particular is revealing. It was written after Richard had stopped in Memphis for a brief visit on his way to New York for the lecture season and heard them express their disapproval of Hangover House, an overly expensive home he was having built in Laguna Beach, California. During the visit something happened between him and his mother and so in the October 15, 1936 letter he begins with "Mother Dear." He tells her "this is a letter just for you. Sometimes I want to love you specially and apart from Dad and discuss things that concern only you and me. We're not a very demonstrative family, and so I have to tell you what I sometimes fail to show."

"I have to tell you what I sometimes fail to show," he says but does not tell her what that is, leaving her to re-read that he loved her "specially and apart from Dad" and that he wanted to "discuss things that concern only you and me."

In the letter he did not discuss anything concerning the two of them but went on to write about Hangover House and its construction. He could say nothing more intimate than what he had already written. He was right in saying they were "not a very demonstrative family." Throughout his life he guarded against demonstrating unpleasant feelings and worked at smooth relationships.

He tried to charm and sooth people. In the construction of *Sea Dragon* he struggled with an increasingly querulous crew and acted as the peacemaker rather than the man who should knock heads together to get things done. Instead, he blithely believed that all would turn out all right, despite his fraying nerves. He says to his mother "we're not a very demonstrative family" and his words carried over to his problems on the docks at Kowloon in China.

In Princeton he was far from Memphis but she thought that one day he would come home. With Wesley Junior recently dead, she wrote she was lonesome in a September 1917 letter and added, "But I pull myself together and know it's for the best decidedly for you to go and finish your education, but instead of you being the orphan chile, I'm the baby about you—I'll try and make the best of it until you are thru and then I do so hope I can be near you always." Here is a curious reversal. She is the baby, suggesting dependence that he was expected to support. For Richard, the expectation was too much. She did not get her wish. He chose not to be always by her side.

Richard's letter home, dated October 15, 1936, indicates a depressive aspect to her personality, maybe mood swings. In this letter he writes, "I was so relieved to find you recovered from the long misery of last summer and returned from your trip so young, and high spirited." The letter tells us that her misery lasted for an entire season and was not simply a temporary thing. The duration suggests a genetic component of depression, perhaps aggravated by the risks her son took. Certainly, she worried about him and probably his continuing adventures unnerved her. At first, she lost Wesley Junior but still had Richard. After Richard died her bereavement lasted years.

She clung to Richard's memory as revealed in a poem "Mother o' Mine," by Rudyard Kipling collected among Nellie's effects in the archives at Rhodes College in Memphis:

> If I were drowned in the deepest sea,
> *Mother o'mine,*
> I know whose tears would come down to me,
> *Mother o'mine, o mother o'mine!*

After Richard's death, she copied it, putting it away with her keepsakes. She took it out now and then to think of his light hair, his fine teeth, his brilliant smile. Years before his death, fear hit her heart whenever the telephone rang or a knock on the door announced Western Union. Then he was gone and no more letters home. No more infrequent visits. No more fear and perhaps that was the only good thing.

She lost both her sons and their pictures were all she had left. Back in 1918 Richard had written her, "What is left of our family is more of a unit than ever."

AMMUDDER

While Richard and Wesley Junior grew, Wesley Senior worked the development of his farm real estate company and Nelle taught music at a women's college, where she became head of the music department. At the college she met Mary Grimes Hutchison, who would figure large in Richard's young life. He grew up calling her Ammudder, dedicating *Seven League Boots* "to Mary G. Hutchison, who with patience and understanding first taught a small boy to love ages that passed and places that are far away." Ammudder was a name from his childhood, probably in his efforts to say grandmother. His grandparents deceased, she was their surrogate. As he sat on her knee, she read him Greek myths of bold men and gods. He traveled the world in his imagination, soaring aloft with Aladdin on a flying carpet, diving into the sea like Neptune with a trident. After he became famous as a world traveler and adventurer, Richard still wrote letters to her, signing them Sonny, offering her a child to replace the one she never had. She never married and had no close living family.

She had a room at 207 Garland Avenue, Memphis but spent much of her time at the Halliburton house. The 1910 census lists her as age thirty-eight and part of the Halliburton household. The Halliburton's became the family she had lost. Richard, in a sense, had two mothers. When Nelle was not available, he had Ammudder. During his travels, she sent him money, and he sent her gifts. In his letters home, he often mentions her and gives her his love.

At age eight she determined to become a teacher. As a young woman, without husband, she resolved to be "married" to her profession. Her father died when she was six, her mother, when she was eleven, her grandmother passed on when she was fourteen. Born in Kansas City, Missouri, after her father's death she and her mother moved from there to the family homestead at Hutchison Station, Kentucky, named for an ancestor. Merely the name of a road by Paris, Kentucky today, the place was close to Lexington. After four years at Science Hill School, Shelbyville, Kentucky, her formal education ended. She became a teacher in Tennessee at Athens Female College, where she met Nelle Nance.

In 1906, Nelle and Wesley moved the family fifty miles from Brownsville, Tennessee to Memphis, where Nelle taught music at a school established by her friend. The school was Hutchison School founded in 1902 by Mary.

Because Nelle taught at Hutchison School, Richard was enrolled in it at six years old. Writers on Halliburton have said that the school influenced his personality and their arguments have gone like this. His teachers were women, his classmates girls. At recess, he played with girls. In class exercises, he worked with them. At lunch he ate with them. As a boy, he enjoyed steady feminine attention, from teachers and students. He was different, and stood out, which must have imparted in him a sense of his own specialness. That would make a case if it were true, but it is not. These writers assume that the school was then as it is now, exclusively female. In Richard's time it was co-ed. In the first few years, both young girls and boys attended. By 1913, Miss Hutchison established it as a college preparatory day school for girls.

According to its mission statement, the school guided girls in Christian principles and ethics, which remains a purpose today. Mary G. Hutchison remained its owner and principal until 1947, when she retired and sold the school to Dr. and Mrs. William R. Atkinson.

To this day, the school figures prominently in the city. Now on Ridgeway Road, in 1925 it was moved to a Union Avenue location, with larger campus, including a main building for administration and classes, a gymnasium, music and art studios, a kindergarten, a lunchroom, and the cottage, which was Miss Hutchison's home.

She is buried in a plot with the Halliburton family at Forest Hill Cemetery, Memphis. Her stone is engraved

Mary G. Hutchison
1872-1962

SCHOOL DAYS & THE BATTLE CREEK SAN

I'm very grateful because I wouldn't take a $1,000,000 for it.
Richard on his restless nature.

Vintage post card of the Battle Creek Sanitarium

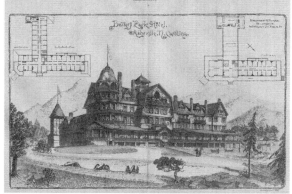

Battery Park Hotel, Asheville, NC

THE HESATATION WALSE

The year is 1913. It is summer in the mountains nestled between the Blue Ridge and the Appalachians. Richard is out of school and on vacation with his parents and his brother, Wesley. Escaping Memphis for the cool mountain air of Asheville, North Carolina, they are at the Battery Park Hotel, built in 1886 in the Queen Anne style. Colonel Franklin Coxe, a railway investor, purchased the highest hill in Asheville and built a hotel in the grand manner with rooms rambling over twenty-five acres on Battery Park Hill. With its steeply sided roofs, its several brick chimneys, it caters to visitors with genteel taste. An orchestra provides music and ballroom dancing. It offers fine cuisine, modern bathrooms, and even elevators. To its south, guests can see Biltmore, the one hundred twenty-five thousand acre estate constructed with two hundred fifty rooms by George Washington Vanderbilt II. He fell in love with the rolling valleys and trees after he stayed at the hotel. In this 1913 summer at the hotel, Richard looks across the hills to the Biltmore Estate and then turns to watch guests walk the hotel's greenswards. Along with frock coats and homburgs, the men wear big bellies, a sign of success, while they escort ladies with diamond brooches.

In that same summer, far away in Moscow, Lenin draws up his resolution for the Central Committee and titles it, "The Task of Agitation in The Present Situation." He opens it with a statement: "The situation in this country is becoming increasingly acute." Lenin is right, of course, but it is becoming acute in the world as well as in Russia. In slightly more than a year, the Twentieth Century will erupt with the mobilization of troops across Europe because of a single assassination in Serbia of Arch-Duke Ferdinand. The acute world situation will make Lenin's task of agitation easier, bringing down the Czar and bringing in the Bolsheviks.

Serbia is far from North Carolina and farther still from the minds of people at the mountain resorts that year. The ladies wear skirts six inches from the ground. Anything higher would be scandalous, like short hair, which riff-raff such as syndicalists and anarchists wear. Ladies' shoes are low-heeled, patent leather, often with contrasting buckskin tops. Well-bred women wear no rouge. Only actresses and burlesque girls wear it. The ladies' undergarments, chemise and petticoat, are thickly ruffled to emphasize their feminine shape and a new corset, a bust-improver, is worn. The brassiere will come later. Gold watch fobs dangle from gentlemen's vest pockets. They smoke Havana cigars on terrace lounges while reading in the *Carolina Gazette* about the suffragettes in London who marched on Number 10, Downing Street to demonstrate against Prime Minister Asquith. It is time for women to vote, the British women insist, and it is time in the United States. On that day, the gentlemen read that Woodrow Wilson supports America's isolationist policy, which they also support because the corrupt Old World should be left to fend for itself. They will re-elect Wilson on the campaign slogan, "He kept us out of war." He will get them into it in 1917.

In about 1912, Vernon and Irene Castle introduced a new dance form called the Hesitation Waltz in which the dancers halted on the standing foot for one full waltz measure while the other hung, slowly moving through the air to the floor. The hesitation lay in waiting for the other shoe to drop. This was a modern innovation to the classic waltz, something fresh, if not daring. Fresh was okay; daring was not. The Battery Park Hotel was far from Bourbon Street in New Orleans or Lenox Avenue in New York where people danced ragtime to the Grizzly Bear, the Turkey Trot, the Bunny Hug, and the Camel Walk. The Hesitation Waltz offered couples on ballroom floors something still stately while a bit more lively waiting for the other shoe to fall. It was an expectation wired into the human brain. It was the foundation of living, always looking forward to the next moment.

Richard wrote his Ammudder about learning to dance the "Hesatation Walse." He had taken dancing lessons and at thirteen was a skilled dancer. In that 1913 summer he and a girl glided across the parqueted ballroom of the Battery Park Hotel, husbands and wives whispering about their youthful grace. As waiters brought the next dinner course, people sat watching the boy and girl. They smiled as the children stepped across the floor. So young and so cute, they said. The boy wore knickerbockers and the girl had a large bow at the back of her white dress. Later, his letter to Ammudder expressed his pride at his skill: "I found a little girl, Cornelia McMurry, over here who had danced with me" at Tate Springs, in East Tennessee, where his parents had a summer cabin. He tells Ammudder, "She and I are the only ones in the hotel who know how to do the Hesatation Walse so we simply delight in showing off. My little pardner went home today so all I have to dance with is grown women." He adds that he misses his dog, Teddy.

His dog was not all he left behind. He was changing from the indoorsy fiddler and wanted other boys to play with. In a letter, he says that at the hotel "boys are a rarity" and then, for thirteen, he shows himself adept at ironic wit: "I think I will go to a museum."

At Asheville on the greens, his father taught him to play golf, both father and son dressed in plus-fours. He wrote Ammudder about the game, "It's splendid, all except the balls which are a great bother, because you lose them and spend three-fourths of your time hunting for them. I lost three this afternoon and they were each a 75 cent ball."

He found friends and did not have to go to the museum after all. He wrote "two other boys and I took a six mile tramp through the mountains and got lost. (That is why it was six miles.) Immediately after we got back we played half a dozen games of box-ball. We then went around the golf course two times."

Playing with his pals does not signal the only change. The boy in 1913 likes the outdoors and cannot rest. "We stopped to watch a fox chase and set out like little fools and tried to keep up with the hounds, after running a mile we came home and played four sets of tennis until it got so dark we couldn't see the ball. We came in just in time to dress and get my supper, and now I will dance until 11 o' clock."

In 1913 Richard was alive with energy and by 1920 he saw his youth as a brief gift. He felt in his body what his hero, poet Rupert Brooke, had articulated as a desire to "do a thousand things" and "walk a 1000 miles" and "sing a thousand poems." The thirteen year old grew into a young man with an urgency, a restlessness, and an appetite that needed life more vivid than dances on a ballroom floor.

Fire destroyed the Battery Park Hotel in 1920, after Richard learned to spell correctly the Hesitation Waltz. The correct spelling came years after he knew how to execute the steps with grace, one foot poised in mid-air, syncopated to fall in measures of time. His body knew the dance before his memory spelled the words.

As for hesitation itself, time has none of it. The hotel's builder, Colonel Franklin Coxe, died in 1903. George Washington Vanderbilt II died in 1914. Vernon Castle died in 1918. Lenin died in 1924. Irene Castle died in 1969.

A SUDDEN ILLNESS

Before Richard's fifteenth birthday in January of 1915 he came down with a malady that perplexed his parents. His heart beat too fast. Wesley and Nelle could not understand why and called a doctor, who gave it a name, tachycardia, and offered a cure, bed rest. Tachycardia is a generic label for a variety of conditions that include sino-atrial tachycardia, atrial fibrillation, atrial flutter, reentrant tachycardia, mediated tachycardia, atrial tachycardia, multifocal atrial tachycardia, junctional tachycardia, and ventricular tachycardia. These all make sense but only to a physician.

These new names for an old condition mean that in Richard's time physicians did not know what he really had—only that his heart beat too fast. Atrial tachycardia is the kind modern physicians frequently diagnose in early teens and young people rarely die from it. Today the upper normal limit is one hundred beats per minute for people age fifteen to adult. Richard exceeded that with the exact count unknown. Other than linking his illness to hyperthyroidism, Wesley does not say much about his son's condition in his book compiling Richard's letters, only that while at Memphis University School Richard "developed a fast beating heart" and that as tachycardia it was due to an overactive thyroid, which can accelerate heart rhythm. Wesley says, "He was removed from school and put to bed." Richard must have found the cure worse than the illness but rest he did. January passed, then February, then March. By April he was not getting any better. There was a place to go, though. People went there to get well.

The place in Battle Creek was called the Sanitarium or the San by its patients, and was written about by T. Coraghessan Boyle in *The Road to Wellville*, later made into a movie. Founded in 1866 on Seventh-Day Adventist health principles, in 1875 its medical superintendent was Dr. John Harvey Kellogg, inventor of Kellogg's Corn Flakes, evolving into the Special K brand of cereals. Kellogg coined the term sanitarium, widely used today. Snap, crackle, and pop as once heard in television commercials were not his idea.

Six stories high, in its day the Battle Creek San was visited by Henry Ford, Harvey Firestone, George Bernard Shaw, Thomas Edison, Admiral Byrd, William Howard Taft, Warren G. Harding, Amelia Earhart, and Johnny Weissmuller, who played Tarzan in movies. They entered through the marbled Grand Lobby and strolled along colonnaded walks, relaxing with sun flowing through windows onto trees in the Palm Garden Room.

Kellogg's Battle Creek idea was that sound health and fitness resulted from good diet, exercise, correct posture, fresh air, and proper rest. Battle Creek came into national prominence as a "place where people learn to stay well," as Kellogg put it. As a testimonial to his principles, he died at ninety-one on December 14, 1943. He held over thirty patents for food products and processes. Add to that his exercise, diagnostic, and therapy machines as well as peanut butter, menthol nose inhalers, and the electric blanket.

Today property of the Federal Government and known as the Hart-Dole-Inouye Federal Center, the building is workplace for two thousand employees of the US Defense Logistics Agency, which provides materiel logistical support to all branches of the United States military, invested—as the government might put it—in maintaining the nation's health. The San's splendid rooms remain, quartered into cubicles for clerks and minor officials. Filigreed gold and blue murals adorn the arches above elegantly curtained windows. Great chandeliers hang from the ceiling of the dining hall, once the largest in the world, which bureaucrats today call the cafeteria. The foyer has a ceiling of ornate and exquisite woodwork. In 1976 the San was added to the National Register of Historic Places.

Battle Creek for Richard Halliburton in April 1915 was cold, far from Tennessee's clime as he stayed with his mother there but it warmed through the summer. That August, a wealthy industrialist, Mr. Johnson, invited Richard on a camping trip into Michigan's North Woods and then into his home in St. Paul, Minnesota. Johnson immediately liked the boy. That Mr. Johnson took a liking to Richard is not surprising, for Richard had an ability to charm people, which remained a notable quality throughout his life. After returning from the camping trip with Mr. Johnson, Richard wrote from St. Paul to tell his parents, "Mrs. Johnson is very lovely to me. She sings and plays and dances. They have everything to make life pleasant—the lake is the greatest factor."

The boy still loves to dance but writes home, "I realize how strenuous dancing can be." He means that he must watch his heart and its fast beat and says, "It accelerates by very little—some, of course. Does that sound as if I 'disregarded my physical affliction and put pleasure first'?" This question must be a response to parental warnings to go slow. In him remains a strong impulse for movement, energetic, fast-paced. He is a curiosity in this, for we find him a sickly boy at fifteen to become a hardy adventurer as a man.

His parents had expectations of him. After Battle Creek he would return to Memphis University School and then attend Vanderbilt University, where his father graduated. With degree in hand, he would settle down in Memphis and go into the real-estate development business with his father. He would meet a sweet young girl, marry, and bring grandchildren to visit them on Sunday afternoons after church. They would have a favorite cookie for each child. It would work out that way in the best of all possible worlds for Wesley and Nellie Halliburton. The Battle Creek Sanitarium opened different doors for Richard.

In a letter home he wrote of things they had not considered for his life. He said, "Now about school. I have not been idle over this subject at the San. I have talked to boys from Calvert and Lawrenceville. The L. boys love their school. I will be near New York, surrounded by friends. I have my heart set on Princeton—50 L. boys go into Princeton each year. About Worcester or Phillips Academy I know very little—they are not Princeton prep schools. It's 3:00 A.M. so I better go to bed."

They could have insisted on their own plans for him but he said, "I have my heart set on Princeton." They could have insisted but they knew better. He wrote "Its 3:00 A.M." Here is a covert message to his parents. He was willful and did as he liked because they were distant and could do nothing about it. It was his way of saying, Here I am, your impish son ignoring parental admonition.

A wise parent knows how much room to give a child. They assented to his wishes.

Lawrenceville it was, then. Lawrenceville had a reputation as a prestigious secondary school in New Jersey and near Princeton University. Located on seven hundred fifty acres in the town of the same name, it boarded boys, grades nine through twelve. Even today, most graduates attend Ivy League colleges or other highly regarded institutions. Its graduates include economics Nobel laureate George Akerlof, Saudi Prince Al-Faisal, Honduran President Ricardo Maduro, publisher Malcolm Forbes, and Disney CEO Michael Eisner.

Halliburton did recover from his fast heartbeat, although it would return upon occasion. He never found a cure for it, but fortunately he seemed to have outgrown it as a major problem as evidenced by his whirly-gig pace through life, often at the limits of physical exhaustion as when he trekked over the Himalayas to Ladakh.

The sojourn at the San underscores that Richard Halliburton succeeded in his adventures not because he was a prime physical specimen but that he succeeded in spite of himself. And success was what he was after. The San led to Lawrenceville and Princeton. The friends he made in those schools, the influences of wealthy chums, left their mark on him, most probably in his desire for money, stuff that kept slipping through his fingers. Strangely, it is also significant in that his stay did not leave him as somebody who worried about his health. To the contrary, he pushed his body to its limit, soldiering on even when sick and exhausted, sometimes becoming terribly sunburned with his fair complexion.

HIS PERSONALITY

In the human scheme of things, some are born lucky, some less lucky, and some unlucky. None of us chose to be born nor did we choose the circumstances of our birth. Among many possibilities, we could have come into the world as American, Canadian, Scottish, French, Mexican, Afghan, Chinese, Indian, Indonesian, African, or Mongolian. We could have had wealthy, middle-class, or poor parents. We are born into chance. Democritus said that everything existing in the universe is the fruit of chance. A Yankees fan might find that to be oh, so true, and say that baseball imitates life. Players have winning streaks and slumps. A hitter may go a season with a great RBI and next season find himself being struck out or sending fly balls straight to an outfielder. That's also life. As Forrest Gump said, Life is like a box of chocolates—you never know what you're gonna get. People and baseball players are like gamblers betting against the house, which has the odds stacked in its favor. Sometimes they win; sometimes they lose. Democritus' universe is the house, and it doesn't care if gamblers or other people go bust.

By accident Richard was born with a predisposition he valued highly, knowing he was lucky. Of his "restless nature" he wrote, "I'm very grateful, because I wouldn't take $1,000,000 for it." It was precious to him because he had visions of the possible where others saw only walls. He felt exuberance, a confidence, in realizing his visions, while his less gifted friends looked ahead to another step along the way to the rest of their lives. There was in him an outlook that welcomed the world with open arms and his vitality fed its own increase.

He was extraordinarily gifted in disposition—his life attests to that, as it is one that few are able to parallel. People could only read about all he did and saw because they were bound to the morning coffee and evening newspaper of their days. In Halliburton they found somebody who had

41

slipped the bonds holding them and with sometimes-wild energy delighted in a life that for them was not only improbable but impossible. No, there wasn't any bad luck for Richard. He didn't see himself with any aberrancy. He saw himself as enabled, unlike those who did not feel as deeply, see as far, and move as passionately as he did.

He knew he had the luck of the draw despite, or because of, infirmities that befell him in early life. They provide an explanation for his personality and his infirmities were documented. They include his fatigue and tachycardia, or rapid heartbeat that sent him in his teens to the Battle Creek Sanitarium. The physician linked his tachycardia to an overactive thyroid. In his twenties Halliburton again fell ill, and a New York City doctor diagnosed him with hyperthyroidism. While in New York struggling to get published, he wrote letters home in which his complaints about restlessness increase. He was lucky in that his form of hyperthyroidism helped give him the buoyancy for which he was very grateful.

His hyperthyroidism offers an explanation for his exuberant personality. In his condition, an overactive thyroid gland (an endocrine gland in the neck) secretes a greater than normal amount of thyroxin. Because thyroxin causes cells to burn fuel and release energy, signs and symptoms of hyperthyroidism are increased energy level, nervousness, increased heart rate, and weight loss.[*]

When happy, he was very happy and felt a great need to be busy and in this he evinces common manifestations of hyperthyroidism. Writing his parents that he had an incessant need to move, to be physically active, he often walked from Princeton to Lawrenceville, six miles distant, where he visited his former teachers and avoided the dorm room of his deceased brother, Wesley Junior. He walked to Trenton, ten miles away. Once, he tramped to Philadelphia, taking all night with barely time to catch the train back to Princeton for his morning's classes. He could stay up nights and be bright and ready next day. He chanced the edge of the possible because his energy demanded release and he considered life more vivid with risk. Not a professional diver nor a good swimmer, Richard leapt off a cliff twice into the Well of Death, better known as the Sacred Well of Chichen Itza, in Yucatán, Southern Mexico—only one instance of his taste for risk.

---

[*]Greater thyroid hormone secretion can mimic symptoms of bipolar disorder. However, insufficient documentation exists for clear support of a down-side cycle in Richard. Biographical accounts are insufficient to support it as well, which is not to say he was without mood swings. Indeed, suppositions and arguments can be made because he does report lows following highs but a fuller assessment requires sufficient documentary evidence and expert analysis. Maybe certain letters were destroyed by Wesley but in any event there is not enough evidence.

Richard's narratives reveal repeatedly that for him emotional drive was attended by risk. With the drive was his habit of thought, which was to plan for the next project, the next travel, the next adventure, and to build his life as he leapt from goal to goal. His goals typically were large, requiring great commitment. In Europe while Mike Hockaday saw the sights, Richard prepared for his future by keeping a writer's journal, writing home that his vocation had begun.

In their globe-trekking flight together Moye Stephens observed that although Richard was not physically strong he had something, a panache that carried him through his adventures. Asked in an interview about Halliburton's impetuosity, Stephens said yes and no to the question. Yes, in that impetuosity involved "everything he did, practically." No, in that Moye qualified his response with "he planned a lot of stuff." This planning was part of the goal-oriented Halliburton. Stephens added, "But he was a very warm natured person, and very generous."

Halliburton would have wholly rejected a physicalist explanation of his life and understandably so, for it wraps all up too neatly, leaving out the mystery of who he was, who we are. It fits all into a neat, explainable box. It omits his sense of beauty and the sublime, his deep feeling of life's brevity, his urgent need to live while he had youth. Only he gave meaning to his life. The cells of his body were servants to his will.

His life was abnormal in the way poetry is. With his personality, enthusiasm, drive, and sensibilities he was dealt a hand in life that few people are lucky to receive. He felt grateful and did not want his life limited in the way many people limit theirs. He wanted to do a thousand things, sing a thousand songs. He saw possibilities and horizons where others felt caution and turned to protection in the herd.

Through his own perseverance and imagination he sought a channel for his biology and to his credit he found one in adventure-travel writing but that discovery lay ahead, not when he wrote from Princeton to his father during World War I and said, "There seems to be something in turmoil inside me all the time. I intend to keep myself in control until the war is over and my education, and, then I'm going to bust loose and let my restless, discontented spirit run its course. The idea of leading a monotonous confined respectable life is horrible to me. Some day the fires inside are going to break out and I'll push my working table out the window and just be a wild man. I've got in the habit of running instead of walking. Something keeps saying faster, faster, move! It isn't nerves. I sleep like a log. I feel wonderful all the time."

It isn't nerves, he writes, meaning he feels no anxiety. Indeed. Anybody with anxieties would never dare to have done what he did. He wants to be a wild man. His roommates are tame men and he exercises will and choice to conform to collegiate expectations but after that watch out. He sleeps like a log. He is on top of the world.

Richard bears witness to feeling more things and feeling them more deeply, having more experiences and having them more intensely. He opened vibrantly to the springtime of his life, knowing it would soon end, and passionately felt the bird of time fleeting with but a little way to flutter. He saw life with limitless possibilities and sought to spend his days joyfully, knowing he could not take them with him. For the breadth and depth of his vision, the vividness of his feelings, he would not have traded places with anybody.

PUPPY LOVE

By 1916, Richard was smitten. Frances Bailey had "brilliant blue eyes and wheat-colored hair." He met her in the summer of 1916, spent mostly in Brownsville, Tennessee. Born in December 1896, Frances was slightly older than Richard and mature enough to be a teacher at Brandon Training School, offering grades one through twelve as well as a preparatory academy in Shelbyville, Tennessee for Vanderbilt University. He was agog with her as the focus of his life. He was sixteen; she was twenty. That summer they swam but swimming was different then. They frolicked in the bloom of youth, with Richard hidden in a one-piece suit, red and white stripes neck to knees and Frances concealed by ankle-length bloomers and a shirt-waisted blouse. They danced in the moonlight. They went on long walks. He tried to think of funny things to say. And when she laughed he heard something new in his life, a strange emotion the romantic in him liked. It was what he had read about. It was love. Love can refer to many things—to passionate desire, to intimacy, to sex and Eros, to parental love, to Platonic love, to religious love. At sixteen, Richard did not understand all this but he did know that she set his heart a-beating. In the first blush of romance, he saw his as a sad tale of unrequited love.

The summer of 1916 could not last. He was pumped with enthusiasm, intensity, and passion, especially for her. It was all too much. By August, he returned to the Battle Creek, Michigan Sanitarium for a check-up and rest. His letter to Frances Bailey is filled with professions of devotion. He is a puppy in love and, although he cleverly uses words in his struggle to understand new feelings within himself, they have the skill of a puppy. He cannot rest at the San because his imagination is wild with her.

"Dear Madam, This letter is from Dick. But I don't like the salutation so I'll begin again. My dear Miss Bailey, I haven't received any. I don't like that either. I'll try again. Dear Frances, but everybody starts off that way.

45

Frances Dear, that suits me, but I suppose you think it is very familiar. I'll try again. My Darling Frances, Breath of my life! Oh go stick your head in the well! I can't get started. I'll wait and let you write me how I should begin my letter to you."

He continues impishly, conceiving of a tunnel to express his scandalous nature. "I have just created some scandal. This seems to be my talent (and I love my calling). There is a tunnel which runs from one of the buildings to another. I thought I would give a girl friend of mine an adventure and take her thru." He describes crawling through the tunnel, then looking through a cellar window at a "missionary meeting on the lawn." He really enjoyed the escapade, but said, "I hope you don't think me a degenerate."

Then he moans like a puppy. "Why don't you write me?," adding, "I wouldn't mind going to school if I had you for a teacher."

The letter spans several pages until it ends, "If anybody were to ask me if I liked you any more, I would say no . . . . But I do love you."

In this as in so much else, he didn't give up easily and instead of resting at the sanitarium he is longing. In another letter, he writes to his "quite Dear Frances" that he is "watching the mails for an answer" to his last letter. He continues, mocking Robert Bond, his rival for her affection: "My brain won't work today I've been sitting here half an hour trying to think of something to say and nothing will come but poetry. Here's one:

> Little Frances mean as hell,
> Pushed dear Robert in the well

No, I don't like to make fun of Bob, so I'll begin again.

> Little Robert hung his sister,
> She was dead before we missed her,
> He is always up to tricks
> Ain't he cute, he's only six. "

In competition for Frances, he turns another boy into somebody even younger than he is. Her love is his goal and he is Clever Dick vying against Silly Bob.

Richard repeatedly asks her to write him but she does not. Her silence only fuels his determination to prevail. He is not prevailing. In his letters, we find his sense of rejection a new feeling for the sixteen year old. The more he beseeches her the more his esteem is threatened.

He writes again, "Queen of Brownsville! How do you like that salutation! I have just thought of another question to ask you. If you are opposed to writing me on general principles, did it ever occur to you that you might at least show a little sympathy, and respond to my attempts to encourage or continue our friendship, a friendship which on my part was and is very close and, well I hope it will be on yours." He is frustrated and says, "Did it ever occur to you that I'm in earnest about you? One could not get me to say the gushy things that most boys write to their best girl friend."

He thinks she should recognize the depth of his feelings for her because they are so obvious to him. He asks, does she "understand how I feel from my straight-forward, possibly silly letters? I express my esteem for you by the fact that I write every day, and not by such disgusting letters as this." Disgusting letters as this. He is disgusted at himself for his groveling but he must make her recognize—as he does—the importance of his feelings. His interior drama should be clear to her but the harder he tries to convey it the greater her distance from the spectacle he presents.

No question but that he had it and he had it bad. She was his romantic ideal, the girl of his dreams, all he expected the fair sex to be. Her continued silence only sank him deeper into yearning's thrall. "My own angle [sic], darling sweetheart, You have not answered my last love note and my heart can scarce stand it for you know I love you more than all the rest of the girls on earth. I think of you every moment and love you, love you, love you. Dear, please promise me never to pay attention to other men, for it kills me to see you forget me when you are always before me, sweetheart mine. You are the only girl I ever loved and you will always be. . . . Your own devoted, Fool."

Other men, he says, for his are grown-up feelings, so he thinks.

He writes a letter to himself, signing it Frances Bailey, and mails it to her because she won't respond. It's the only way he can get a reply. Richard says to himself, "Dear Dick, I received your nice long letter more than a week ago and I intended writing you before but my social duties and my art keep me so engrossed I have no time to waste writing you. . . . Brownsville is very hot and I do as little as possible. Robert Bond and I have grown more or less indifferent since Ridley has been coming to see me. He is the cutest boy I ever knew and I like him so much. . . . I see the twins[*] occasionally and we always speak of you, or rather they do. . . . Well I think I have done my duty but please don't write so often because I can't answer all of them. Hoping that you will write more sense when you do write, I am Yours respectfully Frances Bailey."

After mailing it to himself and receiving it, he then sent the letter to Frances.

"Hoping that you will write more sense when you do write," he says—

---

[*] Atha & Woodlief Thomas. Dr Woodlief Thomas was Chief Economist, Banking & Currency Committee, Federal Reserve Board, Washington, DC.

Halliburton the young pup is able to see his excesses and that they keep her at a distance. He can satirize himself. He understands his own silliness and this self-mockery was a life-long trait as revealed in his books.

The exhibitionist in him enjoys making fun of himself. In *The Royal Road to Romance*, while in Spain he demonstrates self-mockery at the Alhambra. Trying to get a photo of the pool in the Court of Myrtles, he falls into the water. He shouts and his fellow traveler Paul McGrath comes running and found Halliburton "sputtering" in shallow water. McGrath looked on the bold adventurer and broke into belly laughs. Richard cannot be accused of arrogance.

His letter to Frances—the one he first addressed to himself—had affect on her because she did respond, although her reply is lost. By her response, maybe Frances understood that, instead of the passionate, ardently insistent Richard, here was somebody who was capable of self-mockery, of distancing himself from the situation. His letter to himself implies a boy who can step outside his own skin and see his own foolishness and his exhibitionist style in the letter fits the pattern of his exhibitionist behavior in life—in his lectures he performed for audiences and in his books for readers. For readers he demonstrates his French in comic repartée with a girl on the Riviera. He claims to have bought slaves in the Sahara when he in fact did not. All this was part of the public Halliburton, with another self hidden from everybody except those close to him. He was a very private person and, though he needed good friends, he sought solace far from adoring crowds.

Frances finally replied.

After receiving her response, he sits down at his desk to pen a new letter to her, this one just as imploring as the others. It reveals his relief that he has not been rejected but has a lover's despair because of Robert, his rival. "You darlin' child," he begins with a phrase used by his mother, and later returns to "funning himself" when he mourns that "I'd give half my diamond mines if you loved me as much as Robert."

He has no crystal ball for his future but in the letter he reveals his expectations for it, again with tongue-in-cheek. "I went to a very good palmist. He read my hand for an hour, but I believe he read my mind, for he told me every thing I thought about. He told me I would make an unusually good traveling salesman, and, funny, I have been told that twice before and I feel so honored." There is truth in his self-satire. Traveling, yes, but selling in a different way—to find material to use in selling his books.

Travel would indeed become his calling.

In the letter, he expects a certain financial status as an adult: The palmist said Frances Bailey "Did not give a kick for me but would in the future. I could have spit nickels when he told me that. But as he lied in one place, by saying that I would be married on a salesman's salary, I can't believe anything he said."

No salesman's life for him. His eye was on the brass ring, although he had no idea where he could grab it or when it would come by. Something had to be in his future, though, and while at Princeton he became extremely bothered as to how to make that something happen.

Frances returned to teach at Brandon Training School on September 7, 1916. Richard had expected to see her before she left but she had misguided him. Before returning, she was at home, though he thought she was not. This was more than a hint that she did not want to meet him but, a headstrong adolescent, he writes, "Dear Friend Schoolteacher . . . . To begin with I think you are just awful, you wrote me in one letter that you were leaving on the 5th, I planned to reach home the 2nd and come at once to [Brownsville]. The day I left your next letter came, leaving the 2nd, or the day I reached home. Now don't you think you are awful? Why did you change? Here I am sitting up high and dry and no Frances or nothin' but hot weather. . . . So Robert went with you did he?" He asks her "What would [she] have done?" if he had seen her with Robert and says, "I shudder to think, for Robert and I would have fit and bled and hated each other."

Cute, these letters, with a feisty charm like a puppy chasing its tail but smooth they are not. Curiously, they set the tone in his books for recurrent vignettes in which he vies for a lady's attention, often to lose her to a competitor. Perhaps here begins a lack of confidence in any amorous relation with women. Certainly, he was gushed over by middle-aged matrons at literary luncheons but his letters and books never have him hitting it off in a serious relationship with a female his own age.

Frances Bailey became Francis Bailey Appling. She died in 1982. Her daughter, Eleanor Appling, said that her "mother had at least six young men writing to her that summer and fall" of 1916.

When asked by biographer Jonathon Root what Frances really thought of Richard, the daughter answered, "I don't know."

The daughter did come to understand the affect on Richard of her mother's rejection. In Freudian terms, Eleanor experienced a kind of transference by Richard after she heard him speak at one of his lectures. This was after he had become prominent as a wealthy and celebrated author.

To understand the meeting between the daughter and Richard imagine a large auditorium filled with people as his lectures usually were. The lecture ended and a line formed for people, each with a Halliburton book in hand, to meet him and to get his signature on the book. She waited in line and finally her turn came to speak to him. She introduced herself and told him she was Frances Bailey's daughter. He said something and brushed her aside, turning to shake the hand of the next person in the queue.

LAWRENCEVILLE, PALS, & THE BIG SHOW

In Lawrenceville, New Jersey, The Lawrenceville School is a boarding school founded by Isaac Van Arsdale Brown, a town pastor, in 1810 as Maidenhead Boarding School, a rather curious name for a boy's school. In 1883 the architect of New York Central Park, Frederick Law Olmsted, designed the campus into a pleasant green with three hundred seventy-one trees. Funded by wealthy donors, the school developed a system of houses, some named Haskell, Kinnan, McPherson, Reynolds, Dickinson, Griswold, and Hamill. There were housemasters and house presidents from whom school presidents were chosen. Cylindrical turrets above rectangular buildings reflected the Victorian century in which they were built. They were designed with an eye for European tradition, transplanting it to the new continent. Walking pleasant paths, chatting with pals, gazing on dignified architecture, the students had reason to believe in their future as Lawrenceville believed in its own, still existing today.

In fall 1915 Halliburton began school at Lawrenceville and enjoyed good years there. He was happy walking under the cool shade trees, or feeling the sun warm on his cheek, or delighting in the splash of flowers by the dining hall. In summer birds chirped in trees while in winter a peaceful and still whiteness lay over the campus.

Also that year, Private Donald Fraser, 28th Battalion, 4th Division, Canadian Expeditionary Force, jumped into a shell crater to escape German Maxim guns firing six hundred rounds a minute. Years later, grandchildren read in his journal, "At this time a strange incident happened; a German, without [weapons] and equipment, climbed over the parapet on my right and ran into No Man's Land, shrieking and waving his arms, apparently stark, staring mad. He ran about twenty-five yards, wheeled round in a circle several times, the circles narrowing each time, then flopped dead." In that month the British gassed German troops, just as had been done to them. The Battle of Loos had begun and ended with over sixty thousand casualties suffered by the British Expeditionary Force.

Richard read the news and discussed the war with other boys and he was itching to get into the Big Show, as American youth called the conflict. In 1915 a German U-boat torpedoed the *Lusitania*, bound out of New York for Liverpool, costing almost twelve hundred lives, one hundred twenty-three of them American. The boys were confident that the United States would soon enter the war and Richard followed each new battle, imagining himself in a trench about to go over the top carrying the Star-Spangled Banner. Then the 1918 peace was signed on the eleventh hour of the eleventh day of the eleventh month. Bodies were collected and identified. Crosses were fixed to graves. Rudyard Kipling captured the mood of a generation when he wrote, "If any ask us why we died, tell them 'Because our fathers lied'."

In 1915 Kipling's son John, age eighteen, was killed in the Battle of Loos, one of twenty thousand British soldiers dead by its end. After The War to End All Wars, the age of cynicism arrived. Young writers and artists adopted for themselves Gertrude Stein's phrase, The Lost Generation. It is said she used it to describe a young French auto mechanic who did a poor job repairing her car. Une génération perdue, she told his boss.

At Lawrenceville, Richard met Irvine ("Mike") O. Hockaday. At Princeton another friend was James ("Shorty") Penfield Seiberling. They and other good friends were mentioned often in his letters—Edward L. Keyes III, John Henry Leh, and Channing Fullerton Sweet. Sweet died in 1994, age ninety-five, and was a director of several Western United States corporations.

Pals in Lawrenceville went on to Princeton and friendships continued. Through the years until Halliburton's death he remained loyal to them and they to him. While at Lawrenceville he roomed with a boy he pseudonymously called Ship-King, probably scion of a shipping dynasty. When in Potsdam after the Great War, Ship-King had his chauffeur drive Richard and Mike Hockaday around the city. In the late 1980s some of Richard's schoolmates went to Memphis to attend a Rhodes College commemoration of Richard. This in itself was a testimony to his lasting friendships.

Given his charisma, energy, and intelligence, not surprisingly his schoolmates elected Richard as editor-in-chief of the school paper, *The Lawrence*. His father recalled that under Richard the paper became widely recognized as "a vital and useful factor in school life by both the faculty and the board of trustees." In 1917 he was selected to write the words and music for Lawrenceville. Among his son's personal effects, Wesley found a C-flat score titled "Lawrenceville School Class Ode" with "words and

Music by Richard Halliburton." The music was published in the posthumous *Richard Halliburton*, a 1940 compilation of his letters home.

Richard's lyrics are typical of the time and its values. Here on this Twenty First Century shore we can find something lost for some, artificial for others. It implies values and a culture not found at night on prime-time television channels except as satire.

> Great builder of God-fearing men,
> Great advocate of noble life,
> We leave thee now, true sons to be
> Throughout this time of strife;
> To fight the wrong, the right to free,
> Trust us till we come back to thee;
> Lawrenceville, Lawrenceville,
> Trust us till we come back to thee.
> Restraining gates are opened wide,
> Ten thousand paths lead from this door,
> God made us men to face the world,
> Whatever lies before.
> If fight we must beyond the sea,
> Trust us till we come back to thee;
> America, America,
> Trust us till we come back to thee.

If fight we must beyond the sea. That same year the United States declared war against Germany and Richard's idea was transformed by George M. Cohan into a song full of American innocence and cocky confidence, "Send the word, send the word to beware—We'll be over, we're coming over, And we won't come back till it's over, over there."

President Wilson had carefully awakened the nation out of its isolationist slumber even though he was re-elected on the campaign slogan, "He kept us out of war." Richard was neither an isolationist nor a jingoist. He wanted to win glory in battle.

By June 1917, when Richard graduated Lawrenceville, doughboys were behind machine guns in the trenches of France. A year later, at Château-Thierry, the American 3rd Infantry Division with the 30th and 38th Regiments stood fast with French forces troops against the German assault fifty-six miles from Paris. In the battle over three thousand were killed in action with almost thirteen thousand wounded.

John Philip Sousa's band played "Stars and Stripes Forever" at Liberty Bond rallies. Movie and stage stars joined with politicians like Teddy Roosevelt to stir patriotic fervor. Charlie Chaplin, Mary Pickford, Douglas

Fairbanks, D.W. Griffith, all gave pep talks to crowds of people. They pitied weak, old Europe and urged that only America could stop the Bosch. Lillian Gish dramatized Germans as evil menaces. Because of his fifteen unscathed minutes of bullets and glory charging up San Juan Hill in the Spanish-American war, Teddy thought it would be a "bully battle." Then his twenty-year-old son Quentin was shot down and died in a dogfight over Château-Thierry.

Richard's two years at Lawrenceville marked a new freedom for him. In Memphis, his school days had been followed by nights in his parents' home. In Lawrenceville, New Jersey he gained his first sustained taste of independence. He had adult supervisors, including a housemaster, but they had many boys to look after. Back when he was in Memphis, his parents had two, Richard and Wesley Junior.

The two years formed a new Halliburton. At Lawrenceville he knotted bonds with schoolmates. He became close to his teachers and after graduation, wearing his university blazer with "P" as its chest emblem, he pedaled a bicycle from Princeton just to see them. Unlike some youths, he enjoyed conversations with adults. This fits the pattern suggested by his solid relationship with his father. He would not have fit in during the rebellious 1960s with its slogan, Don't trust anybody over thirty.

AT PRINCETON & PRIMED TO GO TO WAR

Richard Halliburton started Princeton in the fall of 1917. President Wilson declared war on Germany April 6, 1917. F. Scott Fitzgerald, class of '17, wrote scripts and lyrics for musicals produced by the Princeton Triangle Club. Fitzgerald contributed to the humor magazine, *Princeton Tiger*, and wrote pieces for the *Nassau Literary Magazine*. He chummed with literary critic Edmund Wilson and poet John Peale Bishop. On academic probation, unlikely to graduate, Fitzgerald joined the infantry in 1917 and was commissioned a second lieutenant. Convinced he would soon die, he did what he had always wanted and wrote a novel, *The Romantic Egotist*, rejected by Charles Scribner's Sons. They did say it was original and if he revised it they would reconsider. Sent to Camp Sheridan in Alabama, he met Zelda Sayre, a beautiful, intense eighteen-year old and the youngest daughter of an Alabama Supreme Court justice. Fitzgerald found himself still alive as Armistice Day, November 11, 1918 came and it was just before he was to be shipped overseas.

After he became rich and famous, Richard met Scott and Zelda at dinner parties a few times. In Fitzgerald's book collection is a copy of *The Glorious Adventure*, with an inscription on the flyleaf: "For F. Scott Fitzgerald the world's swellest fiction writer from Richard Halliburton America's noblest travel writer. June 1, 1927."

Not that it occurred to them, but he and Scott had a point of view in common. While still at Princeton, Halliburton wrote home to his parents about his "modern generation." Fitzgerald called it the Jazz Age and the name stuck. Taking Scribner's advice, Fitzgerald rewrote his book as *This Side of Paradise* and it became wildly successful because it was about the current generation. In Scott's subsequent fiction, Richard's modern generation found themselves in Fitzgerald's accounts of post-war American youth, of flappers, the Charleston, speakeasies, rumble seats, raccoon coats, and sis! boom! bah! cheer-leading. Fitzgerald had captured what Richard and they sensed—a new youth culture in America, of liberated sex or heavy petting made possible by the mobility of motorcars and the lubrication of bathtub gin. Born in 1897, Fitzgerald died in 1940, the year after Richard Halliburton. In 1948 Zelda died as a patient in a mental hospital fire. At Scott's funeral, Dorothy Parker mourned "the poor bastard," borrowing a phrase from Jay Gatsby's funeral in Fitzgerald's novel about him. Both men, Scott and Richard, came to see their way of life as empty, Fitzgerald becoming an alcoholic drained emotionally by Zelda and Halliburton tired of shallow friendships and a clamoring public.

Like Richard, Fitzgerald began with an immense capacity for life. Like Richard, he lived passionately. Fitzgerald's Jay Gatsby had a "romantic readiness." Like Richard, Scott sought experiences, although vicariously through his characters. Both felt keenly that youth does not last, that beauty is ephemeral. They regarded wealth and position as essential to "making it in the world." They both had a tendency to self-destruct because of money. They couldn't hold on to it, which sent them into desperate searches for more.

Richard did not have Fitzgerald's sort of "double-vision," as Malcolm Cowley termed it. Cowley meant that Fitzgerald saw things in two different ways at the same time, a tension combining emotional experience of an event with objectivity and critical analysis. Scott put the matter this way: "The test of a first-rate intelligence is the ability to hold two opposed ideas in the mind at the same time, and still retain the ability to function." Scott was able to do it. While admiring the upper classes, Fitzgerald also saw that they could use people and then throw them away, as his Buchanan's did with Jay Gatsby. In his books Richard was without Fitzgerald's narrative double-vision in part because he didn't explore the world as Scott did. The two men traveled differently, Fitzgerald with his imagination, Halliburton with his body. Fitzgerald's typewriter created the earth on which his characters walked; Halliburton recalled the way it was with his feet on the ground.

He, too, experienced a duality, although not the same as F. Scott Fitzgerald's. He was pulled between a north and a south pole. For him there was activity on the one hand and a kind of mystical solitude on the other. On the north side Richard was after vivid feeling in the heart and throat. In Central America he swam the Panama Canal despite its barracudas, caiman, and crocodiles. Yet he also described sneaking into the Taj Mahal and remaining there undetected through the night, away from tourists, haunted and alone with long-dead generations. This south side of Halliburton has been given little attention. For him the places themselves allowed feelings he thought the ancients felt. With solitary nights in ancient places, he had something he wanted to believe—in undying ages, in spirits of the past—at least in the possibility. He felt the mystery of the ages in Angkor Wat, the Taj Mahal, and the Parthenon and in such moments he found peace he could not have during the day. Adrenalin rushes and mystical solitude. Here is something, a different kind of double-vision. The reader detects it in his books but Halliburton veils it for his public as all part of a merry adventure.

His double-vision manifests differently, depending on the event. Atop the Matterhorn Halliburton is enthralled by the sublime while he has Hockaday puncture his feelings by saying that he, Hockaday, can finally spit a mile. As he adventures during the day he is challenged by risk and revels in adrenalin rushes while at night he contemplates in solitude and silence the long shadows of civilizations that once flourished and are gone. He styles himself a bold adventurer and before a lady's club is introduced as that and when he stands up to speak he announces himself as just a little boy playing Indian. At the Taj Mahal during the night he is seduced by the Temptress Moon, feeling frissons of almost orgasmic sensuality as he slips his bare body into a cool reflection pond and when morning arrives the world returns to its sordid realities in an almost post-coital depression.

In 1918 Richard heard Victrolas playing patriotic songs. There were many. One was "Pack up your trouble in your old kit bag, and smile, darn ya, smile." There were "It's a long way to Tipperary" and "Mademoiselle from Armentières, hasn't washed in thirty years." In innocent bravado, a uniquely American song went, "Johnny get your gun, get your gun, get your gun" with its "Yankee Doodle do or die."

Over there he would find action, a release from the humdrum and so he decided to jump into the Big Show. Princeton opened a training camp and students joined it. His pals enlisted in the army but Richard preferred the navy, as sailors traveled. On October 5, 1918 he wrote home of disappointment caused by his choice. The Army Department intended to send his pals to Officers Training Corps and he said, "If I had joined the Army instead of the Navy I would be packing up for a camp and have my leather putts all picked out. It was the last straw when I heard that. All my friends are in the army and they bombarded me with delightful stories of commissions." Under campaign hats and in tunics with trousers bloused above putties wrapped ankle to knee, his buddies looked grand.

His complaint was not an idle comment. He wrote home that he "didn't sleep a wink" because he was worried at being left out of the fight. He didn't know what to do. His friends had their campaign hats set on a grand adventure while he could only watch them leave. There he was, stuck in the navy. To add insult, one of his professors, Eisenhart, informed his class that "only those men twenty or above could take the naval courses, ordnance and Gunnery, Navigation, Seamanship, etc." Here, he displayed what became a pattern of his life—a casual disregard for what he considered as petty rules. He lied about his age, giving it as twenty so he could attend the naval classes. This disregard might have been fostered when as a boy he heard that his father filched a pie and hoofed it for the train.

He complains that "we are too inactive here, not enough drill" and he jokes that he will "write the Admiral." He wants his commission and soon. He writes, "I have enough sense to know that it's mostly the practical training that is going to make me an officer, so I intend just about living in the observatory with the sextant and compass." He is frustrated that he has not been sworn in, especially in that it "means no uniform." Clothes make the *man*.

At first he had no money for the uniform. As in later life, money was simply something he exchanged for what he wanted. His needs of the moment determined a dollar's use. When he did get a uniform, his father sent fifty dollars for the bill. Richard replied that the uniform cost thirty dollars but the extra twenty would come in handy until his salary from the navy began.

He followed the news of the war and could tell that it was winding down. On October 5, 1918, he wrote home "Wall Street is betting the war will be over in four months. The paper this morning says Germany and Austria are asking for an Armistice." He still hoped but was impatient. In the same letter, he said, "I'm not in the navy yet, and I'm tired of waiting to be sworn in, maybe tomorrow!" But he did what the navy demanded. If he passed his naval exams, he would be sent to an officer's training course. "Four more months and I'll have what I want."

He wrote that he had been a "mess hound for four days" and added, "What a vile job. My old black sweater is caked with butter and fish and soup and molasses. Each 'hound' has to wait on ten people and unless one crashes through and gets his table set up before the hungry get in, there's Hell to pay. So it's a fight to get in ahead and I'm pretty good at that." Yes, he was "pretty good at that." Whether it was sneaking onto a Punjabi train, stowing away on a Malay steamer, or convincing the governor of Panama to let him swim the canal, he had the spunk to see himself through.

He discovered the lure of a military uniform as civilians admired the officer candidates in Atlantic City, watching the boys learn to shoot the sun with sextants. They saw Richard and the others as lads who one day would sink the Hun. That day as the naval officer candidates learned to use sextants, strollers on the boardwalk recalled the news and how they watched survivors in litters. On Black Sunday, June 2, 1918, six American ships were torpedoed and sunk by *U-151*, a German submarine. On June 4th, a lifeboat with twenty-eight survivors from the *Carolina* beached next South Carolina Avenue. The men were transported to the Morris Guards

Armory on New York Avenue while the women recuperated in hotels. Atlantic City bathers were warned that German U-boats were prowling just off the shore. The public had radically shifted from pacifism to militancy and despised anything German so that hamburgers became liberty sandwiches and dachshunds became liberty pups. An Illinois coal miner was lynched because he was a German immigrant.

For a chilly fall trip to Atlantic City, the cadets piled into touring cars, blankets and heavy coats covering them against the wind. Richard bragged that they left "at seven and made the 110 miles in three and a half hours," thus racing along at over thirty miles per hour. He said the trip "was quite cold."

One day at Atlantic City, Richard and his mates heard that the Armistice had been signed. The news had spread through the city and the crowd was ecstatic. Men were shouting. They slapped one another on the back. Women cried and hugged each another. Firecrackers exploded. Strollers passing the Dunlap Hotel could hear the band playing, "She's a grand old flag, she's a high flying flag, and forever in peace may she wave." On the boardwalk the boys were stopped by gentlemen in homburgs with walking canes and white spats over high-top shoes who wanted to shake their hands. They were hugged by women in coats with furbelows and furred collars.

They were trainees, not officially commissioned in the navy. Dressed as naval officers, the boys caught the admiring glances of girls. The lads were neither captains of Gilbert and Sullivan's *HMS Pinafore* nor the very model of a modern major general but they knew they had something.

To his parents, Richard wrote about how it felt to be in uniform on that day walking with his Princeton friend Bill Brooks. "It was the best day in the world to be there." He said, "Everybody went wild. Someway a sailor seems to get more attention than a soldier. Anyway, we were bombarded with hurrahs and questions and acclamations of every sort. Everybody shouted 'You did it!' until we began to believe we really had. We were showered with smokes and candy; were not allowed to pay for anything. As we went in to supper at the hotel, everybody rose and cheered and one table sent ours a big bouquet and another a flag."

Richard and Bill Brooks must have had plenty of chances. They strolled along the boardwalk, "listening to the dance music and hilarity going on in the restaurants." They exchanged glances with girls, most under broad-brimmed flowered hats, wearing high-heeled button shoes. Thinking now or never, they stopped the next two girls "and asked them if they would mind walking with two lonesome sailors. They were very nice looking, and rather startled, but we didn't budge an inch. Later they told us that, but for the uniform and the day, they would have been insulted."

The boys strolled with the girls, seeing and being seen on the boardwalk. Richard said that they "went for a ride in rolling chairs made of wicker," still used on the boardwalk today. They were pulled to a restaurant, a "wild place where everybody was drinking and dancing in celebration of an Armistice that would turn out to be false." Couples on the floor danced the One Step, the Tango, the Two Step, the Waltz, and the Fox Trot. Occasionally they paired-off for a dignified Cotillion. Richard, Bill, and the girls drank ginger ale, ate sandwiches. Himself an accomplished dancer, Richard wrote home that the girls danced very well. The famous Irene and Vernon Castle couldn't have done better. They danced until one in the morning then took the girls home, and crawled into bed at their hotel.

Next day, different news spread. The surrender had been a rumor and the celebration was over the False Armistice of history books. The United Press mistakenly announced a peace had been reached on the 7th of November. The real one on November 11th had yet to be signed. President and general manager of United Press, Roy Howard had reported the signing of the Armistice, hoping to scoop the other papers but instead wound up with egg on his face, having received a report from the Commander US Naval Forces in France, Henry B. Wilson that he presumed to be official.

Had the war lasted, Halliburton would have quit Princeton to get in on the action. He had been primed to go. He wrote to his father "The idea of leading a monotonous, confined, respectable life is horrible to me."

Despite his disappointment at missing military glory, Richard did not gloat because of the defeated enemy. When the real Armistice was announced, he wrote, "Peace is declared again. The report came about eight o'clock this morning." He added, "I am very happy way down deep," and the tone of his letters would change from eagerness to join the fray to speculation over his future.

Next his desire for glory was humbleness. He saw the defeat of the Central Powers differently. He expressed no pride in it. This fits his personality. Vengeance was not among his traits. War for him was what he had read in boyhood books—a test of courage, a chance for adventure.

His difference appeared when he met with the officers commanding the university training units who had been discussing a victory parade through the town of Princeton. He told them he thought it in bad taste. Gratitude for the peace was in order, not a victory march. He had modified effect, or somebody did. He explained, "Whether or not I was the cause, anyway the entire personnel of all the units in Princeton, 3000 men, were drawn up on the parade grounds before a minister who read from the Bible, and a priest who prayed." That was the modification, something reflective on peace at last. The rest came off as intended. "We had a long parade down Nassau Street afterward."

The War to End All Wars was over. For the voyage home from France, the doughboys climbed aboard battleships, the *Connecticut*, the *Iowa*, and the *Missouri* and sailed to Philadelphia without fear of U-boats. Photographs of the era show the decks covered with soldiers, some straddling the barrels of sixteen-inch guns, others sitting on the turrets. Every below-deck compartment was crammed with soldiers and marines headed home.

After Armistice, the navy had little allure for Richard. He no longer had patriotic duty to fulfill, no test of his manhood to meet. And especially, no thrill of waiting adventure. A letter to his parents signaled a change. He wrote, "I shall let circumstances decide whether I stick to it till I am commissioned, or whether I shall try to get back to civilian life. The church bells and whistles have played all day. Some chimes in a church not far off are butchering the 'Marseillaise' on too few bells. It's going to be hard sledding to go on studying war when you see and hear nothing but peace." Hard sledding, yes—he already suspects his decision. He will study war no more.

In this letter he described looking into his deceased brother's room at Lawrenceville the Saturday before, the first time in almost a year, and "it hurt almost as much as it did the last time." Despite the good news of the war, he was tugged by the past. On the one hand, the war was over and he had much to look forward to. On the other, he looked backward. His brother, Wesley, had been dead nearly twelve months. In the letter home he searched for some salvageable feeling, and snatched relief—after months of mounting battles, clearly the shell-pocked moonscape of France would not be repeated on American soil. "What a memorable day this is, peace and relief from almost unbearable worries and horror! We are safe. It has not struck us, thank God."

He said he would let circumstances decide whether he stayed in the navy as a recruit and they did. That November also marked the end of his military career. His navy training "unit is all agog with rumors. Today we hear it's to be disbanded tomorrow. The sooner we are sworn out, the better. Everyone has lost interest in war preparation, and the determination and enthusiasm have given place to discontent and indifference—I guess I'm not any different from the others." His uniform had served him well in Atlantic City with the girls, however. That he didn't pursue a commission was probably for the better, given his maverick disposition. He marched to the beat of a different drummer, a rhythm that only he heard.

PRINCETON PALS

As he matured, his bent was clearly social. He wanted friends. In 1918, when his friends left for army officer training, Richard revealed how far he had come from the young boy who would rather stay inside the house and play his violin: "I'm desperately lonesome with my pals gone, one can make new friends, but not new pals." As a child, he had been ordered out of the house to find playmates. "Kicked out," as his father put it. At eighteen he needed pals. For him, friendship figured large. Good friends were more important than wide appeal. Later, appeal counted only for merchandising his books and he had little interest in popularity contests, so to speak. He had life-long, close friends. As a friend, he could understand the perspective of others, and empathetically listen to them. He was self-accepting and could admit his mistakes among friends, even laugh about his goofs.

With friends he joked and chatted and nothing is more communal than a meal together. The taste of eggs and the smell of bacon find their way into our memories of good times. They are memories to be shared and for him community also took in fairness. In April 1919 he has much to say about fairness and an eating club, The Cap and Gown, a Princeton University institution with attitudes no different than those found in bush tribes. In the club as in the bush, differences with others became tribal. Deep in the human brain there is a notion of people acceptable and unacceptable, good enough and not good enough.

Richard displayed his lifelong sense of fair play when he wrote his parents, "First, about Cap and Gown. There were two cliques, sixteen of us and five of the other crowd, and some members of the two on unfriendly terms. The club wanted some of both cliques, but we wanted all or none and stuck together. It came to taking the sixteen of us or the five of them." His side's tough stand won out with all sixteen accepted. "We had our banquet last night and I was never so happy. Princeton life is really opening up. The clubs cement the friendships one has made during his first two years, and coming not until a fellow is almost a junior, the influence cannot harm." The influence cannot harm. He was learning a lesson outside his classes. Knowing the right people was important both at school and in life.

He had close friends. *The Royal Road to Romance* opens with a description of them. Dormed in Patton Hall that year he looks at his four roommates bent over their desks. His description reveals that he is on good personal terms with each of them, though it also describes them in a way that a young man looks at the future. He sees them dutifully grubbing their lives away. He names each of them and does so with a familiarity, an attitude, that only a good friend could get away with.

He starts with John Henry Leh, who was bent over a text in public accounting, an appropriate study as he was heir to a department store. A landmark in Allentown, Pennsylvania for one hundred forty four years, the Leh family store closed in the mid 1990s.

James Penfield Seiberling, or "Shorty," comes next and, according to Richard, Seiberling would sell bonds after graduation. Shorty eventually became head of Seiberling Rubber and Goodyear Tire.

Another friend, Larry—Edward L. Keyes III—was to become a physician, Richard tells us.

Then, last, Halliburton names Irvine "Mike" Hockaday, a sometime-dreamer according to Richard. Mike climbed the Matterhorn with Richard and later became a successful Kansas City stockbroker. This penchant for imagining probably contributed to their vagabonding together through Europe.

All four are dear friends but he thinks of the fates awaiting them and shudders. Through the years that follow right until his end he stayed in touch with them and they with him. On a trip to Hollywood to discuss a movie deal, he would stop in Kansas City to visit Mike Hockaday and family. On a lecture tour through Pennsylvania he would telephone Leh that he was in Allentown. He stopped to see Penfield Seiberling in Akron, Ohio. He visited Keyes or his parents and had dinner with them.

Photographs of the boys appear in Wesley's *Richard Halliburton: His Story of His Life's Adventure.* Four of them stand together, so very young. Each smiles into the camera. Light traveling at one hundred eighty-six miles per second captured that moment in the summer of 1918. It froze their features and a picture on paper became the residue of that instant long ago. All of them are gone now. Three of them stand in military tunics and jodhpurs. One of them is Richard. The others are Mike Hockaday, and Larry Keyes. A boy in a suit with vest and tie is described as "Shorty." This is James Penfield Seiberling. Their arms are interlocked as if to state they are inseparable. The fifth, Henry Leh, is shown in a separate picture with his wife, Dot, born Dorothy Seler Backenstoe and later a Pennsylvania aviatrix.

He dedicated *The Royal Road to Romance* "to Irvine Ott Hockaday, John Henry Leh, Edward Lawrence Keyes, James Penfield Seiberling, whose sanity, consistency, and respectability as Princeton roommates drove me to this book."

GIRLS & PRINCETON

At Princeton, Richard pursued a girl from Trenton, Helen Pendergast, and his friends took the pursuit as serious. He had a rival, Charles, for her attention. It was a competition he believed he won but he did not.

In his courtship he displays the same density as he did in his rivalry with Robert Bond for the attention of Frances Bailey. He cannot see the handwriting on the wall. He had asked Helen to the prom and she accepted. So far, so good. "Score 1 for me!" he told his dad. That, though, was not enough. His father learned that Richard and Helen were "invited to a friend's home in Philadelphia—score 2 for me!" He got a third point because "Chas. forgot Helen's birthday; I didn't."

There was a slight hitch in the whole affair, ever so paltry to Richard. "However, I think Chas. and Helen are already engaged, which doesn't bother me!" That was November; then came March 1919. He began to see the light. "For a new dance, we find that the prom starts Friday. I asked Esther. Helen is coming up with my rival Charley."

For any other swain "no" would be written in large letters but Richard is not deterred though Helen is already engaged to Charles.

Charles eventually married Helen, who recalled Richard as "quite bitter about it for a long time." This seems to have marked the end of serious courtships. Perhaps he began to think he just had no luck with women. In later years, Helen recalled him as a fine companion, entertaining and considerate. In that regard, he was the nicest she ever dated. He neither smoked nor drank. He was delightfully unpredictable. She laughed at his newest zany idea. Rather than escorting her home from a Friday dance one spring night, he had a better idea. Under the warm, starlit sky, they canoed in the moonlight until dawn. He was a romantic swain but did not win her heart. He had great energy and enthusiasm but a closeness and intimacy was missing for her. She preferred Charles.

In 1922 he wrote from Hong Kong that Helen was "in a class by herself when it [came] to mental congeniality" with him and that she was "the only real girl 'pal' [he'd] ever had, and [he'd] got more stimulation and happiness from her company than from any other girl." She apparently did not get serious with him because she wanted to be more than just his pal, despite the fun times they had.

A girl named Marie attended a Princeton house party. In a letter home he wrote, "Marie was the most popular and by far the most attractive girl . . . and followed around by a flock of men everywhere she went. She has a brilliant mind plus a very demure, shy personality, plus a very stubborn will, plus a tantalizingly attractive appearance. . . . She was so in love with Princeton, and I was so in love with her, oh yes, for the time being of course."

A few days later, a letter home carries other memories, which he was unable to shake. He recalls writing from Battle Creek to Francis Bailey, and compares her to "the girls at our house party [who] were so lovely in their youthful, simple dresses. I hope to heaven I'll get abroad unencumbered by any sentimentalism and not waste perfectly good hours writing to some uninterested girl." Uninterested girl, not uninteresting girl. He says they are uninterested in him. Later in life, he found them relatively uninteresting.

IN FLEW ENZA

They were tumultuous times. The war was over and the great world pandemic was ending. Not war, but a microbe killed the most people, from Europe to Asia to America. Estimates range between thirty and fifty million dead as distinct from eight million in the war. Microbes were a greater enemy than bullets. It was the 1918 flu pandemic. The pandemic lasted from January 1918 to December 1920 and was indifferent to where it spread. People died from it in the Arctic as well as on remote Pacific islands. By May 1918, France, Greece, Scotland, Macedonia, Egypt and Italy had fallen to it. The English fleet saw ten thousand cases in that month. In the three months starting in June there were eight million cases in Spain. It was one of the deadliest natural disasters in human history. The United States was at war but another enemy rose up against it at home as well as rising up in Britain and France. The Allies did not want the Central Powers to know about this and so a news blackout was in place. The public was ignorant about what was happening to them—unlike today, they did not read daily headlines about the disease and the number of deaths, which were frighteningly large, with about twenty-five percent of the US population infected and perhaps six hundred fifty-thousand people dying from the virus.

Wesley Junior died suddenly, as often happened in an age when diagnoses were faulty or cures unavailable. After they learned of the Great Pandemic, the Halliburton family perhaps counted Wesley lucky. He had not succumbed to influenza, the Spanish Flu, as the French called it, or the French Flu, as Spaniards called it. Children had a playground ditty about it.

I had a little bird,
Its name was Enza.
I opened the window,

67

And in-flew-enza.

It was the worst epidemic in American history. It killed more citizens than all the wars in the Twentieth Century combined. It began with fever, sore throat, and headache. Here was nothing serious at first. But it could gallop into double pneumonia. Autopsies often found lungs swollen, gorged with fluid, strangely blue. At first people associated its symptoms with colds, but it was a cold unlike any other. From the northeast, it spread across the nation, West and South, to Illinois, California, Georgia, and Alabama.

President Woodrow Wilson had a problem. The disease reached into the White House, not as a microbe but as a decision. Packed on troopships, doughboys would catch the disease and die, but if he reduced troop shipments, he would tip his hand to the Germans that America was not coming full-throttle. The buck stopped in the Oval Office and it might have been one of the toughest decisions of Wilson's life. Its magnitude finds expression in Jessie Lee Brown Foveaux, who recalled the time. Eighteen and a laundress at Fort Riley, Kansas, she witnessed the flu first hand. She saw many soldiers die. "We'd be working with someone one day, and they'd go home because they didn't feel good, and by the next day they were gone. Every day we wondered who was going to be next." Thousands of doughboys had died of influenza in Europe and troopships were needed to carry more over. Packed on the troopships, many more would die before they reached France.

Some historians have argued that President Wilson's decision was the wrong one, but he finally concurred with advice, which was not to tip off the enemy about the flu by reducing troop shipments. Continue sending troops, he said. He turned to an aide and asked if the man had ever heard the children's ditty. I had a little bird. Her name was Enza. I opened the window and in flew Enza.

The disease slowly faded after the Armistice of 1918, leaving people to face the next decade. Influenza, mustard gas, No Man's Land, they were all behind. People sang the 1921 hit, "Every morning, every evening, ain't we got fun?" The song goes on, "But smiles were made dear, for people like us."

This was the United States, made to be happy, and there was the Old World with all its troubles. America was about the practical, about the chance to get ahead, about making money. President Calvin Coolidge spoke in 1925 before the American Society of Newspaper Editors, with words that made headlines as "the business of America is business." Good old Silent Cal, people said. Yes, prosperity was at hand.

Like the nation, Richard looked ahead. More progress lay in the country's future and Richard was convinced his life would get better. As soon as the dying stopped for the nation, the forgetting began so that today the Great Influenza and the Great War happened in a quaint time and distant place people visit when watching silent-film newsreels in documentaries.

ESCAPED

It wasn't Europe I was after. Mars would have served the purpose. Just some place where I could take the lid off and boil over—with hopes of simmering down. I've simmered a lot but not so much as I hoped to.

Richard in a letter home.

Richard sailing to Juan Fernandez Island

A RUNAWAY FROM EVEN TENOR

In his worldview, Richard was an outsider, somebody looking in the windows of homes and offices, and he noticed the comings and goings of people, the paths they wore between the house and work. For him, it was rather like looking at a man in a telephone booth. He could see the gestures, watch the lips move, but none of it made any sense. The arms, the lips, were empty of meaning. Like the man in the booth, the lives of people formed the same empty gestures. He knew his difference and it worked on him to avoid becoming a man in a phone booth. Soon he would be set free in the adult world and his difference had to find another way of life. The way simply had to be a complete break with his past. He thought about it for months and his thinking hardened into resolve. Yes, he decided, a break, a complete break. When the break came it took his parents by surprise for he had done nothing to alert them but then he was always the polite, considerate son, respectful of their feelings and opinions. Unsure where the break would lead, he was determined to follow its twists and turns. Whatever his path, he could not walk but had to run it. He had no examples, no models to pattern himself after. He had no bohemian acquaintances working in a shabby garret on a painting, or writing a novel, nor was he fond of poverty but had the 1960s counter culture been around when he was young he very probably would have joined it.

Immediately after his break, his search for a better way, his parents thought it a passing fancy. Only later did they look back and see it as part of a life-long pattern. His parents slowly came to understand that their son was cut from different cloth and that understanding was something Wesley explained to his friend Bigg Jimm, James Cortese, who spent evenings with Wesley. One evening, Wesley, or Big Chief, looked from under his bushy white eyebrows and recalled Richard saying to him that he was "hungry for the sea, for foreign ports" and that he wanted to realize his youth while he had it. Sitting there, sipping whiskey with Cortese, Wesley did not ask himself where he went wrong trying to teach an even tenor to his son. "I guess I sorta envied him," he said. He told Bigg Jimm that "Richard had always been restless, inclined to boredom. Why? We could hash it over from his birth to his death and not be any nearer the reason why. But he was one of the elite. Perhaps it was in the genes."

For that predisposition, an outlet occurred on Monday, July 14, 1919, when Richard was driven to the Memphis railroad depot by his mother. Home from Princeton for the summer, he was to visit the Thomas Twins in Brownsville, Tennessee. Richard urged her not to wait with him for the train. She had other things to do, he told her. After all, she and her husband Wesley were traveling over three hundred miles to their Tate Springs summer cabin in East Tennessee by Cherokee Lake. They would be out of town until Tuesday of next week. She needed to prepare for the trip. He would be all right. The train would arrive in thirty minutes. He was only going to Brownsville, some fifty miles distant. He kissed her on the cheek and she left. His offer came as no surprise to her as she knew her son to be thoughtful and considerate.

Later she became alarmed about her son when she heard no news from him. What had happened to him? Where had he gone? Was he dead or injured?

He had not gone to Brownsville. He took the train to New Orleans and from there he signed on as a seaman on a freighter Europe-bound.

He appeared to her as the usual Richard on the station platform. Neither she nor her husband could glimpse what had been going on behind his smiles and gentle humor. Underneath, something happened to bring about this change from his normal behavior, something sudden and unpredicted by them. They understood that his high level of energy, his restlessness, sought release, but they had not been prepared for the direction it took him. The proximate cause for the escape and consequent direction of his life appears as his brother's death from rheumatic fever two years before. The death did strike Richard deeply and brought him into a deep sense of their threesome, all that was left, himself and his parents. Life is short; its ending could come abruptly, without warning. Wesley Junior had lived only sixteen years. The day should be seized before its flame burnt out.

What happened at the train depot. That Monday, Richard watched the Brownsville train slow and heard its steam hiss into the station. He sat on a bench by the station as passengers boarded it and it chugged away. He waited until midnight and then climbed aboard the Meridian & Memphis for New Orleans. Meanwhile, his parents were sound asleep in their bed, confident the Thomas Twins had met him. On his part, Richard expected Wesley and Nelle to be at the Tate Springs cabin but they had decided to stay home rather than leave town.

On Friday, Atha Thomas, one of the twins, knocked on the door of their house. Richard had not showed up. Did he plan to arrive later? Nelle Halliburton looked at the boy, her jaw dropped, her eyes welled with tears. She became terrified, thinking her son had been kidnapped. She escorted Atha in to see Wesley. He, too, was shocked.

Wesley had to sooth her trembling. He thanked Atha Thomas for going to the trouble of traveling all the way to Memphis and saw the lad to the door. After Atha left, Wesley told Nelle that the boy must have run away as a youthful escapade. Richard would come home.

If that's the case, she asked, then why had they not heard from him? Richard was always good about letting them know his whereabouts and plans, even if after the fact.

Wesley thought, and then answered. Richard believed they had taken the trip and did not know that at the last minute they decided against it. He expected them to return next week. He didn't think he had been missed. To reassure Nelle, Wesley avowed his confidence that on Tuesday morning at his office he would find a letter from their son.

Later, Wesley did not tell Nelle that he called every Memphis hotel to ask if Richard had checked in with a woman. He also talked to the Brownsville train conductor to learn that his boy had not been aboard the Monday train.

He and Nelle called all Richard's friends. No, he was not with any of them. Wesley remained stoic. They must wait, he said. They did. That was all they could do. They did not know that this would be the first of many times when they would wait, always fearful that the worst had finally happened.

Wesley was correct. On Tuesday, he found at his Butler Building office a letter from Richard dated July 18th, the Friday before. Worthy of remark is that Richard did not send the letter home because his mother would read it first. He did not want to upset her and hoped that his father could mollify her worries if Wesley got the letter before she could. The reason has to do with arousal of disturbing emotions. This suggests his avoidance in later life of emotional confrontation with others, notably over the construction of *Sea Dragon*, when he could have firmly controlled his skipper John Welch, who was always arguing and berating crewmembers.

In their son's letter Wesley read, "Don't be alarmed at anything. Everything is as it should be." Richard meant that his life was on course. His parents must have thought, well, no, everything is not as it should be. The sun rises and sets everywhere, not on him alone.

Should be. Richard should be in college. They should not be worried. He should not have deceived them.

Their boy continued, "I'm very happy and very well and really am in New Orleans or rather was when this was written."

He tried to ingratiate himself with them. "Surely a boy never had a more comfortable and ideal home life than I have. It's not that. You would not be alarmed if I had gone west, to Montana or Canada, and were away from you for three months or so. This is not different except that my plan is far more interesting, engrossing and active, *active*, that's the word. Please forgive me for slipping off. I considered everything and decided this was the best way." Translated, he meant he did not want a confrontation. He would do it and apologize later.

Elsewhere in the letter he tells them, "I know it was cruel of me to slip off as I did, but I knew too well that if I mentioned my plan and you did not agree with it you would talk me out of it."

His plan—better called his intention, for he did not think that far ahead—was to go to Europe. The letter reveals the dollar details. The New Orleans train took the $15 his dad had given him as pin money for the Brownsville trip. As an ordinary seaman, he had signed on the *Octorara*, a freighter out of New Orleans for Hull, England. His pay was $54 for the three-week voyage. He would have that plus a $65 withdrawal from his Memphis bank. Thus bankrolled, he could step ashore with $95. The math is unclear but that is his total.

It was a rite of passage. He would become baptized into a new life. He wrote them that he was not running away from home. He was running away from his "old self." This former self was reared with a by-the-books mentality. It was afraid to stand on mountaintops, while the new self would ascend the slopes for panoramas that few others had beheld. He would die to the old way and be born into the new. He beseeched them not to stop him because his was not merely an ocean-crossing but an outward-bound voyage of self-discovery.

He explained that it was not a wild impulse. It was not hare-brained. He thought about it for months. It would be a grand adventure, the big one of his lifetime. If only they didn't try to stop him he would return to Princeton for the February semester.

That was what he wrote them.

On the other hand, he said to his Princeton Friends, "I may never see you again." In his mind, it was a passage to more than England. He was emotionally, maybe actually, leaving his old life behind.

What was a parent to do? Demand that he come home? If so, then what would be Richard's next test of them? After all, he was nineteen. The wiser course was to give him their blessing. Let him do it. Let him get all of it behind him. It was only a catharsis and their wild child would return to normalcy. He would go, travel, and then come home. He would graduate Princeton and return to the position his father had waiting for him in Memphis. So they thought.

Wesley's cable is sympathetic, supportive. Sounding like both pal and parent, his father telegrammed him in New Orleans, using a term, "bully," often used by Teddy Roosevelt:

> RICHARD HALLIBURTON COSMOPOLITAN HOTEL, NEW ORLEANS.
> GO TO IT AND MAY YOU HAVE A BULLY TIME. A LITTLE SURPRISED YES. DON'T FAIL TO WRITE US. FOR GOD'S SAKE TAKE CARE OF YOURSELF, BUT GET THIS TRIP OUT OF YOUR SYSTEM. WISHING YOU BON VOYAGE, DAD.

Get it out of his system. The phrase would prove a futile wish.

Wesley's subsequent correspondence, a letter, was another matter. In it, Richard read that his parents were disappointed. They had expected better of their son. This was not how he had been raised. He had caused his mother no end of worry. He should know he had been thoughtless and inconsiderate of the anguish he caused her.

Richard received two signals. One was, Go for it. The other was, Next time think twice about consequences of your actions and their effects on others. He placed importance on the first. He always went for it.

He didn't disregard the second. He advised them of his plan for a new adventure, entertaining their advice, but only after he had made up his mind. In Sicily, he swam between Scylla and Charybdis, then the Hellespont between Europe and Asia Minor, and later the Panama Canal from the Pacific to the Atlantic. He trekked through dangerous, rain-sotted jungles. He assured them that he faced no real danger, that he had the best equipment, the best comrades, and the best preparations.

After running away to Europe, his summer break from school continued into winter. He was still in Europe. Wanting Richard to resume his studies, Wesley expressed concern and cautioned him to return "to the even tenor" of his way, a phrase that captures all he rebelled against.

This time Richard did not avoid confrontation in his reply. His mind was made up and he was in open defiance. He would not return to that way. He never did return to it. He loved his parents and he would return to Princeton but not to their view of life's possibilities. By saying in a letter home that he hated "that expression," he rebuked parental values. "Those who live in the even tenor of their way simply exist until death ends their monotonous tranquility. No, there's going to be no even tenor with me."

Here, he was blunt-spoken and he stood his ground. Something pulsed in his blood they could not understand and it broke free from Memphis in a rage to live. He felt it not just as something in his mind but in his body. It is a restlessness mentioned on October 15, 1923 when from New York he wrote that he saw Ana Pavlova dance and that he was introduced to an editor at Doran by Hamlin Garland, author of *Main-Traveled Roads* and *A Son of the Middle Border*. He says, "I'm wonderfully well. I still have trembly spells but it's not physical exhaustion. It's nervous. Once I'm organized and going I'll calm down, maybe, but I'll never reach the 'even tenor'." He tells them that it is the way he is, the way his body is, and he knows it is not what they want. If biology is fate he loved his destiny.

ORDINARY SEAMAN

Before the *Octorara* hoisted anchor on August 8, 1919, Richard had already discovered that the life of an ordinary seaman was nasty and hard. At the end of *New Worlds to Conquer* he recalled that voyage. "At last, a ship, a very small and unseaworthy one, signed me on, to my indescribable delight. The other members of the crew were the most hardened rogues one could have ever met with, though at first, to my inexperienced and romantic vision, they seemed like knights." * He says of the crewmen that they "very quickly turned out to be not knights at all, but savages who made my life doubly miserable." He claims the seamen abused him, a college boy with educated, "pansy accents." His courtesy only earned him gruff replies and the scorn of tattooed, weather-wrinkled sailors.

Richard tells his readers that he sweated five hours cleaning thirty-eight brushes stiff with hardened paint by using kerosene, hot water, and soap while anchored in the Louisiana Delta heat. Grease and grime raised severe boils on his arms and hands. In a letter home he said he kept iodine for "a beautiful crop of boils." He scraped paint from bulkheads. He brushed on new coats. At about one hundred forty pounds, he had to lift sugar barrels and sacks of bacon, keeping up with husky stevedores. He staggered under containers he carried to the hold crane. He suffered from the heat. His face and arms were sun burnt and peeling skin. His lips had cracked and blistered. He was dirty and reeked of sweat most of the time. Chow was awful. "For breakfast we had oranges, coffee, and ice water, but also condensed milk and a number of flies." In the rolling seas of the Gulf of Mexico he became seasick.

He wanted to see his mother and father.

---

* His "inexperienced and romantic vision": by 1929, when *New Worlds* appeared, he had self-awareness and could look back on his youth with judicious appraisal. .

First the ship's steering gear broke and she lay anchored almost in sight of New Orleans for a three-day repair. Anchor hoisted, the *Octorara* rounded Key West and set northerly for the Bahamas but in the Gulf Stream she developed engine trouble and the open Atlantic was no place to be adrift. The ship made for Norfolk and passed through Chesapeake Bay to drop anchor in Hampton Roads.

After passing through the bay and anchoring in Hampton Roads Richard climbed to the crow's nest of the freighter. He looked north to Fortress Monroe, west to Hampton, and east to Norfolk. He counted one hundred eighty-seven ships anchored in the Roads and was "within a stone's throw of the Atlantic Battle Fleet," with its cruisers, destroyers, and battleships. He was a navy officer candidate at Princeton and the Roads was a reminder of what might have been.

Richard asked the captain for leave while the engine underwent repair. He tells us the skipper gladly agreed and hoped the youth would not return. His parents were vacationing in their Tate Springs cabin and he rode a Greyhound bus—a new transportation system—to visit them, riding six hours with open windows on dirt roads in the 1919 August heat into the Shenandoah Valley and Tennessee. After his last bus transfer, he hired a cab to Tate Springs. When Wesley and Nelle answered a knock on the cabin door they beheld a son with face and arms sun burnt, skin cracked and peeling. Boils covered him. There he was before them, "looking very ill and feeling very chastened." Nelle salved his skin, fed him, and put him to bed.

They talked to one another about their bold adventurer while he slept.

In *New Worlds* readers are told that Richard had resolved he would "abandon this mad career and like a true repenting prodigal" return to his parents "at the first port." He expected sympathy with them and a refuge.

Instead, his mother told him he must return. She wanted his character forged by hardships—something she and Wesley could not do. He tells us that his father might have weakened and let him stay at home but his mother, no. His "mother's composed and unselfish judgment" this time over-ruled his sentiment and he "was sent off again to that cursed vessel."

Matronly ladies in book clubs across America must have chatted about the boy and his wise mother and this was Halliburton's intent.

That was for public consumption. His letters show another Halliburton, eager to cross the Atlantic, both before and after showing up at the cabin. Before, still at New Orleans, he wrote that they were ready to hoist anchor and that "I feel just about as excited as if I were going on a ride on a freight train. I'm perfectly equipped for my, as Dad says, 'personally conducted tour'." After the Tate Springs cabin, back in Norfolk, he tells them, "I have to write fast for the pilot boat may be along any minute and collect the last mail before we sail. Steam is up at last. All my dissatisfaction and restlessness have gone with the approach of sailing."

In a letter from Norfolk to Princeton classmate John Henry Leh, or "Heinie," we find no dispirited Richard. He is cheeky. He writes, "Next time you osculate with Dot, say, 'That's for Dick'." He also instructs his classmate to "recite this poem to her for me. It ought to help me out with her."

> Heinie's girl wears silks and satins
> My girl wears calico.
> Heinie's girl is tall and slender
> My girl is fat and low.
> Heinie's girl is fast and wicked.
> My girl is peeure and good.
> Would I change for Heinie's girl?
> You know damn well I would!"

We know that Heinie married Dot. We can be confident he did not read the verse to her.

On the freighter he met another ordinary seaman, Allen Longbridge from Houston and in his sophomore year at Rice University, who also had "never been to sea before." Allen was "quite cultivated" and made a very pleasant companion, unlike the old salts as well as the other four in his crew, who were "the proverbial seagoing type." He slept with the crew in triple-decker bunks in an aft compartment, which meant by the time a rough sea rolled under the hull they felt the full weight of the ship behind it.

The *Octorara* was loaded with New World lumber for Old World buyers. Forests along the Mississippi were clear-cut and shipped on barges downriver to saw mills for ships bound for China, Japan, Portugal, Italy, and Germany. Clear-cutting led to the Great Mississippi Flood of 1927 and boosted Herbert Hoover, then Secretary of Commerce and in charge of relief, into the national prominence that led to his presidency. For several days, *Octorara* cranes had hoisted lumber and lowered it into the holds until they were packed. Unable to get more underneath, the remaining wood was lashed topside on the fore and aft decks. Richard wrote that the ship was so laden that it almost sank "out of sight." "The decks," he said, were "piled six feet in lumber."

On August 27th, the *Octorara* first mate called down the stokehole and ordered his black gang, the stokers, to shovel coal into the furnace. Below decks was a different world. In the bowels of the *Octorara* men were stripped to the waist, sweating, and begrimed with coal dust, scooping the black stuff into roaring furnaces. Building boiler steam, the skipper relayed another order to the first mate, who told the foc'sle gang to man the windlass. They cranked the anchor out of its muddy goo in Hampton Roads as it coiled itself in the chain locker. Coming about in the Roads, the freighter blew black smoke to clear her stacks. Offshore wind floated the smoke in a long cloud behind the ship as she passed people standing on the ramparts at Fortress Monroe. Leaning on Civil War cannons, people peered through binoculars at her as she trailed wake into the Chesapeake and trained her bow for the Atlantic. The *Octorara* was underway.

AZORES

He had new sights and they were all his, flashing in the sun like gems. They appeared and then fell into the past as new treasures presented themselves. He was afloat in the teeming world of sensations and experiences. In September 1919 on sighting landfall in the Azores archipelago, he became ecstatic, saying it had been "the most glorious day" of his life. "All the happiness of our twelve days at sea, all my impressions and sensations, have been dwarfed by the wonder of the things I've seen today." He and Allen Longbridge had been beckoned by the boatswain's mate to look at the horizon. A grey cloud slowly loomed, changing into a mountain, the Ponto do Pico, and by four in the afternoon the mountain became distinct, rising above the waters. They rounded the island of Faial and by dusk the sun's rays lit the slope of Monte Escuro, illuminating houses, churches, and a lighthouse.

At Faial, they beheld the harbor of Horta, "the most beautiful sight on earth." It was on the other side of the great Atlantic. He gazed upon a new world with new people, all that he had imagined in books he read as a child. His feelings became the guiding principle for his young life. He did not seek rapture in an after-life. Every now and then he was able to find it here.

During the crossing he and Allen Longbridge climbed topside and on the bow "plopped down on a great coil of rope to watch the sun and sea go down." They discussed and argued. Full of themselves, they were young intellectuals, ready to grapple with heady thoughts, "literature and philosophy and geography and the stage." Richard esteemed his own intellect and found Allen about as well informed as he was. He left no records of Longbridge's views, but his own were clear. Real experience came from powerful feelings, with travel through new and foreign lands able to deliver it.

When Richard stepped ashore in the Azores, he didn't dwell on the poverty he saw but expected it, for this was not America. Instead, he described passing along "a particularly slum-like street. The children romped in that street in hundreds. It wasn't long before we were recognized as Americans and a howl of 'mune' (money) went up. We were followed in swarms, and there was not one of them over seven years old. Foolishly, I threw one a penny." The children spoke to the child in Richard. Children responded to the world with awe. As they grew, they lost this, and as he aged he husbanded in himself the openness to experience he felt as a child.

The Azores idyll ended and the freighter sailed on into the North Atlantic. Asleep in his bunk, Halliburton awoke as "a Niagara of water" slammed into a porthole, forcing it open, and splashing into the compartment. Rounding toward Norway and passing the Isle of Man, they entered the North Sea, choppy and downright unpleasant at first and then *Octorara* rode glass-smooth waters north of the English Channel. Richard imagined the Dutch and French coasts to his port. "What a wonderful first view of England," he wrote, "and what an interesting day! Ships by the swarm, little ones, big ones, going and coming in streams." In a larger sense the ship traffic was a metaphor. The world teemed with goings and comings and as Halliburton grew older and increasingly aware of time he noticed more and more the departures. That day and years later others would look upon the busy ship lanes and some, like Richard, would see in them the incessant flux and rapid transit of life.

ENGLAND AT LAST

From the North Sea, the freighter made for the Humber River on the English coast. The crew worked topside preparing the lumber for off-loading. Halliburton wore mittens and several layers of clothes, because "the thermometer dropped a mile." Tugged through shipping canals and locks, the ship moored at Hull, England where Richard explained to the captain that he had been assured of a two-month voyage and had made his plans accordingly. He asked that, because of the delays back in New Orleans and Hampton Roads, he be freed from his return obligation. The captain gave him his extra $25 and had him taken to the American Consul. As he sat foot in town, he was smitten. As his feet carried him farther, he was in love. "I was delighted with Hull and my enthusiasm has grown with every hour." He says, "I'm already an Anglomaniac, and a raving one at that, and I've been here only a week." In his young life he was ready to be unprepared for anything, and that was the idea. Lack of preparation made surprise and beauty all the greater so that things were not fit into preconceived categories.

As in the Azores with urchins, so in Hull he found children and took to them immediately. Walking past an alley, he saw them at a slightly ajar side door of a movie theater, "a bunch of gamins four to eight years old bubbling with excitement," peering at Charlie Chaplin flickering on the nickelodeon screen. That was enough for him—he had to stop and talk to them. He took six in with him to see the tramp in *Sunnyside*, where Charlie plays a hotel clerk in love with the village belle, Edna Purviance. The kids watched Chaplin place a chicken in a frying pan so he wouldn't have to carry an egg from the hen to the pan and they laughed loudly. A four year old sat on his lap and Richard read the film leaders to the boy. Charlie was not half so amusing to Richard "as those kids who almost fell out of their seats."

Leaving the children, he continued to explore the town and met a man he would have fit into his boyhood books of heroes. The man was Field Marshal Edmund Henry Hynman Allenby, 1st Viscount Allenby, nicknamed "bloody bull," rather unfitting, given his upright character. Allenby was respected by T.E. Lawrence, or Lawrence of Arabia, who coordinated and led the Arab Revolt in the Desert of World War I. Of Allenby, Lawrence wrote, he was "physically large and confident, and morally so great that the comprehension of our littleness came slow to him." Allenby led the Egyptian Expeditionary Force against the Ottomans during the war.

Not knowing he was next Allenby warming himself by a fire in a pub, Richard chatted with "a distinguished looking civilian," as they rubbed their palms then held them to the flames. From the man, he learned that a railroad strike had frozen movement of all passenger and freight trains so that no food was transported. Richard was enchanted by England but was unaware the strike resulted from poverty wages, with further cuts threatened. Soldiers sent to guard railway stations fraternized with pickets and the strike was successful, the threat withdrawn. They chatted, the distinguished man and the youth, rubbing hands over the fire and after a while, the General's batman looked into the room and said, "Oh! Therr you arr, General. I think you can go to supper now." The General politely took his leave of the fresh-faced young American and Halliburton said goodbye to him. After asking around, the boy realized he had just talked to the man who delivered Jerusalem from the Ottoman Empire.

Railroad employees were on strike but this did not deter Richard Halliburton. He walked the one hundred forty miles to London, taking eighteen days to do it. This would be the first of his treks in life, and it was mild in comparison to some of the others. For him, the easy way by train or motorcar was boring. He tramped six hours to Manchester, choosing the city on a whim. Of it he wrote, "It has not one virtue except the hundreds of mills which spin our cotton." He saw that, not the vice. At nineteen he had no inkling of the long hours and bleak lives inside the mills, still Victorian in some labor laws. The complexion of workers was sallow and pallid, their bodies stunted in growth, some bent by rickets. Richard then walked 20 miles to Macclesfield, then twenty miles farther, marveling at the green fields, cattle, and medieval churches. To Leek, then to Ashbourne, where he slept at an inn with a sign hanging from the door: Built in 1619. He visited Lichfield, Samuel Johnson's birthplace, and then walked to Kenilworth and Warwick. At Oxford he visited the Bodlian Library and All Souls Chapel, where he gazed up at the Gothic spires.

For us it is an itinerary. For him, it was a feast of the senses. His feet and legs became weary but his body stepped into the past to tread the paths of history.

Whatever his eyes saw, he saw it with his parents. At Tamworth Castle he wrote, "If we ever have a new home we must have the living room about 35 x 25 feet and the walls in solid wood paneling, all the tapestries and plaster made cannot give the warm elegant tone of small paneled woodwork."

Sunday morning he walked out of Oxford and by early evening the next day he reached London. Richard discovered that a favorite play, *Cyrano de Bergerac*, was being staged that evening and he went to see it. Richard saw himself in Rostand's play. Cyrano lived life with panache, with flamboyant manner and reckless courage. A swashbuckler, he spoke Richard's version of romance. He combined knightly chivalry and courtly idealism. Despite Cyrano's improbably long nose, the cavalier expressed an inner beauty, a poetic life, as distinct from Christian de Neuvillette's outer beauty, both men competing for Roxane's love. He knew how to live and his life was his art. True to his chivalric code, Cyrano groaned out of his deathbed to deliver a message from Christian to Roxane. His panache was also literal— the white plume in his helmet. The world could take the plume, the outer panache, from him but not the inner one, the one he lived and died by. Replace *panache* with *uneven tenor* and you get the appeal to Halliburton.

Panache. We can picture Richard in belted Ulsterette coat, leather gloves, and walking cane, the complete young gentleman as he strolled the streets of London. He visited the Victorian Embankment to see a captured German U-Boat, "the sub Deutschland, that came to Baltimore in 1916." Against that reality, he visited the National Gallery where he looked on "The Avenue at Middelharnis" by Seventeenth Century Dutchman Meindert Hobbema. At Princeton, Richard had hung a copy over his desk. In the painting, a country dirt road tapers into the horizon—not an avenue in the modern sense. The blue sky and rural expanse beckon the viewer. Just travel down this road, they say; just travel down it and you will see in a wholly different way.

He spent three hours inside St. Paul's Cathedral, its architect Christopher Wren and, as if sniffing and sipping a bouquet of Chablis, he savored it in solitude, the time for his most delicious moments throughout his life. Finally, the young gentleman delivered a judgment. "I *cannot* appreciate Wren's buildings. The exterior of St. P. is beautiful enough, but all the gilt and gaudiness inside rub me the wrong way. The entire church is not worth the tiny jewel chapel at All Souls College in Oxford. *But* St. Paul's dome is a miracle of architecture."

He climbed the stairs of the cathedral and then a ladder to the clock tower to gaze out on London. The Cathedral clock's minute hand extended eight feet and it weighed seventy five pounds but time had no heft, was absent for him. Here was poetry and his life was in it. Solitude again.

Enwrapped by the panorama that October day in 1919, his world stood still. Finally, "the door man in the gallery below" came laboring up the ladder to see if he had jumped from the top. Poof—with the arrival of the doorman—away goes his poetry. He tells us that the doorman brought him back to the real world. For some reason, Halliburton needed to juxtapose his sensitivities against the mundane. It was as if he feared his aesthetic sense was off-putting to his readers, that in order to sell books, he had to downplay it.

For him, England was quaint, romantic. The Great War had ended less than a year before and in it Britain had lost almost an entire generation in the muddy trenches of France. Still, London plodded on, its citizens recovering from the war and the high-altitude raids of German Zeppelins and Gotha bombers. At night, Count von Zeppelin had sent his bomb-laden ships over British cities. Hitler's Luftwaffe would fly over England again in the next war.

He eventually had enough of London as its quaintness faded. It was not a country road merging into the horizon and he needed horizons. "I *never* saw such traffic jams and so many people. I go miles in every direction and the crowds never seem to thin out." At that time, London was the largest city in the world. He complained about the scarcity of food. At restaurants, "the menu would hide the side of a house and all they have to serve is tea and no sugar and margarined toast." He glimpsed an England he did not, could not, understand. It was an England in deep depression like the rest of Europe, and recovering from the hardships of war, unlike his Land of Plenty.

FROM ENGLAND TO FRANCE IN A FLYING MACHINE

Next morning he walked across the London aerodrome's green lawns to an airline office to look at the biplane that would fly him over the channel to Paris. He gazed at the Handley Page Type 0, a bomber converted for commercial use, parked on the grass and vaguely reminiscent of a box kite with its wings and rear stabilizers. Started after the war, the airline, Handley Page Air Transport, flew routes from London to Brussels and Paris at about £5, a fare many could not afford in 1919, and comparable to over $270 US as this is written. As an airliner, the bomber was not without risk. On one Paris-to-London flight, a Handley Page flew into a snowstorm and the pilot, believing himself over England, landed on a Belgian dike. Another pilot flew through London fog and barely missed St. Paul's Cathedral. With few instruments, these were the days of seat-of-the-pants flying.

Always wanting to know how his body felt, Richard asked if he could fly with the pilot in the open cockpit of the nose and above the twelve-passenger cabin, which was shielded from the weather. He was given a leather helmet, goggles, and a heavy sheepskin coat, which he wore over his raincoat. He and the other passengers stood for several hours, stamping their feet against the biting cold. Finally, they climbed into the aeroplane. While the others seated themselves in the cozy cabin he climbed into the open cockpit and sat next the pilot. That afternoon the pilot taxied onto the grass runway, the biplane bumping severely on its hard-mounted wheels and wooden tailskid. The pilot revved the twin Liberty engines to full throttle and the flying machine began racing down the grass runway. Without muffled exhaust, its engines roared as it bounced along the ground, then the wheels rode on air and smoothness and the pilot turned toward the English Channel.

Richard discovered every chink in his clothing probed by icy blasts. At one hundred miles per hour, the wind found its way around insulation. He thought he had dressed warmly but it was not enough. He tightened the chinstrap on his leather helmet while his cheeks still became numb. Cold be damned, though. He had the view he wanted. He looked down as the Handley Page climbed above the Thames. Below he could see the city, including St Paul's Cathedral and the Tower of London.

In the 1930s he would fly around the world in his biplane but this was his first flying experience. The aircraft reached a mile high, then eight thousand feet. He must have felt like Alice in Wonderland as he looked down to see the world shrink beneath his feet. He noticed specks in the Channel. The ships looked like ants. Ahead lay France and he could already see it.

Then they were over France, where they began to drop lower and the world beneath his feet slowly became larger. At two thousand feet, he looked down upon the Seine, which they followed at one hundred miles an hour. The sun sinking behind them, the air became even colder. He could no longer move his cheeks and nose and his legs were asleep. He beat his hands against his face, and stretched his legs as the Seine led them toward Paris.

He saw the landscape of World War I, ended eleven months before. He looked down on the trenches at Amiens, crossing the terrain as far as the eye could see. He saw the Thirteenth Century Amiens Cathedral with its flying buttresses, where sandbags had protected it from shrapnel and cannonade. Inside, Christ in Majesty presided over the Day of Judgment at the tympanum of the central west portal. As Richard flew above the cathedral at its western entrance a relief depicted a hedgehog ransacking the ruined city of Nineveh. All around the cathedral the city of Amiens lay in rubble. All was so different less than a year later, empty of cannonade, machine gun fire, and hand grenades. Peaceful and still, it was only memory and a few thousand feet below.

The clouds opened and pellets of rain began to drive into the plane, pelting the faces of the two men. There were yet no *pilots*. In a letter home Richard refers to the man as a driver, who "lost his bearings in the semi-dark and had to circle the Eiffel Tower to find them again. The landing field is some three miles outside the city wall." No landing on a Belgian dike this time, nor barely missing St. Paul's Cathedral. Although the driver at first could not get his bearings, they did not crash into the Eiffel Tower and landed safely.

After they landed, Halliburton mentally separated himself from those cozy in the cabin: "One gets the real flying feeling where I sat—may as well as go by train as to sit all closed in." Then came prophetic words. "I'm very happy I did it and I'm going to have a plane myself some day." He carried through with his intention, and dubbed his plane Flying Carpet which, as in the Arabian Tale, would take him to strange and mysterious places.

LEARNING FRENCH

After landing in Paris, he wrote from the Hôtel de Vendôme on October 15, 1919 that during his first night in the city he slept thirteen hours. "I guess the trip tired me, after all," he wrote home. On Wednesday of the same week he told Wesley and Nelle that although he "studied French some twelve months" in classes, he barely knew "how to ask for a glass of water or a postage stamp." He arranged to live in a boarding house where he could "live reasonably and never hear a word of English." He said that immersion in the language was the only way to learn it.

He walked to Versailles, where the World War I peace treaty was signed, and visited the Hall of Mirrors. When he asked directions of a gendarme, the policeman could not understand that he preferred his feet and gave him directions to the tram.

He wanted to see much more but decided to stay in Paris to master French, an example of his life-long resolve. He limited himself to side trips, except for a visit during Christmas to Monte Carlo, Nice, and Marseilles with a Mr. Sanford, an engineer from a California university. We can see them with Ascot ties and wearing three-piece suits with pleated, cuffed trousers. Topped by Homburg hats, they strolled the sidewalks of Paris.

His parents helped him financially. He complained that his shoes needed half-soles because "the walk from Hull to London had quite an effect" on them. Of money they wired, he tells them he "deposited 1800 francs" with American Express. At this writing, the modern dollar equivalent ranges between $350 and $400, an amount that would go far in 1919 France.

Back in Paris, he went to Jack of New York, a tailor, to be fitted for a suit. Jack clearly knew nothing about New York. Richard and he got into a "real Battle of the Marne" because the tailor would not understand that Richard wanted no tight-fitting Frenchman's suit with "bosoms and hips," as depicted in a letter home.

Richard did not back down and went a few rounds with Jack. Finally, Richard took off his coat and handed it to the tailor, "and told him to copy, and if there was one measurement one tenth of an inch different" he would not take the suit. In business deals he stood his ground.

He traveled to the trenches at Lens, trenches that, extending across Europe, once were part of a great, underground metropolis whose industry was destruction. World War I made this underground the largest city on Earth both in population and in area, over 6 million troops of Central and Allied armies, and spreading over 3,760 square miles. At Lens, he looked at mud that once had been a thriving aboveground city of merchants and housewives, of bankers and tradesmen, of children playing and lovers courting. There, he beheld "simply the greatest ruin the world ever saw. A city the size of Memphis. Standing at the center where the 'Grand Place' used to be, one can look for two miles in all directions and see nothing, almost, but a sea of bricks and wreckage. Not one house, not one wall, was left standing." During the war the bursting shells were sometimes heard as far away as London. At Vimy, he "stood on the edge of the great crater, a mile long, 125 feet deep, 600 feet wide"—something he had "longed to see ever since the report of it stirred the world." Longed to see, he says, as if it is the eighth wonder of the modern world, but his imagination became grayed by horrors it could not deny.

Whatever he gazed upon he blamed on the Germans. It had all been their fault. In November, he wrote home that he ground his "teeth over a news item from the *Herald*." The Bosche were without shame, pleading in London that they be able to keep "150,000 milch cows" and not return the animals to France, else "German children will starve." He rhetorically asks, "Did I see one *drop* of fresh milk from Lille to Rheims? I did not." His letter has an angry tone, unusual for him, and it reveals his deep sense of injustice, although he cannot fathom that at the Treaty of Versailles terrible injustices were perpetrated on Germany by the France he defended.

He complains that sometimes he feels he is "making no progress with the language. The worst part about French, real modern French, is that after you have the nouns and verbs and think you are quite ready to say anything, you find that no one understands you because they use the words in an entirely different way from English." He is determined to learn the language and will "get there some day if I have to come to France every summer for 40 years."

In a letter to his son, Wesley says something about Richard's French "frolic," to which the boy replies, "No, Dad, my experience has not been a 'frolic'—altogether, I took it too seriously." This sentiment foreshadows the seriousness of his travels in 1921. While his friend Mike enjoyed a pleasant European tour he was bent on his career as a travel-adventure writer.

In the letter, Richard adds, "It wasn't *Europe* I was after. Mars would have served the purpose. Just some place where I could take the lid off and boil over—with hopes of simmering down. I've simmered a lot but not so much as I hoped to." He could not rid himself of "the tearing hunger to do and do things," as Rupert Brooke phrased it. His seriousness had to do with his body's inescapable rage to live and his need to find a release from norms, the societal chains that bound it.

By January 1920 his first trip abroad was finished. He had not mastered French, for the difference between academic and colloquial French was large—but he had come a long way in learning it.

Apparently, his father had joked with him about not siring any children in Europe. Richard wrote, "Gosh, Dad, don't bring you a daughter" and adds, "you forgot to tell me not to bring home Mt. Blanc or Sarah Bernhardt—but I won't."

He booked passage to New York on the *Savoie*, writing home that his "amazing interlude" was almost over and that he would "be back in the even tenor" of his way at Princeton and wondering if he had "dreamed all this. It's all too fantastic" to have happened to him. He tells his parents to "get out the fatted calf, for, in less than a week after you get this, the prodigal will appear."

While Richard was in Paris, Wesley wrote him telling him to get it all out of his system so that he could return to the even tenor of his ways, with Richard's famous rebuttal, "I hate that expression." Before he left Paris, however, he writes something that qualified the rebuttal. He tells his parents, "When I reach forty I think I will have had enough of uneven tenor." "Nearly thirty years older" than Richard, Wesley is different. So says his son, assuring Wesley that change will come. He is saying, Just be patient, Dad. When he gets to be his father's age, Richard, too, will be writing his own son about even tenor—just what Wesley's father "would have said" to him "if he had been alive" when Wesley was twenty. Richard tells Wesley that his "restless nature must come from one of you—I didn't cause it—but whoever is to blame, I'm very grateful, because I wouldn't take $1,000,000 for it."

The *Savoie* berthed in Manhattan and in the spring of 1920 he was enduring Princeton.

CHOOSING A CAREER

Oh, to live a life that is not routine, not in a rut so deep one can't see over the sides to the limitless horizons beyond.
Richard in a letter home from Princeton.

"Mike" Hockaday, "Shorty" Penfield, Richard, Larry Keyes, Princeton, summer 1916. "Heinie" Leh and wife Dot.

HARPER'S FERRY CROSSROADS, 1920

If in the year 1919, when . . . the Bolshevist bogey stalked across the land, and fathers and mothers were only beginning to worry about the younger generation, you had informed the average American citizen that prohibition was destined to furnish the most violently explosive issue of the nineteen-twenties, he would probably have told you that you were crazy. If you had been able to sketch for him . . . the speakeasy, and Alphonse Capone, multi-millionaire master of the Chicago bootleggers, driving through the streets in an armor-plated car with bulletproof windows, the innocent citizen's jaw would have dropped. . . . You might like it or not, but the country was going dry. Frederick Lewis Allen in *Only Yesterday*

In 1920, the United States' population was slightly more than ninety-two million. Men had an average life expectancy of forty-eight years; women, fifty-two. The average annual salary was seven hundred fifty dollars and in his Follies Mr. Ziegfeld's girls earned seventy-five dollars a week. The divorce rate was a tenth of one percent, or one in a thousand. Towns and villages were worried about motorcars racing through them at thirty miles an hour.

By the time the decade was over, the public had read about Al Capone, John Dillinger, Bugsy Moran, and the St. Valentine's Day Massacre. Some of the readers had been flappers; others, Lounge Lizards. They bought kits for bathtub gin, waited at a speakeasy door for an eye to peer through the slit.

They read about evangelist Aimee Semple McPherson supposedly drowning off a California beach only to re-emerge into publicity in a Mexican village on the Arizona border. Her followers forgave her stunt, and of them she said, "I have the passionate devotion of thousands. If the

94

papers tomorrow morning proved that I had committed eleven murders, those thousands would still believe in me." Families sat around living room radios as Father Coughlin urged they drive moneychangers from temples. Not his temple, of course—only those such as Aimee Semple McPherson's.

Lucky Lindy, or Charles Lindbergh, flew his Spirit of St. Louis non-stop, New York to Paris. Boys and girls did the Lindy Hop, jived to white Bix Beiderbecke in Chicago or black Cab Calloway in Harlem. Strumming his ukulele, Rudee Vallee trilled "The Indian Love Call." At colleges and universities students sang, "Collegiate, collegiate, yes, we are collegiate. Nothing intermediate. Trousers baggy. All our clothes are saggy." Grayed and wrinkled, John D. Rockefeller's picture was displayed in newspapers and magazines for the public to contemplate as a true American hero, setting an example of determined ambition against the day's soft, pleasure-seeking youth.

In 1920 Richard and his father had a long talk about what Richard wanted to do with his life. Their talk occurred during quiet strolls in lovely country far from Al Capone, Father Coughlin, and Aimee Semple McPherson. They customarily spent Easter together and for Sunday, March 28th, they rode the train to Harpers Ferry, at the confluence of the Potomac and Shenandoah Rivers.

In an April 2, 1920 letter to his mother, Richard described the train trip with his dad. "That night it was warm and moonlight and from the observation car we watched the Potomac all the way to Harper's Ferry, which had been called the most enchanting spot in ten continents and I believed it. We climbed to the top of the old town and looked down on the Shenandoah and Potomac River rapids all shiny in the moonlight. Harper's Ferry is so old and interesting it reminds one of something European and ancient. Next morning we climbed by stages to the top of the promontory and the view we got is worth coming miles to see. It must be even more wonderful in flowery spring. It was the sort of view you want to keep on looking at for hours."

They visited the armory where abolitionist John Brown and his men holed up against Robert E. Lee, then a colonel of US troops. By the town, father and son looked down on the rivers. The currents rushed past the town, winding toward the sea, bent on the same direction as Richard's wishes. Long ago, long before John Brown, the ancient Greek Heraclites said you cannot step in the same river twice because it can never be the same waves. Heraclites also meant the flux, the impermanence, of this thing called life and there at the fork in the rivers Richard might have thought about that but it was the future that was good. He had just turned twenty and thought only of where the water was headed.

At the town, they came to more than a juncture of the rivers. Like the decade as it entered the 1920s and Prohibition, Richard was at a crossroads and he planned on the road not taken by most. He agreed with Henry David Thoreau, who wrote, "If a man does not keep pace with his companions, perhaps it is because he hears a different drummer. Let him step to the music which he hears, however measured or far away."

In the letter to his mother, Richard put it mildly: "On the top, we had a very important talk he'll tell you about." What Wesley found out from his son gave the father pause. Running away to Europe in 1919 had changed him, Halliburton said, but it had not soothed his itchy feet as Wesley hoped. Wesley was disturbed by what he heard but said little.

He told his dad that after graduation he wanted to become a vagabond, a world traveler. Not just France, not only Europe. He wanted to see the globe, east to west, north to south. He wanted it all and hardships were part of getting it. No graduation trip for a summer in Europe. Not for him. That was a trifle. The world was bigger than his imagination and that was as he wanted it—what he could not get his mind around.

Wesley had not sized up Richard that way. Refined, aesthetic, the boy had studied classics, poetry, oriental literature, art history. He disliked dirt, noise, and the banal. When the boy was young, Wesley had made him go outside to play. What had become of the Richard he knew? This young man presented a puzzle. He really meant his rebuke when he wrote home from Paris that he rejected their conventional viewpoint.

Wesley had changed his office sign to include his son's name as an inducement for Richard to join him as a partner in his farm real estate business. Their names would be on business cards, maybe as Halliburton & Son—or better, Wesley & Richard Halliburton, Real Estate Developers. Surely the lad would come to his senses and become a steady Memphis businessman once he traveled a little. But no, here they were standing together looking down as the Shenandoah joined the Potomac and the boy was quite serious. Like the rivers, his currents were taking him out to the sea and beyond. Like Richard, like the rivers, Wesley was at a crossroads. What was a father to do?

Yes, what was a father to do? As they stood there, perhaps he blamed his son's attitudes on the times, rife with unrest. Product of the new age, Richard was disenchanted with the old.

As to their names together on a business card, Richard was clear. Not that. Nine to five days in an office or outside it selling something to somebody. No.

What was he to do for the rest of his life? He had been thinking about it, and laid it open for Wesley to see as they looked down on the valley and the rivers. He would travel. And write about his travels. He would earn good money and maybe get the restlessness out of his system. Maybe then he could settle down and make a Memphis career for himself. It was the only way that he could work things out.

"Maybe," he said. He was equivocating, trying to mollify his parents, and perhaps he knew he was doing it; perhaps it was unconscious. For Wesley, the word "maybe" offered hope.

Richard's own words offer testimony as to the course his life would take. As he wrote home from Princeton, "College is little more than a push for momentum so that you can spring into life's activities. 'Routine of life?' Life is not *life* if it's just routine, it's only existence and marking time till death comes to divorce us from it all. Oh, to live a life that is *not* routine, *not* in a rut so deep one can't see over the sides to the limitless horizons beyond."

Richard wrote to Nelle that after the very important talk between father and son, they "climbed down to the river again, right through the rocks and bushes, and had more fun!" Fun. Wesley might have paused on this word if he read the letter to Nelle. The one man middle-aged, the other in the flush of youth, they looked on the same forking rivers and had two different views. Wesley was wise enough to keep his opinion to himself. He promised moral and monetary support for his son's plans, however tentative.

Back down in town, they rented a Ford and drove to Antietam where twenty-three thousand men, Johnny Rebs and Billy Yanks, were killed, wounded, or missing on a single day in 1862. On that September day almost eighty years before, the sun shone as cannon roared. Richard described their visit that March as "a clear, sunny day."

In Philadelphia they listened to an orchestra playing in the Bellevue-Stratford hotel. They enjoyed Schubert's Moment Musical, which Richard had heard in France and "next to Ave Maria, loved best of all." They walked for over an hour "and had a good talk" before catching the train, Wesley for Memphis, Richard for Princeton and his future.

All had gone without a hitch, mainly because Wesley did not let it happen any other way. They parted amicably and Richard continued to write home.

On August 26, 1920, the Nineteenth Amendment was adopted after passage by Tennessee, the thirty-sixth and final state to ratify it. Women had the right to vote. The Eighteenth Amendment, Prohibition, had already been passed. That December 26th in New York City, gangster Monk Eastman was gunned down in front of the Blue Bird café by a corrupt Prohibition agent, Paul Bohan, who saw a mere two years in prison for manslaughter. By that December, rumrunners, bootleggers, and beer barons were already becoming rich from the Eighteenth Amendment. They had no legal competition. All saloons had been boarded-up. Successful in seeing them boarded-up, the Anti-Saloon League and the Women's

Christian Temperance Union were once again outraged, this time at the gangsters, and picketed Capitol Hill.

Richard Halliburton was back at Princeton to become part of the Jazz Age, and Prohibition, called the Noble Experiment by Herbert Hoover, had begun.

MONEY MAKING IS THE HARDEST THING IN LIFE FOR THE UNINSPIRED

Before Richard and Wesley talked at Harpers Ferry they visited Washington, DC, where they called on Senator Kenneth McKellar, a crusty Democrat from Tennessee and member of the Senate Education and Labor Committee. In 1919 over three hundred fifty thousand steel workers walked off their jobs and shut down the industry. In a committee hearing over working conditions, McKellar interrogated steel worker George Miller, who told him they labored twelve hours for $4.20 a day and were laid off if they stayed home sick. Wesley and Richard did not discuss the steel workers with the politician. Wesley probably wanted to sound him out on legislation regarding his own business, farm real estate in Tennessee. After leaving McKellar's office, Richard and Wesley were guided by a McKellar aide, who took them on a tour of Capitol Hill. They had access, not so rare in a day before politicians' time became bought by well-funded lobbyists. Richard wrote to his mother that he "met most of the Senate." After leaving Capitol Hill, he and his dad "had a wonderful walk in Rock Creek Park."

That December Richard learned that Wesley was not prospering. He wrote home, "Gosh, Dad, I suppose business conditions are about as bad as possible. I hope you won't have to sacrifice to get me through school. I'm a rather expensive hobby, I guess. Yes, money-making is the hardest thing in life for the uninspired."

Wesley must have raised his bushy eyebrows on reading the remark. Uninspired? He was paying the young pup's way through an ivy-league school and his efforts were uninspired? Richard would find out for himself about moneymaking and inspiration. The hubris in his boy shone like a sun. Richard thought he would make money because he would be inspired.

Richard had expectations of himself: "but I feel as positive as anything

I'll find something new and use my imagination to make dollars out of it. I revolt at the idea of being a bank clerk or any other sort of 'beginning at the bottom.' I'm going to be my own boss from the first whatever I do. I can't work for anybody else and not have the reins. I'll never be happy or progressive that way."

He compares his generation to his parents' and notes the acceleration of change. They could take things slowly. Halliburton was born on its cusp and the Twentieth Century had happened to him. "The thrills and cream of life, as well as the dross, have been sprinkled through your years for you, and your age, but have fallen on my head all at once." He says they have watched change from the horse and buggy to "the automobile, the moving pictures, the benefits of constantly increasing means, travel, New York and Paris."

The world was changing. The year before, in 1919, an open-cockpit NC-4 flew in twelve hours from Newfoundland to Horta in the Azores, where it took nine days for Richard on the *Octorara*. In 1920 Fascists under Benito Mussolini marched against the communists. In 1920 Karl Binding and Alfred Hoche introduced the notion of lebensunwertesleben, "lives unworthy of life," a wonderfully evil idea that Hitler would adopt. Warning against another global conflict, John Maynard Keynes argued for cancellation of German war debts. Two years before Richard and Wesley visited Harpers Ferry, one and a half million Armenians were slaughtered by Turks without the world noticing. Remembering the Turk success years later, Hitler told his Death's Head units, "Kill without pity or mercy all men, women, and children of Polish race or language. . . . Who still talks nowadays about the Armenians?"

Richard and his ultra-modern generation did not know what lay around the century's corner, but it would come. About to begin adulthood, he could see his own problem. He was struggling with an idea—what to do with the rest of his life—and it had to be something he fervently believed in, something that would shape and transform his life. He looked around and saw people accepting limits. They had traded giving their life to meaning for giving it to the dollar. There had to be a way both to have meaning and to make money. Finding the way posed an immense challenge to him. He was determined to be inspired and he would somehow meet the challenge.

SELF-DOUBT, JOB DESCRIPTIONS, & HARRY FRANCK

In 1921 Jack Dempsey slugged it out with Georges Carpentier at Boyle's Thirty Acres in Jersey City. Seventy-five thousand people paid over 1.5 million dollars to see the Frenchman flattened in the fourth. At Ebbets Field in Brooklyn, Babe Ruth batted his fifty-ninth homer and the 1921 World Series broke records for gate receipts. Man o' War was the horse to watch at The Kentucky Derby. Everybody wanted an Eskimo Pie, a chocolate-covered vanilla ice cream bar, so that in three months the price of cocoa beans on the New York commodities market rose fifty percent. Bathing beauty contests were something new in America and at a competition on the Potomac the girls wore hats to cover their hair, stockings to cover their legs, and tunics to cover their bodies. One daring miss rolled her stockings below her knees.

In his conversations with Wesley when at Harper's Ferry, Richard had been certain about traveling the world as a vagabond but later came to question himself. He had been determined somehow to meet the challenge but self-doubt set in. Maybe something else after all, he thought. The change occurred because in his senior year at Princeton he compared himself to others with greater intellect and broader education. As an editor, engaged in practical rather than academic matters, he was rather like his dad—dealing with the everyday world and not living the life of the mind. Near graduation, he began thinking that he had fallen too far, had been too practical and not sufficiently academic by expanding his mind, studying more. He questioned whether he had wisely spent his Princeton years as he thought about friends and acquaintances who were more mentally developed "than the great mass of their fellow students." The elite were "mostly Phi Beta Kappas, influential speakers, serious students. In which class is included none of my close friends or I." He worried that he might not be smart enough. He blamed himself for being unable to play the piano and lacking fluency in a foreign language. Perhaps he needed to develop intellect and gain an education that the demands of his editorial jobs inhibited. Just before graduation, in April 1921, he wrote to his father, "Suppose this: Why not Oxford—for a year to try it? Take a three months' summer trip and be in England in October. After a year there I'll only be 22 then. I could try for a Rhodes Scholarship which, added to your support, Dad, would establish me excellently. If one year's experience proved unsatisfactory—enough!"

That was one side of him. There was the other in which academic studies and the development of intellect were cast into doubt. In the same April letter, he wrote, "perhaps the higher life has not enough action and freedom."

The other side asked if the higher life was available to him as somebody with modest talents, as he saw himself. Elsewhere, he says of Browning's poem "Paracelsus," that the poet wrote it "at the age of 22! And I began to wonder if perhaps I'd best start selling groceries." He sank into moody ruminations on shortcomings and conflicts and did "get very blue" at times.

In a letter to Nelle for her birthday he said he knew that his mother had taught him "to avoid self-deprecation" but other thoughts wormed their way into his confidence and he struggled with them. In the same letter he deprecated himself again but then caught himself. He put aside his troubles and wrote, "This is your day, Mother dear, not mine." He apologized for the tone, as it was a letter for her birthday and adds, "But the love is here, the sympathy, the admiration."

Speaking of joining the *Princetonian* as an editor, he asks, "Is the Prince board with its grinding demands worth while?" It is not a rhetorical question. It is about job descriptions, so to speak, and he has his father in mind. Wesley had kept to the job description day by day, year by year and his health suffered, not to say his chances to see a wider world. So is "the Prince board" worth it? Richard answers his own question. His answer comes from how he saw his father's experience as honor student at Vanderbilt. At the top of his engineering class, Wesley had been awarded the Founders Medal, of pure gold, the highest bestowed upon a student, requiring hard work and study.

Richard's answer implies rejection of fatherly adherence to routine. "Do you think, Dad, your Founder's medal is worth your bad stomach?" This seems to allude to ulcers from worry. This is another dig such as the one he made with "money making is the hardest thing for the uninspired." As with the other remark, Wesley ignored this one.

In his self-doubt Richard asks, What is worth it? He thinks of the *Princetonian*'s "grinding demands." He must fit its job description, perform certain tasks. He does know that he hates job descriptions because they wear away at his élan and proscribe the future in terms of duties and overarching responsibilities. He does not resign from the board.

His mind becomes a weather vane, turning with the wind of his thoughts. Elsewhere, he admires those of a plodding disposition rather than the Phi Beta Kappans. "Sometimes," he said, "I ardently wish I were one of the phlegmatic kind of students that stick to their books regularly and don't strain over everything and are too insensitive to worry over lack of position or influence. Often they leave college with a better mental capacity to handle life and business."

Position or influence—here is a trait instilled by the values of his parents and in it lay magnetic pull against the free spirit he would like to be. Position or influence counted for something with him. During the Roaring Twenties, *The New York Times* society page regularly listed him as a dinner or party guest at some big-name gathering where he was found among movie stars and politicians, from Rudolph Valentino to Senator McAdoo. After he became a famous author, his entrée was guaranteed and he took almost every entrance he could get. But the 1920s moved into the 1930s and his growing desire for solitude. His gradual and most important lesson in life became that the key to success lay inward with self-companionship rather than with dependency on others. Above all, though, he did not stop believing in the freedom of his feet and in their movement he continued to find pleasure.

When Richard broached travel to Wesley, as a vocation the subject had no shape given by society. Physician, architect, stockbroker—these had a job description. Halliburton began thinking about shape. He looked at his friends. They knew where they were headed. Poughkeepsie, Chicago, Pittsburgh. All that had a local habitation and a name. He had an airy nothing and must write his own job description. They did not think of theirs as grim fate. He did.

His friends' advantage was clarity. On the teeter-totter of swings from self-doubt to choice then back to self-doubt, he had none. They had secure futures. He detested that. They had even tenors. All he knew was that his body demanded unevenness.

Mainly, though, it was the job description. He hated the very idea of it but needed something. What was he to do with his life? He had the vague idea of adventure-travel writing but it lay in the hazy mist of desire. The clear path of his pals drew him into doubts about himself. The more he thought the more he became self-critical.

Richard compared himself to his roommate Mike Hockaday, who some day would be "at the top of a great business where efficiency and faithful obedience mean everything and imagination and inspiration nothing." Of Mike, he said, "his methodical-ness and great sense of responsibility are necessary counterparts to my wild imagination and reckless energy. It's a question which type gets the farther or accomplishes the more." Mike seems to be one of "the phlegmatic kind" to which he alluded, the kind who "don't strain over everything and are too insensitive to worry over lack of position or influence." Had he known about it, Mike might have taken this as a compliment.

Then he met somebody, Harry Franck, who had written his own job description, and it provided roles that Richard himself wanted. Harry carved out his own career and offered Richard a model of what Halliburton could do with his life. A major travel writer of the early Twentieth Century, Franck wrote his own job description by living it. He authored thirty-three books including *A Vagabond Journey around the World* (1910), *Four Months Afoot in Spain* (1911), and *Wandering in Northern China* (1923).

A World War I veteran, at age sixty-one Franck enlisted in the US Army in 1942. To make Franck younger, the recruiter changed his birth date to 1888. Of his war experiences, Franck wrote (with Lt. Porter) *Winter Journey through the Ninth,* about the Ninth Air Force in combat.

Following his freshman year at the University of Michigan, in the summer of 1900 with $3.18 in his pocket Franck worked his way across to Europe on a cattle boat, getting back to Ann Arbor two weeks after classes had begun. Later, he spent sixteen months globe-trekking, stopping to work when he ran out of money. His 1910 book *A Vagabond Journey around the World* sold so well that he continued his travels. He met U Dhammaloka—an Irish hobo turned Buddhist monk and atheist critic of Christian missionaries as well as a temperance campaigner—who actively participated in the Buddhist revival stirring then in Southeast Asia. During construction of the Panama Canal, Franck took a job as a plain-clothes cop in the Canal Zone and recalled it in *Zone Policeman 88.* His book listed as number three among 1913 best sellers. In *Tramping through Mexico, Guatemala and Honduras* (1916), he described his job as overseer of a Guanajuato mine. In his adventures Franck wore the uniform of the French Foreign Legion and of a Devil's Island prisoner.

Franck eventually married. Sometimes his wife tramped with him in his adventures. They settled down and had five children. He died of Parkinson's disease. Born in 1881, he died in bed and in old age in 1962.

Franck was to give a lecture one evening at Lawrenceville and when Halliburton learned about it he knew that he had to go. The man had done what Richard wanted to do. As a boy Halliburton read Franck's books and they helped kindle in him the fire that fueled his discontent with the world as he found it. He pedaled his bicycle to Lawrenceville, bought a ticket, and found a chair in the lecture hall, waiting for the man to appear on stage and step behind the lectern. The room must have been full, for Franck drew crowds wherever he lectured.

Richard listened to Franck and after the lecture he wrangled an invitation to dinner with the writer, about which he wrote home. "Aren't you jealous, Dad?" Another gentle competition the son had with the father. He was beginning to see how he could formulate his own job description when he told his parents, "I'll surely pump information from him."

Were this a novel, at this point in the narrative a major shift in Halliburton could be developed but it did not happen that way. Richard left his dinner with Franck and returned to his old self-doubt as revealed by his letters home. In real life we do not find clear-cut divisions because people rarely experience sudden miraculous transformations, are basked in illuminating light, and see clearly the course of their lives.

Richard pumped Franck for information and neither over the rest of his year at Princeton, nor until the success of his first book, *The Royal Road to Romance*, did he have a glimmer of hope he had developed his very own, unique job description, one that allowed uneven tenor. He remained determined. During his eighteen months of travel that gave birth to *The Royal Road*, he wrote home from Marseilles "This trip is my work. Some Princeton grads from the class of '21 went into banking, some into theology. I went into traveling and writing and I take it as seriously as they do. It must be my income." With each successful book he would be writing his job description but the more his public expected a repeat of the same Halliburton—a persona he came to despise—the more he felt locked-in by it.

Franck had sowed a seed, had told him it could be done. He said there was a way but it was a path Richard would have to find for himself.

In youthful enthusiasm Richard wrote, "If a man does not sing, actually or theoretically, when he works, there must be something wrong either with the man or the work." Like Yeats as an old man, Richard would have "Soul clap its hands and sing, and louder sing for every tatter in its mortal dress." Richard's job description became an unfinished libretto with his life itself as the voice.

GRADUATION

As they were about to go separate ways the Princeton senior class of 1921 looked back on their four years and voted in various categories. They chose one student as "most popular," another as "best athlete, "best lady's man" or "most likely to run for president." Richard was voted "most original."

He and his classmates looked forward to graduation and to the precious few months left of campus life. He also looked backward upon his collegiate years with fond memories. The uncertain world in which he must earn a living lay ahead. He and his pals would have moments to remember.

He was dormed in Patton Hall, named after the university's twelfth president, Francis Patton, who said it was "better to have gone and loafed than to have never gone at all," another way of saying for future national leaders that the so-called "gentleman's C" —a C is for gentlemen—was honorable because of social connections made if not because of knowledge gained. This, in an age when successful families sent sons to university to socialize with other young gentlemen and to develop friendships for future business dealings. In his first book, *The Royal Road to Romance*, Richard looks at his four roommates bent over their desks. His narrative reveals that he is on good personal terms with each of them, though it also describes them in a way that Halliburton looked at the future. He sees them dutifully grubbing their lives away. He names each of them and does so with a familiarity, an attitude, that only a good friend could get away with. John Henry Leh, James Penfield Seiberling, Edward L. Keyes III, Irvine "Mike" Hockaday. In the order named, his dorm mates became department store owner; Goodyear Tire scion; prominent Kansas City physician; and financier as well as father of a Hallmark greeting cards founder. He dedicates his first book to them, "whose sanity, consistency, and respectability as Princeton roommates drove me to this book."

They were good pals and politics did not figure greatly in his friendships although he was on the other side of the political divide. In April 1920, he had traveled to Chicago to attend the Republican National Convention, although he and his family were Democrats. That it was a Republican gathering did not matter much. Politics did not figure greatly because he did not figure politics as great in his life, especially when young. Despite conservative inclinations, he and his family saw Republicans as the party of the loathsome Reconstruction Era Carpet Baggers. Of his fellow Princetonians, he said of the November 1920 Presidential election, "Everything here went 99% for Harding," a Republican who became the 29th President. He was the one percent.

He had much to look back on. In July of 1920 he and his pals had roughed it Teddy-Roosevelt style in Montana's Glacier Park. "We have a world of provisions but four men and two guides." They were going to dip trout lines "in water that never saw tackle before." From this experience he sold an article to *Field and Stream* magazine, which must have whetted his interest in authorship. In November 1920 he and his pals attended the Yale-Princeton game, watching it in sheepskin coats and with blankets. In May 1921 he wrote of his chums and their world, "Tomorrow is a big day for us. [Mike Hockaday's] track team meets Yale and Harvard and the Navy row us on the lake. Heinie [Leh] is captain of our boat."

All the youthful bonds, the fresh expectations, the sheer unburdened joy, all would fall into the unredeemable past. The last few weeks passed in a whir. Near the end of May he wrote of "the happiest seven days I ever spent." He chiefly refers to a girl, Marie. He had spent his time with her and with her hand hooked in his elbow she caught male eyes wherever they went. He was smitten by her. He was in love with her, he said, and then added, "Oh yes, just for the time being, of course." In June 1921, one of his last Princeton letters tells his parents "the girls at our house party were so lovely in their youthful simple dresses." He cautions himself, though. He does not want to get sentimental over them as he looks to his future. His futile experiences with Frances Bailey and Helen Pendergast had left their mark on him.

June came. That month, the New York Giants won two games over Philly, with Dave Bancroft hitting a homer, only to faint later. On Long Island, Helen Keller's home was burglarized. With lovely weather, immigrant crowds took the trolley to North Beach on Long Island. At the other end of society's spectrum, limousine chauffeurs were given traffic tickets from the Elmhurst, Long Island police for driving on the wrong side of the road in order to get their wealthy passengers to the beach on the packed route. Mary Pickford starred in a silent photo play, *Through The Back Door*, and Jackie Coogan played at Proctor's Theatre, New York, in *Peck's*

Bad Boy, next the usual vaudeville bill.

June came and went. Then it was over. As Richard had proposed to his father on the Harpers Ferry promontory overlooking the rivers, he was headed far away from Princeton and Memphis. The plan was eighteen months abroad, some of it with Mike Hockaday. He would travel and write.

By the time he returned home he would have a book manuscript. He knew Princeton was behind him, felt its finality. "Just about a month from today I'm set adrift, with a diploma for sail and lots of nerves for oars. So many men graduating have their lives visioned and arranged with the greatest precision, four years law, father's law office, four years medicine, three interne, practice. Mine is so much more shaky, one and a half [years] travel, nine months writing. If published and success, fine. If not accepted, then what? And at the 'then what' stage I'll be nearly 24 years old." He adds, "When I stop to think about after June 21, I frankly become afraid." In effect, Harry Franck told him he had to write his own job description and he was about to use his new life to begin the first draft. Behind, all was written. Ahead, he did not know what words would form a shape out of the great unknown.

DETERMINED TO MAKE TRAVEL-ADVENTURE WRITING HIS VOCATION

"Follow your bliss," said Joseph Campbell, author of *The Hero with a Thousand Faces* and other books on archetypal myths containing universal wisdom. In his words, he meant that following your bliss "puts yourself on a track that has been there all the while, waiting for you, and the life that you ought to be living is the one you are living." If you feel refreshed in your doings, that is evidence you are following your bliss. To students who took him to be encouraging hedonism, he grumbled, "I should have said, 'Follow your blisters.' " Blisters were Richard's intention. He knew it would be tough and wondered if his travel-adventure writing would become a success. After all, he was aging fast. Soon he would be twenty-four. Then, he answers himself, "Well, that being the case, it's *got* to be a success." The italics are his. It absolutely had to happen. That does not mean he is without misgivings. He compares himself to a child thrown into "a pond to learn to swim."

Wesley tells us that despite Richard's worries on leaving Princeton and his dormitory "So strong were his emotions that he actually ran from 41 Patton Hall as he started for the railroad station." He and Mike Hockaday were going abroad. It would be the traditional Grand Tour for Mike; it became vocation for Richard. Halliburton wrote that he had "a diploma for sail," but Mike Hockaday, his traveling pal, and he soon discovered, as Wesley put it, that "their diplomas were no asset in breaking into the ranks of ordinary seamen." They did not look like seamen. They did not act like seamen. They did not sound like seamen.

EUROPE, 1921

My trip is my occupation in life. I've "gone to work." My aim is proficiency in my present task, not to get through on a certain date.
Richard Halliburton

Richard at Taj Mahal
Courtesy Rhodes College

A LIFE WILDLY IMPROBABLE

In 1921, the same year that Mike and Richard sailed to Europe with romantic readiness for life's great adventures, Eugene O'Neill's play *Diff'rent* was staged. On how environment determines lives, the play featured Emma Crosby with the dreams she had and clutched after. That year, the environment of history continued shaping lives, despite the dreams people had and clutched after. The Irish still waged their war for independence with massacres and violence on both sides. In January, France demanded Germany pay 269 billion gold marks. Impossible, said the German government and declared it an economic enslavement of the German people. They protested and so the French army occupied the Rhineland. The lives of people all over the globe were being propelled forward by historical forces beyond their control. Emma Crosby is guided by O'Neill to the end of the play, where she is defeated and hangs herself, a victim of her environment.

O'Neill speculated on the force of environment on one life's direction— Emma Crosby's. As historical force, environment shapes many lives, from communism to free-market economies, from Stalin's starvation of Ukrainian farmers to Henry Ford's Tin Lizzies. History sweeps us up in its momentum. Richard lived as an adult in an era between two world wars and his life was caught in its historical momentum but he had a direction of his own. Unlike Emma Crosby's dismal existence, his life was wildly improbable compared to most lives.

Imagine yourself like Richard. You climb the Matterhorn in the Alps then later you ascend Mount Fuji in Japan in winter and as well take on Mount Olympus in Greece. Suppose that you decide to swim the Hellespont in imitation of Lord Byron in the Nineteenth Century. You swim the Panama Canal with locks opening for you. In steamy rain, you slog through the thick jungles of the Malay Peninsula, trusting your native guide to detect trail traces, and you barely escape a cobra's venom. Retracing Hannibal's march on Rome, you cross the Alps on an elephant. At the risk of being shot, you climb the dangerous Khyber Pass into Afghanistan. You fly over the Sahara to Timbuktu in an open-cockpit biplane and almost miss fuel dumps. In Vladivostok, just after the Russian revolution, you fear a knock on the door by Bolsheviks and, trying to flee the Soviet Union, almost die of sickness on a tramp ship in the Black Sea. Out of Macao, your ship is boarded by Chinese pirates who rob you and other passengers and shoot five people, killing two. You trek through the Himalayas over forbidden, freezing ridges into Ladakh and Tibet. In Cambodia, you take a steamer upriver to Angkor Wat, deep in the jungle, almost unknown then. You sneak past guards to spend the night at the Taj Mahal. You hunt tigers in Bengal. You hike into lovely Kashmir. You spend halcyon days floating on a houseboat in Srinagar. You witness the marriage of the last Chinese Emperor. You walk the Great Wall of China with the young American woman who tutored the Empress. You are thrown in jail in Gibraltar as a German spy. In Java you stow away on a ship Singapore bound. You camp at Cheops pyramid. You lodge with Dyak headhunters and take the chief for a plane ride. You interview Lenin's widow and the man who shot the Czar and his family. These were only some of his roads less traveled.

Halliburton graduated Princeton in 1921 and the trip abroad set the tone for Richard's adult life. Like Victorian aesthete Walter Pater, he sought to burn with a hard, gem-like flame. His aesthetics, though, were not Pater's contemplative kind. His art was in the feel of his feet against a pitching deck, the wind against his cheek in a Himalayan pass.

He had been reading Oscar Wilde's *The Picture of Dorian Gray*, in which Gray becomes acutely aware that he is young once only. Gray holds that in life only beauty and vivid sensuousness are worthwhile. In a Faustian pact, Gray keeps his youthful beauty while his picture ages. Thus he makes art out of his life as the thing hanging on the wall becomes gray and homely. Words from the book etched themselves into Halliburton's mind: "Realize your youth while you have it."

RICHARD & MIKE ON THE HIGH SEAS

From Kansas City, Mike Hockaday, the sometime-dreamer as Halliburton described him, accompanied Richard abroad. Hockaday's parents gave permission for the trip, expecting him to return and fulfill their plans for him as an investor. With the promise of remittances, Richard's parents gave their blessing, although they could not have stopped him. In his usual generosity of spirit, Richard wrote to his parents that Hockaday's "parents are enthusiastic about his going with me. His methodical-ness and great sense of responsibility are necessary counterparts to my wild imagination and reckless energy." With that statement he expresses modesty and with the next he shows competitiveness and ambition: "It's a question which type gets the farther or accomplishes the more." He looks down the road to success in life and it is not the aristocratic luxury of Dorian Gray but business success as a writer. He returns to generosity in another letter. His parents, Wesley and Nelle, gave him their blessing but he knew his mother was worried. He was almost apologetic to her as he writes, "Mrs. Hockaday has two other sons to comfort her in Mike's absence, and you have no other sons." He then tells her, "However, dad will be a great help, for he is a very optimistic reassurer." Richard meant between the lines that that he had to go and he would.

For the trip he resolved to write a thousand words a day in his notebook, which would provide grist for the book he planned on his adventures as well as magazine articles to finance his travels. He had read Richard Henry Dana's *Two Years before the Mast* and typically self-mocking he would think of his sea experience in terms of an article for the *Atlantic Monthly* titled "Two Weeks before the Mast." He also saw parallels between himself and Dana. Both were Ivy League graduates, Dana from Harvard, himself Princeton. Both followed the sea. Both wrote about it from American ships, one in 1840, the other in 1921. Both were named Richard. Both were twenty-one.

He wrote home that he had the stuff for this career. He could do it, and they need not fret. "Don't you worry, Dad, about my holding my job. I was made to fit it and it to fit me. I've gone at this thing with a seriousness and determination that have characterized the few things in the past which I have reveled in."

Already bent on success, he had a concern he kept from Mike Hockaday. He expressed it to his parents. "I do not contemplate with pleasure the difficulties that are sure to come between Mike and me and to end in unavoidable separation. My trip is my occupation in life. I've 'gone to work'. My aim is proficiency in my present task, not to get through on a certain date. It's going to be 'speed up' from me and 'slow down and stop' from me. It's unfortunate but inevitable."

To begin their adventure, Halliburton and Hockaday sought passage as ordinary seamen on a freighter. The two Princeton men wanted a rough-and-ready adventure. Passage on a luxury liner would have been out of the question. With their Princeton degrees they sought jobs as deck hands but nobody would hire them. There was nothing rough-and-ready about them. They only had to open their mouths and the wrong words came out—right for Princeton but inappropriate for a deck hand. After repeated turndowns, they gave one another soup-bowl haircuts, and wore green flannel shirts. They spoke with salty language and Richard tells his readers that they finally were hired by the captain of the *Ipswich* because of their new appearance and demeanor.

Years later Wesley Halliburton said that the soup bowl haircuts and salty language had no effect. In fact, observed Richard's father, "The Ipswich captain only hired them because he was told to do so. Throughout the voyage he barely spoke to them." As his father noted, Richard liked to embellish narratives. The truth is that they had little persuasion and but for a chance encounter they were destined for a luxury cruise with deck chairs, shuffle board, and ladies on the promenade deck with parasols.

In an interview, Hockaday told James Cortese what really happened: "We wanted to work our way over the Atlantic but we had no luck in getting jobs and had dejectedly bought tickets on the Aquitania." They were not walking among longshoremen on the piers but up on New York's Fifth Avenue when it happened. On the sidewalk Mike met a family acquaintance, Sam Pryor, and they got to talking, explaining their inability to be signed on as deck hands. They had tried and tried again and nobody wanted them. Pryor listened, probably amused, and he gave them a business card with a note written on it.

This was Samuel Pryor Junior whose father was appointed by Percy Rockefeller in 1914 as chairman of Remington Arms, suddenly a lucrative business with the outbreak of war. The Germans accused the United States of shipping arms to the allies and sank the *Lusitania*. Many years later, divers found Remington weapons in *Lusitania's* hold. With George Herbert Walker, Pryor's father was director of American Ship and Commerce Company. Walker was grandfather and great-grandfather of the 41st and 43rd Bush Presidents. In short, Pryor had connections.

Pryor told them to take the card to Averell Harriman. In 1921, at age thirty, Harriman was head of the Hamburg American Line. The two boys immediately called on Harriman, who picked up the telephone as they sat in his office. When he hung up, he told Richard and Mike to report for duty on the *Ipswich* at eight o' clock next morning.

A name to be reckoned with in history and politics, Averell Harriman became ambassador to the USSR, FDR's European envoy, Truman's

Secretary of Commerce, New York Governor, ambassador for US Presidents John F Kennedy and Lyndon Baines Johnson and candidate for the Democratic Presidential nomination. He was also chief US negotiator at the Paris Peace Talks on Vietnam.

Hockaday remembered the morning they boarded the *Ipswich*. The boys tried to look like seasoned salts as old tars watched them climb out of the launch boat and up the ladder onto the deck. Never having been on a ship, Mike had stowed in his knapsack a supply of Mother Sill's Seasick Pills. Climbing the ladder, once he got topside his knapsack broke, spilling his pills on the deck. "I watched as several hard boiled seamen picked them up for me," he recalled. The tars had been warned by the captain about the young swells coming aboard.

Richard wrote that in mid-Atlantic "Mike was green with seasickness and simply had to knock off work and lie down." Nor was Halliburton especially comfortable. Seas smashed against the bow and beams, sending cold spray over the crew.

As the vessel slipped out of New York Harbor, Richard waved "gratefully at Lady Liberty." He said she did not notice him because "she does not flirt with ordinary seamen." The *Ipswich* made through the North Atlantic with its heavy seas, fogs, icebergs, and storms. Even with portholes fifteen feet above water line, they had to remain closed most of the voyage. Rough seas washed across the deck, crashing on the bridge window as the helmsman peered through the wheelhouse glass, bracing himself and holding the spokes steady against the next great wave.

Evenings after knocking off from work, Halliburton wrote in his notebook. He was filled with the excitement of the voyage and recorded his experiences while far greater, dangerous ones awaited him in the months ahead. Among his notes, at the end of July he described the sights off the German coast. The *Ipswich* left the North Sea for the Kiel Canal, a sixty-one mile connection to the Baltic. In his notebook he explains that he and Mike connived work on the ship's bridge to watch land loom. They passed the island of Helgoland to the north as they saw the city of Cuxhaven slowly emerge from the western German coast at the mouth of the Elbe. Richard had never seen so many ships, a great line of them in the Cuxhaven Channel stretching out of the river into the North Sea. On Sunday, July 31st, with the Canal off the port beam, they sailed past it into the Elbe, making upriver to Hamburg.

During the voyage, the ship wireless daily reported the consequences of the Treaty of Versailles, in which Germany and its economy had been plundered by the Allies. Not that the wireless dealt exclusively with the Treaty but that it kept the crew informed of a rapidly inflating German mark. Richard wrote that he heard "the mark is sinking lower and lower until it takes 80 marks to equal a dollar in value." As a young foreign correspondent, Ernest Hemingway reported seeing a German with a wheelbarrow of marks that soon would buy no more than a pack of cigarettes.

Richard was interested in history while current events did not always fill his vision. Soon, in 1923, Hitler staged his Beer Hall Putsch at the Bürgerbräukeller in Munich and though it was put down it was just the beginning for him. The 1920s and 1930s in Germany would fill history books. The decades would spill over into the Second World War and the Elbe River seen by Richard would in 1945 become the meeting place for merging forces of victorious Russian and American troops. While he wrote in his notebook, Richard deeply felt his youth and its brevity. He and Mike spent little time noticing the misery in Germany before moving beyond into the rest of Europe. Here was the world, and here he was, twenty-one. He was in Europe and the rest of his life was about to begin.

ZERMATT

Famous mountains are famous each in its own way. Everest is the highest. K2 is fearsomely difficult. The Matterhorn is beautiful in its symmetry. At 14,693 feet, it is almost a pyramid with four faces aligned according to the cardinal points of the compass, each tremendously steep, each with avalanches tumbling snow and ice into glaciers. There are no easy ways up the Matterhorn. Its weather is unpredictable and fast-changing. As mountaineering became a sport in the Nineteenth Century, other peaks in the Alps were scaled but the Matterhorn remained aloof. It became the ultimate challenge because it demanded great technical skill and because fear rose in the gut of would-be climbers gazing up at its sheer, slick faces. On the border between Switzerland and Italy, it towers over Zermatt on the Swiss side and Breuil-Cervina on the Italian. The Zermatt approach was long considered impossible. The rock was too steep, too sheer, too unforgiving. High mountain weather is forever unpredictable, with sunny skies followed by raging storms. Again and again climbers tried to scale the Matterhorn and failed.

In the Himalayas, Everest has claimed about one hundred seventy lives. The Matterhorn has killed over five hundred climbers since it was first summited and even the first successful ascent was tragic.

Englishman Edward Whymper was a wood-engraver's son. Whymper, an artist commissioned to make drawings of the Alps, wanted to become the first man on the summit. In July 1865 he and his team ascended the easiest route, the Hörnli Ridge and stood atop the mountain, looking out over range upon range of mountains fading into the horizon, with freezing wind roaring in their faces, storm clouds racing overhead, and Zermatt tiny in the valley below.

On the descent, four of seven men lost their hold and plunged down the face to their deaths. Charles Hadow, a Cambridge student, slipped on ice, unbalancing a guide Michel Croz, which yanked a father and son—old and young Peter Taugwalder—both guides, as well as Charles Hudson and Lord Francis Douglas.

Seven men were left hanging by a rope over an abyss. Whymper and two guides threw their weight into holding the others from falling and helped check the fall but there the men hung, dangling as they watched the rope straining against all their weight. In 1865 pitons had not yet been invented. Without these spikes driven into rock, the rope broke and the lower four plunged to their deaths in a glacier almost a mile below. They were Croz, Hadow, Hudson, and Douglas. Except for Lord Douglas, all the bodies were later found. Today, the graves can be visited in a Zermatt churchyard.

In 1931 the difficult north face was finally climbed by two unemployed brothers from Munich, Franz and Toni Schmid. At the 1932 Los Angeles Olympics, Art Competitions and Exhibition, Toni and Franz were awarded Gold Medals, Merit for Mountaineering, for the first ascent of the face. Toni's medal was posthumous. He died that same year, age twenty-two, in a climbing accident seventy-five days before the Games began. His brother Franz died in 1992, age eighty-seven.

Even today, the Matterhorn counts among mountains having the highest number of deaths. Because of the many ascents since Richard Halliburton's day, long lengths of fixed rope and ladders encourage more climbers than is safe. The traffic makes the mountain dangerous. Unlike in Whymper's time, today climbers on the Hörnli ridge have the advantage of a hut, really a solid building, before they begin the sheer ascent on that face. Farther on, they have the Solvay Hut, built by industrialist Ernest Solvay, who sponsored conferences tackling key issues in physics and chemistry.[*] Despite these conveniences, deaths average twelve a year. Many gravestones below in Zermatt provide a narrative of men and the mountain.

In 1955 a twenty-year-old man lost his life in the climb. In August 1997 two Americans died climbing the Matterhorn from the Swiss side. That same year, an Idaho woman and a Californian died climbing it from the Italian side. They fell to their deaths roped together on the east face of the Hörnli Ridge. Also in August 1997 seven other climbers died, including a man, twenty-two, who fell into a crevasse and perished from exposure

---

[*] Ernest Solvay sponsored the Solvay Conferences, about quantum physics, a new and puzzling science. In the famous 1927 Solvay Conference in Brussels, Belgium, Einstein was disturbed by the strange, random world physics was discovering. He argued that God does not play dice with the universe, to which Neils Bohr retorted, "Stop telling God what to do." Bohr meant while physicists could not—and still do not—understand why phenomena sometimes behave as particles, sometimes as waves, facts must be accepted. That's the way it is. The behavior can be described but not understood and remains a mystery raising questions about reality and the nature of consciousness.

before climbers could reach him. In 2005 an Australian lost his footing and when his body was located he could not be identified with his head and face because they had been severely disfigured as he bounced off precipices and crags. In March of 2006 DNA confirmed his identity.

Until his death in 1911 Edward Whymper grieved over his lost companions, never forgetting the tragedy of the very first Matterhorn ascent.

As a Zermatt tradition, the church bell chimes when the townsfolk learn another climber has died on the mountain. Today, the Matterhorn no longer ranks among the most difficult but it remains unforgiving for the naïve and inexperienced.

Richard and Mike were both.

The Matterhorn

MOSEYING TOWARD MORTAL PERIL

Look well to each step; and from the beginning think what may be the end. Edward Whymper

Only after the fact does Richard tells his parents that he and Mike Hockaday knew the Alps were threatened by bad weather. Further, the Alpine climbing season was about to close but they did not hurry as the possibility of there being a climbing season never occurred to them. In *Royal Road* Richard explains that they got in shape for mountaineering by climbing the tower stairs of the cathedrals in Cologne and Strasbourg and in castles overlooking the Rhine. They walked the length of the Rhine and from Strasbourg turned away to tramp through the Alsatian Vosges for "a hundred mile ramble," as he put it, from Strasbourg to the Swiss border. In his letters, Richard said they "scorned the roads" and discovered still fresh World War I trenches, barbed wire, dugouts, and command posts. When at Princeton, Richard ached to get in the Big Show, as he called it, before it was over and here was a testimony to what he missed—testimony, if it sunk in on him. They breakfasted in Schlucht in the Black Forest then walked through thick fog and pouring rain to Krüt, where they boarded a train for Basel, Switzerland.

From Basel, Richard traveled to Lake Lucerne, boated to Brunnen then walked to Flüelen at its southern end. (In *The Royal Road* he called the village Frulen.) He took a lake boat back and on it met an English gentleman. The man was ex-Prime Minister Asquith's private secretary, whom Halliburton found interesting. The gentleman was Maurice Bonham Carter, grandfather of 21st Century movie star Helena Bonham Carter. As Prime Minister Herbert Henry Asquith's secretary, Bonham Carter was privy to the politics and folly that went into the July 1916 debacle at the Somme, with twenty thousand dead on the first day. In 1916, Maurice

Bonham Carter—whose wife called him Bongie—became a Knight, Order of The Bath. Richard took his leave of Bonham Carter at Lucerne and rejoined Mike, traveling with him by train about eighty miles to Zermatt.

They arrived in Zermatt after the end of the normal climbing season. To his parents, Halliburton wrote, "the weather has taken on a decidedly frosty tinge." On September 19, 1921 they checked into a small hotel and asked where they could find guides. Following leads, they asked around, only to find nobody willing to take them up the mountain. The season had come and gone and they should leave too.

TOOTHBRUSHES & SAFETY RAZORS

They did find two experienced Swiss guides, Adolph Schaller and a man named as André by Richard, but recalled as Roman by Mike. A Matterhorn guide of the era was Roman Imbedo, but not any André. Halliburton tells his readers this was Schaller's fortieth ascent. An 1894 magazine, *Around the World*, mentions Schaller's father, also Adolph, who climbed the Dom, near Zermatt: "On 13 January in perfect weather Sydney Spencer, accompanied by Christian Jossi and Adolph Schaller, made the first winter ascent." The magazine has a properly Victorian subtitle: *Contributions to a Knowledge of the Earth and Its habitants.* Having made a winter ascent, the father must have passed the skill onto the son, which helps explain why he agreed to be a guide.

In excellent English Schaller began talking to them, probably deciding they had more youth and stamina than experience. He and Roman sized them up, tried to decide if the boys were up to the climb. They did learn that Richard and Mike had no gear, each with a toothbrush and a safety razor, according to Richard, but at their age, they probably had no need to do much shaving. As seasoned and hardy climbers, Adolph and Roman did not take them on without first testing the lads. The boys appeared determined and in good physical health. First, though, Adolph and Roman wanted to make sure. They decided to run them through a kind of boot camp to see if Halliburton and Hockaday still wished to make the ascent, and if they could do it.

They told Richard and Mike that the cold would bite into their bones. The two Americans needed socks, leggings, mittens, wool helmets, cleated mountain shoes, and ice axes. They had arrived at a bad time, so reaching the top would not only be hardship but also relentless struggle. The boys listened and still wanted to go to the top. Richard and Mike managed to beg and borrow equipment and rented Alpine shoes from the guides.

Today Zermatt is a thriving tourist attraction, then a quiet hamlet where townsfolk rented Richard and Mike the things needed— leggings, heavy sweaters.

Cautious, the guides took the boys up the Gornergrat at 10,135 feet for instruction in Alpine climbing techniques.

The guides remained professional. Halliburton and Hockaday asked them each morning if they could begin the ascent and each morning Adolph and Roman looked up at the Matterhorn and said no.

Fog hung over the valley, followed by heavy clouds, and villagers could not glimpse the Matterhorn. Richard later reassured his parents with a little embellishment, saying the guides refused to go unless the skies remained clear two days. This was not the case, although the guides remained cautious. The night before, rain hammered the hotel windows and the torrent cleared the sky.

Next morning, September 23rd, the boys awoke and went to the window to see the Matterhorn dazzlingly white against a rosy sunrise. Adolph and Roman waited until noon. The skies held.

As a last precaution, as a final warning, they used a tactic to ensure they had determined customers. They took the boys to a cemetery. Standing before gravestones, Halliburton and Hockaday read inscriptions. They read that Charles Hadow of the Whymper expedition had perished on the mountain in 1865. There were others, noted by Richard with initials: W.K.W.—fell to his death from the Matterhorn, 1870; B.R.B—with two guides on June 10, 1891, slipped from the shoulder of the Matterhorn and fell 8,000 feet. Adolph and Roman then took them into a nearby Zermatt museum, which Richard dryly reported as equally encouraging. They gazed upon what remained of the tragic fall from the Whymper expedition. They saw the broken rope that surrendered lives to the mountain on that 1865 day. The museum held the ice axes and clothing of Hudson and Hadow, as well as the axe of Lord Douglas.

Halliburton said the cemetery and the museum greatly sobered him and Hockaday. "It was with our thoughts on the graves and the story of the Whymper party that Irvine and I began the ascent."

TWO SACKS OF OATS

To Memphis Richard wrote, "The reason, Mother and Dad, I went to Zermatt was that I had determined months ago to climb the Matterhorn—which we did!" He tells them he had not mentioned it because they would be worried sick. Always after adrenalin highs, he said, "I've had an experience which perhaps I can never match." Then he hints at the danger, although his parents must have known afterward that it became one in a long line of dangerous experiences. He knew how close he had come to plummeting into a lifeless heap. He wrote them, "Never, never again."

The main season for climbing the Matterhorn falls between mid-July and mid-August. They climbed in late September. Determined to climb the mountain, Richard knew there was no time to lose.

No time to lose, but the mountain stood defiant, ready to test him and Mike, and they would find it a challenge far beyond their imaginings. Richard, though, thought he was ready for it. He claims that as additional warmth he wore his grey suit for the climb.

After a trudge across the Zermatt valley, the climbers started up Hörnli Ridge. The first leg of the climb was strenuous but nothing technical. Climbing the Ridge, they looked down upon the Schwarzsee, a lake with a small chapel on its shore. Beyond the ridge, they scrambled up steep rock, reached a level and, looking back, beheld the Breithorn Chain. The trail led around and above a moraine, the Furggletscher. Pausing to catch their breath, slapping their arms against shivering bodies, they gazed across to see the Schönbiel gleaming in the sun. Exhaling vapor, they looked above to see the Hörnli Hut at 10,696 feet.

From the Hut's perch, the guides roused Richard and Mike at 3:30 next morning. They stepped outside under a starlit sky and Adolph and Roman, Richard, and Mike, tied themselves together with rope. The air froze their cheeks as Earth moved under the Milky Way and the moon slid through black space. Above them, the peak stood dark and silent against countless stars. The next ascent would not be as easy.

Above the hut, the mountain had claimed members of the Whymper party in 1865. Even today with climbing as a well-developed sport, the fittest Alpinist needs a guide for the rest of the Matterhorn. Pictures of climbers on the upper scape reveal a steep, unforgiving surface with little margin for error. A moment's inattention to hand or foot holds, to ice or snow, turns an ascent into a free fall. As the climber looks up, his neck craned backward, his eyes take in a vertical wall, curving his shoulders over empty air. A downward glance reveals more air. The guides led Richard and Mike on a zigzag, following a finger purchase here, a toe hold there, as they slowly, painstakingly, inched their way along a traverse of available rock. From the bottom to Hörnli Hut took five hours to cover about five thousand feet. In five more hours they climbed less than a thousand feet.

From the Hörnli Hut the four men almost immediately began climbing with rope, having to make a left traverse to a small shoulder, which they scaled to traverse left again on to the east face of a couloir soaring up eighty feet. As overhangs forced them to lean out, backs suspended over the valley below, they reached the upper Moseley Slab. Slick as a vertical skating rink, the Slab is named after Walter Moseley, who fell from it to his death a year after graduating Harvard Medical School in 1878. From the Slab almost until the summit, the young men's entire world was the two square feet of granite in front of them, which they made love to all the way up. The sturdiness of ropes and the depth of belay anchors were all that kept them connected to consciousness.

The sun was not their friend. As the day lengthened, it melted ice and snow, increasing the chances of rock-fall. It could heat the atmosphere into violent afternoon thunderstorms or snowstorms. They also risked hypothermia. They could not afford to tarry.

The Moseley Slab had hollows filled with snow and ice. With his ax, Adolph chopped at the hollows to find footing. It was combat in No Man's Land. Yard by yard they crawled upward on elbows and knees, using their teeth to hold things, their lips caressing the rock as they sweated in the frigid air. Adolph and Roman waited to see Halliburton and Hockaday wedged in a crevice then scaled the wall another twenty or thirty feet. The guides then motioned them to another finger hold and drew up on the rope attached to their shoulders. The boys climbed and the guides tugged. Crack by crack, their fingers and toes dug in as they raised themselves up the slab.

One cliff forced Richard up and backward, hanging off-balance above the valley below. He reached for a large stone to pull himself in and it came loose as he held it. With nothing to keep his balance, he lost his footing and as his boots scrambled to regain hold, snow and rocks glissaded off the wall, tumbling and scattering more debris into a minor avalanche. "Adolph! Adolph!" he cried. Schaller tensed himself just before Halliburton fell eight feet, to stop with a jerk at the end of the rope. Richard swung "in the breeze like a sack of cement." By main strength and with aching muscles, Adolph slowly pulled Richard up to a purchase for the toes.

More difficulties were about to begin. They had to get over a shoulder covered with ice. The wind piped into a new roar and threatened to send them skidding off the ice into the abyss. As it raced over their backs, tugging at their clothes, their cheeks lovingly brushed the hard rock.

Left by earlier climbers, belaying anchors hung with ice-caked ropes for them to reach. Oxygen was thin, which made exertion difficult but they had to pull themselves up, inch by inch. Wind swirled snow into their faces, stinging their cheeks with a seeming thousand needles. Their hands wanted to relax the clutch. To just let go would have been so nice but unthinkable.

Then came another challenge, six hundred feet before the top.

They had come to what Richard called "the notorious hang-over," a sheer face with its top jutting over its bottom. Halliburton and Hockaday had nothing left in them. The wind bit into them, the cold shivered them and they tried to haul themselves up twenty-five feet of free-hanging rope. Clutching handful after handful, Richard lifted himself toward the guides but halfway up his arm muscles refused to reach another inch higher. The wind swung him, lazily spinning him out over the moraines. Temporarily blind, he could no longer see. Wholly numbed, his hands desperately clung to the rope as his strength ebbed. Adolph pulled and slowly Halliburton was raised out of the air and onto the rim. Mike was also lifted after his muscles no longer obeyed his will. The boys rested and caught their breath on the cliff precipice.

They panted up a hard, steep climb to the peak and gulping frigid air into burning lungs they looked out at range upon range of mountains under a blue sky.

A hundred feet were left, a hundred feet of deep snow, which they trudged up slowly to the top. Adolph held out his hand to Richard. "We're here," he said, then added, "I congratulate you."

On the roof of the Alps, they looked down on clouds hanging in the valleys below. In the clear sky as they stood they beheld Mont Blanc, its black peak covered with snow. There was the Jungfrau to the north. To the east the Monta Rosa group ranged white against the blue sky while below their feet they looked down on clouds everywhere. Farther off, ranges appeared and disappeared among clouds as if in a colossal magic show.

All his young life, Richard had been after vivid, sublime moments and this was it. They only spent ten minutes on the summit but in the climb then in the view he found a lifetime. To his parents he wrote, "Imagine that, if you can, and you will imagine the fiercest moment of intense living I ever experienced."

Despite its sublimity, he had to pluck something from it for his *Royal Road* readers. It had to be balanced against the entertainer, the businessman, inside his deep sensibilities. He had to lighten it for the folks in Des Moines or Little Rock. He narrated that he thought Mike was also awed by the majesty before them. Hockaday becomes his counterpoint. To offset his own sense of the sublime, even to mock it, he has Mike saying that he had always wanted to spit a mile and now he could.

In his old age Mike Hockaday recalled the ascent of the Matterhorn. He said, "We were hauled up there like two sacks of oats."

RICHARD THE WRITER PARTS FROM MIKE THE TOURIST

Richard had foreseen that he and Mike would eventually part company. For him travel had become a career while for Mike it remained a holiday. He and Hockaday separated in Paris on October 5, 1921 as Mike left for Marseilles. The next week Richard departed for the Pyrenees.

While in Paris, he and Mike dined with Mr. and Mrs. Keyes, parents of their dorm mate Larry, and went to an opera with them. After returning to Paris from the Alps, they shared a pension table with a girl, "pretty and appealing, who seemed shy, quite demure, and proper." Mike nicknamed her "Miss Piety." They imagined her taking Biblical instruction in a convent. To rescue her from such a grave fate, to open her eyes to the world, they offered to dine with her at the Folies Bergères. She blushed and declined. That evening they saw Miss Piety at the Folies as a dancer in a harem scene.

They met another girl with her grandmother, seventy-five. The grandmother had been Lady in Waiting to the Empress Eugénie, consort of Napoleon III, overthrown by the Third French Republic following the 1870 Franco-Prussian War. Years before, posing for Franz Xaver Winterhalter, the Lady was painted with other young Ladies. All dressed in yards of fine silk over stiff crinoline, they prettily surrounded the Empress, petals about a flower. As a courtier, the woman must have helped Empress Eugénie flee Paris for England. Now the old woman had herself, her granddaughter, and a quiet, impoverished life in the country. As a young woman, she saw history made and, as a mature woman, watched the new century repeat the same mistakes as the old but she had made a separate peace, content to entertain with mannerly grace.

For Richard and Mike, the Lady in Waiting "proved so charming and interesting" that they saw her and the granddaughter several times. Mike, according to Richard, was "slightly smitten with the girl, called Suze."

While Richard worked his notes, Mike and Suze went sightseeing in Paris.

Then Mike and Richard said goodbye to one another. They had bought bicycles, Richard naming his Otto, with Mike's as Ophelia. Mike left on Ophelia. After the years at Princeton, those weeks together in Europe, they would see each other occasionally in the years to come. In a letter Richard recorded that change in a single sentence. "Mike left for Marseilles Wednesday night after a sad parting and I feel desperately lonesome in the most sociable city in the world."

Lonely with Mike gone, he visited the grandmother and Suze. Living alone, the two invited him for a weekend in the country at their simple farmhouse. The grandmother's money had abandoned her but the Lady in Waiting remained. She charmed Richard with her genteel attention and Richard reported that he spent "a quiet and sunny and genial day with the cows and chickens." He helped them by stringing clotheslines and fetching water from the town pump. They picnicked in the woods.

He had moods he rarely expressed openly but with Mike gone he lost his upbeat tempo. "Desperately alone," he wrote his parents.

He needed people as he needed adventure. Both served as diversion from Time's Arrow. In solitude he was keenly aware of time's passage. At the Temple of Bayan in Ankgor Wat he felt alone, and his description reveals that being alone raised in him questions about the world and the fleeting traces we make on it. In the jungle he looked at buildings of a lost civilization. All those people gone. He knew that what happened to them would happen to him. He wrote "From the shadows, death and oblivion crept forth to seize the city from the retreating sunshine; ghosts drifted beside me as I moved and dreamed through the gathering darkness."

Moving and dreaming, he was left with himself in France. He would soon travel far from Europe and found something in these other places that was implacable, distant from the romance of the human heart that said nothing in the stillness of dank, oppressive nights and swarming tropical mosquitoes and Richard saw his own brief time on Earth as part of the mystery he could not solve.

After a few days, his idyll with the Lady in Waiting and her granddaughter ended. Halliburton rode Otto back to Paris and its library to do research for his articles. Busy, he would lose himself in his work. Against the lonely Richard lay the youth who tempered his seriousness, who had Mike wanting to spit a mile atop the Matterhorn. He needed the counter-tone not only in his narrative but in his life. It served to pull him away from too much gravity. About his writing style, he wrote to Wesley, "You are right about the 'jocular tone'. That is the first requisite." He would write travel books, and "too much high seriousness can rob them of spontaneity." Seriousness and lightness. Richard gazes upon the sublime while Mike thinks of spitting.

He had written an article, "Adventuring in Republican Germany," a breezy, humorous piece intended for quick sale to a magazine, perhaps the *Metropolitan*. Like Richard, the American public was clueless about the real foment in Germany but anything more sophisticated and insightful would not have been published, especially by somebody without credentials and, besides, the tone suited Halliburton. Visiting the Memphis *Commercial-Appeal* editor, his father had arranged for Richard to be paid as a stringer. Richard sent Wesley his notes on the Matterhorn, telling him that the *Commercial-Appeal* could have them and the photograph with them.

Paris could not hold him once he mailed his manuscript. With Mike gone, he could hurry here, tarry there as he found stories worth writing. There would be other people to meet, places to visit. Paris had charms, but it was not elsewhere. The horizon was.

A career beckoned and the manuscript of his next article awaited. "When I look at the map of the world," he wrote home, "the miles I've traveled already can't be found. It appalls me to begin to realize what enormous distances await me, but the greater the distance, the more to see." Here was a gargantuan appetite. Of his appetite, what we have left are words of the way the weather was and how it felt to be young.

THE ROCK OF GIBRALTAR

Twenty-two seems dreadfully old. I'll be middle-aged in no time.
Richard on his birthday.

1909 Prudential Life Insurance ad with Admiral Dewey's
Great White Fleet

GIBRALTAR

Once called the Pillars of Hercules, the Rock of Gibraltar is as far as you can go in Europe. You travel through Germany, then through France, into Spain, but once you get to Gibraltar, that's it. As you look across the Strait to Morocco, on your right is the Atlantic, on your left, the Mediterranean, and behind you European civilization. In front is Africa eight miles away. For the Romans, the Mediterranean was Mare Nostrum, Our Sea, a claim of Empire well traveled and familiar. They, the Phoenicians and the Greeks before them, looked at the limitless ocean beyond the Rock with fear. Even in the Middle Ages nautical maps marked the Atlantic with the warning, Here be dragons. Gibraltar set the end of a cultural nexus and the verge of the unconscious mind. Beyond it, lay the untapped, the uncharted and, like death, the realm of whatever had not yet been experienced.

For all that, Gibraltar figures larger in our minds than it is in fact. The rock itself is a mere 1,396 feet high and as a British Protectorate it is only eleven times larger than the national mall in Washington, D.C. In history, its strategic importance far outweighed its size, commanding as it does all passage into and out of the Mediterranean. The rock itself has a system of great siege tunnels begun by the British in 1782 as a defense against the Spanish. During World War II the civilian population was evacuated to Britain, Jamaica, and Madeira so that British troops could defend the Rock against the Germans and control shipping into the Mediterranean. The simile "solid as the Rock of Gibraltar" is used today to indicate financial solvency and firmness of character but the solidness has a different origin—military—as in the motto of Her Majesty's Royal Gibraltar Regiment, Nulli Expugnabilis Hosti—Conquered by No Enemy. Gibraltar is solid as a cannon shell is solid but for all that it is rather flimsy within the spectacle of time's passage.

Geologists will tell you that the Rock is a monolithic Jurassic limestone promontory and that fifty-five million years ago it was created when the African tectonic plate collided with the European. Five million years ago the Atlantic Ocean finally eroded the land bridge to Africa and flooded the Strait of Gibraltar, spilling into the Mediterranean basin. On the cusp between boyhood and manhood, Richard said, "Youth is everything!" His life flickered between the slow, geo-tectonic shifts of the planet.

Richard and Mike Hockaday had parted in France but Halliburton found another traveling companion. In Barcelona, he met Paul McGrath after a crowd of Spanish dancers broke up. Holding a Baedeker tourist guide, McGrath clearly was not a Spaniard. In *Royal Road* the meeting is described. Richard jauntily tells Paul that he is a horizon chaser. On his part, McGrath identifies as an architectural student from Chicago.

Halliburton often chanced upon traveling companions and McGrath was another he discovered. He did not like traveling alone and easily made friends while if solo he must go, solo he would. Friends, though, did help support narration, as Paul did, and at Gibraltar Richard's narrative runs him headlong against the law. What he hoped would be a minor problem became jail time. As narrative device, Paul was instrumental in helping Halliburton end his fiasco on the Rock. McGrath's tardy arrival there is key to the story. Without Paul the ending would have been different. Different, in that Halliburton could not have his statement before the British magistrate at the end.

Before arriving at Gibraltar, Richard had been to North Africa, where he had a brief encounter with fezzes and Moors, then returned to Cádiz, Spain, when he took a boat for the Rock. McGrath was to catch up with him in Gibraltar.

On Tuesday, January 3, 1922, six days before his twenty-second birthday, Richard arrived in Gibraltar's harbor. On the voyage around the tip of Spain at Tarifa the sea was heavy and his stomach uneasy from the monotonous diet of meat and Spanish olive oil. That was unimportant, something his will shoved into the back of his mind. Foremost was something else. He wrote home that standing on the bow of the pitching boat, he felt "all the urges that seethed" within him. His energy pushed him while Gibraltar moved through time at a geological pace.

Guarded by the Royal Army and Navy, the Rock of Gibraltar was the gateway to the Mediterranean. As a gateway fortress it provided Britain a lever for diplomacy and the balance of power among nations. The Great War just ended, the United Kingdom did not want another horrific conflict and Gibraltar helped protect against it. Typical of any military installation, and sometimes ignored by photographers, the British military had regulations against the use of cameras. Types of weaponry and their placement must be kept from alien nations, which is why Halliburton got in trouble. Richard wanted photographs because he had a better chance of selling articles with illustrations. Apart from taking pictures, though, he tested authority in another way. With a simple box camera of the era the couldn't take pictures at night but he could have an experience indelible in his memory.

At night he walked the path up Gibraltar and came to a sentry post, the guard unaware of him, with further travel at that hour forbidden. He knew he shouldn't go on, but a little devil whispered in his ear, with a little angel in the other. The devil won. He liked to use the forbidden in his narratives and in his tale of Gibraltar he writes of exquisite temptation to which he succumbed, reminiscent of Adam and Eve and the taking of the Forbidden Fruit. The couple were seduced and they succumbed. In Halliburton's books a motif emerges, one of seduction and surrendering to it. Richard finds himself tempted and he yields to the temptation in order to experience exquisite sensations. He needs a trope and tells us that at Gibraltar the moonlight provoked a madness in him, and the moon herself was a temptress. The temptress moon was a metaphor to suggest the feelings within. She lured him out of normality, out of caution, and he was seized with desire to reach the summit, which he calls sacrosanct, sacrosanct as in a virgin forbidden to be sullied.

Halliburton's descriptions were innocent enough and no girl appears in them but the moon is female and he impulsively surrenders to her in order to experience paradise. In his later narratives, this happens when he is alone, as he was at Gibraltar. As a metaphor, the temptress moon combines seduction with risk. The risk itself is inevitably a challenge to authority. Looking above Gibraltar at the night sky, he saw the moon with her "evil gleam." She whispered to him, "Yield to this exquisite temptation."

Making no noise or sudden motion to alert the sentry, Richard stole through the gate and followed the path higher to Rock Gun Point.

The Rock is said to resemble a crouching lion and Richard climbed until he reached the top at Rock Gun Battery, the very ears of the beast, and wrote home that he beheld "a panorama that I have not the words to describe. The wind tore at me for trespassing but I sat as long as I could stand the elements." He says, "There were the stars which, shimmering to the horizon, met the myriad of lights from the ships in the harbor." It was "a glorious universe" and it was his. He looked down on the Mediterranean to see Africa and Europe and the Atlantic and in the harbor ships rode on moonlit waves. He beheld ships passing out of the Atlantic and through the strait of Gibraltar, creeping toward Egypt and the Suez Canal. Without yielding to the temptress moon he would not have had his "glorious universe." He did "not have the words to describe." This was not intended for stylistic effect. The words are in a letter to his parents, not to his public.

While he had only tropes to suggest his inner life, he meant and felt what he said.

Next day, he went up the Rock again, having borrowed the American consul's Kodak, as he explained in a letter to his parents. He was not especially interested in guns or gun placements but did want the shots he could get of Gibraltar and the Mediterranean. As he wrote home, he took photos "down the perpendicular east side where the whole sweep of the mountain was before me and where I took another roll of pictures."

Early on Sunday he climbed the Rock again to take pictures at sunrise. But "standing on South Point," he became "very careless in enthusiasm" and a couple of civilians saw him with the Kodak. They reported him to a signal station and, alerted, the officer in charge tailed him. When Richard again pulled the camera from his pocket the OIC arrested him but let him return to his hotel room.

As people said in Halliburton's day, he was in a serious pickle. With the arrest he received quite a present. It was January 9, 1922, his twenty-second birthday.

A SERIOUS PICKLE

Richard was not going anywhere. The authorities knew tiny Gibraltar was its own jail and he could not escape without attracting notice. Back at his hotel he placed film in the rain gutter outside his room window. They were pictures he intended to use in his writing on Gibraltar and when, in jail, he could no longer check on them Paul McGrath became key to verifying their safety.

Later, to his parents, he did not express any real concern. He explained that back at his lodging, his optimism surfaced and he put a good face on the situation, thinking that everything was quite simple. He thought it just a minor mistake. Straightforward, he would explain to the British his intentions and that would be the end of it. Like his neighbors back home in Memphis, they would immediately see that he was innocent of any traitorous intent and that his heart was in the right place. It was all in good fun. Just let him go. He could then get on a freighter bound for Marseilles.

The authorities had probably been curious to see if he would make a run for the Spanish border, thus confirming their suspicions. Next morning, three inspectors found him in the hotel writing notes. They, of course, did not know the notes were intended for a book and were not espionage details. They took him before the police chief, who sent the inspectors and Richard back to the room to collect everything in it. In Halliburton's account, he seems to have fit the stereotype of the light-haired Teutonic. He was a German spy with fake American passport and seaman papers. After collecting everything in his room the investigators escorted Richard to the automobile waiting outside. At the police station they took him to an interrogation chamber.

The men tried German on him, one asking him his name. Was ist ihr nahme? Richard did not fall for it. The other tried again, asking how he came by his American passport. Wie erhielten sie ihre passe? Richard stared at the floor.

The interrogation shifted to English. Halliburton answered question after question, telling the truth but not saying anything about rolls of film he hid in the rain gutter outside his room. Nor did he mention his midnight climb to Rock Gun Point. He wanted to convince them of his honesty, good faith, and simple intent but they had not bought any of it despite his bad German. Where he saw a frolic they saw thick subterfuge. Suspicion was their job.

He wrote home that in the afternoon he was arraigned before a judge, who advised him to hire counsel, but he had no money for that. As he stood before the magistrate, the prosecuting officer described him as a spy. After all, he traveled far too lightly, with only a small brown knapsack. An honest tourist traveled with a steamer trunk bearing the colorful stamps of many countries.

Richard finally realized that they would have none of it, no friendly openness, no amount of good will, no protestations of his innocence. He became alarmed but later implied to his parents that it was just a small contretemps.

With one witness absent, the prosecution asked the judge to postpone the trial until Wednesday, explaining this would also allow time to prepare more argument. The magistrate granted it and they handcuffed Richard and escorted him to a tiny cell with four whitewashed walls and one small, barred window.

The warden had Richard's clothes searched—pockets, cuffs, seams, linings. Then the barred door was swung open and he was forced to step inside the cell. The iron-barred door clanked shut with a heaviness and finality. What a day. A morning walk up the mountain had turned into this. He had been grilled as they tried to wear him down with the good-cop bad-cop routine. He had spent hours under their endless questioning and was exhausted. He asked the guard if he could have something to eat.

Tomorrow, the man said, and turned off the light.

A windowless cell and a cot, with Richard Halliburton contemplating his future—it was supposed to be grand. He was left with the dark and with silence. He fretted, paced, but finally fell asleep.

Early in the morning a bell clanged, jolting him out of dreams, awakening him to the reality of his predicament.

To his parents he wrote, "This letter is going to rank among the three most startling that your son has ever written to you. The first was the one from New Orleans about my runaway plans. The next was from Paris saying I had safely climbed the Matterhorn. This, the third, is from Gibraltar saying I am in *jail* in a British military prison."

TRIAL & KODAK

Apart from the film in the rain gutter, before he was jailed he left rolls in a shop to be developed. These the British knew about as they seized the rolls and held them as evidence. He was uncertain whether the British had also found the film outside his room window. About to be arraigned before the magistrate, his planned statement—that the Royal Army had all the film—depended on knowing about their safety. This was where Paul McGrath entered the episode.

Having arrived lately in Gibraltar, McGrath looked for his companion only to find him in jail. McGrath's visit was timely. He could help Richard determine his next move. Richard asked Paul to check the gutter. Were the film rolls still there? Paul left, promising to take residence in an adjoining room and report to Halliburton on the day of the trial. The question was how to report? They would be unable to talk again. They worked it out. Richard would look at him that day. If McGrath smiled, then the film was safe. If he frowned, the rolls had been found and taken.

Finally his trial arrived with Halliburton as his own counsel. How plead you?, asked the magistrate. Guilty, your honor. Guilty of taking photographs. He intended them to accompany magazine articles about Gibraltar. The prosecutor said, no, there was more to it than that. The young man deliberately took pictures, knowing they were forbidden. Not only that, he did it secretly, suspiciously. Photographs in the wrong hands jeopardized the safety of the entire military installation, especially its fortifications. After all, if stealth was not his method, why did he carry no more than a small brown knapsack?

Before entering the courtroom, Richard saw Paul in the corridor. Paul positively beamed. Halliburton wrote home that McGrath "came in all smiles." Richard knew the remaining film lay still hidden in the rain gutter. Richard told his parents that a military policeman explained to the magistrate, "We report that we have every article and paper in the room, including the pictures." Of the eighteen photographs retrieved by investigators from the photo shop, Richard told the judge that he had surrendered all eighteen to them and they were all in the Court's hands. This was not a lie, nor was it the whole truth.

They questioned him for perhaps two hours and became satisfied he was not a spy. The American consul vouched his passport as valid. Despite that, the judge fined him "ten pounds *or* a month in *jail.*" Ten pounds amounted to forty-six US dollars in 1922, which is over five hundred fifty dollars at this writing.

Richard was flabbergasted. Just turned twenty-two, he had expected his little adventure to be seen as a mere peccadillo and instead it was measured with gravity. Thirty days more in jail or a huge fine. To Memphis he writes that he "pulled through uncut, but very *burnt* and the burnt cat avoids the fire." He learned his lesson, he says.

We are told that Englishmen in the court room, officers and gentlemen, offered to pay the boy's fine. Even the man who spoke German, hoping to trick Richard, stood up in the courtroom and offered money.

Between the lines something else is implied here. Richard Halliburton for his readers was a flippant and insolent late-adolescent. That was his public face. In personal encounters he was honest, likable, and not at all off-putting. British officers had gotten to know the lad and could easily see that he was far too innocent to be a spy. They stepped forward with money because they could see he was naïve in the ways of the world.

Richard might have accepted their generosity, for he borrowed only part of the money from Paul McGrath. This is known because in a letter to his parents, he wrote that Paul paid part of the fine. While he was flabbergasted by the severity of the fine, his surprise only confirmed the British officers' measure of him. He had much to learn about life. As for his twenty-second birthday, he told his parents that it seemed "dreadfully old" and that he would be "middle-aged in no time."

As for the photographs in the rain gutter, after he left Gibraltar he mailed them to the British authorities. *The Royal Road to Romance* has only one photograph of Gibraltar, wholly harmless and shot at great altitude from an airplane.

THE TEMPTRESS MOON

*This grim ruthless jungle . . . made me shiver and want to cry out against the doom
that clanked beside me no matter where I turned.*
  Richard in the night at Angkor Wat

Richard with 1920s hair style

NIGHTS AMONG THE ANCIENTS

In his travels, he describes spending the night at the Taj Mahal and his night took in the centuries, wondering beyond his brief, allotted span. He sought something there—call it the secret of the ages. In a seethe of feelings, he can imagine bygone souls speaking to him. In the jungle of Angkor Wat he felt their presence. At the Parthenon, he looked up at a moon that had shone on Pericles and Herodotus and Socrates and he tried to attune himself with something that transcended his brief life. Wherever he spent them, these nights among the ancients manifested his deep concern with mortality.

He had the leisure to enjoy the Taj grounds and the architecture. No tourists pressed against his back, straining over his shoulder for a better view. Although even then the site was popular among global visitors, he experienced no souvenir stands near the gates, no buses off-loading organized tours, no guides with electric mega-speakers.

He was a young man discovering the place and it was his alone. He wrote home "It is so beautiful it hurts." He was transported to another time, another place, as stars blinked on in the dark sky, as the moon lit ripples in the reflecting pond. With midnight approaching, he knew the grounds would close and he must leave but he was not ready. If he left when the Taj closed, he would have to "leave without seeing the palace melt beneath the flood of moonlight." The temptress moon again. Security guards were closing the gates and were escorting laggard visitors through them. A thought came to him, if he did not go, if he stayed, then he "could possess the Taj" by himself alone. Looking for stragglers, watchmen passed by with lamps but he kept out of sight. His parents read that he "spent six hours looking at it the first morning. That night the last of a moon was due to rise at 2:30 A.M. Alone I walked the three miles and wandered around the inclosure till twelve when I hid. I was determined to see what I had come to see." The hours were magic. Over the graves of Shah Jahan and his wife Mumtaz Mahal a light lit the earth. A couple of guards slept at the doors. The world slept but Halliburton was awake. He was able to spend the night with his "marble mistress."

His enchantment continued as he wandered the grounds. An hour before dawn, with the moon at the peak of its course, he felt he had been transported to a place without "time nor space nor substance." He walked next the long reflecting pools extending from the Taj to its outside gate. He sat on a marble bench, gazing at a lily pond with its white blossoms, its water some four or five feet deep, perhaps twenty feet long, beckoning him to bathe in its immortal coolness. He was seduced and he succumbed. He wrote home that he took off his shorts and shirt and "dropped into the refreshing lily-padded water" to float in a reflecting pool and said he "was transported out of this world. It was a taste of paradise." He added, "The sensations were too unreal to last. I know it happened, felt the weirdness of it, but it was like a dream."

Critics called him a liar about floating in the pool because it was too shallow. They were wrong but their barbs stung him. Had he anticipated their charges, he probably would have explained the water depth. Standard tourist photos show the pool of which Richard wrote and it is deep enough for floating. but this was a quibble and they missed the real point. They failed to recognize he meant what he said about the experience. It truly seemed like that for him but for them it was just more Halliburton. His responses were deep, not those of the average tourist, and certainly his descriptions were not intended for mere effect. They could not understand that.

They mocked his prose as Maxfield Parrish in print. But it was pure, unfiltered Halliburton. He did not regard it as sentimental. He meant what he said. An alert critic could have pointed that out as his main fault. His feelings were his truth and he wanted to share them with his readers to raise them to the same sense of the sublime he felt but what he felt was barely communicable and certainly not with florid prose. He is not reaching for the maudlin. His life and his personality indicate that he experienced things intensely. While his writing became relatively matter-of-fact, in his thirties Halliburton still cultivated the sense of wonder he had as a youth. If Richard failed it was that as a very young man he did not understand some readers, critics, lacked his capacity for deep experience and filtered the world through reason and common sense.

AS AT GIBRALTAR SO AT THE TAJ

Against the youth with deep responses was the writer who needed to entertain, sell. We find in *Royal Road* a counterpoint to his night. Dawn rose and his next step came because of his experience with the British on Gibraltar where he was caught, jailed, tried as a spy, then freed. The Gibraltar incident gave him book material; maybe legal trouble would give him material here. Of course he does not confess his motive to *Royal Road* readers but it is obvious. He surrendered himself to the sentries. They marched him through the ironbound gates to the bungalow of the British superintendent.

The sleepy superintendent queried Halliburton but here was no military tribunal as Richard found at Gibraltar. The superintendent wanted to get back to bed. He dismissed the youth after warning him that the act was forbidden and a punishable offense. To his parents Halliburton merely wrote that he "took a cab to go home after a row with the keeper."

The other side of romance is always grim reality. With morning, the Taj "had turned again, to stone." To his parents he wrote that as he walked back to "the ugliness of Agra" he settled into a "depression that always follows intoxication." The morning sunk him into the low that could only be relieved by something else to seek.

ANGKOR WAT

In Cambodia, he took a steamer upriver to Angkor and Angkor Wat, the ruins deep in the jungle and then relatively unknown. Of Angkor he wrote, "All trace of their beginning, all records of their destruction, have been utterly lost in these merciless jungles." As he prowled the ruins he felt "this depressing silence, this ghostly emptiness." It was the shiver of mortality. At the Temple of Bayan he looked through the forest of trees and vines at the faces of gods on the Temple towers, and the cracks in stones gave each of them a "different and contorted expression, some wry, some smiling, some evil. Lianas have crept across the eye of one; lichens and moss have blinded another. They peered at me from the treetops; they pursued me with their scrutiny like a bad conscience, no matter where I tried to escape." What had happened to them, these vanished people? He knew one thing. They were gone. Their spouses and children loved them. They supped, made love, watched the sun rise and then were no more.

UNDER THE MOON AT THE PYRAMID OF CHEOPS

He sought the sublime in Cairo when he left the city for the pyramids to spend a night atop Cheops. Next it crouches the Sphinx, half-woman, half-lion, an omen in Yeats' poem of the modern world as the Sphinx rises amidst reeling desert birds and the poem speaks of a "rough beast" that "slouches toward Bethlehem to be born." Halliburton paused before the Sphinx, whose "inscrutable face" etched itself on his mind. Yeats published the poem in 1920; Richard gazed upon the Sphinx in 1922. Yeats' poem has become a metaphor of the disasters of the Twentieth Century. Halliburton imagined ages long before he climbed Choeps, looking out at the dark desert and up at the night sky with its ancient mystery of time and space.

He imagined that Pharaoh Khufu also liked peace and tranquility and built the pyramid so to sit there during starlit nights and for Richard the night also offered something mystical as well as tranquil. He sat through the night on the pyramid well into the next morning. To his parents he described the desert under the full moon: "The Nile and then the three miles of verdure, then the knife-like edge where the desert begins, the other pyramids" and "the sea of sand behind." At about four o'clock the moon's soft light disappeared and slowly the darkness revealed new tones. "The sun rose over the minarets of Cairo and struck the sides of the near-by pyramids slantingly so that they sparkled like gold; a haze spread all over the velvety valley, dotted with groves of palms and lakelets of irrigation water." He heard a cock crow and as dawn crept into the sky he saw the dark, tiny shadow of a village. Over here, green began to appear amid palm trees. He watched "a long caravan" crawl toward him. Richard recalled Napoleon standing at the pyramid's base, saying, "Centuries look down upon you."

In Richard, then, were an energy and its solace, a restlessness and its peace. One exercised in the light of day; the other found itself in the quiet of night. Under the warmth of the sun, he rejoiced the life within him; in the darkness of the moon, he contemplated his brief existence. This double-vision combining activity and quiet shaped the force that drove him. Without the tension within he would have stayed in Tennessee.

WHAT IS IT ALL ABOUT?

Why seek anything? You never find it.
Richard Halliburton in a letter to his parents

Richard with a lynx kitten

STOWAWAY

Few rough-travelers today are as brazen as Richard. Far from India but on his first global trek, in Surabaya, East Java, with only thirteen dollars, not enough for passage, he sneaked aboard a ship Singapore-bound but was discovered. The captain lowered a skiff into the water, dropped a rope ladder, and ordered Richard to climb down into the launch, which would take him to the pilot boat returning to harbor. Standing on the pilot boat deck, Halliburton looked longingly after the stern of the British ship disappearing into the night. The pilot returned him to Surabaya, where he waited for another chance. This time, he decided, he would not do anything stealthy. He would boldly talk his way aboard.

Obvious to the crew, he went aboard the next ship having spiffed himself with nice clothes, hoping he looked important enough that no questions would be asked. Brazen, this, but he could be that way if needed. He claims he wanted them to think he was owner of a shipping company or a ship's captain. Of course, owner or captain at age twenty-two. He found an unlocked stateroom door, and made himself comfortable. Hidden from sight, he thought all was okay. It was okay until the ship left harbor and he was discovered by the head steward, who wanted to know what the bloody hell Halliburton was doing in his cabin. The steward then dragged him before the captain. The skipper was not amused.

Once again he was dropped into a skiff and rowed to a pilot boat.

An American freighter put into port, which Richard misnamed as the *Minerva* to protect the captain's identity. This captain in fact was Charles Jokstad, who in 1939 as skipper of the ocean liner *President Pierce* would inspect Richard's Chinese junk and declare it unseaworthy. Richard climbed aboard and went directly to the captain, "A grand old man with a magnificent sense of humor," and asked for a free ride, claiming he didn't have passage money. Rather abashed, the old fellow agreed, but only if

Richard followed the rules, which were that free rides were against the rules.

Richard had to stow away in the sick bay until discovered by the first mate, whom the captain let in on the scheme. In front of the ship's company, the properly angry mate took Halliburton before the properly angry captain. The ship's crew heard the proper tongue-lashing but since they were at sea nothing was to be done except let Richard stay. In return for the favor, Halliburton had to fix the skipper's phonograph, and finish reading Thackeray's *Vanity Fair*, which the captain found boring.

The ship sailed to Singapore, where Richard disembarked.

TWILIGHT OF AN EPOCH

Richard had a letter of introduction, often used by his set when traveling in those days. His was from Franklin Seiberling, founder of the Goodyear Tire and Rubber Company and later founder of Seiberling Rubber. The man was father of Richard's Princeton roommate James Penfield Seiberling, who became company president in 1938. With the region's rubber plantations, Singapore was "a rubber metropolis" wrote Richard and he presented the letter to Mr. Donaldson, the Singapore general manager of US Rubber Company. An Englishman, Donaldson took him for a drive around the island, which Richard found beautiful, the weather refreshing. Then the general manager took him to his "lovely home" where Halliburton had tea with the man and his wife.

Singapore had a lively British-American colony. He fit right in. He dined at the house of one of Donaldson's managers, where he had "a very pleasant and argumentative evening," followed by another drive until one in the morning. The class of Americans and Europeans in Singapore glowed in the light of a dying age and their privilege would soon be snuffed out by a new world war and the Japanese invasion. While it glowed, though, he had cachet wherever he went. He could walk into a consulate open to the sidewalk, unprotected by high walls, Marine sentries, and concrete barriers zigzagged against trucks with explosives. A consulate official granted him money for deck travel on a ship. A letter of introduction opened doors to the gentlemen and ladies of any colonial society.

MALAY PENINSULA

The Malay Peninsula dips down on the map from Thailand into the South China Sea like a goose, its head looking for minnows. With its body in Thailand and Burma, the goose neck is long, slender, and wholly jungle. To the right side of the neck lies the Gulf of Thailand. To the left are the Andaman Sea and the Strait of Malacca. At the very end of the peninsula, the tip of its beak, the goose reaches for Singapore, poised there like a choice minnow. In 1922 the shape was the same but the names on the map were different. People had come and gone, with country names giving the illusion of newness. Siam became Thailand. Indo-China became Vietnam; Burma is now Myanmar. On the Malay Peninsula, Victoria Point is known as Kawthaung. Geese are relatively harmless, unlike the peninsula, which is noted for its thick undergrowth, its monsoon rains, its toxic plants, and its poisonous snakes. Halliburton explains that its neck is "no wider in places than the Isthmus of Panama."

At one time rife with unnamed wild life, the Malay Peninsula attracted Alfred Russel Wallace to explore it from 1854 to 1862 and he wrote a book titled *The Malay Archipelago.* Its full title was *The Malay Archipelago: The land of the orang-utan, and the bird of paradise. A narrative of travel, with sketches of man and nature.* Wallace almost beat Charles Darwin to the punch on the theory of evolution.

Form the archipelago Wallace wrote his famous letter to Darwin, which greatly alarmed the elder man, who thought the youngster was about to steal his thunder. Wallace outlined a theory very similar to Darwin's, a theory Darwin had worked on for twenty years but had yet to publish. The gentlemanly thing to do was present Wallace's ideas along with his own to the Linnaean Society, which Darwin did and he was given recognition as the first to formulate the theory. Legend has it that the idea came to Wallace during a tropical fever.

To him we owe the Wallace line, a transitional zone identified between Australia and Asia that marks big changes in animals found on either side. Think marsupials and mammals as one example. Joseph Conrad also owes something to him. For his jungle descriptions in *The Heart of Darkness*, the novelist read *The Malay Archipelago*.

The Peninsula was an invitation to vivid life. Halliburton could feel the strain of muscles as he tramped along a muddy jungle path, watchful for boa constrictors and vipers. It was the counterpoint to his nighttime contemplation of ancient ruins. It was a place for a crossing, not merely from one sea to another, but from one hope to another. Reaching the far side, he could exult in the life beating within him and apart from the dank jungle that had claimed Angkor.

Looking at the map, Richard decided to take a ship to Victoria Point, although that was a problem. The Point was not on navigation routes of steamship lines. He had to invent his own itinerary, which would be Rangoon to Mergui and Mergui to Victoria Point.

Low on money, he bought deck passage out of Rangoon for Mergui on a steamship, the *Adamson*, and fell in with the chief engineer, a hard-drinking old Scotsman who stood second dog watch with a bottle of whiskey. He took Richard under his wing after Halliburton declared "Scotland the noblest country on earth." They became the best of chums and Richard no longer had to sleep on deck. Inside the chief engineer's cabin, they tossed down whiskeys, and shared meals. The price of passage was to listen to the Scotsman loudly recite a verse, "But I would lead the same life over, if I had to live again, though chances are I'd go where most men go." It is by Adam Lindsay Gordon, an Australian poet. Richard held the lines as memorable because he would not go where others went. The Scotsman claimed they were by fellow Scot Robert Burns. Richard wisely did not correct him.

Richard helped the chief engineer empty the bottle and once, perhaps tipsy, almost got himself kicked out of the cabin. When the old man demanded to know if his young companion liked Burns, Halliburton said no. The engineer shouted that Halliburton was an idiot.

The ship dropped anchor at Mergui, then the southern city of Siam, the city having an archipelago of the same name.

Look on a map of the world and you will be lucky to find Mergui, remote and unknown. Detailed maps and charts are old, the last drawn by the British before 1948, when they ceded rule to national governments. The British withdrew in 1997 and in the same year the region was opened to tourists after negotiations between Burma and dive operators from Phuket in Thailand. The archipelago is so isolated that it remains one of the last uncharted places on the globe. Its uninhabited islands encompass ten thousand square miles.

The eight hundred islands of the Mergui archipelago consist chiefly of limestone and granite. Crapforests thickly cover the ground. Mangrove swamps flood the region and coral reefs fill the clear blue waters. Sumatran rhinos have been sighted swimming between the islands as well as elephants, which are said to swim twenty miles. Its flowers and vegetation explode in a riot of colors. Its wildlife includes deer, monkeys, tigers, and wild pigs and swimming among coral reefs a diver sees bull sharks, nurse sharks, and whale sharks along with manta rays and schools of devil rays, frogfish, ghost pipefish, ribbon eels and cowries.

At Mergui, Halliburton found a tugboat, the *Darracotta*, bound for Victoria Point. The Europeans he met in Victoria Point told him he would be committing suicide if he carried out his plan to walk across the peninsula. He smiled and waved goodbye to them. They probably said farewell to him.

Loaned a dugout canoe with two boatmen, he loaded a bunch of bananas and the boatmen pushed off from shore and up the Pukchan River into the jungle.

In bare outline, that describes this event in his young life. In bare outline for his entire life, he lived and he died. It becomes a kind of mathematics, elegant, abstract, stripping his existence to the bone. He lived=2. He died=2. 2+2 =4, wherein 4=the life and death of an entity once known as Richard Halliburton. We thus breath him from a rarified air, far from what he felt, did, and lived, and why.

That is the bare outline. Next is what happened on the peninsula. The why was inside his head.

WHY SEEK ANYTHING?

Burma was then a colony to which Britain sent minor government officials in places forgotten today. Once a civil servant there, George Orwell wrote of it in his essay "Shooting an Elephant," about Burma but really on representatives of empire trapped in far-flung outposts by imperialism. Richard met a handful of forgotten white men living with forgotten Burmese wives, siring forgotten Burmese children. Typically, Richard felt sorry for them. The children had no mental home. They would be rejected in England or America and the Burmese would lump them in the same category as bastards, which they probably were. Looking on them, he began to develop a point of view he had not learned in Memphis and he presents it in his first book, *The Royal Road to Romance*.

Standing in the doorway of a hut, an Englishman hallooed and invited Richard inside. In Halliburton's account to his parents of their conversation, we find another aspect of the adventurer's personality, an existential, questioning counterpoint to the enthusiastic traveler.

They talked as the white man reclined on a wicker deck chair. Halliburton wrote home that the man was an engineer and friendly. He let Richard stay with him two days. The man had been a boy in the trenches of World War I, which left him disillusioned with the "complexities of Western life." Richard describes him as intelligent, well-bred, and well-educated. The man kept "two native women, drank and smoked continually, worked as little as possible." He was open about it all, saying he "sought happiness and insisted he found it." "It's easy money," the man told Richard.

Richard found the man strangely disconcerting. He had planned his global tramp as the beginning of a career in travel-adventures, a career of books written for those who could not go. For his readers he wrote that youth is everything and that life is to be lived. That would be his public face but he had a private face that questioned the worth of it all.

On the Malay Peninsula he had sunk into ruminations on life itself.

He wrote his thoughts about the Englishman to his parents. "Perhaps he is right. Why grind and pant and slave! To what end? Why seek fame and fortune?," he asked.

It was a question in counterpoint to Rupert Brooke's "do a thousand things, sing a thousand poems, and kiss a thousand girls." It was the why of existence, asked for millennia and by great philosophers from Plato to Spinoza.

In the same letter he asks, "Why seek anything?"

Halliburton was the young man who sought the next horizon but he answers his own question about seeking anything. "You never find it."

Ambition was itself a devil, a perpetual goad, an endless torment. He admired the Englishman for deliberateness, for making an existential choice. It was a question of responsibility as understood by Western civilization. The man said to hell with responsibility and to hell with Western civilization.

In September 1922, after crossing the Malay Peninsula, Richard wrote home of himself as somebody "doomed to seek, seek, all my life, never content with what I have, despising it after I have it, seeing a higher place and greater fame every step upward, loading myself with responsibilities and dreading lest I misspend my gifts: gifts of parentage, environment, education, pride." Here was Western civilization as seen from a distant horizon.

He might get satisfaction from his parents and their friends, "but from life, never, for it's an overpowering, brooding enemy that I must strain to preserve myself against."

Life had become an enemy with loss of the urge to do a thousand things, sing a thousand songs. Something happened here and in it we see a deeper, complicated side of Richard unknown to his readers. What clearly happened is an internal discourse that began earlier on the other side of the peninsula at Mergui with another Englishman, a young man named Ainsworth, whom he met at Victoria Point.

EXISTENTIAL QUESTIONS

A well-bred Englishman, Ainsworth owned an island about twelve miles square off the Malay coast. He lived alone except for two Chinese servants and one hundred natives who worked his teak and camphorwood sawmill. Halliburton believed that he had utopia with no need to quest for distant horizons; it was all right there in front of him. He tells his parents that Ainsworth is "a true British gentleman" and he found the man's island "a little paradise. The island is four miles long and three broad, covered with an awful tangle of jungle trees and creepers and vines and flowers. The beach is sand and lined with coconuts and fuzzy evergreen trees. It's very hilly and along two sides the hills form a precipice over water." Ainsworth was thirty and owned "the island, soul and body, and all the natives on it are his subjects. He has two Chinese servants. The coconuts fall on his roof and roll into his lap." In *Royal Road*, Halliburton compares Ainsworth to Robinson Crusoe, except the Englishman had hot and cold running water and dressed in white flannel pants for dinners waited on by servants.

Actually, the scene was less Robinson Crusoe and more Ulysses. The one had to make-do; the other had everything. In his journey home, Ulysses fell under the spell of Calypso and her island and did not leave for ten years. Richard became seduced by the idea of paradise. He began to lose interest in "the isthmus expedition, for indeed this was the perfect life." He looked out on an emerald green sea as it washed between other islands in the distance. He gazed at the white coral beaches under cloudless blue skies. He turned to see thick mangrove forests behind him. In *The Royal Road*, he describes the island as an Eden with teak trees climbing to the sky, their canopies shading the ground, their trunks holding vines reaching up with lavender blossoms.

His existential questions in his letters indicate that this was not merely a trope for his reading public. The implicit issue for him was that a cultured man had chosen to live here. The Englishman was not a civil servant shacking up with a native woman. He had a business and lived on the island because, as Halliburton put it, the place was paradise. In a letter home he writes, "The smooth clean beach was irresistible, and we swam by the hour, sometimes in sunlight, sometimes in moonlight, often in the rain, along the whiteness of sand." For a very young man open to life's possibilities here was a garden of earthly delights.

The gentleman was mannerly and witty and for a while, Richard thought the man had an answer—chuck it all. His parents, his dorm mates, they spoke of career and status. Forget about worldly success and recognition. Ainsworth's island said this is all there is to life anyway. Forget about getting anymore out of life than this abundance.

Gradually Richard saw something that flawed this paradise and in *Royal Road* he provides images to explain it. They swam and enjoyed the beach and, relaxing on the sand, he took in the glistening white sand, the clear blue sea and the azure sky with white clouds floating under the sun. Then he turned to see six crocodiles on another bank, also enjoying the day. Menace lies even here.

The Englishman had a fox-terrier pup and we can imagine Halliburton taking pleasure in playing with it as he did with children. Both have an innocence, expecting no malice in the world. The puppy liked to be petted or to chase sticks. That and happiness were the compass of its world. The dog found a cobra creeping into a hole in the roots of a tree. The pup grabbed the cobra's tail in his teeth and shook it as part of a fine game. The snake bit the dog, which came running back to the men, his tongue lolling, his tail wagging, quite proud of himself. In a few minutes he became strangely quiet and in a quarter of an hour he was dead.

Ainsworth did not dwell on the young dog's death. Halliburton suggests that the man had seen this many times before and knew there was trouble in paradise. On Richard's part, it touched the thing in him where youth lived. He saw that young innocence was not immune to evil. It was a randomness that fell on living creatures and what happened to them could not be weighed, not touched. One moment the dog had been scampering in front of him then it was no more in this other Eden.

Richard was disturbed by it. It had an amoral edge positioned against the values his parents taught him. The World War I veteran and Ainsworth came to outposts on the Malay Archipelago, lived out their lives, and were forgotten. Halliburton was a young man after recognition and a career. He wanted to make his mark on the world, justify his existence. At Princeton he struggled with the question of vocation—the word's root literally meaning a divine calling to one's purpose in life—and finally believed he found it in writing about travel-adventure. He could thereby prove himself worthy of the world's approval. But there was another world that did not care.

Richard, though, was a creature of his biology and while he sought meaning in life his body wanted action. Like Camus, he had an existential question about human enterprise. Richard did not linger on the question long because his body obeyed the neural itch and his mind followed it.

Typically, Halliburton's body demanded attention if ignored too long and Richard responded with his feet. He left the Englishman's island. He had horizons to reach and an isthmus to cross. Questions remained but fell into the background when he was in motion. He scratched the neural itch and where it urged he went. The questions did not go away but he did.

For the moment, his itch led to the Isthmus of Kra, with the Andaman Sea on the west and the Gulf of Siam on the east. He intended to cross its jungles on foot. Ainsworth had a dugout with a deck and roof of banana leaves and he loaned it with two boatmen to Halliburton. Richard could use it to travel the sixty-five miles up the Pukchan River—today the Pak Chan—and from there he would trek across the peninsula. At five in the morning Richard got underway with bunches of bananas as the food supply.

An early morning mist rose over the river, hiding the boundary between land and air so that the solid seemed empty. Richard saw the mist, felt forest breeze wafting across the water and onto his cheek, and then it was gone. Thoughts skittered across his mind and disappeared, like the boundary between land and air. Jungle birds cried to one another and current swept around a tree branch fallen from a bank. He could see Buddhist monks in red robes, with boatmen guiding them upriver to their temple. Lifting yellow umbrellas to the rising sun, they gasshoed toward him and he waved at them. They would sit in meditation as the temple bell echo was swallowed by the silence of the jungle while he hacked with a machete against underbrush.

Passing Victoria Point, Richard viewed the harbor, a tiny refuge from the Andaman Sea. He saw rickety wooden houses on stilts, their mud paths leading to the bank, the houses surrounded by green hills. Along a dirt road the morning sun glinted off statues of Bodhisattvas and Buddhas. Cargo ships loaded boxes of bananas from lighters as other long boats returned to the shore for more boxes. Workers on the ships, people in the houses, looked out the window at his dugout and as they turned toward daily chores it fell into their past.

As Richard's oarsmen rowed him farther upstream he watched muddy banks disappear under a dense canopy of trees, blotting out even the jungle, so that all he could see was the brown of the river and the green of its edges. He had seen a puppy die within minutes from a cobra's bite and he knew the end came to everybody. He had talked to an Englishman who was content far from home but he could not rest.

TAPLEE, IN THE JUNGLE

As the dugout moved upriver, as the river narrowed, the sky became lost under dense canopies of mangrove. Richard swatted at mosquitoes and flies. Crocodiles slipped silently into the water as the boat approached. Parrots screeched somewhere in the jungle and the men heard monkeys chatter. A fish leaped out of the water to gulp a mosquito. Deer timidly approached the bank to drink, eyes out for crocodiles. Elephants drank from the other bank. Cranes and herons reeled into flight upon seeing the boat. Orangutans peered through underbrush at the men. The men could smell rafflesia, a parasitic flower that smells like rotting meat.

That same year, in 1922 in the familiar world, people sat outside Parisian cafés discussing James Joyce's new book, *Ulysses*. In Vatican Square the faithful gathered under the third floor window of the papal apartments to pay homage to Pius XI, the new Pope. Reporters stood around Warren G. Harding as the President listened to the first radio in the White House. History was still in the making.

A boa constrictor hung from a tree. Scorpions scampered across the forest floor, passing an anteater. Upon seeing the men in the sampan, a Sumatran rhino crashed away through the undergrowth. Chattering Gibbons clambered up trees to look at them. On the jungle floor a cobra, hood swollen, reared to strike its venom into an unsuspecting young Gibbon.

At Taplee, a village deep in the jungle, the boatmen banked the dugout. Richard stepped off into the mud and walked toward the village in the clearing.

The boatmen ate food offered by the villagers then said goodbye and knew they would have an easier time of it on the return, for the downstream would float them effortlessly sixty-five miles, past the sea port of Victoria Point to Ainsworth's island. Richard watched them shove off from the bank. He waved at them as the current swept them away, down the Pukchan River. He knew he had only one course left, to the Gulf of Siam on the other side of the jungle.

On a map, the Isthmus of Kra seemed a likely place for Halliburton to walk from the Andaman Sea to the Gulf of Siam. It looked very easy on paper. From Victoria Point to the East coast it was forty miles, a distance pedaled by a bicyclist in a morning. If Halliburton had a bicycle and if he could ride it through the jungle. Instead, even walking was difficult, with the jungle thick, its dangers many, its heat stifling, its trail obscure, lost to mud, and covered by underbrush. The Isthmus is pelted by monsoons and after the clouds clear the sun shines brilliantly on the wet jungle, filling the air with steam rising above the trees.

The two coasts are so close yet so far away. Mindful of the canal across Panama, in our day the Thai and Myanmar governments have discussed digging across the Isthmus at its narrowest point, from the head of the Pukchan River to the Gulf. In Richard's day the river separated Siam from Burma. In our day the names Siam and Burma have been changed to Thailand and Myanmar but the separation remains the same.

Richard had no jungle sense but was determined to cross the gap. Somebody would show him the way. Before the boatmen left him in the village, one of them translated in Malay to the village chief for him. Richard wanted an elephant but was told it cost six dollars and could not be had because the monsoon flooded rivers and streams. After the boatmen left, communication became a problem as the chief bemusedly watched his gestures. They eventually reached an understanding that Richard wanted to trek through the jungle to Chumphon on the East coast. They sat in silence. Richard waited.

The chief explained it was impossible. The old man pantomimed water up to his neck, meaning it was not safe. Richard already knew it was not safe, which was why he wanted to do it. Finally Richard did succeed. He wrote home, "I got a coolie for a guide across. I spent that night on a mat in the second story of the house, with mosquitoes eating me and lizards playing tag all over me. Next morning, my coolie and I started on the trail, a semi-invisible path."

He loitered a day or so in the village, watching rain pelt the river, hearing parrots screech in the distance. He took relief in playing with the village children. He talked to the village men and women, the males wearing chawats, or loincloths, the women with sarongs. In the morning the guide said goodbye to his wife and children. Rains flooded the sky while Richard thanked the village chief, and then the two men walked out of the clearing as the villagers watched them disappear into the jungle.

The guide had agreed to a fee of three dollars, a princely sum if he could find a place to spend it. In his narrative of the trek, Richard praises the man's sure-footedness and understanding of jungle lore but the man's expertise did not do much to diminish the danger.

RAIN, MUD, & SNAKES

We passed through extensive forests, along paths often up to our knees in mud, and were much annoyed by the leeches for which this district is famous. These little creatures infest the leaves and herbage by the side of the paths, and . . . I had one who sucked his fill from the side of my neck, but who luckily missed the jugular vein. Alfred Russel Wallace, *The Malay Archipelago*, 1869

The guide's ample chawat was elaborately folded around his hips, then under his crotch, and tucked in behind, its ends forming a kind of tail. He carried a supply of betel nut, his lips and teeth stained with its juice. Along the route they drank from coconuts and ate bananas. They also had a can of salmon and a tin of soda crackers. The guide with his loincloth, Richard with his pants, shirt, and shoes, each had his own motive. For Richard it was to feel his body challenged by the jungle; for the guide it was the promise of three dollars.

The rain continued as their machetes hacked the brush. The mud sucked at their feet, miring them, pulling off Halliburton's shoes. He had to repeatedly stop, find them, and put them back on. "My low brogues," he tells his parents. "Imagine that! Low quarters for such a trip—got so stretched and loose they stuck in every mud hole and were sucked off." He tells them he used rattan creepers to bind the shoes to his feet. He could now move faster, at one mile an hour. Rain fell without cease. Water gushed down creeks, overflowing the banks. Torrents of mud and rain caved hillsides, blocking the trail. He stumbled over roots, pushed himself through thick bamboo. Falling, slipping, they made their way. They forded streams that had become small rivers and, as they brushed against leaves or branches, leeches clung to their skin, unnoticed by them until they noticed bloody spots on their bodies. A sloth lazily looked down at them from a branch. A Gibbon monkey screeched at them. They frightened a tapir and it scampered into the undergrowth. Trogons and leaf birds chattered and warned of their coming.

As dusk fell they came upon a clearing in the jungle, with about two dozen natives and some shacks. The natives may have thought they had not yet awakened from a dream when they saw a Malay in filthy chawat and a white man wearing shredded khaki pants, both men smeared with mud.

Richard and the guide slept that night in a long house on stilts, more than Halliburton's height above the ground and far from mud and snakes. That was not enough protection. The bed was raised two feet above the floor. Families slept together on long rows of grass matting. Richard bedded next the chief and the chief's favorite wife and the secondary wife and the brother's wife and the grandparents and other families. The rain drummed on the leafed roof but, exhausted, he did not hear it. Breakfast was curry spiced with hot red pepper that blistered his tongue. Here was the region of the Spice Islands so intently sought by Columbus and defended by the Portuguese. He could not eat any more breakfast, though he needed strength for the day ahead.

They found they could not leave. Dark clouds filled the sky, and the wind bent trees as a fierce storm approached. Outside, the wind rose, tearing down bamboo thickets, rattling the walls of the long house. Inside, he said, the sound of the gale was deafening.

By mid-afternoon, the storm gentled to a light patter on the roof and the sun finally peeked between scattering clouds. It was a resurrection, clear and bright against a blue sky. Creatures that vanished before the force of the gale soon reappeared. It was time to go. The two men said goodbye to their hosts, men as well as women naked above the waist. Both men and women chewed betel nut, a stimulant arousing feelings of well-being and energy. Richard noticed their teeth, blackened by its juice. The villagers watched as the Malay and the American disappeared out of the clearing and into the rain forest. As Halliburton and his guide looked for the path a pair of grouse fluttered up, swooping past their faces. Parrots squawked in the stillness. Monkeys scampered up lianas.

Then something happened and the event helps us understand why Halliburton faced risks with optimism that all would turn out for the best.

The occurrence began like this. Halliburton asked if thinking about an event could influence its outcome. In his case, he wonders if fear itself puts a person in real danger. As a counterpoint, he speculates that ignorance is better than knowledge.

Before in his jungle trek he had been blithely ignorant of the danger surrounding him. He had not even considered the isthmus as dense with wild animals and venomous snakes.

Then he began thinking about the danger. After all, he had no sidearm. His skin was bare and exposed. The jungle was so dense he could barely see anything underfoot or creatures behind thick foliage. Thinking about all this, he became afraid and fear, he believed, brought about what happened next.

The guide ahead, Richard sought to avoid a muddy slough that the man had trouble crossing. Instead, Halliburton walked through the grass around the mud. For some reason he looked down at the same moment a cobra was rearing back to sink its fangs into his bare leg. This, for him, was a moment intense and terrible. The moment took only seconds, but his horror took in the miles he was from a hospital, Ainsworth's little dog happy one minute, dead the next. He saw himself dying on the floor of the jungle, far from Memphis, far from help.

For an instant he turned into stone. Then his muscles took over when his mind could not. Something not Richard, not his personality, not his hopes, not his ambitions, something neither in Memphis nor the jungle raised the hand holding the walking stick. Something knocked the snake away with his stick and ran after the guide who had made it through the mud and was far ahead. Something had acted and when mind finally caught up with the running body it was Richard again. He fell to his knees and felt like kissing the mud. What a wonderful world, what a lovely jungle.

Halliburton asks how much does ignorance discourage danger? Or how much does thinking about it cause it to happen? He expresses our hard-wiring. Our brains are programmed for survival and we recognize patterns. Night follows day, scudding clouds bode storms, plants with three leaves cause skin rash. We look for obvious patterns because we like being in control and sometimes believe our thoughts can affect events in the world. A child thinks the rain fell because she is sad. A baseball pitcher believes he has better luck if he chews gum on the left side of his mouth when he throws to southpaws. We all experience it, a phenomenon noted by psychologists and termed magical thinking.

Richard asked if thinking about things influences outcomes. His question does help explain how he could undertake perilous adventures. It went something like this. Do not think about the risk and things will turn out okay. Think about it and they might not. An intelligent man, he was more complex than that in his character and personality but magical thinking apparently did contribute to his psychology, in his case, taking risk.*

---

* Magical thinking: A construction worker secretly buried in wet concrete a Red Sox jersey at the new Yankee stadium. The Yankees found out and didn't want the stadium cursed, so they jack-hammered several feet of concrete to pull it out. It does not stop with sports fans. People yell at their computer because it crashes. They won't buy a house where a murder

The jungle sometimes showed them the sun. More often, they were swallowed by an indifferent grey pall. They might reach the coast or they might not. All was the same to the jungle. They were scratched by branches, bitten by mosquitoes, sucked by leeches. They slogged up hills then down, forded streams, rested to eat bananas, then forced themselves to go on. The second day came with machetes again hacking underbrush. They tramped until the guide could not make out the trail. It became a struggle of life and death, sapping their energy, with nowhere to sleep, no horizon to glimpse. That was when their plight changed. Near the end of the third day Halliburton had little strength left and began to think the jungle went on forever. They could tell the sun was lowering on the horizon because underneath the dense canopy of trees the underbrush was getting dark, the trail harder to find. Halliburton mustered his strength to use the remaining light to see what he could. He climbed a hillock and looked to the east.

Ahead and below, he saw a railroad track tiny and dark in the distance and beyond it the sea. He likened the sight to Balboa casting eyes on the Pacific after crossing the Isthmus of Panama. It was a glad sight and he felt relief to gaze upon the Gulf of Siam.

They struggled down to the track, where he said goodbye to his guide. The two men had spent vivid days together, a time they would remember the rest of their lives, and they said goodbye and that was it. Richard paid him three dollars. They shook one another's hands and turned different directions toward the future.

Clothes shredded, bedraggled, Richard probably followed the track to Chumphon. He looked from the track onto the sea. Soon he would board a ship out of the Gulf bound for the Siamese mainland. He revealed his true feelings to his parents when he described the trek as a nightmare but in *Royal Road* he said he hesitated to recommend it to the infirm and old ladies.

The book remark makes for entertaining copy but it hides agonizing trials and existential depths. The words were for public consumption, apart from the private Richard Halliburton. He had written home to his parents, asking about the worth of it all, asking why not do as the British civil servant and Ainsworth the island owner did. Life is short. Maybe they had it right.

He finally concluded his thinking about the life the two men represented. To stay on an island such as Ainsworth's would have been worse than the trek. In a letter from Bangkok, he wrote his parents about

---

took place. If they miss a bus they tell themselves it happened for a reason. Entrepreneur and Apple CEO Steve Jobs was noted for his "reality distortion field" which enabled him to take on huge risk and succeed in pursuit of an idea. This same magical thinking caused him to delay by nine critical months conventional therapy for his pancreatic cancer. Instead, he chose alternative therapies.

Ainsworth and declared his view of it all: "There is no choice for me, however. To go my way is weariness to the final exhaustion, but to turn back one inch, to be for an hour what my host is I would despise myself to the point of madness."

On his twenty-first birthday, Richard had written home, "Nine more years and I'll be 30 and the last vestige of youth will be gone. At present I can look forward to no joy beyond 30." He added that it was "only existence" for him after that.

There on the Malay Peninsula, though, he was still twenty-two and after Bangkok he sometimes remembered but soon forgot the English civil servant, Ainsworth, the dead puppy, and the cobra.

PIRATES

By what slender thread our destiny sometimes hangs!
Richard Halliburton

Chinese pirate chief, the woman La Choi San

GAMBLING AT MACAO

Fifty miles across the mouth of the Canton River from Hong Kong, Macao has lingered at the dusty reaches of romantic memory. Once Portuguese-owned, it has a certain distance from the Western world, an exotic vagueness that appeals to the wayward imagination. It was a place where few people ever went, rather like Marrakech, or Tierra del Fuego, although in today's con-trailed sky increasingly more tourists jet there. The Las Vegas Sands Corporation has the Sands Macao there. In the 1952 movie *Macao*, Jane Russell is at her busty best, providing prurient pleasure for the schoolboy imaginings of Howard Hughes, who owned RKO Pictures and made the movie. As the title indicates, the story is set on that island. Robert Mitchum has escaped his past, gotten as far from it as possible and, through the generous corruption of William Bendix, Mitchum and Russell are able to engage in a hi-jinx of smuggling. She is a high-roller. Mitchum and Bendix are low company. Together they form a forgettable movie filmed on RKO back lots. It is about the down-and-out, the seamy side of life. It is a kind of film noir and it is not Macao.

Popular history has Macao as a deal between the Portuguese and the Chinese. The Portuguese could lease it if they helped protect Chinese coastal waters from pirates. The island also kept the Portuguese at arm's length from China, thereby avoiding strong cultural contact with the foul-smelling people in armor.

The culture gap was an issue. Gaspar Da Cruz, living in Canton in 1556, mentions that a Portuguese was found armed with a knife, something acceptable in Portugal, but prohibited in Canton. The man had to bribe a Chinese officer to avoid punishment.

The Chinese needed some means to keep these barbarians at bay and so they offered Macao. It would entice the foreign devils off the mainland. That is part of a popular explanation; as for the actual causes of Sino-

Portuguese agreement, accounts differ and they are still being sorted. We know for sure that Macao was given away in a century when tiny Portugal scared the mighty Chinese dragon.

In 1999 the Portuguese returned it to China and that did not make some people happy. Macao-born Portuguese wanted no part of Chinese nationality. To its credit, China was flexible, offering dual citizenship, and accommodated their legal concerns but not because she wanted to do the right thing. Portugal could be a future economic partner for the capitalist juggernaut that communism had become.

Richard wound up in Macao near the end of his first world adventures and in 1922 it was far different than today with its massive casinos and architectural design transplanted from the Nevada desert.

In Richard's time it had nothing such as today's Venetian Macao, a casino resort. With over one thousand slot machines and six hundred gaming tables open around the clock, the Venetian has automated teller machines to help relieve you of money you think you don't need or—if you later realize you need it—to help you enjoy the brief time before your regrets. The Venetian Macao lets you climb into a gondola and have a gondolier pole you along canals that lull the inebriated into a pleasant sense of Italy by the South China Sea.

For Richard, things were simpler. Macao was a brief port of call, rather like a modern McPleasure cruise in the Caribbean. You visited a few hours and were back on the ship. The difference was that there were no McPleasure hordes.

At the American Express in Hong Kong, Richard claimed five hundred dollars. He had sold magazine and newspaper articles about his travels and the cash came in the nick of time. His reaction to the windfall was typical. He decided to spend four hundred dollars on Canton jade and Macao gambling dens. With only one hundred dollars left he could return to life on the edge, which served him because it fit his narrative character, providing the story he wanted to tell—that readers can also follow their nomadic dreams with little to finance them. Of course there was also the lad who pushed the envelope and reveled in risk.

To his parents he describes Macao as "the Eastern Monte Carlo," and that it is where "Fan-Tan is played." When a Portuguese colony, Macao had fan-tan gambling tables and in the mid Nineteenth Century gambling became legalized. Even today its casinos are the place to go for a day trip out of Hong Kong. Likewise in Halliburton's time. On Sundays, people took excursion boats from Hong Kong to the fan-tan houses there.

He had boarded the steamer, the *Sui An*, to visit the island. With its sister ship, the *Sui Tai*, the *Sui An* was a twin-screw steamer built in 1899. The *Sui An* was sold in 1938 and even after that she saw long service until removed from Lloyds Register in 1959. In the early Twentieth Century the two ships carried excursion passengers between Hong Kong and Macao.

At Macao, three hundred seventy passengers left the decks of the *Sui An* for the shore and, knowing they had to be aboard for the afternoon return to Hong Kong, they quickly made their way to the casinos. Fan-tan does not use a roulette wheel to determine the winning number and one version involves a small pile of copper rings dumped on the table. The pile is reduced as four rings at a time are drawn away until four or less remain. Luck and winnings come to the gambler who correctly bets on the number left. As for the bettors, in Richard's day Chinese stood around the table, while Europeans sat in a balcony above it, lowering their stakes in a basket, a trope of their social position and distance from the colonials they governed.

Richard wandered out of one smoke-filled room into the sunlight then back into another. He managed to win forty-five dollars and began thinking himself a sure thing, a high roller. Then the all-aboard horn sounded from the *Sui An* and he saw his chances for wealth fading, but one more bet, only one more, and he could return to Hong Kong rich. He plunked five dollars on a number and lost.

He was mindful of games of chance as he described himself clambering aboard the steamship, its last passenger to return. He wrote home focusing on his initial good fortune, omitting his loss. "Fan Tan is lots of fun and I really won at it." He thinks he might have become wealthy in Macao, and instead he remained a vagabond. After the steam ship slipped its moorings to come about into the sea, its bow parting waters toward Hong Kong, he would meet fate of a different kind, one in which money paled before the true stakes. Chance rolled its dice and the stakes were lives.

BOARDED BY PIRATES

On Tuesday, November 21, 1921, *The New York Times* reported an incident.

> CHINESE PIRATES SEIZE VESSEL, BUT LOSE FIGHT; Disguised as Passengers, They Boarded Boat Heavily Armed. Two Europeans Killed.
> HONGKONG, Nov. 20 (Associated Press). Sixty-five Chinese buccaneers, who might have stepped from some ancient log of the Spanish Main, traveled as passengers aboard the British steamboat Sui-An, when she left Macao for Hongkong yesterday afternoon.

The article explains that pirates held the ship, a steamboat of over two thousand tons, for thirteen hours. There was "a fierce battle" with heavily armed men in which several innocents were wounded, including the ship's captain, a French priest, and another European. The pirates locked up passengers and the crew then turned the ship toward Swatow. After a European managed to shoot the pirate chief, the chief's wife ordered the brigands into their sampans and they escaped.

She was probably the chief rather than a wife, given the account by Russian-born Aleck E. Lilius. His 1930 book, *I Sailed with Chinese Pirates*, explains that he joined the brigands after meeting their chief, a woman named Lai Choi San, probably the same female Richard describes in his account. In his book Lilius used official data to report that on the *Sui An* $34,000 US was taken. Because Milton Caniff used her name in his comic strip of the 1930s and 1940s, *Terry and the Pirates*, Lai Choi San is widely believed to be the source of his Dragon Lady.

Lilius informs his readers that the pirates were very careful, traveling back and forth as passengers on steamers they selected for robbing. After noting crew procedures and positions, they reported their findings to the gang. The gang then smuggled arms aboard—this, by paying off somebody exempt from close inspection—and when the ship was out to sea La Choi San gave a signal for her bandits that all was ready for the final move.

The final move on the *Sui An* occurred ten miles out of Macao on the return to Hong Kong when two Chinese passengers raised a gun on the purser when he asked for their tickets. He ran down a passageway as they shot after him.

Richard had been consoling a young English bank clerk who lost a pile in the fan-tan houses and was bemoaning his newfound poverty on the first-class deck. He and the clerk jumped to their feet at the sound of gunshots.

The sixty pirates had been briefed and knew what to do. Swarms of them invaded each deck. Four Indian armed guards made a pathetic effort to arrest them. Two were killed instantly followed by several more bullets just to make sure. The other two fell to the deck and were beaten to death by the pirates. A Chinese woman, probably La Choi San, climbed the ladder to the pilothouse where she shot the captain. He fell and another thug beat him unconscious.

Her main interest was the Chinese purser, who kept keys to the ship's safe. The purser leveled his own pistol. She shot at him and missed. He shot at her and did not. Hit in the shoulder, she was out of commission as her fellow pirates went about their business.

Passengers huddled together in dark corners, hid in cabins, or flattened on the deck where they had fallen to avoid gunfire. The pirates mugged Chinese passengers and handily relieved them of valuables. In the salon, Europeans reached for the sky as guns pointed at them. Richard lost all his money as well as his hat, coat, vest, belt, and pride. A pirate liked his silver belt buckle and vest just bought in Hong Kong and, poking his gun at Halliburton, ordered him to take them off.

The Chinese found a pack of Camels in Halliburton's pocket. He offered Richard a cigarette then pushed him aside for the next victim.

The next victim had only a dollar and twenty cents, not worth the taking. Not so fortunate was the American who carried two hundred dollars. He pleaded and said it was all he had in the world. The pirates took one hundred eighty and left him with twenty.

The pirates then ordered the Europeans and Americans to their cabins, where they hoped to find jewelry and other valuables stashed away. The Westerners were also relieved of their shoes, hats, and overcoats, leaving them with feet exposed to the hard deck and heads to the chill air. The pirates climbed down into their own boat, each of them teetering under the weight of so many overcoats, with shoes and wallets stuffed in all available pockets, and several hats piled on their heads. As the *Sui An* fled for Honk Kong harbor, Christian passengers might have consoled themselves with the parable about the difficulty of rich men entering the kingdom of heaven.

To his parents Halliburton wrote that he sailed to Macao on "the now famous Sui An," and "she was pirated by 60 bandits and all the American and British passengers stripped of everything. . . . It was the most outrageous holdup Hongkong has ever known and the colony is extremely excited about it, but I'm poaching my own story, 'Piracy à la Chinoise'. "

He still had far to travel and before he arrived back in Memphis he accumulated memories and experiences enough to last most people a lifetime but he had just begun. After returning to the states, he had a book to write and be published before he set out again.

IN SEARCH OF SUCCESS

New York has been inhospitable. It's every man for himself here. They trample on those that fall down.
     Richard to his parents

Richard with cane & spats, next Flying Carpet in crate & about to board
the *Majestic*

STRUGGLING TO PUBLISH

When tried as a spy in Gibraltar, he described himself to the British judge as a writer, an idea he held onto fiercely although his publications then were close to nil. The description was his self-image, which he would carve into the reality of Halliburton the successful author. He knew intuitively what Jean-Paul Sartre said, that first we exist, then we must define ourselves and our lives. He had a definition, writer, and it would shape how he viewed himself and his future. He had made up his mind on a career and that was that. As he traveled during his first trek across the globe he wrote articles as well as notes for his book. Wesley offered him advice on his articles. He politely told his son that they were too wordy. His son politely told him to stuff it. Richard saw Wesley's advice as something to be avoided because he, Richard, knew what he felt and what he felt was good. If it were good then his audience would also find it good. He happily sent his articles on Gibraltar off to find a publisher.

In Marseilles, he checked at the telegraph office to discover a message from his dad waiting. His articles had been rejected.

All his confidence, his pluck, dissolved.

To his parents he wrote, "When I opened Dad's cable and saw both my articles had failed, I sank into a chair more despondent than I've ever been in my life. The world had come to an end. My trip was a blank failure. I'd sacrificed reason and pleasure and company in vain. All the bushel of fine letters from you and everybody else could not console me."

That sadness was one day, not the next. In the morning the sun shone again. The prior night he had gone to bed not planning to get up until noon and then to mope around when he did arise. Instead, he "got up and shaved, had a hot bath, put on fresh clothes, had a big meal and laughed heartily" at his "own desolation of the day before." He salvaged hope in a typical way. Of course things would get better. His account of his stolen moments on Gibraltar was perfect and nobody could have pulled it off as well. He had not suffered a setback. Because of the rejections, he had experienced a lesson about his writing. "I shall profit in the long run for having been jarred sensible." From lemons he would make lemonade.

176

With the rejections he reconsidered Wesley's editorial judgment. He now understood that his articles were over-long, just as Wesley had warned. He told his father, "Please, Dad, when I send you a manuscript, *damn* it as well as like it. I value your estimation highly for I find you are usually right in knowing what is above or below the line of conviction and sanity. Don't think it's fine just because *I* wrote it. Look from an impersonal view as if you were the editor, judging its faults and virtues." He came to believe his father was no slouch in terms of literary acumen. Whatever he thought about his dad before was gone. That was then; this was now, for his father was wise after all. Wesley, a fan of Mark Twain, might have reminded Richard of Twain's remark: "When I was fourteen, I thought my father was the dumbest man on Earth. When I became twenty one, I was amazed to discover how much he had learned in the last seven years."

His dad became his critic, and Richard appreciated the commentaries, at least until he was well established as a popular writer. Either before or after Richard met Paul Mooney, Wesley no longer edited for him. We know that Richard came to rely on Mooney.

Richard Halliburton was uncompromising on certain self-expectations. On the one hand, he politely allowed his father to be correct. "I hate to admit it, but you're right about too much work making me weary. I've slowed up." On the other, he reminded Wesley that the result of slowing was to get behind in his notes. Further, he did not see the world as did Wesley. His father had written him, "This voyage over land and sea is nothing but an unusual post graduate year at Princeton." No, Richard replied. Absolutely not. "This trip is my *work*. Some Princeton grads from the class of '21 went into banking, some into theology. I went into traveling and writing and I take it as seriously as they do. It must be my income. You have set me up in business by furnishing me with money for my education. I must make a success of these articles and then of my book. No, it's no vacation, it's no postgraduate year, it's serious business."

The tone of this reply once again sets son against father. There was love between them but also a rebellion within Richard. He did not want to become like his dad. The irony is that he did emulate his father. He was after middle-class success but outside middle-class avenues.

His spectacular Matterhorn experience was sold as story to a travel magazine. His over-long "German Impressions in 1921" was broken into chunks and the chunks sold to newspapers. Slowly and intermittently he sold but not until *The Royal Road to Romance* did he begin the royal road to success.

STRUGGLES, LECTURE TOURS, & REJECTIONS

He was home from his travels and he did not slow down. For nine hundred dollars, Wesley bought Richard a new 1923 Buick roadster with flashy black canvas top, lacquered wooden spoke wheels, and a fold-down windshield, which the son picked up at the factory in Flint, Michigan after he visited his parents in Memphis in April. On the two-lane gravel roads of his day, without a roof, wind blowing through his hair, he drove to New York City and his future as Toledo, Cleveland, the Mid West, faded from his rear view mirror. New York City was not only on his horizon but he firmly saw it in his future. It would be where he would make things happen. After he arrived, his vision collided with reality. New York City was New York City even then. It was dog-eat-dog, success and failure, with no in-between. He had not complained about that yet. At first it was mainly money. In a letter home he complained to his parents about parking the Buick in a public garage for three dollars a night, the cheapest found, and the cost intruded into his budget. To control costs, he took a room at the YMCA, Young Men's Christian Association, on West 57th Street, near a bottom corner of Central Park. He cut down on expenses by sharing a room with Cecil Crouse, a Princeton classmate. He described Crouse as "the best amateur pianist I've ever known," adding dryly, "but I do not believe we will have a piano." Crouse's Princeton orchestra played at the Savoy Hotel in London one summer. He retired as vice president and director of the Borden Company, which used Elsie the Cow in its advertising campaigns for dairy products, mooing over milk in television commercials.

In his travels Halliburton took notes, photographs, and wrote narratives for what he planned as his book on his great adventure. His oeuvre was to be original; he rejected magazine articles he could draw from. He had piles of photos. He was ready. All he had to do was sell the idea of his book then write it. His time was coming and he was there to meet it. He waited for it and waited for it but it was nowhere to be seen.

On May 10, 1923, he wrote home from New York, "Nowhere in the wilds of Asia was I more homesick than I am tonight. No one with whom to discuss what seem momentous problems—only a little garret room with 7,000,000 people outside I don't know, and don't want to." He was not in a good mental place that evening as he wrote. He needed to earn money to live on while writing his book so he tried to sell articles to magazines and newspapers. He continued, "It would seem that I'd get used to rebuffs but as yet I've not. Successes give me little satisfaction; failures, real depression."

The Hearst Syndicate did not want articles by him. "They wanted only scandal and gossip, but they sent me to the American." There, he told an editor he "had the dope about Chinese bandits." The editor gave him only a few hours to write it, so Richard dashed back to the Y and knocked out a thousand words. Returning to the *American* he only saw a sub-editor who bought the piece for ten dollars. On another day he tried the Bell Syndicate, which was interested in ten articles at fifteen hundred words each depending on what he could write. The McClure Syndicate told him "flat no." As for a possible publisher of his book, he had a connection at Doran, maybe an ace in the hole, at least he hoped so. That, too, did not work, as the connection had an easy out. Richard had to finish the book in time for publication by Christmas, galleys, proofs, rewrites, and all. In another letter he wrote his parents he said, "To date I've made only $10.00, but I've 'prospects,' like the man who promised to pay his board bill when he sold his book which he was going to write as soon as he had the inspiration." He tried the McClure syndicate once more and once more they turned him down.

His parents were in it with him. He told them that. It was not his endeavor but the family's. He is very young and in need of emotional support and especially from them. They were a team, the three of them. He wrote, "Dad, I get such stimulation and gratification from your letters. Don't let a week go by without one for they have become a sort of anchor for me. . . . We'll get there yet—you and Mother and I. Who and what can resist our united determination!" He had ideas, words, experiences, and somebody was sure to buy them. He hoped so. He had a proposal for *National Geographic.* He could write a piece on Fuji and Bali. He could offer pictures, some of Gibraltar. Surely they would interest Gilbert Grosvenor in Washington, DC.

With a girl he had met at Princeton, Marie, he drove to Allentown, Pennsylvania to visit Heinie and Dot Leh on a Friday afternoon, to return Saturday morning. His parents must have had concerns about the two, a young man and a young girl, alone in a motorcar. They stayed overnight, no less. Nelle replied to his letter and wrote something that caused his response: "Mother, I really smiled out loud over your suggestions about Marie and me. We had a jolly sociable time on the Allentown trip and I enjoyed it no end. She talks about her 'Bill' and I talk about my book. Isn't that amorous? I haven't any time for amorousness."

He drove the Buick to the National Geographic Society in Washington and spent a pleasant two hours there with Franklin Fisher, who accepted manuscripts. Fisher wanted to keep and read the Bali manuscript. He also agreed to consider the Fuji piece. From Richard he took eight photographs, including Gibraltar, Carcassone, Vladivostok, and Japan. Richard left Fisher feeling upbeat, though he knew he had to wait four weeks for the decision. He visited the Lincoln Memorial, and declared Washington beautiful, "all in spring clothes."

Back in New York City, he again became impatient and dejected at the brick walls against his would-be career. "Things have gone *so* much more slowly than I hoped for." He adds, "New York *has* been inhospitable. It's every man for himself here. They trample on those that fall down." Still, he would prevail over the Big Apple. He just had to finish his book but in the meantime he needed to eat. Clearly, he would not make enough by writing for newspapers and syndicates. The question became, How, then?

In those days, the lecture circuit was a common means. Radio was brand new while lectures were an institution in American culture, due largely to Chautauquas. Named for its place of origin in New York State, the Chautauqua was what Americans had. It brought entertainment and culture, with speakers, teachers, vaudevillians, and preachers. Teddy Roosevelt said the Chautauqua is "the most American thing in America."

At a Chautauqua, Bohumir Kryl's Bohemian Band played spirited music for audiences. As a ventriloquist, Charles Ross Taggart, "The Old Country Fiddler," sawed at his violin, threw his voice, and laid them in the aisles with his tall tales. People went to hear him but liked Chautauquas for the chance at self-improvement. They offered lectures, travel narratives, and current events. The "Golden-tongued orator" William Jennings Bryan spoke to audiences on temperance. Maud Ballington Booth, the "Little Mother of the Prisons," brought tears to their eyes as she described the wretched conditions of inmates.

Because of Chautauquas, by the time Richard came along the lecture was an American institution and because he needed income he turned to the lecture circuit while writing his book. He called on the Pond Lecture Agency. To Agency executives he described his travel adventures around the globe, climbing the Matterhorn, trekking across the Malaysian peninsula, sitting overnight at the Taj Mahal, trudging across the Himalayas, held at gunpoint by pirates, climbing Mount Fuji in winter, and they threw him out. It was too late for the next lecture season. Come back in time for the following season. Where to turn next? he asked them. The Feakins Agency. Okay. Try there. Feakins. He checked out the address and located the offices. Why, yes, young man, I'll listen to you. William B. Feakins took the youth to lunch. Richard showed him photographs of his travels. Feakins studied them, considered their owner.

Yes, hiring the boy was not out of the question but there was his speaking voice, rather excited, sometimes nervous, too high. Maybe he'd give the lad a shot but first a test. Feakins told Halliburton that before deciding he must hear him give a lecture. Done, said Richard. They shook hands and Richard agreed to notify the Agency of a speaking date for Mr. Feakins to attend.

He rushed back to the Y, which held a talk in the lobby each Tuesday night. Could he have the floor on Tuesday of next week? he asked. The YMCA activities manager agreed on the date and Richard felt relieved. That took care of that. He only had to prove his stuff to Mr. Feakins in one week. He called the Agency and learned that the gentleman would be out of town on that date. Feakins' son could attend, however. Halliburton rehearsed his presentation, went over his notes, practiced inflections and emphases until Tuesday night finally came.

In the huge Y lobby, Richard took his position behind the lectern. Feakins' son sat on a folding chair and waited for him to begin. Richard began talking as a piano banged away in the next room. An advertising bagpiper played outside on the sidewalk. People passed in the lobby, talking loudly. Some people got up from their chairs, making scraping sounds, as they decided to go listen to the piano, or to walk down to the corner restaurant. Others talked to one another, ignoring Halliburton and drowning him out. Richard could not bring audience attention on himself. He could not connect. His voice probably trailed off as he watched one person after another push a chair back and leave.

He did not get a lecture contract from Feakins.

He did get a polite brush-off from Feakins' son. Knowing that the lad had not spoken in an auspicious situation, the son referred him to *Boy Scout Magazine* and provided an entrée with the editor there. The *Boy Scout* editor listened to Richard's talk of his experiences, examined photographs of many lands and peoples, and let their conversation last a good hour. Finally, he told Halliburton, "You are just the man we want. You dropped from Heaven to answer a serious call for just such a person." However, the editor wanted support in his choice. He arranged for them to have lunch with higher-ups Monday next at the Algonquin Hotel. Richard had great hopes that an initial success would lead to many lectures and even movies.

He and the *Boy Scout* executives talked over several weeks but nothing happened.

Mr. Feakins returned from his trip. The two, father and son, must have discussed Richard's misadventure at the Y, and the son acknowledged the unusual difficulties Halliburton had to face there but despite that advised his father that Richard was not ripe for a Feakins lecture. They gave him another referral, this time to a Mr. Powlison, president of the Child Welfare Association of America. Yes, said Powlison, he could get Richard a dozen places to speak, the first at an orphan asylum, and the sooner the better. For once Richard wrote with understatement when he said of the job, "I took it."

This would be a shining moment. If anybody could relate to kids, Richard could. Richard invited Powlison to hear him speak and then he persuaded Mr. Feakins Senior to attend.

He drove two hundred miles up the Hudson to the orphan's school, Sheltering Arms, in Hoosac Falls. At 7:30 in the evening, he stood before two hundred children from five to fifteen years old. Powlison and Feakins sat in the back. The kids sat before him, rowdy, excited, eager. As soon as he began to speak, they became silent, rapt in attention. Richard drew from his repertoire and told vivid, imaginative stories. "I knew I had them, for not a person moved. Their eyes were big as saucers, and I saw that Feakins saw *that*." When he finally moved into his finale, then closed, he looked up at them, entranced, their mouths agape. He waited. They broke into wild applause, applause that only delighted children can make.

Powlison rushed up to him, said it was "the best talk he'd ever heard made to children." He wanted Richard in his work with orphans. Most definitely. Feakins was clearly pleased. Richard's odds were improving. This was it, he thought. It was in the bag.

He offered Powlison and Feakins a ride in his Buick roadster and waited for the offer as they chatted. Nothing.

Feakins did say to meet him at the agency office in a few days. That was a carrot but money problems were getting serious. A couple of days later, he wrote his parents. He told them he worked hard on the book and got another chapter done. Telling them he visited the parents of his Princeton dorm mate Larry Keyes, he added "I am going to the Ritz to a dance tonight, friends of the Keyes. I've been to the theater once and the movies once. I have neither time nor money for such. My garage bill was $15.00."

He woke up "absolutely broke," which he called an "amazing experience," the comment suggesting he was in one of his exhilarated moods. His parking garage bill, the trip to Hoosac Falls, and clothing, had "eaten up" his "last dime." He took his photographs to a syndicate and "was thrown out." He got the same treatment at the *Times* and *New York World*. He had drawn a cartoon called Pure Prom that he tried to sell to *Life* and *Judge*. Once again he heard a sorry and no thanks. He made a little money with the *Tribune*, which bought four photos at $40 total and the cartoon for $25. He had some cash again.

Feakins finally agreed to hire him for one speaking engagement in fall 1923 for $25. The twenty-three year old saw it as a great breakthrough. "It's a *start*, and that's the vital thing up here in this cauldron of competition and exaction. Dogged perseverance won the day. We're working on circulars now." In another letter, he wrote his parents thanking them for a check. As for the Buick and its expensive parking costs, he motored to Princeton and left it in storage at Trenton until his parents drove it back to Memphis.

He wrote home "I often look out my window and shake my fist at the New York skyline and soundly damn the entire place." *National Geographic* sent back all of his submissions. They explained that they had too much copy on Bali and Fuji. They offered him $2.50 each for twenty photos but he declined; he would not sell his efforts that short.

Lecturing well was a sometime thing for him. Feakins hired him for other engagements and he occasionally became nervous, his voice high-pitched, and he could lose his audience. This happened from time to time over the course of his life. In November 1923 he wrote his parents, "For the first time in my lecture career, I talked, Wednesday evening, without stage-fright—at an enormous Boy's Club here in the slums. They were young and responsive, so it was real fun after the distracting stage-fright I went through at the church in Newark. Lecturing is a tempestuous, nerve-wracking business." He recalled a speaking engagement in Brooklyn with two thousand people who had not come to hear him but to see a Jackie Coogan movie that followed him. It seemed "everybody in Brooklyn was there." Four-year olds squirming in their mother's laps or jumping on the next seat. Old ladies shocked at some of his tales. "It was an *impossible* audience. As I walked on the introducer said, 'One hour! Not a minute over.' Seeing the clock hand approaching the fatal three-thirty, I hurried too much and fell back into inarticulation."

At one lecture in the Waldorf-Astoria, New York, before the Eclectic Club, he found himself confronted with three hundred "conservative, mature women" whose president's mouth fell open at his fresh, unwrinkled face when she met him. "It was lucky for me she didn't see me before making the contract—she wouldn't have dared employ such a *very young* man." Quick witted, Richard mentioned his mother as "president of the biggest club in the South." This helped and gave the Eclectic Club president an out. She introduced him as the son of Nelle Halliburton, president of The Southern Club.

His time in the Big Apple was not without his mingling in its high society, which did not occur often during his struggles for success, but was enabled as his income and celebrity grew. He and Cecil Crouse occasionally dined at the Princeton Club in New York, and one evening they attended the Manhattan Opera, where they saw Anna Pavlova dance.

He did not relent. With characteristic intensity, he lectured and wrote, lectured and wrote. He burned the candle at both ends, getting up early, then writing, rewriting, and completing chapters. He prepared for lectures, spoke and, back in his apartment, wrote late into the night.

In his 1923-1924 schedule he had mild encouragement here and there although he still had not sold his book. *Travel* magazine bought a piece on the Malay peninsula along with five pictures. Lawrenceville, his prep school, booked him at $100 to speak on December 15th. The editor of *Asia* bought his good photo of Fuji. It helped that he spent an evening with the man and his wife, and that the editor was Princeton class of 1906. The *Philadelphia Forum* wrote an encouraging letter, "Thank you heartily for the article. It will do splendidly and I shall use it in the November issue." Mr. Huff, of the *Forum*, also arranged a couple of speaking engagements for Richard in Germantown and Wyncote, and expected to have more later. He had recommended Richard to Mr. Froelich of *Asia*. Feakins found him some engagements, $150 for two in Kansas City January 7th and 8th, $100 for St. Louis on the 9th. He was scheduled for another in Westover at $100, at Taft School for $75, then Shady Side at $35. "So far," he wrote his parents, "we have $1160." The *we* referred to the three of them. He added, "I'm going to throw all my efforts with Feakins." The lecture circuit was it, then. It became a means of livelihood, as it was something to foot the bills while writing and trying to sell his first book. As for the lectures quelling his writing energy, he wrote his parents "Don't worry about Destiny choking off the book. I'll choke Destiny first."

His own biology choked him. His body and its nerves could not keep up with his drive.

Richard's doodle in a letter home on his frenetic life.

BURNT OUT & BACK AT THE BATTLE CREEK SAN

After his lecture engagements were over for the 1923-1924 schedule, he went to Siasconset, an island off Nantucket, to continue his writing. He wrote home, "For nine weeks I've not left my desk. I don't take any heavy exercises or long walks. So long as I'm quiet inside and out I feel—or rather don't feel—anything. The moment I get tired or in a tension the old troubles begin." The old troubles were what took him in his teens to Battle Creek and the San. He ignored them and doubled his efforts, reporting that he was moving fast, "about out of India, Malay, Siam, and Angkor." He was soon into the Java and Bali pages.

Throughout 1924 the old troubles steadily worsened. In July he wrote from Nantucket "for nine weeks I've not left my desk." His will held him to it and he ignored signals from his body. In August he became extremely tired and nearly sick after motoring down to New York. The next day he sailed with friends off Long Island and discovered he had difficulty climbing aboard the yacht. His pulse "was beating a mile a minute" and he "felt very bum in general."

After he returned to Nantucket a doctor listened to him as Richard complained about "extreme nervousness, a fast-beating pulse, and a general weakness." Without examining him, the doctor announced that Richard had all the symptoms of goiter. Goiter?, Richard asked himself. He said, "There is something raising hell with my nerves and it *might* be goiter, though to save my life I can't find any swelling and neither can anybody else." Richard had to ask the physician to examine his heart. The man did, thumping his back, listening with stethoscope, and assured Halliburton that it was "sound as a dollar." No murmur. Not enlarged. He decided to return to New York to get a second opinion. He would look up a goiter specialist. Whatever he had, it was getting worse, and he was concerned.

He drove back to New York, where a physician diagnosed him correctly.

He alarmed his parents, telling them he was told what caused his "trembles and debility this past year." The doctor told him he had no goiter problem but he did have an overactive thyroid. The man found "a marked oversecretion of thyroid" and recommended that he go to Battle Creek. Richard was relieved that he finally had a name for the "overstimulation" he had felt "for a year without knowing it."

His Ammudder had visited him at Siasconset to be by his side while he was ill and she accompanied him to Battle Creek. She had set him on her knee when he was a child and read to him adventure stories, which helped shape the world-traveler he became. He tells his mother and father that he is glad she is with him and we learn that he started feeling weak way back in Japan. He regretted that he had to put the manuscript on hold but accepted that nothing could be done for the delay.

In August 1924, Richard wrote from Battle Creek, "I did not greet the San with much enthusiasm this morning. The idea of my having to come here at all and having to disrupt my beautiful summer plans nearly kills me. But I'm here and I'm going to go at getting back to 'normalcy' with all the determination I've gone at everything else. I'm afraid you're worrying unduly."

He described the San's Dr Elmer Eggleston as the "same gentle self" he had chatted with when there the first time as a boy, and said the doctor had gotten Wesley's letter and had been expecting Richard. Everything was closed as it was Saturday, the Sabbath for its Seventh-Day Adventist founders, though he and Eggleston chatted for a quarter of an hour. On Sunday they would have serious conversations on Richard's health issues.

He did not put the book on hold after all. He kept at the manuscript and had written himself into China. He still had money problems and could not tarry at the Sanitarium, noting that "Feakins counted up $2300 in engagements, so I've got to get back on high in time." He knew he was in good hands in Battle Creek, though. Elsewhere, he added humorously, "I suppose we ought to leave a few of our millions to the San out of gratitude." His parents were comfortable but had no millions. Without diversion, without a social life, he was able to concentrate on his manuscript. Finishing the first draft, he wrote, "This is one big burden off my chest." He felt the book was over-long so Richard wrote Wesley that he needed him to "cut and prune" the manuscript. On top of first-draft completion, he had his lecture tour. He wrote Feakins that he would not let any physical disability interfere with it. Ever the optimist, he was now buoyed in his travail because, having revised it, he had his "complete manuscript to play with." He would also have the pleasure of selecting among his pictures for the book. He did not stop to consider he had not found a publisher.

He arrived at Battle Creek in mid-August and by October he was home in Memphis and then returned to New York. He might still have had his "trembles" but he had calmed and strengthened enough that he left the San. Richard's symptoms did recur at times throughout the remainder of his life and for somebody so active, so driven, so focused, it is not surprising. They did not deter him from many busy lecture seasons, nor from several more world adventures, nor from writing other books.

After Battle Creek, he met with his dad in New York. Then Richard resumed his lectures, stopping at the Drake Hotel in Chicago, where he wrote his parents, "Dr. Seabury gave me some nerve exercises which I'm practicing hard. If I could only follow all his instructions, I'd get strong again."

He wrote his parents that Seabury told him to "live by artistry, not by emotion." Seabury meant that Halliburton should attend more to the style of his life and writing, becoming an objective observer of them rather than plunging into them. This, just as an artist must maintain critical distance from his art. The doctor told Richard that he had "lived, lectured, thought, moved, entirely on emotion" until "bled to exhaustion." For Halliburton, such a life with distance was not permanent but only, as he put it, "until my emotional state can recuperate." For him there could be no permanent separation because he was what he felt, as was his writing. His life itself was his art and could not be experienced as a painting, but only with acute openness to all its feeling and sensation.

He still had a book to finish and publish. In New York, he and Wesley edited the book, cutting some stories, shortening others. Wesley hired a typist to put it all back together. They had the finished product bound, then boxed it and mailed it to Boni & Liveright. "About a ton of material was discarded," Richard wrote his mother. The editing done, he could step back from the book. He was quite optimistic about its. The Boni & Liveright editors were not interested

Century House rejected it. The manuscript became dog-eared by the fingers of so many editors. He read it repeatedly, trying to figure how to improve its sales chances but he had no clue.

He had given the book his best shot. He called it *The Royal Road to Romance*. Editors had told him it contained too much philosophy so he culled what he could. He had been told it was youthful and naïve but he resisted changing its tone. He stubbornly insisted on his title because *he* was romantic. He continued to shake his fist at New York and a world that could not share his vision.

Waiting to hear from publishers, he took Seabury's advice but despite his need for rest he missed the total absorption in the book. "I feel lost without it. But I'll get busy on another right away." Soon the public would see his name in print, he believed.

During lecture tours he complained of throbbing headaches and committed himself to an Indianapolis hospital for a painful sinus drainage. Even there, he was determined to get on with his schedule. On one tour he developed laryngitis that allowed only a whisper. After five days, he resumed his engagements but got no better. He was hospitalized for three days but, restless with inactivity, he began speaking again, still hoarse. Groggy, filled with sedatives, he dismissed protests of physicians and nurses as he dressed himself and returned to his hotel.

With auburn hair and blue eyes, his skin suffered regularly from over-exposure to the sun and easily became crimson but he ignored this and at Tiberias he swam the Sea of Galilee, becoming baked with second-degree burns, his skin a riot of blisters. He was bed-ridden, nauseous, and feverish for two days afterward. He was weak and could eat little for a week. In Soviet Georgia, the Gossudarstwenoje Polititscheskoje Upravlenije or GPU, the secret police, confined him to a dirty hotel room in Batum for two days while he awaited a ship to Istanbul. He contracted the flu and the ship's captain saw him pale, bent over with illness, and refused him passage because he had a communicable disease. Alone, without nurse or friend, he had to wait another three days, by which time he was seriously sick but he strolled aboard the next ship, faked a cheerful face, announced himself in fine fettle and after he got to his cabin he collapsed on his bunk. In Istanbul he was hospitalized for three weeks.

In his romantic readiness, his sometimes-innocent enthusiasm for life, there was a very tough individual. Despite his search for intense experience he could control his feelings and emotions, his pains and pleasures, and even put a lid on them, to see himself through the worst of times.

SMASHING SUCCESS

No matter where a young man might turn, he would find fresh tracks in the dust—the marks of Richard Halliburton's boots; and he would find signposts pointing down side-roads to publishing houses. The paths of glory still lead but to the grave, but they lead first to the Savoy-Plaza; there one finds Halliburton, the snows of Popocatépetl still clinging to his coat sleeve, the waters of the Panama Canal still gathered in little beads on his eyelashes, a young adventurer home on schedule, surrounded by his memories, his little sandwiches, and his book-chat ladies. "Talk of the Town," E.B. White. *New Yorker*, Dec 14, 1929*

1925. The year, like all others, had something for everyone. In Indiana, things happened as they did everywhere else but, like everywhere else, they happened in their own unique way. In 1925 the Indie 500 was won by Pete DePaolo at 101 miles per hour. That same year in Indiana Ku Klux Klan Grand Dragon David Curtiss Stephenson was sentenced to life imprisonment for the abduction, rape, and death of Madge Oberholtzer after she learned he belonged to the Klan. A few years before, heiress Louisa Fletcher fled her Indiana mansion dressed in overalls and when found she claimed she was "tired of being a poor little rich girl" and wanted to live like everybody else. In 1925 she married a German blue blood and became Countess Von Schmettow of Berlin. Apparently she changed her mind.

The year had something for Richard in Indiana. In 1925 Richard finally sold his first book to Bobbs-Merrill in Indianapolis. His fortunes had turned.

It did not began with fireworks. He took fourteen sample chapters to Scribner's. They would let him know soon. They did and it was another no thanks. Before he got the rejection, he wrote, "I've had so much on my mind and had so many rebuffs that one more won't concern me. It will add the necessary incentive to my writing." Despite his brave words he was depressed after hearing Scribner's criticism of his manuscript. They spent three hours with him, faulting "youthfulness and immature style."

In 1925 he could not get used to opening envelope after envelope to read another no thanks. Boni & Liveright rejected his book, as did many other publishers. Just start anew, he must have thought. Chuck it all. Nobody wanted his first book so he might as well do another. He decided to do that very thing. A new adventure would lift his spirits. A new adventure and another book, this time in search of ancient myths such as the voyages of Ulysses. Then he tried Bobbs-Merrill.

"Founded in 1838" was printed on its letterhead and until its name was dropped by purchaser Macmillan in 1985, Bobbs-Merrill had a back list that included L. Frank Baum's *The Wizard of Oz*, Pietro di Donato's *Christ in Concrete*, Irma S. Rombauer's *The Joy of Cooking*, John Erskine's *The Private Life of Helen of Troy*, David Markson's *The Ballad of Dingus Magee*, and Ayn Rand's *The Fountainhead*. It published the Hoosier poetry of James Whitcomb Riley, known for the phrase "life of Riley" due to his idyllic settings. Ford Maddox Ford, Mary Roberts Rinehart, Booth Tarkington, and Earl Derr Biggers were also published. Prospering, Bobbs-Merrill used its money to move in 1926 from University Square in Indianapolis to 724 Meridian Street.

Returning from a lecture in Cleveland, Richard stopped in Indianapolis. He called on Bobbs-Merrill and met with some editors. After Halliburton left, vice president David Laurence Chambers, Princeton 1898, read an alumni bulletin that Richard was scheduled to speak about his world travels before the Princeton Club of New York. Chambers telephoned Thomas R. Coward in the New York office about it so he would attend. Chambers then also decided to hear Richard.

Having arrived late, Chambers said later, "I found young Halliburton going great guns in the final period of the extempore talk. He looked like an Apollo. His light hair made an aureole around his face. His eyes flashed. He was on fire with enthusiasm. Impetuous words, full of life and color, poured from his lips. The effect was electric. His breathless enthusiasm was contagious." After the applause had died he and Coward waited to speak with Richard. Flush with adrenalin, Richard greeted them and they settled into business. Coward and Chambers wanted to read the manuscript. Why, of course, said Halliburton

After each man read it, they discussed the manuscript. Then Richard received a telegram.

NEW YORK, APRIL 24, 1925 RICHARD HALLIBURTON

PARKVIEW HOTEL, MEMPHIS, TENN.
ORGANIZATION ENTHUSIASTIC ABOUT YOUR BOOK
AND FOR ACCEPTANCE IF YOU WILL CUT IT. SHALL WE
SEND MANUSCRIPT TO YOU OR ARE YOU COMING
NORTH? PLEASE WIRE REPLY. T.R. COWARD

They wanted the book and although Richard and Wesley had edited it they wanted to do more rewriting. There was a problem. Halliburton had decided on the book title as *The Royal Road to Romance* and would not budge. It would not sell, the Bobbs-Merrill editors felt. It was juvenile, a rebuke to adult sensibility, and should be revised to something less florid. No, said Richard. For him, the title said it all. His was a way forward out of the world to which most people are condemned and the title offered the avenue. Absolutely no change in the title. The book provided both a manifesto and a method and that was that. Its title declared his life to the world. It embodied his belief and his practice. Let others read and learn from him. The Bobbs-Merrill editors shrugged, then caved.

In Indiana Richard worked with editor Hewitt H. Holland. Later editor of *Century Magazine*, Howland was brother-in-law to humorist and playwright Irvin S. Cobb, author of the Judge Priest stories made into a movie *The Sun Shines Bright* by John Ford. Of Howland, Halliburton said, "I've never in my life enjoyed more ten days of pleasant and profitable activity." At a dinner evening with him and his wife, Richard and they chatted into the night. He found Howland to be "an affable, lovable, understanding gentleman" and they "worked together beautifully." Howland gave Richard "almost too free rein to keep it in the singing, capricious style" he valued "so highly." Halliburton was especially pleased with the price. With twenty-four full-paged photos they would sell the book for five dollars.

Halliburton sent a bragging note to the editor of the *Princeton Alumni* magazine for the comments section on the class of '21. The message read, "Bobbs-Merrill has signed on the dotted, and it's all over but counting the royalties." He had no doubt of his eventual success.

Week after week *The Royal Road to Romance* appeared on *The New York Times* bestseller list. Other editors had turned it down. It had been rejected repeatedly but thanks to the acumen of the Bobbs-Merrill editors, it met with the success they anticipated.

One of the enthusiastic editors was Thomas Coward. Like Chambers and Howland, Coward saw the originality of the work. In 1925 Coward was fresh out of Yale working for Bobbs-Merrill in the New York office and culling for manuscripts worth publishing. Coward was not a paper-shuffler and found something in Richard's manuscript that others did not. The editor had an edge, a competitive talent that not only alerted him to the value of Halliburton's book but caused him in 1930 to found Coward-McCann with James A. McCann, former Bobbs-Merrill sales manager.

David Chambers had come to the company as the personal secretary of W.C. Bobbs, the president. A Phi Beta Kappan, he graduated magna cum laude from Princeton in 1898 and, a major stockholder, became vice president of Bobbs-Merrill in 1921 while remaining an editor. At Princeton he was first place Baird Prize winner, a competition in oration. The university published a work by him, *The Metre of Macbeth: Its Relation to Shakespeare's Earlier and Later Work*, still available. Chambers is said to have had a quick temper at first but after a doctor cautioned him about heart attacks he learned to control it. In 1926 he wrote to H.S. Baker of the New York office that "one of the trials of life is the necessity of constantly showing an accommodating spirit to authors." In 1935 he gained full control of the company when he became president. In 1939 historian Thomas D. Clark sat down across from Chambers and described the man at his desk as tall, stooped and graying. "His shirt tail was out, his hair was rumpled and he looked at me over his pince-nez glasses as if I had brought a dead fish into the parlor. He made me sit down across the broad, tousled desk before him and talked in such a low voice that only by the grace of God could I tell what he was saying."

Chambers belonged to a bygone era and frowned upon the cynicism and tough prose of younger writers such as Ernest Hemingway, James T. Farrell, and John Dos Passos. No wonder, then, that Chambers liked the freshness and enthusiasm of Richard Halliburton.

The Royal Road would be published in Denmark, Holland, Sweden, Norway, Germany, Italy, France and Czechoslovakia. Richard was somebody who could deliver the goods, as a publisher then and now might say. Following that book, published under his name were *The Glorious Adventure* (1927), *New Worlds to Conquer* (1929), *The Flying Carpet* (1932), *India Speaks* (with Richard Halliburton), (1933), *Seven League Boots* (1935), *One Hundred Years of Delightful Indigestion—Memphis Priceless and Treasured Receipts*, (Introduction by Richard Halliburton, World Traveler, Author and Epicure)(1935), *Richard Halliburton's Book of Marvels: the Occident* (1937), *Richard Halliburton's Second Book of Marvels: the Orient* (1938). Posthumously, Wesley published *Richard Halliburton: His Story of His Life's Adventure, as Told in Letters to His Mother and Father* (1940) and *Richard Halliburton's Complete Book of Marvels (1941)*.

Richard was confident now, sure of his direction, convinced he had been right after all because there was a message in his writing that appealed, that sold, and all the publishers who rejected his manuscript were wrong.

When his first book appeared, reviews were not even. Some critics said Richard tended to exaggerate situations rather than describe them as they were. Here was a travel-adventure writer who could not be taken seriously. Atop the Matterhorn, he describes himself as awestruck by the panorama in the frigid air while Mike Hockaday is quoted as saying, "Gee, Dick, I can actually spit a mile."

Critics had fun with his prose. *Time* magazine mocked Halliburton's travel on the cheap as "around the world on $40" and did not relent. It was "the biggest kind of super-romantic money's worth that 'self-satisfied people, caught in the ruts of convention and responsibility' can buy anywhere currently." *Time* referred to Richard as Dick Halliburton, Princeton grad, who "romped around the world in tramp ship forecastles, called it *The Royal Road to Romance*, said he was 'living poetry instead of writing it.' He talks volubly, cracks many jokes, threatens to write a novel called Hell." The *New York Herald-Tribune* said the book was juvenile and lacked good taste. The *Saturday Review of Literature* called his observations superficial. The *Dallas News* dismissed him as a college boy from a rich family, which was not true—not the rich part.

A *Los Angeles Times* reviewer wrote of his own pleasure which "may be likened to the enjoyment of small children watching a magician who brings rabbits from empty hats and does all sorts of mysterious things." Among favorable reviews, *The New York World* said the narrative was full of life. It had "swift movement, unending variety." The *Detroit News* spoke of its "captivating charm"—"Halliburton's tale of travel and adventure is one of the most fascinating books of its kind ever written. It is a glorious story of the irresponsibility of youth, of the dauntless spirit of the age, told with a captivating charm and a wing and a dash that takes one's breath away." *The Chicago Post* wrote, "Impetuous to utter recklessness, laughing at hardships, dreaming of beauty, ardent for adventure, Halliburton has managed to sing into the pages of this glorious book his own exultant spirit of youth and freedom." The *Columbia College Spectator* wrote that the book "is the best substitute available for those who are unable to make a similar trip." Richard would have gone a step farther for those who could see his meaning—do not substitute; just do it.

He appealed to readers both young and young at heart. Among these was Susan Sontag, one of American's most influential intellectuals, National Book Award Winner, author of seventeen books, and human rights activist. Her books include *The Benefactor, Death Kit, The Volcano Lover,* and *In America*. She read him when she was a girl and he remained an enduring influence because he urged that nobody lose their wonder. When asked what books had changed her life, she accorded Halliburton first place. She learned from him that a writer could lead a privileged life, endless in "curiosity and energy and expressiveness and countless enthusiasms." Halliburton visited Lenin's tomb. He climbed Popocatépetl. He walked the Great Wall of China. He flew over the Sahara. He wrote about them all. As she put it, "Halliburton made me lustfully aware that the world was very big and very old; that its seeable wonders and its learnable stories were innumerable; and that I might see these wonders myself and learn the stories attached to them."[*]

Halliburton influenced the life of travel writer Paul Theroux, prolific with books that include *The Old Patagonian Express, The Mosquito Coast, The Great Railway Bazaar, The Kingdom by the Sea, The Happy Isles of Oceania, The Pillars Of Hercules* and *Sir Vidia's Shadow.* In *The Tao of Travel* he writes of Richard Halliburton as a major influence on his life. Elsewhere he said that when a teenager he read *The Royal Road to Romance* and accounts such as bathing in the moonlight at the Taj Mahal and swimming the Panama Canal gave him a sense of direction for his life.

After he became a celebrity, Halliburton visited Chicago on a lecture tour. On Michigan Boulevard, Brentano's main bookstore placed a huge photo of Richard next a poster proclaiming *The Royal Road to Romance* as "The Outstanding Travel Book of The Year." At Marshall Fields department store he was given a grand reception. The socialites of Lake Shore Drive came to see and hear him despite a blizzard and he spoke of his boyish adventures to their matronly delight. They bought his books and asked for his autograph. He inscribed their copies with "Here's all that's fine, books and old wine, boys be divine to_____," filling in the blank with the lady's name. He was toasted at the Chicago Adventurers Club. In Cleveland he was guest speaker at the annual Rotary Convention. Over fifteen hundred people heard him at the April Philadelphia Forum. National Geographic Society members turned out to hear him.

In the first blush of success, he relished his public. He was interviewed by Bernarr McFadden's *Physical Culture* magazine, and declared that he needed no training, only inspiration. *American* magazine described him as "a slender, blue-eyed boy who has dared to live his dreams, who has fought and laughed his way from Spain to Siberia." He was asked to speak at a department store in Boston with six hundred seats in its auditorium. Eighteen hundred people showed up. Even John Grier Hibben, the president of his alma mater, Princeton, sent him a note, "I almost read your fascinating book in one sitting and I congratulate you upon the remarkable opportunities you yourself created to see this wonderful world of ours." From France, Princess Murat invited him to visit her at her estate in the banlieues of Paris. Alex Thiers, grandson of French President Poincaré, also invited him. English playwright John Van Druten proposed he come

---

[*] In *Gravity's Rainbow*, on page 266 of the original Viking edition Thomas Pynchon writes this: "It is the well-known frontispiece face of insouciant adventurer Richard Halliburton . . . Richard Halliburton's Jodhpurs are torn and soiled, his bright hair greasy now and hanging. He appears to be weeping silently, bending, a failed angel, over all these second rate Alps."

to Europe so they could tour Norway.

As a teenager John Nichols Booth listened to Richard lecture at Cleveland Heights High School in Cleveland, Ohio. He recalled that when Halliburton walked on the stage girls shrieked as they later did with Frank Sinatra. He had charisma, Booth said, adding that he was an especially handsome man. After being introduced by the principal, Halliburton talked about climbing the Matterhorn. His punch line was about Mike Hockaday saying he could spit a mile from the peak. Inspired by Halliburton, Booth also traveled the world.

By 1935 more than half a million people had heard Halliburton lecture. He had a contract with Bell Newspaper Syndicate, which distributed columns, fiction, feature articles and comic strips to newspapers for decades. Bell editor and publisher, John Neville Wheeler, knew popular taste and signed up Halliburton for pieces on his latest adventures, which were run every Sunday. It was good money. Richard had only "to fill a page every week for 52 weeks—about whatever I please." The pieces helped fill out the book he would write about his next travels, *The Glorious Adventure*. Despite his insistence on the word in the first book, he was practical enough to avoid *romance* in another title so, to avoid redundancy, *glorious* served his meaning.

He settled for all that but he had another side, one that looked at it all with disdain as he grew older and faced still another publishing deadline. He liked the dollars that came with recognition but saw through the ballyhoo of his popular success. He was bothered by it, although it had been what he wanted. At Princeton, to a *Daily* reporter he said his book was not literature. Fanny Butcher of *The Chicago Tribune* asked him to write a piece for her Confessions column. He wrote, "I wish instead of The Royal Road to Romance, that I had written Don Quixote." Behind his flamboyance became hidden a Knight of The Sad Countenance. He tilted his romantic lance at distant horizons but all of them eventually turned into windmills with nothing more than money in them.

He did not write literature, he told the *Princeton Daily* reporter. His high-society evenings, his recognition, diverted him from reminders of what he did write. As his body caught up with him in his thirties he re-read *The Royal Road* and wrote, "It seems surprisingly young. My lack of variety in expression, my roughly connected ideas, etc., strike me as never before." He had changed from the young man who would not budge on the title *The Royal Road to Romance* because it signaled his manifesto and method. "Of course," he wrote, "I am trying to see how severely critical of myself I can be—and I find it very easy."

As he grew older, Richard puzzled over his success but his father knew. In the 1960s Wesley told James Cortese that "Richard happened along at the right moment in time with something the world needed and wanted:

romance, adventure, and escape from the humdrum of life. In an era labeled 'the Roaring 20's,' in a world that was yet large and unexplained and unknown, Richard Halliburton had the youth and enthusiasm and the verve to explain the unknown." Wesley said, "Richard dealt in superlatives." Something, "no matter if it was just a walk to the corner drugstore, was the best, the most wonderful, the most beautiful." In all its youthful enthusiasm, the Jazz Age needed spokesmen and Richard Halliburton became one.

Cartoon of Richard diving into Well of Death, better known as the Sacred Well of Chichen Itza, Yucatán, Southern Mexico

HOLLYWOOD SPEAKS

Hooray for Hollywood . . . Where everyone at all from TV's lassie to Monroe's chassis is equally understood. Go out and try your luck, you might be Donald Duck.

Music by Richard Whiting and lyrics by Johnny Mercer

"Has Richard Halliburton written anything lately or has he settled down?"

1930s Cartoon: "Has Richard Halliburton written anything lately or has he settled down?

CELEBRITY

Halliburton dined with the famous, some of them forgotten. *The New York Times* Screen Notes column on October 13, 1932, announced, "Dorothy Jordan, Irene Rich, Ely Culbertson, Richard Halliburton, and Lola Hays will be the guests of honor at the luncheon of the Associated Motion Picture Advertisers at Sardi's today." While Halliburton was on his Washington, DC speaking engagement, President Herbert Hoover invited him to the Oval Office. Richard "had a chat with him, surrounded by six bodyguards." That same day, he lunched with Huey "King Fish" Long, former Louisiana governor, then a senator, who would be assassinated two years later, with his last words, "God don't let me die. I have so much left to do." The month before, Richard had dined with Lowell Thomas, broadcaster and journalist who had interviewed Lawrence of Arabia in Palestine. He and Lowell previewed Thomas' movie, *Mussolini Speaks*. A Russian princess interviewed him for *Liberty* magazine. He dined with Corey Ford, once a fierce critic of his books. In gossip columns, names of the rich and famous became linked to his and many would be remembered: Herbert Hoover, Charlie Chaplin, Basil Rathbone, Mary Pickford, Douglas Fairbanks, Art Linkletter, Ramón Novarro, Lowell Thomas, Huey Long, Charles Mayo of the Mayo Clinic.

While in Southern California, Richard visited Erle, a distant cousin. Erle Halliburton founded the corporation US Vice President Dick Cheney once headed. The Halliburton Corporation became principal contractor for the United States government during its occupation of Iraq. On January 19, 1927, with his wife, Vida, Erle motored Richard to a party in Richard's honor in Redlands and thrown by an ex-Senator from California, James D. Phelan.

On impulse and during the depths of the Depression, Richard

bought a new, luxurious Packard four-door touring roadster. He bought it in LA and drove it to his cousin's mansion. On the drive, the crankcase drain plug probably loosened and oil leaked steadily from the engine. After visiting Erle and his family he left it there, promising to have it towed away. It sat as an eyesore for months until Erle had it hauled off. That was one thing. The other was that Erle watched Richard regularly rise from and sink back into debt.

Richard Halliburton was accepted by the smart set and his dashing reputation preceded him. The week before he motored with Erle to the bash at Senator Phelan's, Richard had dined with F. Scott Fitzgerald and his wife Zelda. Two years before, Fitzgerald had published *The Great Gatsby*, his masterpiece, just before his friend Ernest Hemingway published *The Sun Also Rises*.

In 1932, on New York station WOR Halliburton told the radio audience how he took the very first high-altitude photographs of Mount Everest while freezing in an open cockpit biplane. It was indeed a brave new world with planes and radios and flying above Mount Everest. It was a time made for the likes of Richard Halliburton. Sir Edmund Hillary and Tenzing Norgay would not climb Everest until 1953. In his speaking engagements Richard had been greeted almost as a discoverer of the Dark Continent, as Africa then was called. He made the unknown known. He opened eyes to the world. He had a niche in popular awareness and his question remained, How to use that niche? One way was to star in a movie.

RICHARD IN A STARRING ROLE

India, Mother of 10,000 Sins
INDIA SPEAKS
Starring Richard Halliburton
Directed by Walter Futter
Movie Poster, 1933

The movie was schlock and he knew it but the fact he starred in it showed he had become a brand. He talked on radio. He appeared in newspapers. His fame was evidenced by a large picture in the October 18, 1925 *New York Times*. The rotogravure shows him between columns on the Acropolis in Greece. The caption reads in part, "Richard Halliburton of Memphis, Tennessee after swimming the Hellespont, reaches Athens to reports he had had been drowned in his exploit as the first American to do as Byron Did." The news bureaus thought he had been caught by the current and drowned but, as Mark Twain said of himself, the reports of Halliburton's death were greatly exaggerated.

He was asked by Walter Futter to star in a talkie, *India Speaks*, playing opposite Rosie Brown, of Italian heritage, who stood-in for Jane Wyman in several MGM movies. Futter directed and produced *Africa Speaks*, a jungle travelogue still viewable on the internet. It was so popular that it invited parodies in the British spoof *Africa Shrieks* as well as the cartoon series *Africa Squeaks* and Abbot and Costello's *Africa Screams*. Apparently, *India Speaks* was so bad nobody even wanted to parody it. The film was almost lost but Rhodes College has remnants of a copy.

Richard got an offer of ten thousand dollars for six weeks of acting in the film. An independent producer for United Artists, Futter approached Halliburton with a contract and, long story short, Richard accepted in October 1932 and reported to United Artists studio on November 3rd. He wrote that Futter could make use of film footage that "has been collected for years—India, Tibet, the Himalayas." His role was to provide a dramatic and narrative link between the clips. Filming would start on November 7th.

He canceled his lecture contract. He spent his last night on the tour in Durant, Oklahoma and that was far from the warm clime and bright lights of Los Angeles. On the flight to Hollywood, he sat next Bebe Daniels, who had starred opposite Rudolph Valentino, sang in a Busby Berkeley musical, and was caricatured on a 1921 *Vanity Fair* cover of celebrities. On its cover, Daniels was surrounded by Fatty Arbuckle, Douglas Fairbanks, and Jackie Coogan. Daniels and Halliburton did not speak much to one another because with little insulation against sound the cabin was too noisy. Without pressurized cabins and engine superchargers the plane could not fly above turbulence and it was bumpy. Flying through storms rather than above them, airliners were tossed up, then thrown down, and passengers became airsick.

Futter approached Halliburton about the movie because he counted on Richard's name and on book sales as part of the promotion. He talked to Grosset & Dunlap about a book with shots from the film and the publisher said yes, advancing a thousand dollars for the book, which Futter agreed to split with Richard. This deal did not go down well with Richard's publishers. Bobbs-Merrill believed the book would cut into revenue from their reprints of Richard's other books. David Chambers, Bobbs-Merrill editor, gave Richard a five hundred dollar advance to lure him away from their rival but Halliburton went ahead with the Grosset & Dunlap deal. The picture book, *India Speaks*, flopped, though it sold for a dollar.

The film *India Speaks* depended on a thin plot line, partly of romance between Richard and olive-complected Rosie Brown as an Indian maiden. From Los Angeles, Brown was apparently smitten with Richard, and this was her one and only main film role. Of her, Halliburton writes, "only one chapter has a love-girl in it—and she's sweet too—named Rosie Brown. She's dressed up like a Kashmir girl, and I have a romantic scene with her in a garden." Their rose garden love scene was like the boy-girl romances in Richard's books in which something intervenes to keep Richard from intimacy with the girl of his affections. In this case, their ardor is suddenly extinguished by a downpour, handily achieved by a fire hose. Futter called for a re-shoot of the scene so many times that Halliburton became drenched and sick. He caught a cold that become a pneumonia sending him to Cedars of Lebanon Hospital. Rosie daily called the hospital to ask about his health. After the film was put in the can, Richard continued to get letters from Rosie.

The talkie travelogue was filmed on United Artists back lots and at Yosemite Valley in Northern California. Richard described Yosemite Valley as "the wildest of the wilds." Access to Yosemite can occasionally be difficult even today when paved sections are washed out by rockslides along high canyon walls and a sometimes-roaring river. The narrow road cuts along the Merced River underneath sheer mountain cliffs. It rises, drops, and snakes for miles and can be impassable in winter. In 1932, over unpaved roads, the going was rough. Once there, the temperature fell to ten below zero and they had no heat at all. They spent three days in the valley and Richard was glad to leave. He had his young and busy life to live. Bridal Veil Falls, Half Dome, and El Capitan did not notice his departure and stood as they had for millions of years.

At the official premier of the movie, he appeared on stage at the Roxy Theater in New York City to pump the movie. On 50th Street, just off Times Square, the theater held almost six thousand seats. "Roxy" was the nickname of Samuel L. Rothafel, a "movie palace" impresario. It was magnificent and dubbed the "Cathedral of the Motion Picture," with columns in its large rotunda lobby fitted with a huge oval rug and a pipe organ on the mezzanine. It was demolished in the 1960s.

On Sunday May 7, 1933, he wrote, "Our theater today has been only moderately filled, about two thousand people at each of the five performances." He spoke about two and a half minutes and was straightforward and honest. He said, "Not all the adventures in which I take part on the screen happened to me personally. I am chiefly an actor playing a part." The lights in the Roxy blinded him. He was in the spotlight, highly visible to the audience, but he could only see a large black theater. He had to wear makeup and he could not go out on the street between shows. He did have "a fine, big dressing room" where he could "read and write letters," but he did not "get much relaxation." Walter Futter paid him eight hundred dollars for five days of introductions. The audience listened to him in real life on stage, and then watched him on the screen. Their impressions are lost but critical reception is not.

In his May 8, 1933 *New York Times* review of the movie, Mordaunt Hall describes the movie as "scenes of life in India and Tibet, with a running comment delivered by Richard Halliburton." He calls it "a curious concoction of fact and fiction which is now on exhibition at the RKO Roxy." Misspelling the director's name, Hall tells us that the film "was produced, or rather assembled, by Walter Putter, who, after collecting a generous footage of scenes made in India, engaged Richard Halliburton, author and adventurer, not only to deliver a running microphonic comment but also to assume the rôle of the harassed hero who pops up during several melodramatic incidents which were photographed in Hollywood."

With that introduction, we know what will follow.

Hall says that, despite many authentic scenes, "It is somewhat disconcerting to be called upon to believe what the screen voice is saying at one moment and then appreciate that in the next breath one is listening to a fanciful escapade."

"Speaks" in the title of *India Speaks* heralded something new in the world. It was the age of Vitaphone, of sound-tracked film reels, and Futter exploited the technology. Mordaunt Hall is bothered by the "the terrific enthusiasm for sound." In the battle between lion and tiger, "Mr. Futter has overdone the inoculation of sound." Futter's enthusiasm is counterpointed elsewhere when "the scenes are silent and later one hears the breaking of a tree as it is pushed over by an elephant." Hall adds "To enhance the effect, notwithstanding the height at which the two birds are flying, one hears the frightened cries of the smaller bird before the eagle catches it." Sound was a new toy and Futter played with it, sometimes successfully, sometimes not. Hall felt that *India Speaks* should have spoken less indiscriminately and more quietly.

Hall complains that in one scene Halliburton is handled roughly by natives but glaringly obvious is that the treatment is not part of the collected footage. Richard is posing for the camera. Moreover, he stood on stage introducing the film and explained he only played a role. Richard was candid with viewers because he could see where critical response would be headed. On his part, Halliburton had hedged his bets on the movie, describing *India Speaks* to the press as a photoplay, thereby merging fact with fiction. He had no great expectation for its credibility as documentary or attraction as drama.

In the movie Richard's script appeals to the prejudices of the times. He talks of millions of Hindus who starve to death while in temples the beds of sacred cows are prepared with clean straw and they eat clean fodder. He speaks of the law of the jungle as he describes a fight between a lion and a tiger, both in a pit and unable to escape one another. An eagle dives upon its prey, a pigeon positioned for the bird's easy grasp. Halliburton wakes up to find that a vampire bat had fastened itself to his throat. The audience learns of Indian lore which says that once bitten, a man's soul is possessed and he is doomed to be reincarnated as a bat. Richard awakens, mouth aghast, eyes wide to see the bat on him. Such was the movie.

Hall gave his opinions and descriptions of the film but it was a bit of ephemera. He could not anticipate any historical interest in it. Regarding the movie, here are some historical facts. Futter was born in 1900 in Omaha and died in 1958 in New York City. J. Peverell Marley, a cameraman, was one of only six cinematographers to have a star on the Hollywood Walk of Fame. Seventy-eight minutes long, the movie was released on April 28, 1933, showing in Finland next year. It had a second release in 1949 titled as *Bride of Buddha* and also as *Captive Bride of Shangri-La.* In Britain it was titled *Bride of the East.* One of its tag-lines is, "A virgin chosen to bear a living GOD!"

In his review Hall nails his lid on the coffin when he says, "It is somewhat disconcerting to be called upon to believe what the screen voice is saying at one moment and then appreciate that in the next breath one is listening to a fanciful escapade. It is a mixture which does not 'jell'."

Richard & Rosie Brown in *India Speaks**

---

* As Rose Schulze, with her second husband she retired to San Juan Capistrano, California.

BOOK TWO

Richard & Sea Dragon, Kowloon, 1939

OVER THE HIMALAYAS

When the gold was stolen, the giant ants would give chase, and they could run faster than any man.
Herodotus

Richard atop Zozi-La Pass, one of the highest in the world

THE GIANT GOLD-DIGGING ANTS OF LADAKH

Throughout history Ladakh has remained remote, distant, and not even a curiosity to the wide world. Still, it was probably known to an educated few in the ancient world. Before the vast library at Alexandria was fully and finally destroyed in 391, Ladakh was written about in books remembered to be there. Of existing ancient works, Herodotus writes in his *Histories* that it is a land of wonderful ants. Endowed marvelously, these ants call to mind the spice worms on Arakkis in Frank Herbert's science-fiction trilogy *Dune*. Herodotus says, "Here, in this desert, there live amid the sand great ants, in size somewhat less than dogs, but bigger than foxes. . . . Those ants make their dwellings under ground, and like the Greek ants, which they very much resemble in shape, throw up sand heaps as they burrow."

That isn't the end of it, for the marvel of these ants is greater. Herodotus explains that "now the sand which they throw up is full of gold. The Indians, when they go into the desert to collect this sand, take three camels and harness them together. The camels were necessary. When the gold was stolen, the giant ants would give chase, and they could run faster than any man."

They might have been the Eighth Wonder of the ancient world, these ants, but then Antiquity was full of wonders.

Still, unlike Herbert's spice worms that control stuff with ability to fold space, expand consciousness, and extend life, Herodotus' view of the ants is more practical. Steal some sand and you are rich if you can outrun the ants.

Sometimes called "Little Tibet" because of its Buddhist monasteries, Ladakh sits near the borders of Russia, India, and China and is visited by few tourists. Portuguese merchant Diogo d'Almeida is the first European known to have visited it and this after 1600. He lived there two years and reported that "It was a land run by strange Christians whose monks recalled those of Portugal."

An Italian Jesuit, Ippolito Desideri, traveled there in 1715. In his climb over the mountains he described a rope bridge strung between two mountainsides, made of two thick willow ropes four feet apart. From the large willow ropes, loops of smaller willow rope were tied every foot and a half. To walk on the ropes invited vertigo. It required a gait and a style that can be best described as hanging on for dear life.

"One must stretch one's arms and hold fast to thicker ropes while putting one foot after another into the hanging ropes to reach the opposite side. With every step the bridge sways from right to left and from left to right. Besides this, one is so open on all sides, that the rush of water beneath dazzles the eyes and makes one dizzy." Elsewhere, Desideri writes that they "traversed a deep and narrow gorge between steep mountains." His fellow climbers shouted at him and he looked where he had just stepped to see a huge mass of snow falling away, crashing into the rocks far below.

In the upper Indus Valley, Ladakh today is held by India. It sits in the Kashmir region, which is contested by Pakistan. A district of frequent border skirmishes, mountain troops dress in white to blend with snow. On one side, the Himalayas stretch skyward; on the other, the Karakoram Mountains make an almost impenetrable boundary. Ladakh is inhabited by people of Indo-Aryan and Tibetan descent. It is one of the most sparsely populated regions in Kashmir. It earned its sobriquet Little Tibet because Buddhism heavily influenced its people. Ladakhis are mainly Tibetan Buddhist with the rest principally Shia Muslim. Abundant rock carvings bear evidence that Neolithic human beings lived there, a mixed Indo-Aryan population of Mons and Dards, mentioned in Herodotus, as well as in Nearchus, Megasthenes, Pliny, Ptolemy, and Puranas.

Access is easier than when Desideri found it in 1715. It is easier than in Richard's day. In 2006 India opened the two hundred eighty-eight mile Srinagar-Leh highway to Ladakh. The highway is closed from November to May because of snowfall. "Easier," though, is a relative term. Some of those who have driven it in recent years describe Zozi-La Pass, at near 12,000 feet, as almost a nightmare.

In 1842, a man with a brief name—G.T. Vigne, Esq., F.G.S.—wrote a book with the brief title, *Travels in Kashmir, Ladakh, Iskardo, The Countries Adjoining The Mountain-Course of The Indus, And The Himalaya, North of The Panjab. With Map.*

In his book on Ladakh, Vigne writes, "On the banks of the Basha is produced more gold-dust than in any other part of Little Tibet . . . the value of the quantity collected, and of the time expended is so nearly balanced, that I have never seen any gold washers but once, and that was near the village of Kerris."

Vigne observed the Himalayan marmot, about the size of a large housecat and similar to the North American prairie dog, both types digging holes in earth for their colonies. The creature has a dark chocolate-brown coat with yellow patches on its face and chest. Local tribes collected gold excavated from their burrows.

He recalled Herodotus saying the giant ants "make themselves habitations under ground, throwing up sand like the ants of Greece" and noted that in Ladakh some of the diggings around marmot burrows contain gold dust.

Vigne concluded that the "ants as big as foxes" were marmots.

Gold-digging ants swarming a horse.
From *The Travels of Sir John Mandeville*, c. 1357

SRINAGAR AND PREPARATIONS FOR LADAKH

Richard traveled at the twilight of Vigne's zeitgeist, or spirit of the times, while colonialism did not know it was in its last breath. He could still find YMCA, Young Men's Christian Association, lodging in places like Singapore or Calcutta and it was common enough that he inquired after it even in Srinagar, which he visited with David Russell, a young traveling companion whom he met in Agra, India. In pursuit of YMCA lodging while exploring Srinagar, they spotted a sign, Civil and Military Agency, rather like armed forces travel and recreation services offered by the military today. The British were mindful of maintaining morale and, through the agency, offered travel diversion to military and civilian personnel.

Halliburton met Russell before he became famous and while still gathering adventures for his first book, *The Royal Road to Romance*. Richard and David went inside to ask if Srinagar had a YMCA. No, the agent replied, but he had a tent, fully equipped and waiting for a new British physician. They could sleep there until the doctor arrived. As things turned out they did not need it as they spent delightful weeks on a houseboat. He wrote home that they "accidentally met a Mr. Catlin, American, living in a deluxe houseboat on Dal Lake. 'Come on over,' he invited us, 'and live with me.' So we did; all free, private gondola, rich food. All yesterday we were on water with six oarsmen behind us. Garden after garden, fountains and flowers, such as Versailles never dreamed of, built by the builder of the Taj Mahal and as beautiful in their way." He tells his parents that Catlin is "a brilliant talker." He had "done everything and been everywhere, had very eccentric and persuasive ideas," and they listened "to him from dinner to bedtime." Catlin promised Richard and David jobs in the states if they ever applied for them.

Richard said that Mr. Catlin let them use his wardrobe to join the social life of the Anglo-American community and pay calls on others. They played golf almost daily.

Richard paints Srinagar as a kind of Shangri-La, an Eden from which only a fool would want to escape. This is his standard tactic to foreshadow change from the idyllic to the risky.

As they played golf, as they dined with ladies and gentlemen of the British colony, he and David saw the Himalayas in the distance, and in their life of ease they became discontented. They wanted to climb over the mountains. Mr. Catlin thought them crazy. He was middle-aged; they were very young. He thought Srinagar the best of all possible worlds; they wanted to explore the best of all in the world.

Ladakh was on the other side of what they saw in the distant Himalayas and they wanted to go there. They heard that in Ladakh every woman had three or more husbands. Six out of every ten men were Buddhist monks. Leh, its capital, sat at 11,000 feet elevation. Grain was raised at 15,000 feet. They had to cross a snow pass at 11,500 feet, a desert pass at 13,000 with air so thin it sapped energy. They would not find paradise but would meet challenges and that was good.

No matter that Leh was two hundred eighty-eight miles away and along a narrow mule trail often buried under snow. No matter that they must cross three mountain ranges rising to 14,000 feet. No matter that only twelve foreigners a year could travel to Ladakh.

Twelve. That information clinched it. Boundaries, numeric or geographic, whetted the desire to challenge them, at least for Richard. He was unsure, though—unsure if they could do it. He wrote home that they "*hope* to get there. The country is so sparse and the natives so inhospitable to Europeans that the number allowed to make the trip each year is limited to twelve." As he would find them, however, the natives were friendly enough. Of the twelve applicants, he and David persuaded two people to give up their places for them. As the two people gazed at the distant mountains, thought of the difficult and dangerous passes, they probably were easily convinced.

The British agent told the youths they could travel there for seventy-five dollars each, the cheapest possible way, with mules, guides, and equipment. That was a princely sum for them. It was a number to overcome by pluck and craft. Richard told the agent they were journalists. The Civil and Military Agency could get free publicity if it only loaned them the necessaries. Almost as a stage whisper in his book, Richard adds that his public was about as small as those interested in the Greek Testament. In a letter he says the Agency gave them thirty dollars of supplies free in exchange for mentioning it in his book. He repeats their offer in *Royal Road*, and true to his word Richard plugs for the travel office and he shouts it in capital letters, giving the agency's name and declaring it the best place in Kashmir for touring needs.

They scrimped to get to Ladakh. They decided on one cook and two other men. Just two pack horses with some yaks. They agreed to budget for sixty cents a day for fifty days.

Word traveled fast. Many men claimed to be cooks, hoping to be hired. The boys chose the one who spoke the best English, which was not very good but, as Richard wrote home, the man was an excellent cook. He dubbed him Holy Moses, probably not because of the Abrahamic connection between Islam and Christianity but to give his readers from Midwestern farms and villages a chuckle.

Richard & David Russell, houseboat, Srinagar

INTO THE HIMALAYAS

On the trek over the mountains, they encountered more than they had reckoned for. One hundred thirty miles out of Srinagar, Halliburton woke up very sick, probably bad food from the good cook, but trudged fifteen more miles. At the next stop he plopped onto his blankets, wishing he were home. Next day Richard and David looked up on mountain after mountain, with a whitewater river coursing far below past boulders and around cliffs. They found paths barely wide enough for their feet. A misstep and the traveler fell down a precipice, breaking a leg or tumbling into the river. Nothing could stop the fall except a ledge or the bottom, for there were no bushes to cling to in that barren region. Then it happened. A packhorse tripped on the narrow trail and tumbled into the roaring icy waters below, carrying tent and provisions with her. Richard and David scrambled, slipped, and rolled down the steep slope and jumped into the river to save the horse, which was protected by a cove of rocks from the rushing current.

That was not the end of it. They had to spend the night on one of the highest mountain passes in the world, at 11,578 elevation. This was the Zozi-La Pass ("Pass of Blizzards" in Ladakhi), blanketed with twenty feet of snow in winter. Today, with its countless switchbacks barely wide enough for one vehicle, the pass is dangerous in good weather and closed to traffic six months out of the year because of sudden blizzards. The blizzards trap the unsuspecting and leave them frozen to death in their trucks to be dug out of snow banks in spring.

In his 1926 book, *The Devil's Guard*, Talbot Mundy described his experience in the pass: "When we camped one evening, within two hundred paces of the entrance of the pass, snow had already begun to fall and the wind was howling through the gorge with such force that we could hardly pitch camp on the only level place beside the road where there was any shelter. It was impossible to drive pegs, so we weighted the tent down with rocks and used most of our loads for a wind-break. Then we blanketed the ponies, fed them extravagantly in a hollow fifty yards away, and turned in, all in one tent." One of his party died during the night and was buried under rocks next morning.

In a letter home Richard wrote, "On foot we might make three miles per hour but our laden horses must be constantly spurred on over the rocks and prodded up defiles and over 13,500 foot passes to make even two miles an hour; so that twenty-mile stretch in a day means ten hours of restless motion." Richard and David found the trail up to the pass lined with pack animal carcasses and human graves. They spent the night in the pass, rain falling in torrents on their pathetic campfire, wind blowing their tent down on top of them, the cold turning zero at their bones. Mr. Catlin had given them a bottle of brandy, which Richard said fortified them through the night. He claimed it saved them from total extinction.

THE WOMAN WITH FIVE HUSBANDS

Dawn revealed a different world. All was calm and clear. Weary, surrounded by indifferent, solitary peaks, they climbed steadily into the mountains, noticing the vegetation grow increasingly sparse as the sun traversed the sky. Only the hardiest pines and shrubs could grow in the thin air. In a mountain pass, which must have been Pensi-La at 14,436 feet, Halliburton said "On the tenth day the summit of our trail to Leh was reached, fourteen thousand feet!" He tells us that they beheld range after range of Himalayan mountains, extending much farther than their eyes could see. Black and gray and capped with white, the peak of Godwin-Austen reached over 28,000 feet. On survey maps it is called K2 and Italian climber Fosco Maraini prefers that name because "it makes no attempt to sound human. It is atoms and stars. It has the nakedness of the world before the first man—or of the cindered planet after the last."

As they climbed through passes their lungs fought for oxygen. The chemical explanation is that at higher elevation oxygen molecules are farther apart making it harder to breathe but their lungs did not understand that. The boys knew nothing about high altitude edema, or fluid build-up, for nobody had yet heard the term. Halliburton does not mention it but they had headaches as their bodies grew weak and tired from the altitude. They had to concentrate on placing one foot in front of the other. Through Richard's fatigue, the intense light turned the sky into a blue unlike anywhere else.

One day, trudging through pines and flowers, they looked below them to a vast, stark floor bereft of foliage and knew they were nearing the end of their journey. They gazed upon Ladakh, its region a high-altitude desert because rain clouds of the Indian monsoon are blocked by mountain barriers. Edward Frederick Knight had remarked on the landscape and on the typical weather. An English barrister, soldier, and journalist he wrote

218

about his 1891 travels to Ladakh in his *Where Three Empires Meet*. Of the land he says "It was one of the usual cloudless Ladakhi days: the sun's rays, passing through the thin air, which lessened little of their power, fell upon us with scorching fierceness, while the wind at this elevation was keen."

Halliburton and Russell saw Leh far away in the desert, the air so clear that they could make out every detail of its buildings. The clarity made the villages seem close. In fact, they were miles distant. A letter explains that they "saw Leh from six miles across the desert that, at 12,500 feet, spreads before it. It looked only a mile away but it took us three and a half hours to arrive. Distances in Ladakh are strange and wonderful. One can see every detail of villages."

After they reached Leh they met a missionary couple, Mr. and Mrs. Kumick, who had arrived in Ladakh in 1909 and had been there thirteen years. The couple had never seen an aeroplane and only a few motorcars. They had not left Ladakh or even seen Srinagar and would soon return for a year's rest in their native England. They gave the boys fresh milk, potatoes, and greens from their garden. They were tending a patient, else they would have boarded Richard and David. The couple was probably part of the Moravian mission, established in 1875. The Moravians built a hospital and church as well as an English school in Leh, and collected material as they researched the history, culture, and archeology of Ladakh.

Richard and David Russell had a different kind of research in mind, one that caused a twinkle in their eyes. Their curiosity was aroused back in Srinagar when they heard that Ladakhi women had several husbands. Here was a subject worthy of investigation.

In *Royal Road* he explains that a woman of Ladakh thought twice before she married because she wed not only the man but his brothers as well.

Declared illegal in 1941, today polyandry has largely disappeared in Ladakh and was on its way out in Halliburton's time. The missionary couple told him that monogamy had become the convention as polyandry posed moral problems. Moral problems, because with less right to connubial access, younger husbands became habitually unfaithful. With a surplus of unmarried women, unwed mothers and unsupported children were on the increase, thereby threatening the social order. What began as a practical custom became impractical. Richard said that in the not-too-distant future polyandry would become antiquated.

The two youths asked the missionary couple for help in visiting a polyandrous household but the Kumick's could not as they knew only converted Christian families, a religion and a monogamous practice Richard had no interest in, for it bespoke Memphis and the familiar world.

As in many customs, a practical reason accounted for multiple husbands. Polyandry arose through extended families in which a group of brothers farmed the land under the leadership of the eldest, the prime inheritor. To prevent dividing the land for separate families, they kept it whole by living in one household with one wife and many children. It worked because not all husbands were home at the same time. Despite brotherly bonds, the connection only went so far when a man had sex on his mind. There was a line they did not cross and it was the threshold. When a man returned home he left his shoes on the doorstep to warn the others away.

In his 1891 journey, Edward Knight met a woman who explained the situation to him and the primacy of the eldest brother. "She told us she had three husbands, but that all were now away getting wool. She explained to us that when her eldest, or principal husband, was at home the other two had to keep out of the way. Thus, if he happened to return first from his wool-gathering, he would place his stick or winter boots outside the house door, to intimate to his juniors that he had taken up his residence . . . and that their presence there was undesirable until he should go away again." As for the younger brothers, they could only find the main chance when they thought the others were elsewhere.

Richard and David did have one resource—the Muslim porter who spoke a little but not much Ladakhi, the man whom Richard called Holy Moses. Through Holy Moses they asked a storekeeper if he shared a wife with other men. Yes, he said. Well, then, the youths thought, here it was, the opportunity. They struck a deal. During their stay they would buy from him if they could visit his family. He agreed.

Built of rock, the storekeeper's house was large, palatial according to Richard, which well it might have been given the cottage industry for the poor wife in producing children for all her husbands.

The storekeeper graciously introduced them to his family. The other husbands smiled and welcomed them and the children looked curiously at them. The woman's face was blank. Prompted by the Americans, Holy Moses suggested in halting Ladakhi that they be invited to the family meal. Mindful that Richard and David had promised to buy their goods from the storekeeper, the men agreed. They sat down to eat, bountifully served with rice and unleavened bread. The bounty was one thing. The three strangers sat apart from the family. That was another. Sitting with the family, they would have eaten as fellow husbands with the same connubial privileges.

The wife wore a perak, artistically elaborate, assembled from dark leather, stitched with long rows of turquoise stones. She quite literally carried her wealth on her head and only took it off at night. In the headdress center was sewn a ga'u, an amulet box for good fortune. The perak was fastened to her head by silver chains and stiff earflaps.

Richard does not tell us how many rows of turquoise beads the wife's held, but the number of rows determined a woman's social rank and economic status, with five the highest, three the lowest.

The perak had religious power as well. It brought her into affinity with subterranean deities that protect humans. Richard correctly stated that the headdress was "the most important part of any Ladakhi woman's costume." In rags or riches, all women wore one.

Typically, Richard teased her and wanted to know if money would pry the perak away. He offered her five hundred theoretical rupees, theoretical in that he was broke. No. No way. He raised the ante, upping it to a thousand. Uh-uh. Forget it. Out of the question. It was after all something spiritual, hardly a bauble to be sold. He jumped to a million. Her husbands were amused. She was not.

Okay, at least one prize. Richard asked if he could take their picture out in the courtyard. Four fathers, one mother, many children. The wife loudly disapproved. Absolutely no way. The white man had wanted her perak; he could well want to do further evil. He was a kind of anti-Buddha with dangerous mischief. The little black box of the Kodak Brownie could capture their spirits. The husbands prevailed and the family passed into the courtyard for a photograph that after all the fuss might now gather dust in the Halliburton archives.

Richard, David, and their guide said goodbye and left the husbands to their wife, the woman to all her children.

AND THE LOCKS OPENED

In 1928, American travel writer Richard Halliburton paid 36 cents to swim through the Panama Canal.
  Entry in *Guinness Book of Records*. Richard swam it as the *SS Halliburton*.

SS Halliburton, foreground, swimming Panama Canal

BECOMING SS HALLIBURTON

The Panama Canal is fifty-one miles long. To get from New York to San Francisco around Cape Horn a ship must sail almost fourteen thousand miles and off Cape Horn it is tossed by the treacherous seas and howling winds of the Roaring Forties. So Richard decided to take the easier route, as Groucho Marx might have quipped. He became the *SS Halliburton* and locks of the Canal opened to let him swim through it, Pacific to Atlantic.

The big ditch was dug not only because it offered a shorter and safer route but also because Theodore Roosevelt saw it as important in international relations. The American fleet could be moved quickly from the Atlantic to the Pacific in case war erupted with Russia or Japan. In 1898, in response to the *USS Maine* sinking in Havana harbor, the battleship *Oregon* was dispatched to Cuba but took sixty-seven days to reach Havana from San Francisco. Speak softly but carry a big stick, T.R. said about foreign policy. He made his stick bigger by a short cut through the Isthmus of Panama.

In Richard's day the Canal was new. The United States took over construction from the French in 1904, soon after his birth. Things could have been different. He might have swum through Nicaragua because at first that country was chosen, having many lakes ready-made and needing less digging. Politics and money caused him to swim through Panama. A French interest group did not want Nicaragua and lobbied hard against the idea, trying to turn the US Senate's attention to Panama. They made persuading Washington worthwhile for an American lobbyist and lawyer—some part of $40 million of worthwhile—if he, William Nelson Cromwell, could carry it off.

Philippe Bunau-Varilla was the linchpin of the French group. He spent a lot of time in Washington in the fall of 1903. Some call him a scoundrel; others call him a genius. Whatever the opinion, the Panama Canal would not have been dug without his connivance and strategies. A French engineer and soldier, in 1884 he worked for Ferdinand de Lessep's Panama Canal Company. The man who dug the Suez Canal, de Lesseps saw another opportunity in Panama and began the Culebra Cut in 1882 but his company went bankrupt in 1888 because he insisted on a sea-level canal rather than a system of locks. Creating a new company, Bunau-Varilla saw a windfall in the making if he could prevail on the Americans to resume in Panama. That was not so easy. Influential Americans favored Nicaragua because the country was less difficult to dig and with less volatile politics. Bunau-Varilla campaigned against them in a tour he made of the Northeast. He carried pictures and postage stamps of Nicaragua's Mount Momotombo erupting. The volcano was next the proposed route. He talked to Roosevelt. He talked with Secretary of State Hay. He talked with politicians. Eventually Washington came around under his persuasion.

There was a problem. It was that Panama was a province of Colombia and the Colombian senate refused to ratify canal construction. The government there wanted a piece of the $40 million action and did not want to cede power to Americans over the Canal Zone. Colombian, not American courts, should have legal sway. Indignant, Teddy Roosevelt believed their real scheme was money and thought it all part of a shakedown. In one of his gentler descriptions of them, he called the Colombians "foolish and homicidal corruptionists." The United States government said no to the Colombians—no to a piece of the action and no to control of the Zone. Now T.R. had a question. How to get the Canal built?

In football terms, there is always an end-run. Roosevelt's wide receiver was Bunau-Varilla and the French consortium forming the New Panama Canal Company. Teddy looked the other way while they stirred unrest against Colombia, lubricating it with a quarter million dollars under the table to nationalist agitators in Panama. Key to the insurrection was a revolutionary junta headed by José Augustin Arango, an attorney for the Panama Railroad Company, standing to make huge profits from the canal.

Colombia was out and Panama in. President Roosevelt said, "No one connected with the American Government had any part in preparing, inciting, or encouraging the revolution." The Panamanians allowed the United States control of the Panama Canal Zone on February 23, 1904, in exchange for $10 million. Though French, Bunau-Varilla represented Panama, signing a treaty with US Secretary of State John M. Hay. In exchange for a pile of money, Bunau-Varilla and his cohorts sold the New Panama Canal Company to the United States, including sovereignty over the area. While getting all this done Bunau-Varilla had not set foot in Panama, not for seventeen years, and he never went back.

On August 15, 1914, the *SS Ancon* became the first commercial ship to transit the Gatun Locks of the canal. The same month, World War I began, with Germany declaring war on Russia and Belgium, with Russia invading East Prussia, and with the British Expeditionary Force arriving in France. Teddy Roosevelt had his Canal and President Woodrow Wilson had a heap of trouble to keep America out of a war T.R. wanted to jump into with his Big Stick.

Born in 1859, Bunau-Varilla died in Paris on May 18, 1940 a very wealthy man, less the one leg he lost in 1916 at Verdun, and twenty-seven days before Hitler's panzer tanks and jack-booted troops paraded down the Champs-Élysées as the French lined sidewalks, looking on in despair at the red flag with a black swastika.

Twelve years before Hitler marched in Paris, Richard wrangled a ride on the navy cruiser *USS Cleveland* as it passed through the canal from the Pacific to the Atlantic. Standing on its main deck as the ship passed through locks, Richard thought about swimming the Canal. It would make a great story for his book, *New Worlds to Conquer*. As Halliburton stood there, a sailor could see he was of slight build. Although Richard was not a good swimmer, not athletic, he liked the idea. Never mind barracuda, caiman, and crocodiles because they would add to the story. When he talked about it, people told him he was crazy but he knew they would say that. They told him that nobody in his right mind would expect those giant locks to open for a swimmer. Well, they had a point. He would check it out. Where's there's a will, there's a way, he might have said, and he had plenty of will.

Then he heard that somebody had already done it. Days after the Canal opened in 1914, James Wendell Greene and J.R. Bingaman swam it ocean to ocean. Both Canal employees, they were given the go-ahead by the Secretary of War because it would make good publicity. Still, there was a restriction. The locks would open only for ships, not them. They had to go around each lock. They had to climb up the ladders and swim when the locks were not in use. The two men must "not establish a precedent" said Zone Governor George W. Goethals. As government employees, they could only swim on Sundays before the workweek started so taxpayers did not have to pay for their sport.

Greene swam the Canal again in 1918 to promote Liberty Loans, a wartime fundraiser. A postal department mail clerk, he was also a champion long-distance swimmer. Before Greene, an army captain named Alfred Brown swam thirty miles of the Canal, still under construction in 1913. A lifeguard, Brown described himself as the "champion long-distance swimmer of the world." Both Greene and Brown could make claims as long-distance swimmers, something Richard could not do. Brown had another advantage over Richard. He swam it before the Canal was open to traffic. Elaine May Golding also swam it in 1913. Billed by the Zone press as the "champion lady swimmer of America," she favored the breaststroke, which brought her head under water. She became badly sunburned and said the water stank.

Bingaman appeared before Congress in 1914 to argue for money so that he and other Zone athletes could compete in the Panama-Pacific Exposition next year in San Francisco. In 1916 he quit his job and left the Isthmus while Greene remained to become the Panama Canal's first Treasurer. Greene retired from civil service in the Panama Canal Zone in 1952. Elaine Golding married a man named Samuel Burnett Tuthill in 1923 and died in 1951.

Richard located James Wendell Greene and talked to him. A large man with a big chest holding a good set of lungs, Greene sized up Halliburton's build but said go for it. Richard went for it. He was resolved to do it and he used a sidestroke obsolete in 1885.

The Canal administration knew a good thing when they saw it. Here was a world-renowned writer and traveler and therefore here was good publicity. Halliburton got an audience with the governor of the Canal Zone, General Meriwether Lewis Walker who, according to Richard, warned him that his physique did not lend itself to the grueling effort.

Chief of Motor Transport Service in World War I, Walker was awarded the Army Distinguished Service Medal for his logistical accomplishments in the war effort. Walker was noncommittal to Richard and thought he had gotten himself off the hook by saying he had no authority, meaning he could not permit the swim nor could he forbid it. A young man swims through the waters and that was it, nothing that involved special permission.

He was not off the hook. Richard made a request that left him dangling from it. Halliburton wanted to use the locks. He wanted them to open and close for him, not just to climb out and dive back in on the other side of a lock as Green and Bingaman did. Walker could not shrug this off. He had to decide, to commit.

It was indeed a preposterous request. Tons of water must pump in to raise Halliburton's body to the level of the next lock while he treaded water, waiting.

Governor Walker was aware of the absurdity but for some reason he agreed to the request. Richard received a letter from him authorizing the swim. It did not make sense in the scale of things so a little topsy-turvy logic was needed. Richard had to register his tonnage.

The regulations were that locks opened for a ship so Richard became one, making his transit legal. Richard passed through the locks as a vessel, *SS Halliburton*, and was assessed toll at thirty-six cents total for one hundred forty pounds or seven one hundredths of a ton. That would put the whole thing on the up-and-up. For 1928 the US Panama Canal record indicated an average cost of ninety-five cents per ton for laden vessels and seventy-two cents for ballasted vessels. At twenty-two thousand tons, an empty, or ballasted, ship cost almost $16,000. In an August 25, 1928 letter to his parents he wrote, "27,000,000 cubic feet of water were used to lift me the 85 feet into Gatun Lake, and just as much mechanical labor, just as much expense, just as much everything, as to lift the biggest ship that ever passed through."

He was ready to go and the Zone governor assigned him accompaniment. Together, they made an uncommon scenario. Take a man about five-foot nine, a sharpshooter well over six foot, and a Jamaican oarsman of average height. Put the first man in water filled with barracuda, caiman and crocodiles. Put the other two in a rowboat alongside him. The five-foot nine man was *SS Halliburton*. The sharpshooter was Thomas Wright, Sergeant US Army. The oarsman was Quentin, from Jamaica, "who after ten years of service to the lighthouse department knew every inch of the canal." They had to be especially alert for crocodiles in the Gaillard Cut.

The governor wrote Halliburton, "It is understood that any expenses in connection with this expedition will be borne by yourself, and that the Panama Canal will not be held responsible for any damages sustained." The caveat inserted the usual precaution. In its own way the statement was prescient given what Halliburton escaped and endured.

DO YOU WANT A TOW?

Starting from the Pacific, he swam for ten days with rest ashore at night and during half of the ordeal—for that is what it was—he returned to a hotel in Colon, getting a few winks before arising at four in the morning to plunge back into the Canal.

With fair skin, on the first day he incurred a sunburn that worsened with each return to Canal waters. His entire back festered with blisters and the stinking water infected them. Above Gatun and after nightfall, he crawled out of the water weakened, sick. He developed a high fever. He had thought that almost total submersion would protect him. He had covered his face and shaven head with oil, which only magnified ultraviolet rays. Next morning, smeared top to toe with petroleum jelly, he dove back in. "Every stroke was torment," he wrote. He struggled the canal's fifty-one mile length.

He avoided Gatun Lake's channel, swimming distant from ships, while crewmen and passengers waved at him as they sailed past. He wearily waved back. At Bohio Point a long line of ships passed him, the crews and passengers lining the rails. They knew who he was, what he was doing, for newspapers and the radio daily informed the public of his progress. Coming abreast, each ship gave a loud blast from its whistle, a salute to *SS Halliburton*. The people hallooed and waved. Navy pilots, men he had befriended, circled overhead, landed their floatplanes and shouted, "Do you want a tow?" before they took off again.

He swam in any weather and one day storm clouds gathered, darkening the sky, and dumped torrents, wind tossing the water, rain pelting him. The air was thick with rain, objects barely visible when the black shape of a massive ship loomed high, headed directly toward him.

He was not visible from the ship's pilothouse far above and its bow broke through the rain, plowing straight on. He scurried toward the rowboat but the ship saw the boat and veered toward Richard. The hull's wake, its churning screws, its vibrating steel, pulled at him as it lumbered past and as Richard looked up at its towering stacks he felt suddenly drained in the choppy water. After the rowboat landed, he crawled weakly onto a bank and quit for the afternoon to nurse his sunburn and sores.

Near Balboa he heard the sergeant yell as the water splashed with barracuda leaping dead ahead. Richard was jerked out of the water into the boat by the sergeant, who had no time to use his rifle. Halliburton waited, hoping them gone, and after a while slipped off the boat to tuck himself between Quentin's rowing oar and the hull. He swam as Sergeant Wright splashed water at the bow to keep the jaws at bay.

Thoroughly exhausted, sun burnt and sick, he swam his sidestroke as along the canal people waved at him. Each day Zone radio kept the public informed of his progress and haggard appearance. As he neared the end of his swim, news spread and in Balboa, crowds gathered to await him. They milled around on the shore looking for a sign of him and finally there he was swimming resolutely and tiredly toward them. When his arm struck land many hands reached in to pull him from the water.

AT FIRST THEY LAUGHED AT SS HALLIBURTON

After he rested, he wrote home consolingly on August 25, 1928 from the Tivoli Hotel in Panama City, "It's over. I'm not harmed one speck, the sunburn and sore limbs are departed and I'm where I was before beginning. It was a whale of an adventure and one not likely to be duplicated. The humor, the sport, the novelty of it seem to hit everyone."

Not quite. For Panamanians what started as humor and sport ended with deep admiration, as told by John Nichols Booth, who also traveled the world, inspired as a boy by Richard's lectures and books.

In 1936 Booth asked a hotel clerk in Colon if the man remembered Richard. The clerk answered that when people first learned about what Richard attempted to do, they laughed at him, thinking it stupid and a great joke. Each night for the first half of his trip he was brought back to the hotel and they saw him blistered, haggard, dead-tired. He could barely walk and he could not sleep. He was a thin man, the clerk recalled, and not athletically built. After that, they praised Richard Halliburton to the skies.

The Panama Interoceanic Canal Museum, in the Casco Viejo of Panama City, documents Panama's history as a transoceanic route. In this excellent museum are found memorabilia from colonial Spanish times, such as muskets, sabers, cannon balls and coins. There is an exhibit dedicated to the building of the Panama Railroad, with charts, maps, and photos of the Canal excavation, as well as stock certificates from the bankrupted French Canal Company and a copy of the Hay and Bunau-Varrilla treaty.

In the museum is a photo of Richard Halliburton, described as an adventurer who swam the canal in the 1920s and paid the lowest toll ever, thirty-six cents, based on his weight.

PRELUDE TO THE FLYING CARPET

With a winged ship, I could still be a vagabond, but a vagabond with the clouds for my province, as well as the continents.
Richard in his book *The Flying Carpet*

Moye, two Persian princesses, Richard

RICHARD NEEDS A PILOT

A major turn in Moye Stephen's life began one morning in 1930 when his phone rang and echoed into his future. To Richard's thirty, he was twenty-four, an airline pilot for TAT, Transcontinental Air Transport later becoming TWA, Trans World Airlines, and the years ahead were too abundant to count. In his unpublished memoir, he explained the event this way.

He heard a voice saying, "I would like to speak to Mr. Moye Stephens."

"Speaking."

"I'm Richard Halliburton. I'm contemplating a vagabond journey around the world by air, and I want you to be my pilot."

We can assume that Halliburton was too mannerly for such an abrupt proposal but Stephens does convey the surprise he felt on getting a call from the famous Richard Halliburton. Indeed, he says that the exchange was only a little less startling than if the caller had been President Herbert Hoover. He writes, "Richard Halliburton was unquestionably the leading travel author of the time. His name was practically a household word in the United States and was far from unknown in many foreign countries. His books had been translated into eighteen languages."

Richard planned another book based on a round-the-world flight in his plane, called Flying Carpet after the mythical rug in Mid-Eastern tales. In a story of the *One Thousand and One Nights*, Prince Hussain buys a magic carpet and in Jewish legend Solomon's green silk carpet had a golden weft, sixty miles long and sixty miles wide.

They met to discuss a deal at the Hollywood-Roosevelt Hotel. With his usual confidence, Richard presumed that Moye had agreed to the offer. He had a "rough itinerary," saying that they would fly to a place that excited them, then stay until they tired of it. This was not the predictable future Stephens saw in store for himself. Still, he had been reared on risk by the barnstorming aviators who took a liking to the boy at Rogers Airport in Los Angeles. He had a talent for adventure, given the newness of flying and its attendant dangers.

Despite that, he was, if anything, cautious. As a stunt pilot for silent movies, Moye survived because he carefully planned an aerial maneuver. He did not consent to Halliburton's offer immediately. It sounded like the opportunity of a lifetime but he thought of the great job he had landed as airline pilot. What about that? he asked. He could not just snap his fingers and turn his back on it.

He was well aware that a great stroke of luck, an airline pilot job, let him escape law school and turn to flying, the love of his life. He had a wonderful job and he risked losing it if he agreed to pilot Richard. He allowed that Halliburton's enthusiasm was "infectious" and it was "difficult to resist" but still he had to think about it. Richard understood but asked him not to take too long.

Moye was told by Tommy Tomlinson of Transcontinental Air Transport that they could give him a year's leave of absence for the global flight with Halliburton but no more. This presented a problem. The Flying Carpet journey would take more than that. Moye would have to quit TAT if he wanted to go. He thought about it. What did he have ahead? A steady job. A career. Maybe some day a wife and family.

He talked to his parents. They had him and Halliburton for dinner. He thought about it some more. He knew the pioneer days of aviation were ending. Things would become increasingly ordered, safe, predictable. In a way, piloting the Flying Carpet around the world would be like his teenage years at Rogers Airport with Bud Creech, Frank Clarke, Eddie Bellande, all those early pilots, all over again.

As an old man recalling aviation's early days, he said that "Perhaps the trip, in satisfying the thirst for adventure, would, to a degree, compensate for the passing of a wild blue yonder which could be relived in memory only."

He agreed to pilot Richard Halliburton around the world. "The decision did not come easily, but in the end the dreams won out." He would look back on his life and ask what if he had done this rather than that?—stay with the airline or Northrop Aviation, which he helped found.

To Memphis Richard wrote, "I went to the mat with Moye Stephens and his family, and after several long and earnest conferences, I won him over as my pilot. He had just been offered a $12,000 a year job with his Transcontinental Flying Company and naturally, debated, at age twenty-four, whether to throw up so valuable a position or not. He, himself, is very eager to go, but his father and mother had to be convinced. I offered him $100 a month, and he accepted. I could have gotten one hundred pilots for nothing, but after inquiring about Moye from innumerable sources, I am quite sure he is the best equipped pilot on my horizon." Halliburton adds, "I have turned over to him the entire equipping of the ship, because I have learned that there is no person in California more trustworthy. I got a wonderful bargain." Yes, he did. Moye gave up $12,000 a year for $1200 a year.

He and Halliburton were both products of their era. With aeroplanes, motorcars, radios, and moving pictures, the world was on the cusp of something, and their world flight would be part of the newness. They both liked an edge in life, something different, but Moye was prudent where Halliburton was optimistic. Still in his twenties, Moye had seen too many pilots crash and die because of minor oversights and had himself flirted with disaster because of something, say wind sheer, that he did not take into account. He learned to think ahead. He was always planning, always mindful of minor engine noises or strut vibrations, always concerned about the next flight plan. Richard trusted people and in Stephens he was lucky to find somebody worthy of his confidence.

Flying Carpet over Baghdad
Courtesy Rhodes College

MOYE STEPHENS' BACKGROUND

In three typewritten pages titled "Notes on Highlights of Career" Moye writes that he was first attracted to flying at the "Dominguez Aviation Meet of 1910 held on the southern outskirts of Los Angeles" where at three years old he wondered at strange kite-like contraptions that went up in the air with men in them. While a Hollywood High student, he worked at Rogers Airport, at the corner of Crescent and Wilshire, near the high school, and about a quarter mile east of the La Brea tar pits, as "a combination grease monkey and beast of burden" to earn flying lessons. "The rate of pay was one minute of instruction in return for one hour of work." His father didn't want to pay for the lessons because he disapproved of the strange contraptions.

The Federal Aviation Authority did not exist then and certification to fly depended on a solo followed by a handshake if you landed without crashing. He was certified by Jim Webster, Rogers Airport owner, and Eddie Bellande, his instructor, under a form embossed with a seal and with the letterhead, Rogers Aircraft, Inc.

Graduating at 17 from high school[*], he was held back a year by his parents before he could attend Stanford in 1924, graduating with a law degree because his father wanted him as partner in the firm. At twenty in 1926 he bought his first plane, a war surplus Thomas-Morse Scout S-4C, for $450. The money came from his first job as a pilot flying in Cecil B. De Mille's *Corporal Kate* with movie stunt pilot Leo Nomis, who sold him the plane.

His "Notes" tell us that before her 1937 disappearance, Amelia Earhart consulted with him "on the portions of her route which coincided with those of the Flying Carpet," the plane he flew for Halliburton around the world. He gave flying lessons to Howard Hughes, Cliff Garret, Jerry Vultee, and Jack Northrop—the first a movie mogul and billionaire, the

---

[*] According to his statement in his unpublished manuscript.

others, founders of aircraft companies.[*]

In 1929, age twenty-three, he was hired as pilot for Maddux Airlines. He had only flown single-engines, not a Ford Tri-Motor passenger plane. A chief pilot had him ride shotgun on a trip to San Diego, another to Alameda. Then he told Moye to take-off and land three times at Grand Central Air Terminal in Glendale. The next day he was an airline captain with "a load of unknowingly trusting souls in the passenger compartment." There were no copilots. Next him he had "a mechanic flying shotgun."

In 1937 he married Contessa Gadina de Turiani, known as Inez. Although his notes do not mention it, she was born in Trieste, Italy, on the Adriatic near Slovenia, and was first married to millionaire Ross Hadley, co-founder of Pacific Airmotive. Stephens and his wife went to Australia for their honeymoon because Lockheed sent him there to promote sales and to check-out pilots of two airlines, Union Airways and Ansett Airways, in their Lockheed 10's.

In 1939 he was "instrumental in the promotion and organization of Northrop Aircraft, Inc., in consideration of which [he] was awarded a stock interest in the company and was made assistant corporate secretary." He was then "elected to the board of directors."

As a test pilot with Northrop, he flew the Flying Wing, the N-1M, and "did the major part of the experimental test flying in the two year test program." This was a very early prototype of the US Air Force B-2 Stealth Bomber. He also was test pilot for the P-61 Black Widow night fighter, a twin-engine twin-boom World War II night interceptor and the first specifically designed to use radar in lieu of visual identification.

His three pages of "Notes" do not say much about a lifetime but they say one thing about Moye Wicks Stephens. Aviation was his life.[*]

Moye, 20, in his Thomas Morse Scout

---

[*] The notes do not tell us that in 1926 while at Stanford he published with J.M. Hiatt a short story, "Ghosts of the Air," in *Weird Tales*, an issue that included H.P. Lovecraft's story, "Moon-Bog." In 1990 he appeared on PBS *The American Experience* in a program called "Lindbergh" as a commentator on the aviator.

[*] Additional information on Stephens can be found at the back in Miscellany.

RICHARD & PANCHO BARNES

In his life Richard met many unusual people but maybe the most remarkable was Pancho Barnes and she is worthy of note because of her personality and character. She had two precepts in life: When you have a choice, choose happy, and Nothing exceeds like excess. She lived on her own terms. Unable to get a divorce from her minister husband, each Sunday she climbed into her biplane, took off, and dove down over his church, buzzing it with the engine's roar, drowning-out morning services.

Through Moye Stephens, Richard met various aviators, including Pancho Barnes. Moye and Pancho had known and respected one another for some time, the acquaintance made easier by Pancho's almost open house to guests, drinks, and food. Knowing Richard, Moye probably felt that Halliburton and Barnes would find kindred spirits in one another and he was right. Pancho had a sense of humor and fun that appealed to Richard. An intelligent woman, she could talk flying with Stephens and range over many topics with Halliburton. Noted for her generosity and interest in others, she was well liked and admired.

Richard was taken with Pancho, not that he was in love but that she was an unforgettable person. Nobody she met could be indifferent toward her. She made lasting friendships wherever she went. She also did not suffer fools gladly.

In a November 1932 letter from Hollywood, Richard wrote his parents that he visited Pancho Barnes, "the woman flyer I'm so fond of, and she took me to Ramón Novarro's, a lot of drunk movie people were there, so we left early." The line was clearly for mom and dad. Richard added that on December 4th he would take her to Moye's wedding to an Italian contessa although he would miss it, "an especially fine one."

On Thanksgiving he drove Pancho fifty miles "down the coast to her summer home, which was her Laguna Beach mansion overlooking the

Pacific." In this letter home he plays bad to the good boy he was in the earlier correspondence, as if he vacillated between two roles regarding his parents. "We took off our clothes and pulled clams from the rocks, then put the clams in a big stew pan to steam, and had that for our thanksgiving dinner." One imagines his parents raising their eyebrows, asking, What kind of woman is this?

On November 30th he told them, "Pancho and 4 of her friends are coming in for dinner. I just tell my perfectly marvelous cook [Pancho] and forget it. All the big time movie people I used to know I've not seen this time, much prefer to sit quiet and do my job. They can wait."

Born Florence Leontine Lowe, Pancho was supposed to have grown into a debutante whose coming-out would be into the best Southern California society. She was supposed to have married well and become a society matron. Her husband would be a wealthy developer, investment banker, or attorney whose family was Old Money, and who had the proper connections. Her children would play croquet on a great swath of San Marino lawn during a lawn party while her servants walked about balancing silver platters with martinis, whiskeys, and gin, as they paused politely before a guest, offering a drink. She would smile delicately at a gentleman describing his polo pony. She would raise her finger and give a friendly nod to guests just arriving. She was supposed to have done all that, but she did not.

She grew up on South Garfield Avenue in San Marino, California in a three-story thirty-five room mansion with eighteen-foot ceilings, wood-paneled walls with hand-carved moldings, and a massive crystal chandelier hanging from one ceiling. A harpsichord chime summoned the family to dinner. Silver spigots serviced upstairs baths of marble. Water lilies decorated a large patio pool. Guests ambled to tennis courts for a few sets or to the stables, where they rode a mile course.[*] In Laguna Beach stood another fine mansion on the cliffs above Emerald Bay. Next it she had a landing strip for her airplane.

Florence was born to rebel but her mother had the upper hand for a while, at least, and decided that an arranged marriage would cool her daughter's spirit. In 1921 Pancho wed Episcopalian Reverend C. Rankin Barnes of Pasadena and ten years older. The newspapers announced that a society aviatrix married a Pasadena reverend. Three nights after the marriage, they finally slept together and begot a son. After that night they slept apart. William Emmert was born nine months later and grew up close to his mother, dying in 1981 when his WWII fighter, a P-51 Mustang, crashed.

Of an academic bent, the reverend left his name on obscure books no

---

[*] As the mansion was remembered by the daughter of a servant.

longer available. One is *A History of St. Paul's Church, San Diego*. Another is *Ethelbert Talbot, 1848-1928: Missionary Bishop, Diocesan Bishop, Presiding Bishop*. He also wrote *The General Convention: Offices and officers, 1785-1950*, as well as *Practical Standards for Diocesan Social Service Departments*.

Theirs was not a match made in heaven.

Florence became Pancho after friends wanted to hire on as seamen on a banana boat. Pancho, the only woman, decided to join them. Hair cut short, baggy pants, she was hired as Jacob Crane. At sea, she and her friends discovered the ship ran guns to Mexican revolutionaries. At San Blas, she and crewman Roger Chute jumped ship, fearing it would be sunk by gunboats of Federales. Deep in Mexico, both riding horses, Chute said she looked like Pancho, Don Quixote's squire. No, she said, you mean Sancho Panza, but she liked the name because it gave the raspberry to her mother's proper lady.

Born wealthy, going slowly broke, in 1930 Pancho entertained lavishly at her San Marino mansion. Because her place was a magnet for those who lived on the fringe—aviators or others—and, given the people Richard preferred, perhaps he would have learned about her and met her anyway. Pancho disdained a low profile. In his unpublished memoir, Stephens wrote that he and his pals "would join the practically continual evening festivities at the San Marino home of Florence Lowe 'Pancho' Barnes." Big-hearted, she offered food, drinks, and parties. Had her parents still been alive, they would have disapproved of the goings-on but they weren't and the property was all Pancho's—the mansion in San Marino, California, and the one in Laguna Beach.

Moye Stephens recalled one bash at her mansion, saying "The lengths to which she went in protecting Frank Bell provided another demonstration of her big-heartedness." Everybody was having a high time when the door chime rang. Opening the door, they found Frank Bell, a bootlegger. Bloody from several bullet wounds, staggering on his feet, Bell reached to push the door button again, but they grabbed him and helped him to bed upstairs. Pancho called a doctor who would not report gunshot wounds. Patched up, somewhat recovered, Bell explained what happened. Returning from flying lessons in Long Beach, "business competitors" pulled alongside his car and opened fire with a Thompson submachine gun. Bell crouched down and fortunately no bullet penetrated his heart or lungs. Bell was finally strapped into an electric chair by the State of Illinois and there was no crouching in that.[*]

---

[*] After October 29, 1929, Black Tuesday, Pancho bought "apartment buildings to put up her friends who were pilots," says Lou D'Elia of the Pancho Barnes Trust Estate, "and paid for their groceries, to get them and their families through the Depression." She ran out of money around 1934, trading apartments for an alfalfa farm in the Mojave Desert near

Despite her lavish lifestyle, in her middle years she became an able businesswoman after she lost most of her fortune and, next Edwards Air Force Base in the Mojave Desert, built the Happy Bottom Riding Club because General Jimmy Doolittle once told her he had a happy bottom. It was also known as Rancho Oro Verde Fly Inn Dude Ranch, where she eventually built a dance hall with glamorous hostesses, a gambling casino, a swimming pool, horse stables, and a championship rodeo stadium. She became a kind of mother to Chuck Yeager the first pilot to break the sound barrier in the Bell X-1 and she was played by Kim Stanley in the movie *The Right Stuff*, about test pilots and early astronauts.

Big time movie people were not Pancho's thing. She did not care if you were a mogul, a star, or a janitor. She did not like airs. With her what you saw was what you got. One of the habitués at her mansion was a husky eighteen-year-old named Marion Michael Morrison, attending the University of Southern California on a football scholarship. Seeing that money was tight with him, Pancho helped him out. Fifty years later, she sat in the Universal Studios cafeteria eating lunch when a big man walked up to her table, quite sure of himself. He asked if she remembered him. Gray-haired, bent over her plate, she sat back and paused to look theatrically at him and slowly, feature by feature, sized him up. Yes, she did. "You are Marion Morrison," she said. Of course she recognized him as John Wayne but as one of Wayne's movie personas might have said, his ego had gotten too big for his britches.

Pancho Barnes & her Travelaire

Muroc, where she one day built her Happy Bottom Riding Club.

240

THE FLYING CARPET

We had a strong headwind, the day was terrifically hot, and it took an enormous amount of concentration to follow the piste, and I had to sit in a very uncomfortable position with my neck craning over the edge of the cockpit all day long—ten hours and a quarter of flying.
    Moye Stephens on trying to follow the faint track across the Sahara Desert to Timbuktu

Crashed French plane, Sahara. Crew died of thirst awaiting rescue.

FLYING CARPET PREPARATIONS

Before meeting Stephens, Richard had difficulty choosing an aircraft, largely because he lacked aeronautical expertise. He had bought a plane but sold it because he was unsure about it. From Chicago in September 1930, he wrote home that he was rid of his old plane and "had to lose $1500 on the deal, counting paint" but "it was a good riddance. I flew on to Wichita and then learned of a grand big Stearman plane with a 500 horsepower motor for sale by Cliff Durant (Durant Motors) of Detroit. It was the sort used by the U.S. to carry mails. I sped on to Detroit and Northern Michigan near Mackinac and saw the plane and Durant. It's worth (he paid) $25,000. He liked my idea and offered the plane free if I'd take his own pilot who has already broken it in."*

Richard declined Durant's offer and kept looking. His distant cousin Erle Halliburton offered Richard the use of his private airplane. On October 26, 1930, Richard wrote home, "I went to Erle Halliburton's ranch Saturday morning and didn't come back till Monday night. We had a grand time. He said he 'thought it could be fixed to get me a plane free'. And after a week's time, he did get me one—his own Lockheed. It's the plane he and his pilot have flown all over America in."

This was a Lockheed Vega, seating four passengers and a pilot. The Vega was a high-winged monoplane, powered by a Pratt & Whitney Wasp engine of four hundred fifty horsepower. It was indeed a fine plane for its time and, with its closed cockpit, offered travel in relative luxury. Richard

---

* An auto industry pioneer, William Durant founded General Motors and Chevrolet and later left to manufacture his own line of Durant motorcars. Heavily invested in the stock market, on Black Tuesday, October 29, 1929, he and the Rockefellers bought huge numbers of stocks to prove their confidence in the market. The market continued to fall and by 1936 Durant was bankrupt, living on a small pension Alfred P. Sloan provided from General Motors.

went on, "He has bought him a new tri-motored Ford for his own use, and no longer needs the Lockheed, which he insists is the best, fastest, and safest plane I can get—and he's giving it to me with no strings whatsoever. I've told Moye Stephens about my new plans. He doesn't want to go in anything but an open Stearman, thinks the Lockheed too big." Moye's choice turned out to be a modified Stearman C-3B.

A rugged biplane with simple straight wings, the C-3 had a tough undercarriage with oleo shock absorbers and two open cockpits, its pilot in the rear. Stearman manufactured PT-17s, simple and dependable planes liked by the military and used to train pilots in World War II. They still fly today.

Moye held that, rugged and uncomplicated, with two open cockpits, the Stearman was the ticket for their flight. Produced by Lloyd Stearman in Wichita, Kansas, an earlier version had been used by the government as a mail plane, helping it become known for reliability. In 1929 Stearman Aircraft was bought by the company that became Boeing. With the plane, flights were made to Europe and even to the North and South poles as well as across the Pacific.

He wrote his parents that the Stearman "itself, retails for $4500 without the engine, and I got it for $2800. It is the same ship Erickson showed us that had been standing in the hangar for a year. I was suspicious as to its condition, but Moye gave it a scrupulous examination and declared it good as new. It has never been flown. The engine I bought at a similar discount. It, too, sells for $4500—the 'J-5' 225 H.P.—the same engine that Lindbergh used to fly the Atlantic. It had been flown thirty-five hours, which had merely broken it in." He tells them "The engine cost $1500. I have my own instruments, which are being installed for a complete dual control."

Dual control? The comment is curious in that Richard had taken flying lessons and flunked so badly he decided to hire a pilot for his next adventure. Still, another instrument panel was practical in that Halliburton could hold the plane steady while Stephens rested.

Not only the Stearman's size was found congenial by Moye but also its engine. Powered by an air-cooled radial engine, the plane did not present the complications of a liquid-cooled machine of the era. The J-5 Wright Whirlwind operated at lower revolutions per minute, eighteen hundred, a less wearing speed. With the J-5 not as prone to overheating, Moye leaned fuel mixture, although this increased temperatures. Fuel efficiency was critical. They did not want to run out of gas above the middle of nowhere. At twice the horsepower, Erle Halliburton's Vega burned too much fuel and Moye knew that over the Sahara they would find fuel dumps sparse and far between one another.

Richard Halliburton had an eye for how the Stearman would strike people of foreign lands as the mechanical bird appeared overhead then landed to roll up in front of their villages. He wanted its appearance to be memorable. That, of course, also made for good publicity. He wrote, "I am leaving the wings as they are but painting the body a bright scarlet, with black struts. I think it will be very beautiful."

He waxed enthusiastic. This would be a grand journey and he was filled with plans. In the same letter, he soothed his parents' fears: "Moye and the mechanics all agree it is going to be a flawlessly equipped ship and the sturdiest and the safest." He adds, "Yesterday, Moye and I acquired fur-lined flying suits, since, because of the late date of our departure, we will have cold flying from here to New York, and from London to Morocco. The mechanics and Moye are working day and night, and we expect to be in the air in about ten days."

He assured his parents that Moye came from good people. The Halliburton's would approve of them. Moye's father was a successful attorney, his grandfather a judge. "Mrs. Stephens, who is a most wise and charming woman, wanted us to stay for Thanksgiving Day, that she might give us a farewell party. I had hoped to be home for Thanksgiving, myself, but couldn't make it, and to be with the Stephens, to whom I have become truly devoted, is the next best thing."

Most important, he assured them that with Moye as pilot the risk was minimized. Stephens' parents had "not the slightest uneasiness over the hazards of our expedition; they have seen Moye flying almost daily for eight years, and think no more of it than they do over his driving their motorcar. Time and again, he has demonstrated his clear and cautious head as a flyer, and they know that he will not take the slightest chance."

Then they were ready to go. In December 1930 they flew in the Stearman to have Christmas dinner with Wesley and Nelle in Memphis but fog grounded them in Fort Smith, Arkansas so they arrived on the 26th.

From Memphis Moye wrote his parents "Dick is the fair-haired boy" in the town.

On the 27th they flew to New York where Richard talked to editors about deals covering the flight. Then it was to Washington, DC to meet officials at the Departments of Commerce and War who could help ease their passage through foreign lands. Richard said they "are helping us in every way they can." In New York, the Stearman was hoisted aboard the *SS Majestic* and stowed in the cargo hold next its wings, which had been removed. Next day, on January 30, 1931, the ship slipped its hawsers for Europe, where the adventure would begin.

MOYE WRITES HOME

Like Richard, Moye was the dutiful son, writing regularly to his parents during his travels. His parents kept the letters and read each one word by word, vicariously experiencing the journey of The Flying Carpet. Here is an early letter, before their son's grand foreign adventure began.

"Dear Mother and Dad,   Jan. 2, 1931

I am awfully sorry that I haven't gotten around to writing you before, but I have been so darned busy that this is really the first opportunity I have had. Of course on the way, flying all day and dead tired at night I couldn't do it, and since we have been here in Memphis it has been one continual round of gaiety interspersed with periods of work on the motor, which has been behaving badly." Moye continued, "First of all, I almost gave up and called the trip off when it came to actually leaving. I certainly wanted to stay home just about that time." Then he returned to problems with the engine, "Shortly after passing through Cajon Pass the first signs of motor trouble appeared. It manifested itself in a sort of skipping or irregular pulsation of power, but it got no worse and after a certain point I continued on to Kingman where we stayed over night (our late start and head winds making it inadvisable to continue)." The letter is signed, "Your Loving Son, Moye."

Not running perfectly smooth, the motor worried Stephens. They flew cross-country and, landing at various airfields, he had mechanics check the engine. Some mechanics installed larger carburetor jets; others cleaned the spark plugs; still others squirted penetrating oil on the valve seats or checked the magneto. Nothing worked until on the East Coast when a Wright factory mechanic correctly diagnosed the problem as shellac applied to tappet guides during engine assembly. Under extreme heat, the hard shellac became a gooey mess slightly interfering with valve timing.

Although the engine ran well enough otherwise, Moye was determined to get the problem solved before leaving the states and before it could cause serious trouble. The letter reveals an attention wholly different than Richard's. Moye's aptitude was for things mechanical and aeronautical.

In New York, he wrote that he and Richard "escorted a couple of young New York heiresses to a night club where we had dinner and danced. One of them, Doris Duke, is the daughter of the American Tobacco Co. magnate and is reputed to be the richest girl in the world, the other, Lita Morse who is also not exactly a pauper." His friend Rich Hobson assured him that Lita was "the most popular debutante in New York during the past season. I was with Lita and we all had a great time."[*]

From New York, Stephens writes that a friend, Benny Hys, "tells me there is quite a bit of agitation for the forming of a pilots association, not a labor union, something more dignified but by means of which the pilots can set up certain standards such as the number of hours required for all different types of commercial flying, the maximum number of hours to be flown per month." Today, we take airline safety and pilot hours for granted. His letter tells us that things were different back then.

Before they embarked, Stephens' main task was to see the Flying Carpet lifted onto the ship and safely stowed. While Moye watched, the winch operator must have caused him to curse several times under his breath. As the operator hoisted the plane, Moye "thought we had lost the poor old Stearman once during the process of loading. The man on the winch became very nervous and started to lower too abruptly. When he checked it, the tail sunk down and the [plane] started to career about in a most alarming manner, just missing stanchions, ventilators, and what not." After several more near-disasters, for Moye "a period of years," the deck crew "finally leapt in, seized the airplane, and dragged it to safety. How it escaped being bent double around a stanchion is one of the most marvelous things I have ever seen." Once the aircraft was aboard and fastened down, Stephens relaxed. The 56,000 ton ship was "quite luxurious" according to Moye.

Then with Richard, Moye left on the *Majestic* for an adventure that would take almost two years to complete.

---

[*] Doris Duke was daughter of tobacco and hydroelectric tycoon James Buchanan Duke, after whom Duke University is named. In 1930 she was presented to society at eighteen as a debutante. Married twice, her affairs included Olympic medalist and Hawaiian surfer Duke Kahanamoku, Hollywood star Errol Flynn, World War I Flying Ace Alec Cunningham-Reid, General George S. Patton, bebop Jazz pianist Joe Castro, and author Louis Bromfield. She was horticulturalist, art collector, and philanthropist. Her life spanned varied interests, including work as a journalist, surfing in competition, playing jazz piano, and conserving wildlife.

He mentions dining on the ship with Ken Litour, the *Colliers* magazine fiction editor who later bought F. Scott Fitzgerald stories. Litour, he tells his parents, was in the Lafayette Escadrille, a French fighter squadron during World War I. Stephens implies the toll combat took with a description of Litour: "He is thirty-six and his hair is almost snow white."

In London they dined and partied and then flew across the English Channel to Paris in February 1931. Stephens assured his parents that flying across the Channel was safe but what he wrote next did not convince. He said that if he and Richard had not landed at the French aerodrome of St Inglevert, "very fast speed boats" would have been sent to look for them. Moreover, "there were many boats in the channel and had the motor quit at any time I could have landed alongside one." As the aircraft sank beneath the waves, they only had to swim for the boat. Stephens' mother was probably not reassured by this.

In Paris he and Richard were befriended by the Count and Countess De Sibour, "who you may remember flew around the world in their little [Gypsy] Moth in 1929 following the beaten path (shipping across the oceans of course.)" In fact, the Vicomte and Vicomtesse de Sibour had done so in the summer of 1928, probably the first round-the-world flight by a married couple. They wrote a book about it called *Flying Gypsies*, and their feat helped spur Amelia Earhart to her fated 1937 flight. Both the Vicomte and his wife were seasoned pilots. Moye continues, "And what an interesting couple they were." He says, "One of the pilots in England gave me a letter of introduction to them, and Dick and I called them up the day after we arrived." Moye's parents read that "they have been simply marvelous to us, just can't do enough for us." De Sibour "flew during the war and was shot down." As for his wife, Violette De Sibour, she is "an American girl who was raised in England. She is the daughter of Selfridge (the owner of the huge London department store)." Stephens wished he "could find another woman like Violette." If he could, he would be "sitting on top of the world. She is very pretty, as nice as she can be, multi-multi, flies her own plane (and loves it) and is crazy about big hunting." In a March letter, Stephens says she and her husband will "fly completely across the Sahara from Abyssinia."

On March 29, 1931, he writes that the aircraft engine "vibrated considerably" ever since leaving the Wright factory, which removed the shellac on the valve guides. He called on "Doc" Maidment, "the Wright factory expert in Europe," who found "the propeller did not fit onto the crankshaft correctly." Ever vigilant to mechanical problems, Stephens was unlike Richard, who drove his new Packard until the motor burned out, leaving it at the California ranch of Erle Halliburton until Erle had it towed away.

They soon left Europe to begin the great adventure into Africa. Their last European aerodrome was in Malaga, Spain, and "it was certainly heavenly—the aviation field covered with fresh green grass and wild flowers right on the edge of the Mediterranean, a quaint old tumbled-down hangar surrounded by trees, and the mountains in the background—it was swell." Next morning, the Flying Carpet flew across the Mediterranean to Rabat, French Morocco. They avoided Gibraltar air space, off limits to civilian aviators, and where the British jailed Halliburton for "spying" on its military defenses.

Landing at the Rabat aerodrome of the French army, they "were greeted by very nearly the entire post and were immediately carried off to the officer's bar and plied with beer and enthusiastic questions" until they "could hardly stand up." French officers arranged hotel reservations for them, notified the Shell petrol representative that they had landed, and gave them maps.

This was the new age, the age of the aeroplane, which joined people from far-off lands, and it is hard to imagine such a reception for anybody today, no matter what part of the world they fly in to.

The world was indeed different with the advent of aviation. Doors opened wherever they traveled. The French Prime Minister, Aristide Briand, intervened to cut government red tape. Landing at Oran, Algeria, they were asked "Where are your papers?" They did not know the commandant at Fez, French Morocco had slipped authorizing telegrams between pages of the plane's logbook.

The French commandant at Oran wired for clarification while Stephens and Halliburton looked for their papers but not in the logbook. On the second day, when the telegrams were found in the logbook, the Oran commandant said they "didn't look official enough." Moye and Richard began sending wires of their own and, on the third day, the Oran commandant did an about-face. Suddenly they were free to go. Aristide Briand had wired the commandant, asking why they were being held up.

Richard and Moye were cleared for the next leg into the Sahara and in the morning they were getting ready to take off when a wire arrived warning of a severe sand storm. It lasted three days. They had been delayed once before when "a fresh out-burst of fighting had commenced directly between Fez and Colomb Bechar." The French Army was in North Africa to control the colonies but even then Arabs did not like to be colonials. Finally, the two young men "received a favorable weather report and dashed out to the field to get a nice early start—only to find that one of our tires was absolutely flat—punctured by a huge thorn picked up on the field somewhere." They "managed to get it fixed by noon" and followed the railroad tracks to Colomb Bechar.

After flying over what Moye described as "beautiful mountainous country" in Algeria, they saw a large valley below with Sidi Bel Abbes, the Foreign Legionnaire training base, and then came the Sahara. "At the end of an hour we hit the desert, and what a desert it is!" Stephens said. "Nothing but sand and barren rocky mountains. For the next four hours it was the same. Towards the end we passed over a few oases and finally arrived at Colomb Bechar. It is a large oasis right at the edge of the Sahara proper, and what a welcome sight it was after hours of headwinds and monotonous desert."

Moye wrote that a French army pilot drove them to a hotel in town but it had no rooms available because French men and women had booked there to celebrate Easter—this was the day after. The proprietor gave them "a couple of mattresses and some blankets" and let them "sleep on the dining room floor." After sleeping accommodations were arranged, Lieutenant Bodin, the French pilot, drove them to his house for dinner with three other pilots. They had "a wrinkled old Arab for a cook and a German Legionnaire for a second maid."

From Colomb Bechar, on April 9, 1931, Stephens wrote home that in Meknes, French Morocco, he met a French Army Lieutenant named Hamilton, "a very peculiar man, as any young American must be who will spend as much time in the Foreign Legion as he has. He is a very superior type of man, well-bred and educated, and has a very thorough knowledge of current world affairs. He flew in the Lafayette Escadrille during the war, Incidentally, he is the associate editor of the official books of the Lafayette Escadrille. It is a beautiful set." Stephens told his parents the French Foreign Legion had a reputation based on myth—it was not "a living hell." Hamilton and other officers pointed out why this was not so. If it were so bad, then reenlistments would not be so many.

"When the men go into the desert for one purpose or another, the French government sends along five women to each battalion (you will remember such an episode in the picture Morocco, although, as I remember it, the explanation for their accompanying the troops was a bit more romantic than the actual truth.)" He adds that it cannot be so hard on the men but "quite a job for the women though, n'est-ce pas?" He later witnessed the hard life of enlisted Legionnaires and then disagreed with Lieutenant Hamilton's evaluation of the men. His opinion on the life of the women did not change.

Moye described Colomb Bechar "as yet unspoiled by civilization." He said, "There are no electric lights, no baths, only one or two autos, and absolutely no sanitation. The number of flies is terrific. Ditto for the odors. But yesterday Dick and I left the village, which is on the desert to one side of the oasis, and went for a long hike (four or five hours) through the palm trees along the river. It was beautiful beyond description. I say river, but it is really a series of lakes with just enough current to keep the water clear. It wells up out of the sand at the head of the oasis and seeps back in again at the bottom." It seemed like a South Sea Island, the trees leaning over the water, the Arabs cultivating small patches of land along the banks. This was an early impression of Colomb Bechar and it was about to change.

Against this idyllic scene was war, the reason the Legionnaires and French Colonial soldiers were there. Algerians did not like the French in their land. Stephens wrote, "Colomb Bechar is quite near the site of the war and soldiers are coming in and going out all day long. Every morning the army planes leave to bomb the natives and return in the afternoon, many of them with bullet holes through the wings and fuselage." To cover the bullet holes, "the mechanics put a little heart-shaped red patch" and "some of the planes look as if they had the measles." He tells his parents "Don't worry about us being shot, because in the first place we have no desire to collect any lead, and in the second, the French government won't allow us to fly over the dangerous territory."

Moye tells his parents that "it is pathetic to see what lengths a few of the officers go to amuse themselves—siccing their dogs (they all have dogs) on the waiters in the cafes, making them bark during musical numbers, striking matches for their companions' cigarettes and then blowing them out before the companions have a chance to light up; yelling and having convulsions of laughter over small and uninteresting things—in short, acting like schoolboys aged about ten."

Stephens says, "Dick has at last commenced writing on the book, and at present is down among the bulrushes beating his head on a rock, and, as the sound of rock being chipped sets my teeth on edge, I have left him to chisel out the chronicle of the Flying Carpet in solitude." With this statement, he lays to rest any claim that Paul Mooney[*] wrote *The Flying Carpet* from the ground up. Stephens concludes the letter with, "You no doubt by now think that I'm lost, strayed, or stolen; in reality I'm in Colomb Bechar—whether or not there is any distinction I haven't been able to decide. Loads of Love, Moye."

---

[*] Paul Mooney is covered later in this book.

TIMBUKTU

Their destination was sixteen hundred miles away in Timbuktu, at the edge of the Sahara and near the Niger River, today in the nation of Mali. As a name, Timbuktu pervades popular understanding as a place so remote that it borders on legend more than reality. As an idiom, "going to Timbuktu" in the early Twentieth Century meant to travel where no road leads, where time is forgotten. Indeed, in the imagination of recently bygone decades it did not exist but was a place mysterious and mystical, rather like the fictional Shangri-La in the remote Himalayas, a place romantic to visit, but only in movies or novels. Timbuktu cannot be real, so popular thinking went, because nobody had ever been there. But it was real, not imaginary, and the two young men wanted to fly there, this in 1931 when Africa was uncharted in Western imagination.

Established by Tuaregs perhaps as early as the 10th Century, the name *Timbuktu* has a curious explanation. According to popular etymology, an old woman, Buktu, lived in the place, and throughout the region she was known for her honesty. Centuries ago travelers plied the route from south to north and back again. They left belongings with Buktu, the old woman, as the goods were too cumbersome to carry north on camels. Returning, they claimed them from her. When a Tuareg was asked what he had done with his belongings, he replied that he had left them with Buktu. He left them *Tin Buktu*, or at the place of Buktu. Fused, *Tin Buktu* became Timbuktu. That is one version of the name. Another is that in Berber *buqt* means far away, so *Tin-Buqt* means a place far away, so far that it is at the nether end of earth. That certainly described it in books and magazines of Halliburton's era.

It became celebrated as a remote, romantic place, and being so far it never collided with the icon people nurtured. They owned it as their own private, imaginary place. It became legendary for tales of fabulous wealth.

251

It was fabled as a city paved in gold and in 1824 the French Société de Géographie offered ten thousand francs to anyone who reached Timbuktu and returned alive. Wanting the prize, in 1825 Major Alexander Gordon Laing led a caravan over two thousand miles from Tripoli to Timbuktu, taking more than a year, men and animals dying of heat and foul food. His competitor, Commander Hugh Clapperton, died in Sokoto of dysentery. In 1826 Laing was murdered in the desert, after expulsion from Timbuktu. René Caillié, a Frenchman and baker's son, made it to Timbuktu in 1828 and got home alive, winning the ten thousand franc prize, the Legion of Honor, and a government pension. His book, *Journal of Travel to Timbuktu,* or *Journal d'un voyage à Temboctou,* was a bestseller. Laing had written of Timbuktu as marvelous; Caillié said it was a poor, mud village.

It had been a robust slave market before the arrival of the Portuguese but Portuguese slavers found Atlantic harbors a more convenient alternative than the Timbuktu slave market as their human goods could be moved directly from the harbor to ships without the bother of overland herding of humans, which was left to Africans who captured the men, women, and children.

FUEL, THE SAHARA, & TIMBUKTU

Richard and Moye sat in the middle of a desert with a wind-up Victrola playing Schubert's Eighth Symphony. Wherever they looked, they only saw sky meeting horizon. Wherever they listened, they only heard wind and shifting sand as background to Schubert. The sun slipped below the horizon and they sweated less, felt the cool breeze, knew that night would vex them in a different way, the oppressive heat of daylight shifting the air to a nighttime weight on their skin as it tried to breathe and they tried to sleep. Schubert played again as a soft adagio while they watched the silent oncoming of night. They were somewhere in the Sahara with its 3.5 million square miles. Next them sat the Flying Carpet, its exhaust pipe no longer creaking as it cooled, now at rest after flying them from Fez, in the Atlas Mountains of Morocco.

In the morning, they shook sand from their clothes and hair and climbed back in the plane, Stephens, in the rear cockpit as pilot, Halliburton in the front. The Pratt and Whitney cranked, the cylinders sputtered, caught, sputtered, caught, and finally roared to life, the exhaust stacks spouting flame and smoke as the biplane's backwash scattered a storm of sand behind them while Stephens turned the plane, racing for the sky. The altimeter read five hundred feet. Seven hundred fifty. One thousand. Two thousand. They looked back on their wheel tracks already fading, and turned ahead toward Timbuktu. They followed a desert trail, a thing with faint, sandy traces as fleeting as the grin on Alice's Cheshire cat.

They had not counted on the sands of the Sahara, which shifted, covered everything, and once shifted, shifted again. The plane was their lifeline and fuel was its own. Fuel was the problem. At a French Foreign Legion outpost the commandant had allowed them to use Legion fuel tanks strategically placed along the route of their flight south to Timbuktu. Once a fortnight, Legion lorries drove along a track of sand from the Niger River north to Fez, then back again. For mobility of its troops the Legion had stashed gasoline in tanks every four or five hundred miles.

The track was difficult for the trucks to follow and if a driver lost the trace he and his Legionnaires might drive in endless circles seeking it until they ran out of petrol and slowly became bones bleached by the sun.

Halliburton wrote of a French army biplane whose pilot tried to land after he lost the track but its wheels caught in the sand and it ground-looped, its tail pointed skyward. The passenger, a general, broke his shoulder. With the pilot was a mechanic. The three of them had one canteen between them. There was no shade, except for a small area under the wing. The sun baked them; the wind seared their skin. The pilot dutifully recorded their last moments in case somebody found their remains. A Foreign Legion rescue team located their bodies. According to the pilot's notes, the general was the first to die, the mechanic next, the pilot last.

In his memoir as well as letters home, Moye's narrative describes a flight by no means easy. Moye wrote, "That night we realized that we were really in the desert. We lay on our beds gasping without a stitch of covering and didn't get a very good night's rest." They were up before daybreak for "what proved to be the hardest day's flying I have ever experienced. In the first place, we had a strong headwind, the day was terrifically hot, and it took an enormous amount of concentration to follow the piste, and I had to sit in a very uncomfortable position too with my neck craning over the edge of the cockpit all day long—ten hours and a quarter of flying." It had not been easy to follow. "The piste in places had been obliterated by the wind and sand and I had to keep one eye on the piste behind us while we proceeded, and search for the piste ahead with the other." He said, "There is absolutely nothing of interest in the Reganne Gao stretch—sand, and that is all."

The Stearman had a sparse instrument panel, including magnetic compass, a gyro-horizon, airspeed indicator, and altimeter. In a featureless landscape they were needed because little was felt for the senses to confirm except they were up and below was down. They kept their eyes on the track, circling back to find it when it disappeared.

Always nagging was the question, Had they missed the fuel deposit? Mile after mile, they wiped at goggles and strained to stay alert to the vast monotony below. Wind could cover the track. As Halliburton explains, "Moye's eyes and mine were fixed grimly on the wisp of a track. We lost it, wheeled about to pick it up, lost it, found it, lost it, hide-and-seek all morning long." Moye wrote, "An iron tank was almost indistinguishable in color from the sand and was easily buried by a storm."

They had expected to find the next fuel deposit at half-past eleven. It was after twelve. They worried that they had over-flown it and knew that it would be easy to do after a sandstorm. Stephens kept his eye on the tank gauge and, while scanning the desert below, he had Halliburton take the controls. After he grew weary and lulled by the endless drone of the engine, it would be Richard's turn to search the sands.

Halliburton often credited Stephens with a calm and a skill in getting them out of many dangerous situations and, gazing down at the Sahara, Moye again came through. Stephens peered ahead and saw a half-dozen jerry cans littering the track, although no fuel deposit could be seen. It was a slim hope but Moye landed to heft the cans and see if they had enough gas to pour into the biplane. Together, the cans might provide a little feed to the Stearman's nine-cylinder appetite. While taxiing toward the cans they spotted a dune that did not fit the landscape. They looked closer and saw a pump handle poking out of the sand, then taxied up to the dune and climbed out. Digging sand away from the handle they found the fuel tank. They filled the Flying Carpet's tank one jerry can at a time as heat waves shimmered into the air. They could not linger. They had only "time to be conscious" they were hundreds of miles "from the nearest human being."

Again in the air, the Stearman slowed, bucking a head wind, and the miles crept by as the nine-cylinder engine guzzled gasoline. Halliburton had the sensation that the plane seemed to be standing still. As the sun lowered in the west, they struggled against the wind. By seven all they could see over the dark sand was more sand. The moon was rising and they knew they had to land or else lose the trace.

That night on the desert, unsure of finding the next petrol storage, they rationed their food to a cup of water and a tin of beef. They filled bags with sand and placed them on the wings to anchor the plane against the wind. Unable to sleep, gazing at the stars, Richard understood the Sahara finally.

Richard wrote that he might as well be on "a dead star wandering in space. There would be the same relentless progress of the murderous sun by day, and of the frozen firmament by night, in cloudless, seasonless silence. There would be the same appalling expanse of fixed, enchanted waste, without end, without change, without hope." At night the black infinitude of space opened over the desert. In sunlight, it scorched the lungs and killed life. They went to sleep with their parachutes for pillows.

In the morning, the propeller again turned, the engine sputtered then caught into a roar. The biplane taxied for take off, blasting sand into a cloudy wake, racing, bumping along the track. The two young men looked back, looked ahead, and looked down, trying to keep sight of the desert track.

As the sun crept into the sky, they saw something on the horizon, something that was not more sand. It was a twisting thing that convoluted its way east to west and they realized it was a river. It was the Niger and not a mirage. They were nearing Timbuktu, which sat next the river, though the place was still some three hundred miles upstream.

Stephens climbed Flying Carpet to ten thousand feet and eventually they could see the city in the distance as it slowly moved toward them. Gradually they descried mosques, minarets, and a market place. They circled the city and at five hundred feet they could see in the market place natives wearing boubous, white-robes, looked up at the Flying Carpet. People pointed at the thing in the air, shouted at one another to see it. Others were leaning out windows, climbing on roofs, to watch the scarlet biplane with black struts.

They passed through a great dark cloud, blinding them. It rose skyward, rising from chimneys and housetops. These were storks, thousands of them that soared into the sky, blackening it. The thunder from the plane's exhaust stacks had stirred them. The storks acted as one mind, a ganglia of neurons, emotionally charged, swooping and turning in the sky as a single thought of fear. The mind soared above the plane and waited until its fear passed.

Upon landing in a rough field, bouncing as the biplane slowed, Stephens taxied to a stop. Ignition toggled off, the propeller spun then halted. People ran toward the scarlet thing descended from the sky. It had roared over them as they craned their necks to follow it swooshing past, as it climbed, turned, and aimed back at the field. They watched it bounce along, roll toward them, slowing until it came to a rest. They stood watching two men climb out of holes in the thing, then jump onto the ground. In the sudden silence, holding their leather helmets with goggles, the men shook sand off themselves. Then Moye uncoiled some rope. Having experienced the fierce winds of the region, he and Richard tied down Flying Carpet's wings and tail, using pegs pounded into the earth. The crowd waited to see what the two would do next. Richard was clear on his next move. He had a story in mind and it would be about Père Yakouba.

PÈRE YAKOUBA

In June 1931, Moye Stephens' parents received a letter that described Timbuktu and explained that they found very few Europeans but "one of these people is a very famous character known as Père Yakouba," who had lived there thirty-six years. Stephens wrote that the Father had gone there as a Catholic missionary but after "a couple of years he decided celibacy was the bunk." They dined with Yakouba and his African wife, finding him "very well informed and apparently intelligent."

Richard had done his homework. Before leaving the states he determined a tale worth telling. He had a story similar to that of Dr. Livingstone, who in the Nineteenth Century had been presumed lost. European and American newspapers asked what had happened to the man, until journalist-explorer William Stanley found him at Lake Tanganyika. Stanley's words, "Dr. Livingstone I presume?" became famous in the annals of exploration. Such accounts fascinated readers of the era. Richard had another encounter in mind, and with it he could sell articles to magazines and include it in his book.

His Dr. Livingstone lived in Timbuktu and was the French ex-priest. The ex-priest was written about in *Time* magazine on October 29, 1934, in a review of a book by William Seabrook called *The White Monk of Timbuctoo*. The review explains, "Père Yakouba, is an old (69) and somewhat remorseful man now. He was never pious. When he first went to Africa (1890) as a strapping young missionary he had already a quiet reputation as a priest who did not take his vows of celibacy very seriously." The review continues, "But his genius for languages and for mixing with native Africans made him useful. He took to medieval Timbuctoo like a duck to water, and sturdily resisted all attempts to send him elsewhere. When threatened with a transfer to Palestine, he announced that the only Jew he had ever loved was Jesus."

257

Jesus, okay, but he certainly loved women. French officers of the Timbuktu outpost complained that the Father stole their girls. Forsaking his vows of celibacy was one thing. Working their turf was another. Both dispositions got in the way of a good reputation but that did not bother the Father. He had moved to Africa to live life his way. So it happened that when his Timbuktu superior died, Père Yakouba was not promoted into the man's position. Rather, he was ordered to Algiers.

The father did not go. Instead, he resigned from the Church, dressed himself like a native and became, not a fisher of men, but a fisherman. As he explained to his biographer, "I quit the Church because I didn't want to leave Timbuctoo and didn't want to give up women." Casting nets into the Niger, bringing fish to market, with a large libido he took shelter with a large woman, Salama, but to earn his keep and her bed he had to do something besides fish. Seeing a certain advantage in his priestly renunciation, Salama required practical conditions for their relationship.

She made him accept a civil job as interpreter and demanded his week's pay. On her part, she handled him, the household, and their eight children. He became head of Sankore University, commandant of Fortress Goundam and interpreter at court trials. He turned from chaplain to warrior in expeditions against the Tuaregs. By the time Richard and Moye met him, he was the most celebrated citizen of Timbuktu. With a large house of mud walls, a large family, and a large wife, he was well respected. He had a good library, plenty to eat, drink, and smoke. His door was knocked on by the occasional foreign visitor.

Still, whatever the front he presented to Richard Halliburton and Moye Stephens, he was not happy. To his biographer, he summarized his life, "In the end it was not well."

Here was no Kurtz, Conrad's character in *The Heart of Darkness*. He did not look about him and think he had descended into barbarity. He had it made but nearing seventy years of age, had concluded that all was not well. An ex-priest in Timbuktu, errant from his God, perhaps, and with plenty of worldly comfort, at the other end of life he lacked something.

Richard tells us that he came to Timbuktu as a Catholic missionary. As the immense land swelled into his life he forgot France, forgot churchly ways, forgot family and kin. There was nothing, no motorcars, no telephone in Timbuktu. Cut off, he was left to scholarship, and became an expert on native languages and cultures. Civilization was his baggage and he kept it in books on his shelves, using it to interpret the land's ways and tongues for Europeans but felt something was missing.

When the two airmen met him he wore long white robes and a long, grizzled beard. Rather portly, he greeted them with warmth while his wife brought out their best liquor and spread the table for tea. They sat in the study. According to Halliburton, a baby leopard and a monkey crawled into her lap, quite ample. As Richard sipped the tea and drank the liquor he looked at the study. He saw shelves with books and pamphlets, as well as notes. They were either written in, or were written about, the languages of West Africa. Yakouba answered all their questions about Timbuktu and about the history and culture of the region.

The two old people in Timbuktu talked to Richard and Moye. They made small talk, laughed at one another's jokes. It was a fine day, with the excitement of two young men descending from the sky in an aeroplane and bringing news of the outside world.

Yakouba died in 1945 at age eighty, when war raged across the globe and after Richard Halliburton had been lost at sea. On that day in 1931 he was the cordial host, the resident scholar, the white man, the town celebrity. The two young men bade goodbye to him and his wife. They climbed into Flying Carpet at the edge of town and took to the air. Père Yakouba and Salama climbed to the roof to watch them. Moye waggled the wings at them; Richard waved. Then they disappeared into the distant sky and the old couple went back downstairs. As the days, weeks, months, and years passed, Father Yakouba looked back on his life and said that in the end it was not well.

Elsewhere on that day in April 1931, Haile Selassie was preparing the first written constitution of Ethiopia, soon to be invaded by Mussolini's troops. A new flag was adopted for the Second Spanish Republic, which would fall to the Falange of General Franco and to Hitler's Condor Legions. The Japanese Imperial Army was mobilizing for the invasion of Manchuria. Everywhere it was not well.

Père Yakouba with white beard
(born Auguste Dupuis)

ELLY BEINHORN MEETS RICHARD & MOYE

But I'll play St. Louis Blues for you on my phonograph each day, and you must play Falling in Love Again for me, and love me very much.
Elly Beinhorn to Richard and Moye

Elly repairing her Klemm

GERMANY'S AVIATRIX

In *Flying Girl*, translated out of the German and published in 1935, Elly Beinhorn describes a 1931 meeting with Stephens and Halliburton in Bushire, Persia, now Iran. She met "a white man seated at a writing table. He was fairly young and he was wearing an open leather jacket." This was Moye Stephens. She could see he was tall when "he rose and greeted me first in English, after which we continued the conversation in French, of which at that time I had a better knowledge." I had a better knowledge. This comment suggests a competition, which Moye describes in letters home, more of which shortly.

She learned that Stephens was another aviator, which "explained the leather jacket with the zip fastening." Moye explained to her that he was pilot for Richard Halliburton, "a very well-known American author of travel books, and the owner of the aeroplane." Indeed, Richard received generous royalties from his books published in Germany. For a year, he and Halliburton had been "engaged in a flight around the world. Richard was in Teheran at the time but would soon return. The flight was intended as the subject of Halliburton's planned book The Flying Carpet."

Stephens asked her, "Do you happen to know a German woman aviator who made a forced landing" in the Sahara "early in the year? I have forgotten her name."

Elly said she had heard of the incident but coyly did not confess herself as the German aviatrix. Stephens recounted how, the week after the aviatrix left, he and Halliburton had landed at Timbuktu in the Stearman biplane, Flying Carpet. In North Africa they had been told "at every aerodrome" that Elly "had just been there."

She finally confessed that he was talking to that very woman. In *Flying Girl*, she writes, "In this age of flying our earth is no longer such a big place." Her readers around the world read this and felt they were beholding the future.

She said she would feel safer if she could travel with them. Would that be all right? In case she were forced down once again—or if they were—traveling companions would provide good help. Stephens was agreeable to her joining them, two planes in the air above jungles, mountains, and valleys, as they would be taking the same route to Singapore, alone or together. She was not sure how Richard would feel about it. At the moment, he was only somebody whose books she read or heard about.

Returned from Teheran, Halliburton met her the next morning. She writes that she had awaited his arrival "with mixed feelings." She did not know "what view he would take of this extra item in his world-flight programme." Moye knew. He had been traveling with the man long enough to understand Richard Halliburton was willing to help. Richard agreed at once. "To him the rendering of this assistance seemed as much a matter of course as the picking up of a glove," Elly wrote, implying his gentlemanly manner before ladies.

She did not meet Richard and Moye at the hotel in Bushire because she had flown there. Instead, she had ridden there in a rickety Model T after her Klemm developed motor trouble forcing her down at Bandar Dilam.

As its propeller slowed then stopped, Persians ran up to the plane and were surprised to see a young woman in Jodhpur pants and leather jacket. She pulled off her leather flying helmet and goggles and stood before them, all five feet two of her. After lifting the cowling flaps, she took the carburetor apart, checked the gas line and plugs, and still had problems. She turned to the crowd gathered around her and the plane and made gestures after failing with words. Not knowing any Pharsi, Elly tried to explain with her hands. They thought she was lost. She said she had mechanical troubles. Kaput. Not okay. Bad. She pointed at the Klemm. Her only hope was to contact the German embassy. She found a man who grasped what she wanted. He explained it to the others. A Persian agreed to give her a lift. She bounced along to Bushire in a rattling, over-loaded Model-T Ford, and there she met the two Americans.

A mechanic as well as pilot, Stephens flew her in Flying Carpet back to Bandar Dilam to see if he could fix the Klemm. Though she was clearly an intrepid young woman, she wrote, "I sat helplessly in the passenger's seat in front and had to let myself be flown by a strange man." After setting the biplane down and walking to the Klemm they found themselves accosted by uniformed officials who wanted to see their passports. She had hers but, in their hurried flight to reach Bandar Dilam, Stephens had forgotten his. This could have meant imprisonment for Moye but one imagines that Elly with her charm talked the officials out of it. The officials shrugged but did not leave, waiting to see what the two would do next. She and Moye turned to examine her Klemm.

In a letter home, Moye describes her aircraft as "a beautiful little plane—a Klemm low-wing monoplane." Elly was confident she fixed the problem before leaving the plane and just needed to fly it away so long as she had Moye, "a person with experience," to give it a final once-over. Moye wrote, "The motor started all right, but missed terribly and spit back through the carburetor continually."

The same letter implies Moye finds her attractive. With Moye, she had been working on the engine and he refers to her "somewhat besmudged little nose" attended by a femininity he could not help noticing.

He wanted to check the spark plugs. She assented but insisted they were okay because she had already cleaned them. She pulled the plugs to let Moye inspect them. She was right. "She did an excellent job on them, even to adjusting the gap to the exact distance."

He asked about the carburetor jets. With "increasing dignity" she said they were also okay. He didn't know how to reply as he noticed the curve of her breasts and so he checked the gas filter instead. It was clean. He looked at her and caught an I-told-you-so glance. He then knew he "couldn't possibly look" at the carburetor jets "without a complete break in relations." That was something he wanted to avoid. Instead he disconnected the gas line and fuel gushed out. No problem there. With cowling flaps up, she looked at him from the other side of the engine, a slight smile on her face. Finally, though, he had to check the jets. Unbolting the carburetor he "furtively extracted the jets" and found a grain of sand in a jet hole. Elly watched him clean the jet and was "still skeptical but clambered into the cockpit" as Moye wound the starter crank

"The motor sputtered a few times, caught hold, and settled down to a steady purr."

She throttled down the engine and shouted over the cockpit, "We are two good mechanics."

Moye pretends to be completely deflated by her remark but his letter implies he wanted more than to fix her Klemm.

As Moye knew, this was not her first forced landing. Back in the Bushire hotel he told her that in Africa he and Richard learned of her trouble when she flew en route to Timbuktu. The name Elly Beinhorn awaited them wherever Flying Carpet set down. They learned the lady flyer had been thought lost with no hope of finding her in the vast expanse of desert sand. Soldiers at Foreign Legion outposts spoke of the little woman in the little Klemm who landed at their field, then left next day, but one day did not arrive at the next destination as expected. She well might have died but she did not.

Her forced landing in the desert occurred suddenly. She was flying above the desert, lulled by the monotonous drone of the engine, when she came awake to the exhaust's sputter, and then the motor stopped. She looked at the dropping needle of her air speed indicator. She checked her fuel gauge. The ship had enough gas. Then she heard only the rushing wind. Without an engine, she had little time to line the nose up for a dead-stick landing and the Klemm was dropping fast. On roll out, the plane ground looped against a rough patch of desert, propeller digging into sand, cowling crumpling. She was jerked violently toward the windscreen but her safety harness kept her face from it.

She spent the night huddled next her Klemm, a small low-wing monoplane powered by a ninety-five horsepower Argus engine. She was left in silence with only her canteen and the dry heat parching her throat. After several days a few Tuaregs came upon her. Leper outcasts, they helped her find a caravan where she hitched a ride on a camel the remaining forty miles to Timbuktu.

Finally in Timbuktu, she waited for a French Foreign Legion convoy scheduled to return to Morocco. According to *The New York Times*, February 17, 1935, the Klemm factory sent her another KL-26 monoplane, top speed one hundred eight miles per hour, so she could continue her aerial journey. * She flew the new Klemm from Timbuktu to continue her global flight.

During the 1930s, hers was a household name on many continents and remains so in Germany. She was a daring young woman in the mold of Amelia Earhart, her friend. Like other such women of her time her goals were not properly feminine. Aeroplane pilot was a most unwomanly thing. Not only that, she wanted to fly around the world. Alone. Her mother wept and her father, a well-to-do manufacturer, threatened to send her to a psychiatrist but an aunt had died and left Elly a little money. She would learn to fly.

It all began when she heard a lecture by Hauptman Hermann Kohl, who had just flown the Atlantic. He opened her eyes to a world of possibilities far from the ground. Like a bird, he became unshackled from earth and soared free from its clutches. Most of all, though, there was the fact that he flew over the Atlantic from Ireland to Canada and had even been awarded a Distinguished Flying Cross by American President Calvin Coolidge. He showed her that there was a world to see.*

In 1929, renting a small Berlin flat, she took flying lessons and soloed

---

* The Klemm Leichtflugzeugbau GmbH (Klemm Light Aircraft Company) built sports and touring planes. In 1919 Klemm's first design, the Daimler L.15, used a single cylinder seven and a half horsepower Indian motorcycle engine. Klemm later moved up to a twelve horsepower Harley-Davidson. Elly's KL-26 with its ninety-five horsepower Argus is gone. Only one KL-26 survived World War II and it no longer exists.

* A Catholic and a man of character, Kohl fell out of favor with Hitler and lost his job with Lufthansa airline. He died in Munich in 1938.

just before her money ran out. Her instructor suggested she get an aerobatic license and stunt fly. Soon she was making good money at weekend air shows all over Germany.

Elly Beinhorn

AIR SHOW FOR THE MAHARAJAH OF CALCUTTA

There was a problem. The three wanted to fly over Nepal and Mount Everest but more lofty obstacles were the British and Nepalese governments, which prohibited it. They found a way to avoid the two governments by gaining permission from the Maharajah of Calcutta. As Moye explained, "If we came to grief and had to land we could plead our invitation from the Maharajah." The old man had never seen an airplane before and they could impress him. Moye explained, "Elly and Dick lost no time in taking advantage of the opportunity and struck while the iron was hot." They would fly in an air show for him and his court in exchange for permission.

Moye did stunning aerobatics, maneuvers he learned stunt-flying in Hollywood movies. Richard had not known him capable of them. With full rudder and full opposite aileron, he yawed the biplane into a hammerhead. Swooping into a half loop upward, followed by a half roll, he had the crowd with mouths open as they saw him climb into an Immelmann turn. From behind their tent, the Raj's court heard the engine roaring toward them, then rush overhead, swooping down onto the field before them, only to climb skyward until Moye dove the Stearman into an outside loop. Then tipping the biplane into a steep dive, motor roaring, he plummeted toward the Maharajah's tent, pulling out at the last minute as the crowd ducked.

Elly had also been trained in aerobatics and in a 1932 *New York Times* article she described her experience with the Maharajah. "When I got out to the flying field," she said, "I was marched up to the marquee where the Maharajah was seated, surrounded by his retinue. He rose to greet me and was most charming to me and looked so kindly with his long white beard. He said (he speaks English well) he had been told that I was going to do some stunts for him and he was eager to see them."

She added. "When my turn came I went up in some trepidation, wondering what I had forgotten since last doing stunts. But it went famously. I did everything pell-mell—I looped, turned, rolled, flew upside down, stood the plane on its tail—and the spectators got excited when I would come swooping straight down within yards of them; and at the end, I went quite close to the ground and spun directly over the Maharajah's head." She whip-stalled the Klemm only three hundred feet off the ground, something the larger Stearman could not do.

The Maharajah agreed to let them fly to Mount Everest and over it if they could.

MOUNT EVEREST

Wings of the two planes glinted in the morning sun. Rising to eight thousand feet, Moye looked back at Elly in her Klemm. She held her gloved hand thumbs-up to show she was okay. He eased the stick toward his stomach. The biplane's nose edged up and the engine labored slightly. He looked back at her again. Again, she was okay. He eased the stick again. Past Richard's head in the front cockpit, Stephens looked toward the Himalayas. Richard had talked to him about once trekking over them to Ladakh and maybe Moye wondered if it was any warmer down there. Halliburton had walked over them; now they were about to fly above them.

The Klemm followed the Stearman as it climbed toward Everest. The altimeter showed nine-thousand feet. Ten thousand. Eleven thousand. Moye looked back at her again. She waved at him to go on. Although her KL-26 had a service ceiling of almost eighteen thousand feet, she decided to wait below. As it climbed the Stearman began laboring. Its engine was not supercharged for high altitude. The engine breathed with difficulty just as the two men with fur-lined leather did in the thin air. The biplane struggled to eighteen thousand feet.

Despite leathered fur, Stephens' hands and feet were numb as the climbing plane struggled to maintain airspeed. Then Richard unbuckled his safety belt and stood in the cockpit to photograph the mountain. Like a parachute brake, his erect body stalled the ship and it dropped like a stone. Richard felt the cockpit floor falling beneath his feet and he pulled himself back into his seat, re-buckling his belt. To recover from the stall, Stephens shoved the stick forward, sending the Stearman into a dive toward the mountain, hoping for enough clearance to pull out. When he pulled back on the stick there was no response from the plane. They kept dropping toward the slopes of Everest. After picking up speed, Moye pulled the stick into his stomach and the biplane's nose rose, then rose again. A near-collision but Richard was happy. He took the first aerial photograph of Mount Everest, fuzzy as it was from a vibrating cockpit, but it proved to his detractors that he had indeed been there. The Stearman continued to labor in the thin air. Climbing higher was impossible. Straight-ahead, collision with the slope imminent. Moye banked the biplane back down the mountain.

Elly and her monoplane had been circling and waiting for them. She followed them down to warmer air.

The three sped over the Bay of Bengal, their shadows tracing along its shoreline. They flew to Burma, visited Rangoon. There, they saw the Shwedagon Pagoda, an immense Buddhist Temple twenty-five hundred years old. Leaving Burma, they flew over dense, steamy jungles to Siam, and in Bangkok they parted company, at least temporarily. The King and Queen of Siam gave a party for Elly but Richard and Moye could not attend because the next leg of their journey required floatplane pontoons, which awaited them in Singapore. An unknown challenge, the pontoons demanded time for fitting. Richard and Moye said goodbye to her in Bangkok, hoping to see her soon in Singapore.

She rejoined them in Singapore, where Elly and the two young men parted for good but not immediately. She had wanted to get on with her journey but according to Halliburton, they put "What Good Am I without You?" on the phonograph to lure Elly into still another day with them. On their part, they could not depart as the pontoons had been shipped to Singapore without support struts. They had to find a way to fabricate the struts and, without skilled welders and machinists, the difficulty was agonizingly slow to resolve. Eventually Elly could wait no longer and did leave. Their route would take them to Borneo and the Philippines, hers to Australia.

On their last morning together they escorted her to the airstrip. She stepped onto the wing of her Klemm, climbed into its cockpit, started the engine, and waved to them as she taxied into take-off position. She climbed into the sky and they watched her Klemm disappear.

From Batavia in present day Indonesia they received a note from her: "My dear Papas: Batavia was easy, only six hours, but it seemed [such a] long time with no Flying Carpet to keep me company. The world became very big and very empty again, after I left Singapore. What Good Am I, without my two papas? And what will you do without Elly? Who will keep Moye from talking about aviation, and who will make Dick wear his sun-helmet? I'm sure you both [will] go to the dogs. But I'll play St. Louis Blues for you on my phonograph each day, and you must play Falling in Love Again for me, and love me very much. I kiss you both on your sunburned noses."

mishap with a rope twisting around the Stearman's propeller.[*] Both were dressed in flying gear. The Rajah, Charles Vyner Brooke, was in England with his oldest daughter. The Ranee appeared with their two other daughters, Princess Elizabeth, eighteen, and Princess Valerie, sixteen. Wearing a garland of orchids and a diamond necklace, the Ranee met her guests as a Filipino orchestra played for the hundred couples dancing on the floor of the banquet hall. On the walls of the hall hung portraits of Sarawak history, its white Rajahs gazing upon the resplendent couples. Borneo's European elite glittered in jewelry, Parisian gowns, medals, scarlet dinner jackets and gold-trimmed epaulets. When the time came, and with a Princess on Moye's arm, another on Richard's, the two aviators—Stephens in flight togs, Halliburton in patched corduroy—led the Grand March in a scene reminiscent of an Indiana Jones movie. Ranee Sylvia insisted they stay the night in the palace.

She was the polite hostess, asking about their travels. Richard asked her to dance and she gave him her arm. He escorted her onto the floor and as they glided across it he commented on the portraits looking down on them. She smiled and explained the history of the Sultanate and the pirates and the insurgents and how she loved her kingdom. She asked about Flying Carpet and their adventures. When Halliburton invited her to take a plane ride she accepted.

This was a measure of her personality. For a royal, there was something bohemian in it, a disregard for propriety and her ministers, who were concerned and urged her not to go off with the two men in an airplane. They came out of nowhere; they could disappear back into it with her aboard. The Rajah was in England. If anything happened to her, the country would be without a ruler for weeks. The thought of shocking headlines in the local newspaper only made her the more resolved. Sensation. It would create that. It was unheard of in a country that needed it. Yes, she would fly. Presently the proposed flight was on every tongue—Malay, Chinese, Dyak, and English. Think of the headlines, she thought. Wouldn't they be divine?

Of the plane ride, the *Sarawak Gazette*, May 2, 1932, gives the Ranee's account, which indicates national stereotypes of the time. "Had I said to an Englishman, 'Oh, how I'd simply love to fly!' he would have replied, after five minutes of the heaviest cogitation, 'Look here old thing, hadn't you better think it over. I mean to say it's an awfully beastly responsibility for a chap, by jove it is'." She continues. "Not so America. I had hardly

---

[*] In Pontianak, Dutch East Borneo, the Stearman had anchored in a river. Stephens started the engine to hold the plane against the river current and had Halliburton stand on a pontoon to lift and coil the anchor rope. Richard lost his balance, the propeller ripped the rope from him, tearing streaks of skin from his arm, with the forty-pound anchor flying past his head, fortunately only grazing it.

finished the sentence before Dick Halliburton had whisked out his notebook and was 'go-getting me into that plane.' 'Fly,' he said. 'Gee girl, that's easy—Monday—stone steps—nine o'clock—we'll take you up.' I hadn't time to protest—I hadn't time to be alarmed—that's America! At nine o'clock, I was on the stone steps. I couldn't feel anything except that tremendous sinking you have when deep down in your soul you know you are partaking of forbidden fruit. Suppose something happened. But there, nothing would happen. Wasn't I being piloted by one of the men who had taken part in 'Hell's Angels'?" (Moye had stunt-flown in Howard Hughes' silent movie extravaganza.)

The citizens of Sarawak must have clucked their tongues as they read this.

She explains, "My one consolation over the whole affair had been that at any rate I should have Dick Halliburton to cling to. Picture my embarrassment when I was pushed into a tiny seat in front of the pilot—alone!"

More clucking of tongues.

Of the view, she states "Kuching was beautiful from above. The Astana looked like a mushroom on a fresh green slope. I saw all our Malay boys waving from the garden and I tried to wave back, but the wind nearly tore my hand from my wrist, and one of my rings blew right off from my finger. I saw little white figures darting from the offices."

This, then, was the Ranee of Sarawak.

Perfectly respectable, the newspaper did not mention its own opinion of the whole affair.

When Richard and Moye said goodbye to her, they promised her one last view of Flying Carpet, so they swooped the biplane, circling it over the palace grounds. "The Ranee and the two princesses ran out on the lawn, waving good-bye with big white scarfs." Moye dipped his wings and swooped across the lawn. Richard tossed out the leather helmet the Ranee had worn. He turned in the cockpit, the slipstream tugging at his leather jacket. He saw her pick it up to read what he had written on it. "Long Live The Queen! From The Flying Carpet and Its Crew." Then with his feet on the aileron pedals, Moye banked the plane away and over the jungle.

On Christmas day 1941 the Japanese captured Kuching while the Rajah and Ranee had exiled themselves abroad. Theirs was the twilight of imperialism but the fact is that in 1946, the war over, they were warmly welcomed back as hundreds of small boats watched their progress up river and on the banks crowds waved at them. As they climbed ashore they were saluted by twenty-one guns. But the economy had been devastated by the Japanese. Its reconstruction was beyond their capacity. Rajah Vyner took the only solution available. In February of 1946 he announced to the people that Sarawak had been ceded to the British Crown, whose rule lasted until 1963 when it became part of Malaysia. Sir Vyner Brooke returned to England a broken man. He lived the rest of his life as a recluse. He died in London in 1963. All three White Rajahs, the original, his nephew, and Sir Vyner, are buried in St Leonard's Church in the village of Sheepstor, Plymouth, England.

After an unhappy childhood—at twelve she tried suicide, first eating rotten sardines, then lying naked in snow—Sylvia Brooke had found Sarawak "like a dream come true." Back in England, she spent her days purposeless, bored, with nothing to plan, nobody to help, no visitors to receive. She had only the past. She had her memories of Dyak gongs, distant drums, flowers in girls' hair. They lived separately in London, Vyner on Albion Street, she in a flat in Archery Close, both of them near Hyde Park. She did not stay there. Lady Brooke died in 1971 in Tuffet Cottage, St. James, Barbados.[*]

---

[*] She was the only child of great financier Joshua Bates.

LENIN'S WIDOW & THE MAN WHO SHOT THE ROMANOV'S

I am standing on the grave of the Czar
Pyotr Zacharovitch Ermakov, interviewed by Richard

Czar Nicholas II & family

RICHARD & WHITE RUSSIANS

In Siberia in December 1922, Richard Halliburton visited White Russians. Their armies fought the Bolsheviks who seized power from the Mensheviks after the fall of Czar Nicholas II. How Richard got there safely was a marvel of luck and no tribute at all to caution. The American consulates in both Peking and Harbin had flat told him that they could not give him a visa, could not approve the visit, and that he should not go. If he did, the American government assumed no responsibility and he might rot in a Russian jail or simply go missing, dead or lost to the world. He even applied to the Bolsheviks, who also refused entry. His appetite whetted by the challenge, he would get there somehow. Vladivostok or bust. Chang Tso-lin's bandit army controlled the railroad and on his train Halliburton was stuck in a dining car with a bunch of these brigands. He is twenty-two years old and traveling through a warring China with its anarchic factions. The brigands were rowdy, armed, dangerous, and getting very drunk. He says he had nothing more exciting than that.

First, he had to reach Harbin in North-East China. In 1922 Harbin was a Russian city despite its Manchurian location. At one hundred thousand population, it was easily the largest city of Russians outside their motherland. In 1897 the Russians needed a town on a river as administrative headquarters to build a railway for China. They needed a river so sea-going ships could bring supplies. Soon, the city had an opera house, fine stores with signs in Russian, wide boulevards, carriages with ladies and gentlemen. The Chinese granted Russians the right to their own government, police force, and law courts. Then came the 1917 Russian Revolution.

As the White Armies retreated, White Russians fled to Harbin, swelling its 1922 population to about one hundred fifty thousand.

When Richard reached the city he was surprised to find Harbin a very

Russian city, despite being in China. As a child he had looked at book illustrations of Russia and all he had seen in the pictures was there. With its U-shaped yoke poised high above the horse's head, a droshky rumbled down the street. With poppy-headed domes, churches invited the faithful to prayer. To ward off the biting cold both men and women covered their heads and ears with ushankas or balaclavas. He met men who had icicles hanging from eyebrows and beards. He was not in the land of Bolsheviks but instead was among those who had taken refuge from them. White Russians, most belonged to the aristocracy or to the intelligentsia and were penniless, struggling to survive, seeking any kind of work.

Harbin had a YMCA, where Halliburton went to seek shelter. Richard learned of an impoverished Russian princess who was teaching Russian to the YMCA manager's wife. If she returned to Russia she would be executed as an enemy of the people. She had only her language. Okay, now repeat after me, she would intone to her pupil, Ya ni gavaru pa ruski— I don't speak Russian. The manager told Richard that a general in the Czar's army worked for him as a janitor. The man had once owned a ten thousand acre estate. Harbin was filled with people such as these, having left one world, dead to them and waiting for another powerless to be born.

Many White Russians clung to Christianity and loathed Bolshevik atheism, blaming it for the horrors perpetrated on their motherland. The Orthodox Church and its teachings provided a sanctuary for their distress, Richard discovered that for himself when he attended church in Harbin.

A year before in Granada, Spain, Richard had attended church on Christmas Eve, the warm Mediterranean sun casting its light through stained-glass windows. A year later he wanted to attend a Christmas celebration in this frigid place. When he first arrived in Harbin it had been twenty degrees below zero Fahrenheit.

With a blizzard raging outside he entered an Orthodox chapel and watched the others. The faithful stomped the ice and snow off their boots as they closed the door. Their hands brushed at icicles clinging to beards. They walked along the church wall, stopping at each icon, kissing the feet of each saint. They crossed themselves, knelt, and touched their foreheads to the floor. He found the music superb, moving, and was perhaps surprised to hear the same doxology as in the Presbyterian church of his youth,

> Praise God from whom all blessings flow,
> Praise Him all creatures here below,
> Praise Him above, ye heavenly host,
> Praise Father, Son, and Holy Ghost.

The wind roared against the windowpanes but above it rose a clear, lovely woman's voice, and a man's singing in a fine, rich bass. The music spoke back to an indifferent blizzard blowing against the windows.

The human dignity and spirituality of that scene stood in stark contrast to another encounter in the city. The one scene exalted hope and belief in what humanity can become. The other sank into the grim reality of what it too often is.

In Harbin he met a Russian nobleman whose son had become hardened, perhaps by atrocities he witnessed while escaping the Bolsheviks. In listening to the son, Richard probably saw into how pliable human nature is—how it can be shaped by circumstance to countenance the unspeakable.

Halliburton described himself as becoming pale upon listening to the story of the couple's son, Dimitri. The young man had seen violence enough in his short life; he had learned hatred enough at the hands of the Reds. Maybe, as he listened to Dimitri, Richard was minded of the faithful in the little church, seeking to do God's will.

Quite blasé, the boy told Richard about the beheading of six Chinese. He had watched them decapitated before a large Harbin crowd and he himself was standing in the center of the gathering. The crowd hungered for entertainment and they were it. With fanfare, trumpeters preceded a cart led through the streets, as people fell in behind the thing. On it were chained six Chinese, accused of being bandits. Freezing, bones trembling from fear and cold, they were dragged off the cart, presumably by fellow Chinese as the execution was rather Mandarin-style. They were forced to kneel, hands tied behind, necks bent to the pavement. The first blow fell, the head plopped off, and blood almost spurted onto Dimitri's clothes. The boy told Richard he jumped back and Halliburton's opinion drips with distaste because the boy then explained he had to go to a tea party afterward, and didn't want his shirt spattered. Having experienced too much violence in his young life, the boy admired the swordsman's skill as he lopped off each head.

In Harbin, Richard went to the Bolshevik passport bureau and discovered bureaucrats were the same everywhere. The Russian clerks did not know the rules on Americans without visas but they did have politics to play. The US government did not recognize the Bolshevik government and so here was fair game. By being difficult, they might force the American consul to make a request for Richard, a kind of de facto recognition of their right to exist. That, Richard knew, would not happen. The American consul in Harbin said absolutely not.

Cigarettes and an Englishman came to the rescue. At his hotel, Richard met a young man who lived in Harbin and knew the Bolsheviks and was even on friendly terms with them. When Richard told him of the dilemma, the Englishman told him to buy a pack of cigarettes. Richard found a tobacconist in the city and bought a pack, probably American tobacco, maybe Camel or Lucky Strike, or Fatima, then in favor worldwide. Pack in pocket, Richard returned to the Englishman and together they went to the Bolshevik passport bureau. The Englishman walked up to the Russian with whom he was chummiest, slapped him on the back, and dropped the pack on the table in front of the man. That was it. Richard was gleeful—until he got the bill. Twenty-five yen, or thirteen dollars, charged by the passport bureau. "That floored me," he wrote home, "but it was too late to turn back."

He was ready to enter Russia and Vladivostok was its first city. Instead of December 1922, had Richard entered Vladivostok in October 1922 he would have found American soldiers there but they left before he arrived, along with many Whites and other Russians who resisted the Bolsheviks. The city had been their last stronghold with White regiments crumbling under the Red Army advance. They knew Vladivostok would soon surrender. By December when Richard arrived it had.

EYE WITNESS TO HISTORY:
BOLSHEVIKS & AMERICAN SOLDIERS IN RUSSIA

By the time Halliburton set foot in Vladivostok he saw no White Russians. The city was run by Bolsheviks after their army outnumbered and defeated Czarist troops. With defeat soon, as White forces fell back toward the city, Admiral Stark, age sixty-eight, was called out of retirement to mount an evacuation of nine thousand in the White Russian population: men, women, children, civilians, Cossacks, sailors, and soldiers. He gathered thirty ancient warships of the Siberian Squadron, anchored twenty years, rust creeping through hulls. Entire families waited at the docks to board the first ships. They crammed aboard wherever they could, topside or below deck. He promised those left behind that other ships would soon follow. On October 24, 1922 the fleet hoisted anchor, arriving seven days later in Wonsan, Korea. Unseaworthy or out of fuel, eighteen ships remained there, families looked after by the Red Cross. For the other ships the next port was Shanghai but the vessels became tossed by a fierce typhoon before reaching the city. *Dydymov* and *Asia* bobbed like tin cans as three-story waves swelled above them then crashed down on their decks. They capsized or took on more water than the leaky bilge pumps could handle. Thirty teenage officer-cadets and a group of orthodox nuns drowned. With ten of the original thirty ships and three thousand people, the remnants of the Siberian Fleet anchored in Shanghai.

It was over. A way of life had ended. On January 15, 1923, Stark ordered the flags of Imperial Russia lowered in Manila Bay before he auctioned the rest of the aged fleet, some for scrap metal, and gave the money to support the refugees. On November 13, 1928, he died in Helsinki, Finland. Eventually the Vladivostok refugees emigrated to various places, some to Melbourne and others to Hong Kong or San Francisco.

In Bolshevik-controlled Vladivostok Richard walked on the city's first street, originally named Amerikanskaya, after the corvette *America* that visited its port in 1871. On city streets he saw great numbers of poor, ragged people with nowhere to go, wrapped against the frigid air, begging on the sidewalks.

He encountered a soldier from President Wilson's American Expeditionary Force to Siberia. The man was heavily wrapped in rags, trying to sell something. Richard noticed the fellow spoke English with an American accent. Curious, Richard started a conversation. The man had deserted from the American army in Siberia and was eking out a living by selling supplies stolen from the Red Cross. Richard walked on; the man continued hawking his wares. Perhaps the deserter was arrested by the Bolsheviks, tried, and executed as a capitalist spy. Perhaps the Red Cross took pity on him and booked him passage back to the states. Perhaps he froze to death one night on a Vladivostok street. His life was not even obscure. It is forgotten, once mentioned in passing by Richard Halliburton.

The story of American troops on Russian soil is not well known. To bolster White Russian troops fighting Bolsheviks, Wilson's AEF Siberia was sent there, comprised mainly of the 27th and 31st Infantry Regiments, with volunteers from the 12th, 13th, and 62nd Regiments. On December 31, 1917 American navy cruisers dropped anchor next British and Japanese ships in Golden Horn Bay at Vladivostok. He sent troops to Siberia chiefly because along the Trans-Siberian Railroad the United States had a billion dollars worth of guns, three hundred locomotives and over ten thousand railway cars that had been given to the Kerensky government. It would not be good if they fell into Bolshevik hands.

There was also Wilson's concern for the Czech Legion, formed largely of émigrés to Czarist territory, settling in Ukraine and loyal to the Czar. They fought on the side of Britain, France, and the USA. They fought well but fell victim to the November Revolution. Gaining governmental control, the Bolsheviks pulled out of World War I, leaving the Legion with no support, no supplies, no reinforcements. The Legion fought on, this time with the Whites and against the Red Army.[*]

Vladivostok had a YMCA and its director invited Richard to stay with him and his wife. Richard was ready for a rest and gladly accepted but was

---

[*] The Entente promised them and their countrymen a homeland if they fought the good fight. Their homeland became Czechoslovakia. During the war some troops of the Legion wound up in Siberia, many in Vladivostok, and the soldiers had to travel through then hostile Bolshevik territory to reach Europe. To help a safe journey to their new homeland, created in 1918, President Woodrow Wilson and Allies landed troops in Northern Siberia, the only time in official history that American troops fought the Soviet army. After the fall of Soviet communism, a monument to the Legion was erected in Vladivostok. The last Legionnaire died in 2001, fifty-three years after Czechoslovakia fell under the boots and tanks of the Soviet Union.

awakened about two in the morning by the tramp of marching boots in the court below his window. He rushed with his host to their second story window to look down on eight soldiers and two officials about to enter the building. His heart sank; his hands shook. His wild dreams had all been a terrible mistake. He recalled the warnings of the American consulates at Peking and Harbin. He remembered that they could offer no help to rescue him from a Siberian prison or from a firing squad. Maybe he would disappear forever into the archipelago of prisons.

The boots stomped up the stairs, reaching his landing. The door was rapped loudly, demandingly. He knew they were about to arrest him as a spy. He heard the Y director talking in Russian to the officials. What could the man say to rescue him? Nothing.

Then they left. They had the wrong apartment. They went up to the third floor. A few minutes later, they dragged a Russian down the stairs, frog-marching him away to be interrogated, beaten, and deported to some freezing cell.

Richard had seen the reality of Bolshevism when he first got off the train. At the Vladivostok station he looked across to the next track with boxcars packed with starving and frightened men and women. Stripped of their dignity, they had become enemies of the people. Highly educated or aristocrats, they were now cattle awaiting shipment to an outpost. Thousands of miles of arctic wind blasting through cracks in the boxcars would greet them each day and night. The trip would take four weeks for the few who survived it.

Unlike Harbin, in December he met no White Russians who invited him into their Vladivostok homes. They were gone, either escaped to Shanghai or drowned at sea. He would have had a story to tell had he been there in October to see the frantic scurry of families as they packed up for Admiral Stark's ships with the advancing Reds almost on the city doorstep. Vladivostok held out against the Reds longer than any other Russian city but its turn eventually came to fall.

THE GRAND PATRIOTIC MEETING IN VLADIVOSTOK

Richard stayed in Vladivostok through New Year's 1923 and wrote home that he went to a Bolshevik mass meeting. He saw red flags hanging everywhere in town, walls plastered with posters advertising the event. On New Year's Eve he had an early supper, then braved a growing blizzard to get an early seat for the mass-meeting. He looked around to see the proletariat everywhere, laborers, dockworkers, mechanics, their wives and children. The walls were festooned with crimson bunting with a yellow hammer and sickle. He looked at the ornate balcony, built to seat fine ladies and gentlemen. He noted the chandeliers, once designed for elegant balls with women in gowns, men in tuxedos, dancing to a waltz. From them, large red flags were festooned and underneath them a rag-tag bunch awaited the program.

At ten that evening the program began. He heard one Bolshevik song after another. He watched movies of the Red army entering Vladivostok. He heard patriotic speeches pledging allegiance to the great worker's republic. The audience clapped, shouted, and cheered. They tilted vodka to their lips and the more they drank the more patriotic they became. Outside, the temperature had sunk below zero. At eleven, the commanding general of the local Red army spoke. He rose from his seat among the workers and strode boldly to the podium. He was young, with a dominating glance. He carried himself with great dignity. He dared the enemies of the people, the capitalists and other warmongers, to try to subjugate the people again. He went on like this while couples drank from bottles until just before midnight when he motioned toward a great brass band, which struck up the Internationale as the clock tolled twelve.

The Internationale unites the human race.
So comrades, come rally

And the last fight let us face
The Internationale unites the human race.

Richard left. Outside, the wind froze his eyelashes, the snow pelted his cheeks. His head down, he pushed against the gale, struggling back to the YMCA director's apartment, where he fell into slumber. Back when he was a boy he felt the warm breeze blowing off the Mississippi and went to bed at night dreaming about a bright, gentle world in his future.

LENIN'S WIDOW BEFORE RICHARD MET HER

Over sixty, Lenin's widow wore "a very simple check dress." She had "big overhanging eyelids and her lips were slightly twisted. She was a kind, courteous woman with sympathetic smile. She made an impression that she had worked hard throughout her life—unselfishly hard. She had sacrificed herself for the greater good of others."
    "Lenin's Widow Talks to a Welshman," by Gareth Jones,
    The Western Mail, November 7, 1932

Now in the Hoover Institution archives, Palo Alto, California, a 1923 secret memo says Lenin's wife begged Stalin to poison her husband to put him out of his misery. The memo was written by Stalin to the Politburo but Lenin's widow said no such thing and the memo strongly implicates Stalin as Lenin's poisoner using cyanide. Stalin pretended to be sympathetic and concerned, claiming Lenin and his wife begged him for poison but sympathy was unknown to him. *Stalin* means man of steel, a name he adopted. In the memo he tells the Politburo he was indecisive about their request and did not have the strength to carry it out.

Stalin had his own reason to carry it out. This is the man Lenin called the most brutal member of the Communist Party. On December 25, 1922 Lenin recommended removing Stalin as General Secretary of the Central Committee. He observed that Stalin was more than brutal. The man was accumulating too much power, which would prove highly dangerous in such an individual. Evidence points to Stalin as a psychopath. He ordered the Ukraine genocide by famine with twenty-five thousand people dying daily and three million children starved to death. Ukrainian farmers did not want to collectivize so he locked up their granaries. Afraid of being shot for trying to find food, parents sent children out into fields to forage grass and berries.

Apart from fear of Stalin, there was also a personal matter. That same month, Stalin had shouted obscenities—including "syphilitic whore"—at Lenin's wife, Nadezhda Krupskaya. Lenin demanded that the man of steel apologize or else all relations between them would end. They did end but not in the manner Lenin expected. Next day he died and Stalin's doctors called it a fatal stroke.[*]

To show his respect Stalin ordered that Lenin's body be preserved and put on display at the Lenin Mausoleum. Embalmed with formaldehyde, methanol, and other solvents renewed regularly, it can still be viewed next the Kremlin during visiting hours.

Dedicated to her husband's memory, Nadezhda Krupskaya wrote a book about him, fondly recalling his strong sympathies for working people, especially the down-and-out. In her *Reminiscences of Lenin*, she remembered their days as expatriates in Zurich, Switzerland where they took meals at a boarding house. "We ate there for about two months," she wrote. "The food was plain but sufficient. Ilyich liked the simplicity of everything there—the fact that coffee was served in a cup with a broken handle, that we ate in the kitchen, that the talk was simple, talk not about the food, not about how many potatoes had to be used for this or that soup, but about matters that were of interest to the boarders." The few boarders kept changing and soon they realized that they had landed in the lower depths of Zurich. One of the diners was a prostitute. She did not hide her profession and was concerned about her mother's health. She wanted her sister to find better work than she had.

With her conscience, Nadezhda Krupskaya was one person. Stalin's minions were many. After the fall of the Soviet Union, government archives were declassified, allowing historians to examine them. Their discoveries made facts out of whispers heard by every Soviet citizen during that era, whispers that another husband was missing from wife and children, another mother from husband and family, another child from parents. Some historians estimate deaths between 1937 and 1938 at between nine hundred fifty thousand and 1.2 million. At Butovo Shooting Range near Moscow over twenty thousand people were shot and buried from August 1937 through October 1938.

Such was the USSR that Richard visited, one largely hidden to him, just as it was when, an older man, he visited it again in his thirties, but this time he had barbed comments.

---

[*] With Lenin out of the way, the brilliant and charismatic Trotsky was left and of course Stalin saw to that with the 1929 Moscow Show Trials, in which Leon Trotsky was exiled and far from Russia in Mexico City he stated that Stalin poisoned Lenin. Lenin took care of that annoyance when he had Ramón Mercader plant an axe in Trotsky's head.

RICHARD MEETS LENIN'S WIDOW

In St Petersburg, then called Leningrad, Richard arranged an interview with her and in his 1935 book, *Seven League Boots,* he is no longer a raw youth as he describes his first impression: "When I entered her office (she is commissar of education), I saw a strange figure waiting to greet me. I say strange because the figure offered such a sharp contrast to the very young and very alert girl-secretaries outside. She sat, leaning on her desk, as if extremely tired, a black shawl held close about her shoulders and snow-white hair falling in careless wisps about her strong but kindly face. Her weary lids were half closed." Here was a woman who had fought all her long life for what seemed to be, for most of it, a hopeless dream. "She had been worn out by the murders of so many and by the cynics in charge of progress."

By the time Halliburton met her, Madame Lenin's body was slowing. She suffered from an illness, Grave's Disease, which affected the thyroid gland, causing her neck to bulge as well as her eyes. In females the menstrual cycle can also be disrupted. Perhaps this is why she and Lenin never had children. Her appearance caused her to be code-named "Fish." It had probably been assigned by Stalin.

In his interview, Richard found that Nadezhda Krupskaya had one main interest, which was helping women. She was an early feminist and wanted to see women educated and emancipated. Richard tells us that this did happen. In ironic comments, Halliburton states that Russian women leapt "overnight" to "absolute equality with men in every respect. Women became economic, political, and legal equals." The Russian "Mrs." or "Miss" had given way to "comrade" and "citizen." From gender difference to unisex.

Richard saw no men in Comrade Lenin's Department of Education. Looking out the window of her office, he observed a new building under construction with brick masons working on it. They were women. Streetcars carried passengers from home to work. The operators were women. Out on the Neva River, women captained barges and boats plying the current. They were majors in the air corps, generals in the army, an Ambassador to Sweden, a Secretary of the Treasury. And women mixed concrete, riveted girders, hammered nails.

That was the true Soviet proletariat. The arts—music, poetry, painting, operas, and ballets—were engaged in principally by men. As Richard put it, "women are too busy mixing concrete and riveting girders." His irony might have been missed by NKVD agents but it was not lost on the simplest of his American public.

He listened to Madame Lenin describe how "the mother works all day in the new subway shoveling government gravel" while the father works "all night making government shoes." They passed one another in the hall climbing up or down from their "one room allotted by the government."

"Perhaps," Halliburton mused, "Russian women are happier, now that they have all the privileges of men, and none of the privileges of women." While he clearly liked her and was sympathetic toward Nadezhda Krupskaya and her commitment, he saw what she could not.

This voice in *Seven League Boots* comes from a Richard Halliburton unknown in his earlier books. It is satiric, biting. It tells the reader about grim realities, about the very un-romantic lives of millions with no hope for grand adventures, who lived in humble obedience to the state. This is the truth he wanted to tell readers who only bought his books for the fluff. The change in voice signals a change in person. While he still lived with uneven tenor, the youth who looked for beauty and innocence became the man who no longer beheld life as a golden apple waiting to be bitten.

The book was reviewed by a James Gray writing for the *Dispatch* of St Paul, Minnesota, with this headline: "Halliburton Shows Signs of Shedding Spectacular Style." The headline adds, "Latest Book Has Less of the Personal than Predecessors."

Gray explained, "Perhaps his advisers have indicated to him that it is time for a man of 35 to begin acting his age. At any rate, he makes his first sincere effort at straight-forward reporting."

The reviewer adds that many chapters "have written color sketches that are superior in every way to the superficial sketches Halliburton has made. But no doubt his easy, skimming way of suggesting a great familiarity with foreign scenes will still please his enormous audience."

Gray is right about the change in Halliburton. In some passages in *Seven League Boots* Richard writes with explicit social comment, as in this one: "All refined, cultivated classes, all money classes" were "killed or exiled. Only peasants and factory workers remained with their hands on control levers of hydroelectric dams, on steel plows of collective farms, and on thick cables of iron foundry forges. They were the Proletariat that would eventually take over the world, with help from the elite—Soviet leaders and

Soviet intelligentsia of course."

Richard listened to Lenin's widow extol the advances made in Russian education. He offered no transcript of the interview but we can imagine the topics she covered. In factories, workers studied. They worked days and went to evening class in the same place. Going to the country, they spread their enthusiasm, where in villages they taught peasants to read and write. Illiteracy was waning. Libraries were on the increase. The workers would no longer be suppressed by the educated elite. They, too, would progress, albeit without the decadence of avant-garde literature, effete futuristic music, and modern art.

Instead, machines. The future depended on these things. Marxist dialectical materialism demanded them. Matter, not spirit. It was the foundation of society. Schools would be attached to factories. Students must visit these, the means of production so often mentioned by Marx. Workers learned they owned the means of production, not any capitalists. From each according to his ability, to each according to his needs, as Marx put it.

Madame Lenin would have families and workers living together in communal houses, with one floor dedicated to day care for the children. Trained psychologists would watch over them. Evenings, of course, could be spent with their parents. Aldous Huxley wrote about similar things in his dystopian *Brave New World*.

In the end of his account, Richard called Nadezhda Krupskaya "the most winning old lady I had met in many a day." She had true sympathy for the workers, and for women. She believed in a future for them that she would not live to see. She had to believe in it as a future beyond Stalin, for government led by his ilk would be grim.

Lenin's widow survived Stalin until February 26, 1939. That evening she invited her friends to attend her seventieth birthday party. Stalin did not attend but sent a cake. Later that evening she was stricken with severe food poisoning and died the following morning. She was hospitalized and operated on by Kremlin doctors who assured her death. The grieving Stalin carried her ashes at the funeral.

Nadezhda Krupskaya

RICHARD FINALLY MARRIES

In Leningrad, a "charming and intelligent English-speaking Russian girl" accompanied him to the Marinsky Theater to see a ballet, *The Hunchbacked Horse*, by Cesare Pugni. The interior did not fit with Soviet progressive modernism. Chandeliers hung from the ceiling and balcony tiers with exquisite yellow damask silk covering the walls and the orchestra chairs. The theater fell into darkness as lights dimmed, the curtains parted, and the stage lit up. Watching the dancers pivot and pirouette on stage, Richard imagined the audience in Czarist times, polite society in their "richest jewels, whitest gloves, their most lavish gowns and uniforms." Here the Czar and Czarina with their son and daughters had come frequently to sit in the Imperial box and applaud the lavish spectacles. In the Marinsky that evening "not one woman wore anything but the plainest, cheapest, sack-like dress." Near Richard, two women, after working all day in a factory, took off their shoes. As for the ballet, it was "superlatively good." He observed, "Here is one Czarist art the Proletarians have not let die," though he would have "enjoyed it more had the audience not eaten apples all during the performance."

Richard's comely companion belonged to the Communist party and outside the theater they chatted. He said to her that the Marinsky Theater must have provided stunning sights. There, Anna Pavlova had danced *The Dying Swan*. There, Vaslav Nijinsky had leapt across the stage in *Giselle*. There, Feodor Chaliapin sang with his powerful bass in *Boris Gudonov*. The girl belonged to the New Russia, the Russia of the future, and against the decadent past. She had never heard of Pavlova, or of Nijinsky, though Chaliapin, well, yes, the name was familiar. She vaguely recognized it as his name had not been expunged from history because, hedging his bets, he did not denounce communism.

Marriage had come to be seen as a bourgeois institution in its formalities. A Soviet woman could keep her mate or divorce him. Divorce was Reno-style, even easier.

The escort and Richard visited a marriage and divorce bureau. That would make a good narrative for his book. Richard described the sixty-second marriages. The couple stood before an officious female clerk with a registration book. She asked them if they were in good health. Yes, why not? She looked at their IDs, took down their ages and names. The woman could elect to take her husband's name or keep her own. They paid one ruble, signed the register, and the next couple in line took their place at the table.

Richard thought about it and asked his interpreter if she would marry him. He looked at her; she looked at him, and hand-in-hand they stood in line. If the Soviets kept such records this would have been the shortest courtship ever entered in a ledger. Halliburton already told his readers she was pretty and that she spoke English; we do not know her perspective but she agreed to tie the knot. With his instant fiancée, he shuffled behind couples shuffling toward the clerk shuffling papers.

They gave their names. They signed the register. He paid the ruble. Done deal.

They walked into the next room to divorce. With his lady interpreter he waited in line. Halliburton described the routine. After a long line and a long wait, the comrade stood before the clerk and said he or she wanted a divorce. The comrade clerk asked if there were any children. No. Okay. The clerk pulled out a post card and wrote on it. If the woman's name was Ivana, it read, "Dear Ivana: You and your husband are divorced. Regards, the Government."

If yes, the courts did not simply favor mothers in divorce cases. Maternity was one thing but Marxist-Leninist ideology another. They awarded the child to "the parent most able and likely to raise it according to Proletarian standards." Translated this meant that a spouse could charge the other with being a bad Communist in order to win the child. Being a good parent was being a good Communist.

Bastardy allegedly carried no stigma as the Soviet was supposed to turn a blind eye to unwed mothers. They were on the same footing as married mothers. A frolic in a rented bed, saying good-bye next day, and birth labor nine months later were all another sign of comradely equality.

At their turn his guide demanded of the clerk that she wanted a divorce from her husband. She was asked if she had any children. No. They signed the register. Done deal.

Richard complained to the clerk that he wanted a postcard so next day he received one in the mail at his hotel. It told him he was divorced. He had a souvenir from Moscow.

The scene is almost Marx brothers with Groucho turning to wink at the audience.

At the bureau, he noticed the many couples waiting to be wed. He looked at the women clerks behind the tables. He glanced in the direction the couples would be looking, a wall behind the clerks. He read it.

On the wall was a huge poster rendered in Soviet graphic realism, letters in vivid red, highlighted by sunny yellow, against a sick, black background. The poster asked,

ARE YOU DISEASED?

A CELLAR IN YEKATERINBURG

Richard Halliburton was the first in the free world to report the truth of how the Czar and his family were assassinated. For years, many did not believe Halliburton's account but he in fact did have an audience with one of the assassins.

On July 17, 1918, the day promised to be sunny, the sky blue. That morning, birds chirped in the trees of Yekaterinburg on the east side of the Ural Mountains and on the verge of the vast Russian steppes extending into central Asia. Surrounded by taiga (boreal forests), and small lakes, Yekaterinburg was a pleasant town where lovers could walk arm in arm under the broad sky or in winter cuddle cozy and warm by a fire. They could stroll past a large house, manorial in size, owned by a well-off engineer named N.N. Ipatiev and recently seized by the Bolsheviks. On that July day they could not imagine the future significance of the house as a place where something terrible happened or that the Politburo would order Boris Yeltsin to demolish it in 1977. They could not foresee that the Church on the Blood of the Fallen Family would one day stand on its grounds. All that would occur years later, after the fall of the Soviet Union.

Very early that morning it happened. Inside the house Czar Nicholas II and his family were awakened at about one in the morning, long before the sky turned blue, before the birds chirped. The Romanov's would not see the sky nor hear the birds.

The Czar, Czarina, their family and servants, were awakened and ordered downstairs to the cellar and told that unrest in Yekaterinburg made living on the top floor dangerous. They would be moved to a safer place. The family understood that the Czech Legion, an element of the White Army, was nearing the city. As for safety, by this time they knew better.

Czar Nicholas II carried his son, Alexei, age fourteen, in his arms. The boy was a hemophiliac, a bleeder who had been ill for most of his imprisonment. The Czar and the boy were dressed in soldier's tunics, gymnastiorkas, and wore soldier caps. The boy's mother, Czarina Alexandra, followed them. Born a German princess in Hesse, she had on the same blue dress she had worn for weeks.

Next came the girls, Olga, Tatiana, Marie, and Anastasia. Their retainers followed: Dr Botkin, the family physician; Anna Demidova, a tall, blonde maid; Alois Trupp, the manservant; Ivan Kharitonov, the cook.

The Czarina pointed out that there were no chairs, so two were fetched from upstairs, one for Alexandra. The Czar put his son in the other, and then stood so to shield him. The Czar's daughters held two small pillows, and placed one on their mother's chair, the other on their brother's.

Behind Czarina Alexandra stood three daughters, the girls ranging from nineteen to twenty-three. The fourth daughter, Grand Duchess Anastasia, held the family dog, Jemmy. Age seventeen, she stood by the tall maid, who clutched two pillows in front of her. Behind Alexei, the boy, stood Doctor Botkin. The cook and the servant stood against the wall to the left of the cellar entrance.

The Romanov's waited with the Bolsheviks and then the door opened as other men walked in. The family's eyes fixed on the new men standing in front of them.

One of them was Pyotr Zacharovitch Ermakov, Commissar of the Verkh-Isetsk iron works, with a Mauser pistol. Russian archives hold a photograph taken later of Ermakov. It depicts him in knee-length jackboots, Jodhpur pants, and a tunic with a broad belt. On his head sits a garrison cap. He is a sturdy, fit young man with high, Eastern European cheekbones. He stands in a clearing called Pigs Meadow. A forest rises behind him. Beneath his feet is an unusual hump in a dirt road, higher than the level surface on either side. On the back of the photograph, he wrote, "I am standing on the grave of the Czar."

Next Ermakov in the cellar was a sailor named Vaganov, also holding a Mauser. Both were friends of the leader, Yakov Yurovsky, and had been included to help dispose of the bodies. The men could see a window behind the family and through it the night outside. Above the night, the stars glimmered light years away.

The family knew the men with guns would come eventually. They just didn't know when. They had been waiting a long time for it to happen. The Czech Legion might have rescued them had its soldiers known of the Romanov's' exact whereabouts but instead the Legion sealed their fate, for it was battling closer to Yekaterinburg. The local Reds must execute them before the Czech Legion and White Russians took Yekaterinburg. The Legion was loyal to the Czar, who had commissioned it. The locals were only too happy to carry out orders from higher-ups in Moscow. It would have been bad business for the guards and commandant if the Legion and the Whites discovered them imprisoning the Czar and family.

The Imperial family was evidence that had to be taken care of before the enemy captured the town. The girls did not weep, nor did their mother. They remained still. They stood resigned. The pale, weak Czarevitch sat on his chair, his fourteen years mustering all the dignity they could. His father stood waiting, knowing nothing could be done. Nobody asked for mercy.

They faced five Bolsheviks and seven soldiers, Hungarian prisoners of war—unable to speak Russian—chosen because the local Cheka, or security forces, feared Russian soldiers would not shoot the monarch's family. The Hungarians looked at the girls, so young, so pretty, about their own ages. They looked away and didn't think. They nervously waited, some with Nagant revolvers, others with Mauser automatic pistols.

It was all over now. A few months before, the monarch and his family still felt something. Now they just wanted it finished. In April 1918, when the Czar and Czarina arrived at the Ipatiev house, they had been thoroughly searched. One of the men rudely jerked the Czarina's grey suede handbag out of her hands. Czar Nicholas' blood rose and he demanded of the commandant that the impertinence stop. They were at least owed common courtesy. The commandant swaggered, shouted, and pointed his finger at his own chest. The people were the masters now. They could do as they pleased. Inside the Czarina's handbag they found only a handkerchief, smelling salts, and heart pills.

A series of swaggering commandants followed, including a drunken watchman and a former factory worker, whose men followed the women to the lavatories. That was just the beginning of the family's descent. They might have kept hoping, waiting—until they were ordered into the cellar. Once down there they knew. It would be either there or they would be taken to the forest.

Yakov Yurovsky's job was to herd the family and their retainers into the cellar. "I prepared twelve revolvers and designated who would shoot whom," he later recalled. Because of the short distance in the cellar, side arms would be used rather than rifles.

Yurovsky leveled the barrel of his Nagant at the family. At forty years old, tall and sturdy, he was a quiet man who kept his own counsel. He had dark hair and wore pince-nez spectacles over brown eyes. He lived in Yekaterinburg with his wife, three children, and mother. His sister was Mistress of Novices at the city's Novotikhvinsky Convent.

In 1891, when Yurovsky was a boy in Tomsk, he stood among the crowd welcoming to their city the future Nicholas II, a boy himself. He heard church bells pealing welcome; he saw miniature Russian flags waving at the royal procession. Thirteen years old, he stood in the doorway of the watch repair shop where he worked and watched the Czarevitch pass him in a brightly painted troika. Years later, he remembered how handsome Nicholas was with his neatly trimmed brown beard. He cheered as Nicholas nodded and waved at the crowd.

In the cellar on that 1918 night, he stood looking at the family, at the Bolsheviks, at the soldiers, and waited to give the command. Three days before the execution, he said to a priest, "It is important that one must pray, and one must save one's soul." Before the shooting, he told the other men that the Czar and Czarevitch were his to kill. Shortly after the massacre, a guard found him upstairs on a sofa, a cold compress on his head.

Following instructions, the driver of a Fiat army truck had pulled up in front of the cellar door. Everybody inside could hear it. On hearing it, the Czar stood and his son reached for his cap. The manservant stooped to pick up the Czarevitch's pillow to take with them. They waited for the order to exit but it didn't come. The truck driver raced his engine and the Fiat's exhaust rose to a great din, drowning out the rustling of tree branches, the hooting of owls, hiding the gunshots inside.

Nicholas was shot first and fell in silence. His son sat petrified in the chair. Yurovksy walked up to his chair and put a bullet in the boy's head. Grand Duchess Olga, Dr Botkin, and two servants died at once. Drunk, Ermakov killed Czarina Alexandra with a pistol shot to her left temple. He did this before she could finish making the sign of the cross. He repeatedly stabbed her body and the Czar's, breaking their ribs.

The assassins had not counted on the cellar's brick walls. As soon as the firing began, bullets ricocheted. A bullet hummed past Yurovsky's head and grazed the hand of another assailant. Smoke filled the cellar until it was hard to see. The women were screaming.

Anastasia, Tatiana, and Maria did not die easily despite bullet after bullet fired into them. Bullets bounced off them because they had sewn jewels into their corsets so they could hide them as the Bolsheviks moved the girls from place to place. Anastasia huddled herself against the wall, arms over her head. Anna, the maid, had hidden jewels inside two pillows she carried in front of her. That did not save her. She was stabbed in the throat.

Outside, the truck engine roared. Off in the taiga, wind sighed through branches. Far above, stars shone in the dark sky. It didn't last long. Soon there was only silence in the smoke-filled cellar. The driver cut the motor to an idle.

HALLIBURTON INTERVIEWS ROMANOV ASSASSIN ERMAKOV

In November 1934 Richard Halliburton wrote home that in a few days he would be traveling to Sverdlovsk, formerly Yekaterinburg. The city was renamed to honor Sverdlov, the man who ordered the executions. The house still stood where the Romanov's were murdered and Halliburton had a chance to interview an assassin, Pyotr Ermakov, an interview he provides in *Seven League Boots*. Why Richard was allowed to learn about the assassination remains a mystery lost somewhere in Soviet archives. We can be sure it was arranged by higher-ups, somebody in the nomenclatura of the politburo, and that permission was granted by Stalin, for nobody dared anything so boldly revealing without his approval. Pyotr Ermakov was instructed to tell all and he did. The facts Richard heard stand today—the general location of body disposal, the use of gasoline and acid, the truck bogging down, the jewels on the women, as well as sundry other data.

Halliburton wrote home, "The man who murdered the Czar and all his family, the actual assassin, who was jailor, executioner, undertaker, cremator, has kept silent for seventeen years. I got him on his sick bed, and heard his story poured out." He adds, "He's never spoken to any other person" and "It was *history* he told me."

The original privilege of the interview was not Richard's. Instead, a correspondent for the *Chicago Daily News*, William Stoneman, had learned about it while in Moscow. Maybe Stoneman thought the whole thing a hoax and put Richard on to the story for that reason. Probably so, for a first-hand account of the Imperial Family's assassination would have been a scoop worldwide. Living amidst Communist lies and propaganda, perhaps Stoneman doubted anything so candid. The Soviets were never so generous as when they were devious. Because of his suspicions, he passed the tip along to Richard who was visiting Moscow. Stoneman flubbed his chance, though he had a long and illustrious career. In 1942 he was evacuated from Dunkirk along with British troops. He died in 1987 in a Paris suburb, age eighty-three, having retired there in 1969.

Accompanied by a Soviet interpreter, Richard took the thousand-mile trip by train from Moscow to Sverdlovsk, today returned to its name as Yekaterinburg, and where in 1960 CIA pilot Frances Gary Powers was shot down flying over the city in his U-2 spy plane.

Richard and his interpreter found Ermakov's apartment, built by the Soviets for the proletariat. The interpreter was assigned him by a bureaucrat, perhaps by somebody who did not like the man, for accompanying Richard to reveal deep government secrets could not have been a choice assignment in a paranoid state. The Sverdlovsk apartment was a typical worker's dwelling. Its quarters were tiny, with a hall and two small rooms, almost bare of furnishings.

Knocks on the apartment door brought Ermakov's wife to it. She opened it and reluctantly let them in. Here was an American sent to talk to her husband, who had helped murder the Romanov's. No good could come of it. She had seen too many of her friends and family taken away for trumped-up crimes against the state and feared being charged as an accessory to something or other. She was uncooperative and did not want to let them into her husband's bedroom. Halliburton looked around the dingy, cramped apartment, and heard the man shout to his wife to allow the strangers into his bedroom. Ermakov had his orders and he had to carry them out. Richard had been told Ermakov was dying and wanted to make a deathbed confession. He beheld the man languishing in bed, coughing, and Richard tells readers the man presented a miserable sight.

On seeing the man, Richard was convinced Ermakov did not have much longer to live. In fact, he lived another sixteen years after the interview. Certainly, he would not have defied the Soviet to cleanse his soul. It simply was not done. The Gulag system of prisons awaited those who exercised their conscience and in it they would die faceless and forgotten. He was told to feign his deathbed and that was what he did.

In those days of Soviet machinations an excuse was needed for telling the truth. Still, among people in Yekaterinburg the truth was common knowledge as Ermakov told the story to anyone willing to listen. Among other venues, the man liked to talk before boys gathered around Youth Pioneer summer campfires, which was where Alexander Avdonin—who discovered the graves in 1979—heard it.[*] Ermakov described the assassination to the boys and explained that he was charged with disposing

---

[*] Many years later Avdonin dug in the area described by Ermakov as the burial ground of the Royal family. "I was praying to God that nothing would be there," Avdonin recalled, "but of course there was."

of the bodies.

Richard listened at the bedside through the interpreter. He described the interpreter, who "looked sick and pale" and "was repeating rapidly in low, flat whispers every word of Ermakov's labored phrases. I myself was wondering how much more of these cold-blooded horrors I could stand. There was no promise of respite."

The interpreter was probably less concerned about gruesome details than that he would be liquidated by the whimsy of a bureaucrat in the NKVD for having heard them.

Ermakov said that thirty-eight pistol shots were needed to kill eleven people because the women had hidden jewels close to their bodies. He said that after the assassination about a dozen men were detailed to clean up the cellar with its blood everywhere, on slippers, pillows, handbags "swimming around in a red lake." The bodies were wrapped in blankets and piled onto the truck. At about two in the morning he and the sailor Vaganov drove it to some abandoned mines at a spot known as the Four Brothers, in the Koptyaki forest, a few miles from town.

They had not planned on a nigh impassable trail to the mines, only eleven miles away. The truck bogged down again and again so that they arrived as dawn broke. They would be visible to anybody hiking in the woods. So much for that, then. They returned with the truck the following night. The White Russians must not know of the disposal site

In the dark, they dumped the bodies off the truck, piling them beside firewood and tins of gasoline, as well as sulphuric acid. They didn't burn them yet. Ermakov left Vaganov and a squad of soldiers to protect the site. He drove back into town to see Yurovksy. They had to get rid of the evidence at the Ipatiev house. It had to be done quickly. The Whites and the Czech Legion were closing-in on Yekaterinburg.

Ermakov returned that evening to the mines. By lamplight they stripped clothes from the corpses. They then discovered the reason for their bullets' impotence. Into the clothing of each Czarina, diamonds, necklaces, gold crosses, and other jewels had been sewn. The men tossed the clothes on a heap of pine straw soaked with gasoline. Ermakov flung a match onto the pile. He sent jewelry, icons, diaries, and letters to Moscow.

They poured five tins of gasoline over the corpses as well as "two buckets of sulphuric acid." Ermakov had to insure that "not one fingernail or fragment of bone could be discovered by the Whites." He turned body pieces over in the flames. They took what ashes they had and shoveled them into the now empty tins of gasoline and acid then loaded the ashes onto the truck. The driver carried the ashes to a road where he stopped. Ermakov dug his shovel into the ashes and pitched them into the air. With each toss, wind caught the Romanov remains and lofted the ashes into the sky above woods and fields, where they slowly fell, spreading over the Russian earth.

Ermakov did not explain to Richard that they had to bury some remains because all could not be burned quickly, and he did not disclose the burial location. The bones became ashes too slowly and White Russian regiments surrounded Yekaterinburg. Dawn approached with the Whites even closer. So, they buried what had not burned. That was the night of the 17th. Word spread fast about the burial, with rumors about the location. The enemy must not know the location so on the 19th they returned to the Four Brothers to retrieve them for burial elsewhere. At the new spot the bones remained undiscovered for decades.

The spot had not been planned. The truck became mired in mud at Pig's Meadow and finally free of it the men asked a railway guard for railway ties to make a bridge across the mud. This ersatz bridge turned out to be the burial site. Before placing the ties they dug a pit six feet deep and eight feet square, dumping the bodies into it, then filling it with dirt. Over the dirt they placed the ties for their bridge. Thus the bones lay until 1979 when Avdonin found them. He covered them back up to wait, as he put it, until circumstances in his country had changed. After the Soviet Union's collapse, in 1991 he disinterred them and they were given a Russian Orthodox funeral and properly buried by the state.

Shortly after the assassinations, the Red Guards were ordered to evacuate Yekaterinburg. The Czech Legion and the Whites had them outnumbered. On the 18th of July in 1918 the Legion and the Whites learned that the Czar had been assassinated and they fought furiously toward the town. They seized the railroad into it so to thwart escaping Reds. To break through the White ranks, Ermakov and his men had to climb onto horses and dash headlong in a cavalry charge through soldiers blocking the road. Next day, Czarist troops entered the town and made straightaway for the Ipatiev house. They saw the bullet holes and asked questions.

They soon learned about the abandoned mines and the burnt corpses because rumors had spread throughout Yekaterinburg. Somebody whispered into a neighbor's ear; the neighbor stopped to chat with a friend, and shortly it was an open secret.

Ermakov told Richard about the White investigation but did not mention the principal investigator of the murders, Nikolai Sokolov, thirty-seven years old at the time. Sokolov began a disciplined and thorough investigation. He questioned witnesses, some of them captured Red Guards assigned to the Ipatiev house. He inspected the cellar wall-by-wall, room-by-room, door-by-door. He went to the abandoned pit mines in the forest, even discovering where the truck had stalled during the night of the 19th.

Sokolov's investigation was exhaustive but he failed to uncover a Bolshevik lie, that the eleven bodies were completely burned in two days and two nights. It was also a lie told by Ermakov to Halliburton.[*]

In fact, later tests simulated the burning and proved it impossible to destroy fully so many bodies in so short a time. Sokolov's error was not to look under the railroad ties.

Nikolai Sokolov did not live out his life in Russia. In 1920, the White army defeated, he fled ahead of the Red Guards, finding asylum in France. Penniless and sick, he wrote for history his account of the investigation, published in French, its title translated as *Judicial Inquest into the Assassination of the Russian Imperial Family*. He concluded that the Imperial Family had been murdered in the Ipatiev house and their bodies entirely destroyed. He died in 1924, leaving a twenty-three year old widow and two small children.

Back home in the United States, Richard read the critics of his day who thought he made up the story, just as the Hellespont "drowning" had been part of his attempt to stir publicity. There was also lingering opinion based on his early writing style. They confused his enthusiastic prose and his tendency to "paint the rose," as his father put it, with falsehood. About facts, Richard did not lie. Because of his undeserved reputation, though, little attention was given to the revelation.

If the Soviets had been waiting for the news to hit the West like a blockbuster, they were disappointed.

After the interview with the assassin, Halliburton and his interpreter went to the Ipatiev house, which Richard called the Yekaterinburg "prison house museum where the Imperial Family had died." They were shown through the house by a guide. Richard found that it was not a museum for the family but for the glorious revolution, with "posters and diagrams on the wall, announcing the glories of Communism, and showing how many more tractors and ingots of steel were made under Bolshevism than under Czarism, and how many more airplanes and suits of underwear . . . as if, in this house, anybody cared."

Hearing the house guide extol the superiority of communism, Richard soon grew weary and asked to see the Czar and Czarina's room, where Yurovsky had Dr Botkin bring the message for the royal family to assemble below. The guide didn't know about any of this, had never been told. His job was not to memorize the last petty details of the murdered family but to extol a future without them.

---

[*] Until recently, two of the Romanov's had not been found—Prince Alexei, the Czar's heir, and his sister, Princess Maria. In 2007 Sergei Plotinov stumbled on a hollow covered with nettles. He dug and hit something hard. Forensic evidence revealed that the two children met the same fate as the rest of their family. Their bones had been covered with acid and burned.

Having listened to Ermakov, Richard didn't need the Ipatiev house guide and could find his way about, with his interpreter following. He descended into the cellar. Down there, he imagined them on that 1918 night. The Czar and Czarina here with the Czarevitch. The duchesses over there. The physician at that spot. The maid at this one. He saw the smoke, heard the gun reports, the roaring truck engine outside under the dark, silent night. He recalled Ermakov's statement, "thirty eight pistol shots to kill eleven people." He looked at a display case on the museum wall. His interpreter translated the headline of a July 19, 1918 Yekaterinburg newspaper.

EXECUTION OF NICHOLAS,
THE BLOODY CROWNED MURDERER.
SHOT WITHOUT BOURGEOIS FORMALITIES
BUT IN ACCORDANCE WITH OUR DEMOCRATIC
PRINCIPLES.

Democratic principles. He smiled.

HANGOVER HOUSE

Just to mix with people for excitement bores me painfully, and from them I shrink further and further each year. It has always been my true nature and only in recent times have I learned that in solitude lies my peace of mind. This in part explains why much of the joyous wonder has gone out of my writings. It would have gone out anyway because I am older and less astonished and amused by what I see. All these things I thought about before deciding to build a house and live in it at least from time to time.

October 1936 letter from Richard to his parents.

Hangover House at top, Laguna Beach

PAUL MOONEY

As a young man, Paul Mooney appears in a photograph as slight, not husky, but with a trim, athletically able body.[*] The photograph shows him and another youth in bathing trunks, the friend in the seat of a playground swing, Mooney standing on the seat, his right arm reaching up to hold the swing chain. An ornate Chinese dragon tattoo crawls the length of Paul's right forearm. This, in a day different than our own when it was wholly déclassé. Sailors and slum-dwellers sported tattoos but Paul's was probably cosmopolitan, influenced by the cultural diversity his anthropologist father found in Native Americans.

Paul Mooney met Richard long before the construction of Hangover House, perhaps earlier than 1930 at Pancho Barnes' mansion, although that year offers a date certain because they can be put together there and then. With the building of the house in Laguna Beach, Paul becomes tied to a distinct episode in Halliburton's life and in that period he lived in the house while editing as well as ghostwriting Richard's *Book of Marvels*. Mooney's handiwork is in some of Halliburton's other books but without acknowledgement within them. Some authors have suggested the change in Halliburton's style as almost solely due to Mooney and no doubt Paul did contribute largely to stylistic content but Richard himself had changed, thereby affecting how he wrote. As for Mooney's influence, that would not have happened if Halliburton remained the man who insisted on the effusive manner of *The Royal Road to Romance*. No doubt, too, that Mooney was the better writer, using words carefully, sparingly, and with effect. All that can be interesting in its own right but the stylistic co-mixture of Mooney and Halliburton does not provide a leitmotif for their companionship. What seem of more interest are the lives themselves.

---

[*] The photograph appears in *Horizon Chasers*, by Gerry Max.

Paul entered Richard's life not as simply another friend but as a life-companion, somebody he could talk to on quiet nights and who could listen and understand. On first meeting Mooney, Halliburton's parents probably had suspicions about the relationship and feared their hopes for grandchildren were doomed but their son had traveled the world and saw many ways to live so that by the time he met Mooney and found an affinity in Paul he also found someone with whom he could rest, although maybe before their relationship solidified both Halliburton and Mooney had occasional dalliances with others.[*]

Their life together was filled with memories they jointly owned and they could think back on the time they went for a drive in a roadster under the moonlight or when they attended a party at movie star Ramón Novarro's house but what they did and how they remembered it is lost to us. Of their life together we have some documentation but Wesley Halliburton probably saw to disposal of letters about Paul written by Richard.

We know that Mooney was born in Washington, DC on November 26, 1904. Paul was the son of James and Ione Lee (Gaut) Mooney. James Mooney was born in Richmond, Indiana in 1861, the son of Irish-Catholic immigrants James and Ellen Devlin Mooney. With a high school education, James became a well-respected and self-taught expert, living several years among the Cherokee, Kiowa, and Sioux and is well-known for two reasons.

The first is that James did not agree with his government employer, the Bureau of Ethnology, or with Washington politicians, that the tribes must shed their "savage" ways. Instead, he believed in the value and wisdom of their culture and traditions. Theirs was a way of life worth preserving and he argued against an easy explanation for the demise of the American Indian—that it was fate. Ardent Irish-nationalists, his parents had taught him about Ireland and fate. Fate be damned. The more difficult explanation lay in white man's history and power structures. Instead, the US government had obligations to Native Americans.

The second is that his monographs on the Cherokee, the Kiowa, and the Ghost dance became classics, and were derived from his having lived with the tribes, where he smoked peyote[*], and got in trouble for it from his

---

[*] Silent film star Ramón Novarro has been linked to Richard, the difference being that Paul was an enduring companion. Novarro was born José Ramón Gil Samaniego on February 6, 1899 in Durango, Mexico. Novarro was a male heartthrob in movies such as *Scaramouche* and *Ben-Hur*. His death resulted from two brothers he invited into his home when he was sixty-nine. Looking for a big cache of money, they tortured and murdered him.

[*] Peyote got James Mooney in trouble because he believed an anthropologist must experience whereof he speaks so he got high on it in religious rituals. Its use was illegal and when many of his fellow scholars read his account, they thought he had gone out of bounds. The Ethnology Bureau was publicly embarrassed and let him know. For a time his reputation suffered but he did not lose his job.

employer, colleagues, and respectable readers. He wrote in the third person historical and in flowing, succinct prose. This proved so effective that a Mooney Award is given to anthropologists with accomplished writing styles. The lucid, un-pedantic sentences of his monographs might have influenced his son, for Paul wrote well.

James and Ione had five children, two boys and three girls, with Paul as the elder boy. The parents were concerned about the development of their children and family memory has James as a loving father. James died in 1921 of congestive heart failure, age sixty. This was about the life expectancy of a male in that era and, although some writers have suggested Paul had fears for himself because of his father's early demise, sixty was a normal life span for the era. That Paul had a fear of congestive heart failure is another matter because he witnessed his father's gradual collapse into death. Ione was left to care for the entire family and not long after, 1923 or 1924, Paul began roaming the world, perhaps set adrift by his father's death. He took passage on a freighter Turkey-bound. Back stateside, he moved from New York City, where he wrote ad copy, to Paris, and then Brittany. Within the decade he wound up in California and there his fate became entwined with Richard's.

Pancho Barnes' mansion provides a likely scenario for Richard meeting Paul as Pancho's was a magnet for those who found they could fit in there, with interesting people to meet and drinks to lubricate conversation. Halliburton and Mooney became regular companions and Richard came to depend on Paul for editing skills.

Mooney's literary sensibility is evidenced by his 1927 privately published book *Seven Poems*. Of them Gerry Max says they "speak of adventure, unrequited love, triumphant love, carnal love, death and burial." With Halliburton he had adventure, probably love, and certainly death and burial but in the sea. As for his triumphs, like Richard he lived life the way he wanted it.

Richard began working on the manuscript of *The Flying Carpet* while circling the globe with his pilot, Moye Stephens, and had been sending copy to Paul for editing. From Singapore in January 1932 he wrote about Paul as an able writer and an asset to the book's style. He told his parents that Mooney "is a writer himself" and that they should "treat him entirely as my friend and guest" when he visited Memphis.

In reading Richard's letter, Wesley and Nelle must have puzzled over why Richard would tell them to treat Paul as his friend and guest. Of course they would be mannerly and of course they would treat Mooney well but when they met him they understood what lay within their son's choice of words. Paul was not what they expected.

We have no record of the parents' descriptions though, in a 1986 interview with Michael Blankenship, Moye Stephens recalled his impressions of Mooney. Stephens used Pancho Barnes to deliver his own opinion. He explained that Barnes "had a heart as big as all out-of-doors. I mean she'd take in stray puppies or anything of that nature. She had a couple of them around her house, and Paul was one of them."

Moye added, "Paul was . . . I don't know if you'd call him a hanger-on . . . there wasn't anything special about Paul Mooney. He wasn't an impressive figure in any way." When Blankenship asked why Mooney figured so importantly in Richard's life, Stephens replied, "Well, Dick was a dominant sort of person and Mooney was anything but. So maybe that was what brought them together. Of course, Mooney was undoubtedly intelligent. I mean I'm sure he helped Dick considerably in his writing."

This must have been the impression of some who met Paul but his life and his writing indicate other layers to his personality. He liked danger and adventure, as shown by his early travels and by his dogged determination to persevere in the *Sea Dragon* expedition. For Mooney, one foot followed another. In 1923 he graduated Washington DC Central High School and dropped out of Catholic University and from that time forward returned home occasionally. The Nineteenth Century words of Horace Greeley—Go West, Young Man—remained as a spur to the population. Whether he ever read Greeley or not, Paul went. For him, travel was a fit theme. It was also Richard's theme, but for Halliburton it was a way of life that extended beyond itself to a purpose in life.

Others had impressions different from Stephens'. Boyhood pals called Paul "Peck's Bad Boy"—the mischievous child of a fiction series—and remembered him as a good friend and a showman with a penchant for recklessness. According to Gerry Max, as a boy Paul jumped from the roof of his house to the neighbor's and back again. He liked fast cars and aeroplanes. His boyhood friends confirmed later descriptions of Mooney. They remembered him as a master of jibes, having a verbal instinct for the jugular. He thought sarcasm the only defense against stupidity.

Stephens indicated the two men as different but in their difference lay their compatibility.

Mooney had his aloof moments and sulked while Richard readily engaged people. Mooney was temperamental while Richard was typically even-natured. Accounts have Mooney as quiet, unassertive, and quite willing to blend into the background while Richard enjoyed good repartée and bright conversation. Mooney also did, but on his own terms. Clearly, Paul was more complicated than Richard in both intellect and personality. Against his double-vision, Richard had a kind of inveterate sunniness, which he clung to until experience talked him out of it. Paul began his adult years with a convoluted, sophisticated response to life. The tone of his life suggests his world was not comfortable, without the ease of familiar dispensations. With age he grew increasingly fond of drink and used it to forget. As for his life itself, Paul Mooney's took a course far from the spotlight that followed Richard Halliburton. He liked it that way and was quite happy to let Halliburton have all the illumination. As he grew into his thirties, Richard became world-weary and they shared a desire for quiet companionship far from the public eye.

Another difference between them was this. Paul Mooney did not have Richard's focus in life. Richard had a burning drive. For Mooney, there was just the pleasure of being where he was in a new and foreign place. Paul did not have Halliburton's commitment to a life vision, probably because he was estranged from the ambitious values Richard held.

Their backgrounds were also different. Paul's father was employed by the government, the Bureau of American Ethnology, and lived among Native Americans to carve out his own scientific career, staying with it for life despite having more than a degree of maverick in him—as evidenced by his open acknowledgement that he smoked peyote and by his contrarian attitude toward Native Americans, publicly championing them. Richard's father was a self-employed businessman with a mercantile, success-oriented view of life. Richard found the maverick inside himself on his own. To want both—to be a maverick and have business success in life—set Halliburton up for a difficult conflict.*

Mooney and Halliburton would not have become intimate companions had they only been different. They had things in common. Most obvious, they both shared a disregard for symbols associated with middle-class respectability—family, children, church—the pillar of the community sort. They both had sexual relations with their own gender, while Richard was bisexual and Paul apparently was not. Both enjoyed fun and both were sociable, each in his own way. Both also liked to escape into solitude. They

---

* Gerry Max (*Horizon Chasers*) indicates that Mooney helped ex-Nazi Kurt Ludecke, an avowed homosexual, write *I Knew Hitler*, a massive eight hundred thirty-three pages published in 1937. In that year *Time* magazine wrote about Ludecke that "Hitler" and "Nazi big shots" called him "Der Amerikaner" due to his US savvy, snappy dress and "nervy wit"—an image sold by Hollywood and bought by Europe. The review explains that Ludecke "managed the first meeting between Hitler and Mussolini, headed the first Nazi propaganda missions abroad, the Nazi press bureau in Washington." We read that "he was sent on a begging tour of the U. S., where he negotiated—unsuccessfully—with Henry Ford, the Ku Klux Klan, small fry from coast to coast. On a second trip—this time to escape the still more savage intrigues of his comrades—he hit on the idea of an 'American folkic program,' to be headed by Flyer Lindbergh, spread the good word about Hitler but got little money. In Detroit he married a plain, sensible librarian." The irony is apparent. Sensible librarian to offset his zany schemes. Eventually Hitler threw him into a concentration camp from which he escaped in 1933, coming to Manhattan. Although accounts elsewhere have Ludecke as merely a playboy and opportunist, the *Time* reviewer is favorable toward his book, saying "his story is the most amende and grimly absorbing Nazi confession that has yet appeared in English." On reading this, Paul Mooney must have smiled.

each had a sensibility for poetry, art, and the theater. They liked physical challenges and risks. Both were fond of animals.

Paul Mooney holding wooden Hangover House sign

PAUL MOONEY & HANGOVER HOUSE

Paul Mooney's wanderlust carried him to Los Angeles and the times must have suited him. Mack Sennett also found them suitable because he did not see much future in filming cowboys chasing Indians on the beaches of Long Island and instead had his Keystone Cops chasing robbers across back streets near Hollywood. In 1912 Sennett moved from New York to Los Angeles. Hollywood was new, having been found as a place where the weather was good for movie-making and confetti had to be dropped as snow in front of cameras. Later, in Mooney's day, narrow gravel and dirt roads reached from the Midwest across to the West but you could ride in comfort on the railroad to Southern California, just as Judy Garland sang it—the passengers were traveling there on "the Atchison, Topeka and the Santa Fe." It was a new place for a new and restless generation. Many sought the California sun, including Halliburton and Mooney.

As in his ghostwriting of Richard's books, Mooney was also a principal in the building of Halliburton's Hangover House in Laguna Beach. With Richard on tour, he received checks from Halliburton to support himself and to administer details of house construction, as well as advise Richard on construction progress.

In 1936 when Halliburton decided to build the house, he hired Mooney's friend William Alexander Levy, a recent graduate of New York University School of Architecture, to design and erect it for him. (The architect became known as William Alexander.) Richard wanted something bold, modern, and the architect agreed to come all the way from New York. According to Gerry Max, Alexander had been modeling for painters while designing interiors as a day job and had failed the state licensing examination for an architect. He had never been hired to design a house, let alone build one. He never again built such an exceptional structure.

The house would stand on a ridge some six hundred feet above the

310

Pacific Ocean and it would precipitously overlook Aliso Canyon, today with luxurious homes. Of concrete and steel, the innovative house included such features as a dumbwaiter, heatilator, and a bastion-like retaining wall. Today architectural historians consider it among the early masterpieces of modern design in Southern California.

BUILDING HANGOVER HOUSE

In 1989 *The Los Angeles Times* described its driveway as a private road so steep that "it threatens to flip cars end over end." The writer said Hangover House at 31172 Ceanothus Drive in Laguna Beach is "an architectural wonder" and that "few people these days have cause to brave the dizzying drive." By 1989 not many readers had heard of Richard Halliburton so the writer informed them that he was "one of the most famous adventurers and authors of his time" and that he climbed the Matterhorn, swam the "alligator-infested" Panama Canal, and flew up Everest in an "open-cockpit biplane."

Constructed from 1937 to 1938, it stands on the edge of the continent, as far as wheels could get him from Memphis. Atop a bluff next the Gulf of Santa Catalina, it overlooks the Pacific Ocean and the houses below. Halliburton called it Hangover House for its physical presence.[*] It was daring, bold. Standing on its balcony, a guest could commit an excellent suicide just by stepping over the railing.

During its construction, the house had so many gawkers that a ticket booth was erected at the base of the ridge, probably to control crowds and because Halliburton saw a few dollars in the enterprise, which was costing him dearly.

It does not mingle with the houses below but stands aloof, magisterial above them, all huddled safely and conventionally together at sea level. It is precariously perched on a cliff, a study in high architectural adventure, fitting its owner's sense of the bold. Most important, it did not move. There, his feet could stop. His eyes could take in the ocean horizon from his balcony.

---

[*] The association of hangovers with the morning after is inescapable and Paul Mooney claimed its name came from parties held there.

It was the kind of house Ayn Rand's Nietzschean characters might build and in her fiction one of them did. Gerry Max tells us that William Alexander was interviewed by her one day during its construction. She climbed the steep drive to talk to him about it and according to Alexander one of her houses in *The Fountainhead* is based on it. The Heller House of her character Howard Roark is also perched precariously.

It marks Halliburton's first home, and its construction came not from his restless energy but from needing a rest for that energy. Hangover House reflected a man who craved peace and intimate companionship far from admiring throngs in lecture halls. As he aged he saw each new book as Halliburton imitating Halliburton, the romantic voice becoming stylistically hoarse. He also moved from public man of adventure to a man weary of the public mask he wore. Once fresh and new, the world had become tainted with familiar patterns that offered only a return to the same bounded world no horizon could transcend. It left him ambivalent, one side competing against the other. On one side remained the restless, driven Richard, seeking adventure and needing more money. On the other he had seen it all, done it all, and found it all empty. In far-off lands lay only more of what he left behind at the last port of call, in the last jungle, on the last frozen steppe. Something else there was. Something he craved, and it was peace and intimate companionship.

In an October 1936 letter, Richard writes of his weariness, his growing awareness of it, and his desire for solitude. Because of that, "much of the joyous wonder has gone out of my writings." He is no longer a believer in his youthful way of life. He tells his parents that his zest "would have gone out anyway because I am older and less astonished and amused by what I see." He adds, "Despite my constant contacts with people I have almost no friends, friends who really are a vital part of my life." He shrinks from them "farther and farther each year." And so in search of rest he came to the hill overlooking the Pacific on which he built something that did not move.

Halliburton's idea for the house goes back as far as 1930. At Laguna Beach he was with Paul Mooney, both on horses. He wrote home, "I was riding horseback one day ten miles south of the town on the beach. I looked up and saw a ridge rising broadside eight hundred feet from the shore." He and Mooney rode up the ridge and looked down on the view. Of it, he said, "It is a sensational vista and stops people in their tracks when they stumble unexpectedly upon it. I went back over and over just to look at the peaceful valley on one side and the full sweep on the ocean on the other, six hundred feet above both." Then we read Halliburton the businessman. "I finally found out who owned the mountain, and, taking advantage of the panic, offered $500 for three hundred feet upon the ridge and three hundred feet down the mountain side facing the ocean. Since I bought it, three hundred houses have gone up along the coast just below, and a big real estate combine is putting half a million dollars into the valley below."

Halliburton the businessman also justified the purchase because he was uncertain about the Depression-era economy. In a letter home, he describes the stock market as "jittery" and that he would not invest his royalties from *Seven League Boots* in shares but instead would buy $10,000 more life insurance and put $8,000 aside for Hangover House with its lot. "The house is to cost $6000, the road up to it, water installations, garden landscaping, etc., another thousand."

Its final cost was $36,000, $29,000 more than he planned, more than a four hundred percent cost over-run. At that percentage, today a house estimated at $360,000 would over-run to almost $2 million.

Hangover House sits on a third-acre lot and contains two thousand square feet of living space, with three bedrooms and two bathrooms. Today and depending on the market, the house remains worth millions of dollars. It was built of one hundred tons of concrete and fifty tons of steel.

The Laguna Beach Department of Parks and Recreation lists the house among its historical residences, noting that this part of south Laguna Beach is called Coast Royale by old-timers. The Department describes Halliburton's house as a "moderne house with a brutalist influence." The brutalist influence refers to its unpainted concrete walls. The house is "composed of many square and rectangular angles, larger panes of glass." We are told, "The house straddles a ridge with steep sides and is built in a very precarious position."

Halliburton wrote "The long side of the house is built sheer with the precipice" and that in the living room "the entire end is glass and overlooks the ocean." He described each bedroom as "equipped for a sun porch" and that "the garden runs along the edge of the ridge with the precipice and valley on one side and ocean on the other."

Before he returned to the lecture tour, he "remained in Laguna long enough to see the road, very zigzag and steep, finished and the foundation going in. The house will be finished some time next spring. I will not see it until late April when my tour takes me west. I have thought of calling it Hangover House, because it overhangs the precipice. The furnishings are to be extremely simple. No bureaus or dressers, only built in cabinets and no bedsteads."

Hangover House was a challenge for Alexander, then in his late twenties, who accepted Halliburton's commission of fifteen hundred dollars and left New York.

Before he could build it, Alexander had to get to the site, which meant blasting a road up the ridge. That wasn't all. Next the cliff, Alexander's crew had no room to work and so he had a retaining wall built, seventeen feet high and hooked into the bedrock with concrete beams. Alexander then had the workers pour the concrete as a monolithic structure.

Listening to Alexander, Richard consented to things then unheard of—garbage disposal, central heating and a dumbwaiter connecting all three floors. It all sounded good to him but he did not like the bills.

Wild cost over-runs can be traced to Halliburton's evolving construction decisions but the fault was not altogether his. Richard quarreled with Alexander over expenses. Alexander has been described as a perfectionist with a fixed vision of his creation who resisted short-cuts to reduce cost. Although this was Alexander's first project, it can be argued that what he lacked in fundamental knowledge he might have gained by trial and error in constructing the house at Richard's expense. The differences between Alexander and Halliburton became so great that Richard cut off funds for the project and asked Alexander to leave. They did make up but unplanned expenses continued.

Back from a lecture tour, Richard found a physician with a stethoscope listening to the concrete walls while a workman on the roof made rattling noises. Alexander explained that the electrical conduits got buried in the concrete and they were trying to find the electrical outlets. From above, the man jiggled the wire while the doctor pinpointed the sound. When the job was done, Alexander asked, "How much do we owe you?"

"Nothing," said the physician. "It was fun."

Because Richard's engagements kept him away, Paul Mooney was left to edit Richard's *Book of Marvels* and to administer financial affairs. Complaining to Halliburton, Mooney said, "Alexander is incompetent," while Alexander countered, "Mooney is officious and domineering." Interestingly, both men were good friends and remained so.

During construction Richard wrote letters, trying to keep peace between architect Alexander and writer Mooney.

His parents were at first happy to hear about it, as a house meant their son was settling down and might marry. Years later, Wesley said to his friend James Cortese at the Memphis *Commercial Appeal*, "Once upon a time, back in 1933 I wrote a letter to my son Richard, lamenting over the poor prospects of ever having a grandson which I very much desired. With the waters of a third of the century already passed under the bridge, Richard, completely engrossed in making plans for another trip over the Earth in his *Seven League Boots*, replied: 'Don't be so downhearted about your lack of grandchildren, Dad. There's a lot of time. I'll grow weary of this headlong life. The current gets stronger that way.' "

Wesley told Cortese, "That left room for hope at least." Their hope was kindled when Richard "wrote of the house he was designing to build on his lot, Hangover House." Their "hopes took on a brighter hue. Why a house unless there was to be a mistress in that house?"

He was the only son they had left. They wanted Richard to marry, settle down, raise a family, visit them with his kids and often.

In 1936 Richard wrote them and his words indicate dismissal of his earlier suggestion about eventual marriage. He writes, "Likewise the women situation is no cause for alarm. They play a very small part in my life, chiefly because their minds and natures bore me worse than men's. They are extremely rare and never younger than myself. Please don't be distressed because I'm the way I am. Just be grateful that I'm so much happier than most people and growing on a continually up-climbing curve rather than marking time with the masses who have all come from the regulation mold." Wife and family were merely part of the regulation mold.

His parents gave up all hope after visiting Richard at Hangover House. Maybe they didn't like Alexander. They probably didn't like Paul Mooney. With their Southern gentility, they didn't like any of his friends. "Richard's following," said his dad, with their "sophisticated airs and brittle manners." Brittle, indeed. This suggests Mooney, self-described as temperamental. The friends were everything that Memphis was not. Wesley and Nelle went home to their quiet Court Street house under its shade trees. His parents thought these people had rendered their son into a cynic, morose and apart from all they held dear.

After visiting Mooney, Alexander, and other friends, Wesley and Nelle detested the place as a symbol of bad influences on their son. They were not unhappy to get rid of it. After Richard's death, Zolite Scott, a ballerina, and Wallace, her husband and Marine Corps fighter pilot, bought it in 1941 with their offer of $7,500. For the Scott's, though, it was a fortunate purchase. In 1989, surrounding properties sold from $750,000 to $1.5 million. That year, Zolite, their daughter, still owned it.[*]

His parents had no use for the house because in it they heard a difference that spoke more than Richard's uneven tenor. The walls whispered that they would never have grandchildren and with his friends they began to understand why.

Had they thought about it, they also might have understood their son as somebody who traveled the world and saw cultural norms as functions of their time and place. This fit the pattern of his life. He was an adventurer by personality, not just vocation. On the other hand, he tried to have it both ways. The house reared priapically into the air, scorning the

---

[*] Scott's son Mark recalled his father barrel-rolling a plane over the canyon below Hangover House. He and his sister Zolite grew up in it. The father fought in the Philippines, where Japanese strafed and bombed his Marine Air Group 32. Wounded at Luzon, Lieutenant Colonel Scott earned a Distinguished Flying Cross and a Legion of Merit. He had little time to enjoy the house after buying it.

conventional, while the businessman in him feared his readers' judgment.

His parents saw the house as a curse on their son, as it demanded payment for its exorbitant costs. The zigzag driveway up to it was a trope of the serpentine ways of his restlessness. The house stood aloof from the others below; it didn't join, just as Richard had stayed indoors and away from playmates during his childhood. It was a California house in Laguna Beach, far from Memphis, and offered wide vistas that Richard loved. At ocean's edge, it spoke of breath and life like nothing in Tennessee and to pay for its expense Richard began his final adventure.[*]

---

[*] In 2012 the house's new owner planned major redesign. However, a stop-construction order was issued because of the house's historical significance. In April, 2012, the stop-construction order was over-ruled allowing the house to be changed after completion of an impact study. An architectural historian feared Laguna Beach would lose one of its real architectural assets. Then the impact studied was ruled as unnecessary.

THE SEEDS OF A NEW ADVENTURE

The Golden Gate Exposition at Treasure Island could provide a profitable venue for anybody enterprising enough to take advantage of it.
Walter Gaines Swanson

Girls in a plastic-bodied car at the 1939 San Francisco World's Fair
(Golden Gate International Exposition)

Golden Gate International Exposition, Treasure Island, 1939,
as seen from Yerba Buena Island, site of the Bay Bridge tunnel

318

GOLDEN GATE INTERNATIONAL EXPOSITION

Unity of the Pacific nations is America's concern and responsibility. San Francisco stands at the doorway to the sea that roars upon the shores of all these nations; and so to the Golden Gate International Exposition I gladly entrust a solemn duty. May this, America's world's fair on the Pacific in 1939, truly serve all nations. President Franklin D. Roosevelt

The Golden Gate International Exposition was held on an island in San Francisco Bay to celebrate the opening of two new bridges spanning San Francisco Bay. Dedicated in 1936 the Bay Bridge connected San Francisco with Oakland on the east shore. In 1937 the second bridge, Golden Gate, was opened, then the longest suspension bridge in the world. It spanned the strait flowing the Bay into the Pacific Ocean so that ships from Asia and the South Pacific passed under it and later, in WWII, bomber pilots did victory passes under it after the long flight from Honolulu or Johnson Island. The bridges were opened to much ballyhoo, for they demonstrated things to come. The public proudly believed in progress. Things were better and would continue to improve. It was the American Way, after all, and these two engineering marvels were proof. The Exposition opened on February 18, 1939, lasting through October 29, 1939. It opened the next year on May 25, and closed on September 29, 1940.

On September 1, 1939 Hitler's blitzkrieg fell upon Poland with cannon from his Panzer tanks butchering Polish horse cavalry. In Munich beer halls wermacht soldiers clinked beer steins together and sang "Deutschland über alles." On June 21, 1940, Der Fuhrer's jack-booted troops marched into Paris and—in mockery of past French military victory over Germany—through the Arc de Triomphe and down the Champs-Élysées. World War II became a counterpoint to the American belief in progress.

319

The Exposition was held on Treasure Island, flat and artificial. Named after Robert Louis Stevenson's pirate novel of that title, it honors the Scotsman, a San Francisco resident, 1879-1880. Built in 1939 expressly for the Exposition, the island was dredged into existence from shoals on the north side of Yerba Buena Island. Today in a car headed to San Francisco on the Bay Bridge, a driver can look down on Treasure Island just before he passes into the tunnel dug through Yerba Buena.

Built by the federal government, Treasure Island became a terminus for the flying boats of Juan Trippe's Pan American Airlines, charging passengers $1500 for a round trip flight, San Francisco to Manila. With their transoceanic flights, the flying boats captured the public imagination and Hollywood knew it. In 1936 Humphrey Bogart and Pat O'Brien starred in the movie *China Clipper*. In real life, from Clipper Cove, with an American flag painted on the nose, a flying boat taxied into the bay, picked up speed, became airborne, and wealthy passengers looked down on the Golden Gate, then they gazed ahead at endless expanses of blue water as the clipper droned across the Pacific to Hawaii and Hong Kong.

When war erupted in 1941 Treasure Island was taken over by the navy, becoming a naval station until 1997. During World War II its training schools fed sailors and marines into classes in electronics and radio communications. Sailors from Nebraska farms were ordered there before shipping aboard destroyers, cruisers, and aircraft carriers bound for the battles of Midway, Coral Sea, and Iwo Jima.

FDR's hope for "Unity of the Pacific nations" was lost and finally in 1945 two bombs, Little Boy and Fat Man, one dropped on Hiroshima, the other on Nagasaki, brought Japanese emissaries, in top hats and frock coats, to surrender on the battleship *Missouri* in Tokyo Bay.

In 1939 Americans could not believe anybody might attack them. In the dark of movie theaters they watched flickering Warner-Pathé newsreels as Japanese troops marched through Manchuria, or as Mussolini strutted on a balcony in Rome, but they were separated by oceans, after all, and nobody would want to attack big-hearted America. Americans just wanted to be left alone; they bore no ill will. That was the popular sentiment. The Depression was ending. The world lay bright ahead. That was what they believed but not what they got.

WALTER GAINES SWANSON

In 1936 Halliburton's editor, David Chambers, suggested a book for boys and girls mainly of high school age—something that would show them the wonderful places on earth by somebody who had seen them. A compilation of illustrations with text, it should make money for both Halliburton and Bobbs-Merrill and that was the main thing.

After being given more thought, the book became two, one for the Western world, one for the Eastern. The volumes would be jointly titled *Richard Halliburton's Book of Marvels.* His name was in the title because Richard appealed to kids. Every schoolchild was familiar with Halliburton the adventurer, who had written in prose they could appreciate— enthusiastic, wondrous. Former CBS news anchor Walter Cronkite spoke of avidly reading Richard's books when a boy. The list of admirers includes travel writer Paul Theroux and intellectual Susan Sontag.

For young people like Sontag, Theroux, and Cronkite, Richard wanted to include in the first volume two new marvels, the Golden Gate and the Bay Bridge. The structures were not sunk in the deep past but were fittingly American, modern engineering wonders, and typical of things to come. Halliburton could see construction pillars of the Bay Bridge from his San Francisco apartment. The papers were filled with reports of its progress, the cost over-runs, the engineering difficulties, so that he wanted to visit it and the Golden Gate to understand and experience the challenges they presented. The bridges did not speak of dead history but of the future as young America led the world into it.

The job would not be difficult. Richard would not have to travel again, at least for a while. He could visit libraries, examine the stacks of tomes, writing his books with available materials, and this appealed to him. He really wanted to rest, to enjoy Hangover House, and to enjoy some solitude. He could write the book in the summer of 1936 and, money always needed, return to the lecture circuit in the fall.

Research for the book took him to the bridges in San Francisco Bay and a meeting with a public relations representative for the project. The representative had a rather cumbersome title as Vice President-General Manager of the San Francisco Convention and Tourist Bureau. His name was Walter Gaines Swanson and he was responsible for publicity of the coming Exposition as well as construction of the two bridges. With his job he had also to figure out how to explain costs, contract delays, and worker deaths. He had to keep the bridges in the public eye. In Twenty-First Century parlance, they had to be "spun." To keep things spinning, he was always on the lookout for the main chance, the big story, the opportunity to pitch. He was paid for being good at his job and with the World's Fair and the bridges he had a wide responsibility.

Halliburton telephoned the California Toll Bridge Authority, identified himself, and explained that he was writing another book. Could they let him visit the bridges? He was referred to Swanson. As it turned out, each had what the other wanted. Richard needed a story. Swanson could help him find it. Swanson needed publicity. Richard offered name recognition. The public-relations man could issue press releases such as "Richard Halliburton on Golden Gate Bridge" and "Richard Halliburton Visits San Francisco-Oakland Bay Bridge" or "Halliburton Amazed by Engineering Marvels." Swanson could get free coverage for the projects in the *Chronicle*, the *Call*, the *News*, the *Examiner*, and the *Oakland Tribune*.

Swanson asked Richard if he wanted to walk on the unfinished Bay Bridge. Always game and certainly willing to see his subject at close hand, Halliburton agreed. Jonathon Root stated that next morning when Richard arrived at the bridge, he found not only Swanson but ten reporters and photographers. With their note pads and cameras they were busy recording his every move and Hollywood movies of the era let us imagine a dialogue.

"What do you think of this bridge, Mr. Halliburton?"

A camera bulb flashes.

"Oh, it's quite a feat. Yes, quite a feat."

A photographer has Richard smile, posing with hand on the rail, a bold explorer gazing at the sky.

"When will you begin your next adventure?"

"Well, that's a tough one. I don't know yet. I'm still thinking about it. I'd rather like to take it easy for a while."

"Mr. Halliburton, will you hold it there, yeah, right there, so I can get a shot of you shaking hands with Mr. Swanson?"

"How's that?"

"Yeah, good. Thanks."

Swanson brings attention to his interests, "This is a suspension-cantilever bridge, and it will stretch eight-and-a-half miles from San

Francisco to Oakland."

They left the reporters. Richard walked with Swanson to a cable. Swanson pointed to the cable and its catwalk. "It's safe," he said. "Don't worry." The bay lay two hundred fifty feet below and twenty-two workers had fallen into it.

They climbed onto the catwalks. Without obstruction, wind blows hard over open water and it blew against them. Root says that Halliburton clung to the catwalk railings. He gazed down with Swanson on the bay.

When Swanson asked if he wanted to visit the Golden Gate Bridge the next day Halliburton accepted.

When Richard met Swanson for the Golden Gate Bridge tour, he was introduced to San Francisco Chronicle photographer Barney Peterson. With Peterson, Halliburton stepped onto a cable to follow its catwalk up toward the tower. Smaller cables formed the handrails on either side, with the suspension cable, at three feet in diameter, climbing swiftly toward the sky, then it descended on the other side of the tower.

Peterson wanted some photo opportunities. According to Jonathon Root, Richard was agreeable to this but not to what Barney Peterson said next. The photographer wanted Richard to grab one of the cables dangling from the main cable then swing out over the water.

"You must be crazy," Richard said. "That water is three hundred feet down."

"You won't fall," said Peterson. He got his camera ready. "I thought you would do anything."

"I don't know where you got that idea."

"From your books." Peterson grinned. "I'm one of your more faithful readers."

Peterson held his camera in one hand and, grabbing the cable in the other, he swung out over the water. He said, "If I can do it with one hand, you can do it with two."

Richard grabbed the cable and kicked free of the catwalk, dangling there for Peterson's photograph.

Walter Gaines Swanson

FUNDING FOR A TRANS-PACIFIC VOYAGE

In Swanson's meeting with Richard lay seeds of the next turn in Halliburton's life. Some scholars like to play what-if games with history. If Cleopatra's nose had been a quarter-inch longer, Mark Anthony would not have fallen for her and the course of Roman history, ergo Western history, might have been different. Richard Halliburton made no impact on the course of civilization but the same consideration applies here with regard to a man outside history. If Walter Gaines Swanson had not met Richard Halliburton the outcome of Halliburton's life might have been different. He might have died an old man, which is not to blame Swanson but to blame the gods that roll dice.

In the what-if of things, if Richard had not been thinking about a new kind of book, he might not have met the bridges' publicist. It was a plan for the book that brought him to meet Swanson and in their conversations Swanson proposed a trans-Pacific voyage to the Golden Gate International Exposition. It would provide excellent publicity for the fair and it would be a boon to Swanson. Halliburton saw what was in it for him. His livelihood depended on publicizing himself and an ocean voyage would provide fine advertisement. He could sell articles and write a book about it and, though he had written his parents of his tiredness, he had debts and a standard of living to maintain. His Laguna Beach home, Hangover House, was the most recent example of his need for money.

His parents, Wesley and Nelle, strongly disapproved of the voyage across the Pacific. Don't worry, he wrote his parents in effect. All is well. It will work out. I'll sail safely across the Pacific and into San Francisco Bay, and you can watch me tie up at the Treasure Island pier. Just you wait and see.

After Swanson broached the idea to Halliburton, they talked about Richard sailing into San Francisco Bay from China and tying up at a

Treasure Island pier for the Exposition. A world's fair, people from all over the globe would come to see it. Richard could charge families to sightsee the bay on his Chinese Junk. People would look down from the Golden Gate Bridge as he sailed under it from China. As they stood by the Palace of Fine Arts, they could see the strange craft on one of its sightseeing tours with families. From Fisherman's Wharf or the Oakland Bay Bridge, crowds could see it as he sailed past Alcatraz. Halliburton didn't have to worry about publicity because that was Swanson's job and because the exotic vessel in the bay would provide its own publicity.

All that was fine possibility but there is fancy and there is fact. Richard was a businessman who marketed himself and he thought in business terms. What about building the thing? What about paying workers? There must be many other expenses he had not yet considered. What about them?

Swanson tried to find backers and he thought of China Town. He contacted some well-heeled Chinese businessmen on Grant Avenue and arranged a meeting with them. In July 1936 Richard went to Grant Avenue to talk with investors, the Chinese Six Companies. They would get great publicity. Newspapers, magazines, radio, books. At the World's Fair he would charge sightseers for a trip around San Francisco Bay, maybe only to sail around Alcatraz. He needed $35,000 from the investors. That would cover the junk, the crew, and the voyage. They listened carefully, applauded politely when he was done, and asked him to leave the room. In his head as he waited, Richard began planning for the voyage. After all, it seemed appropriate. They should be interested. He would sail from Shanghai or Hong Kong and they would have interest in the connection to their mother country. He waited outside but found out in October. It was not practical they finally told him. A gambling casino with fan-tan would have been okay, but this, no.

Richard did find financing. He incorporated his adventure as The Richard Halliburton Chinese Junk Expedition addressed at 739 Market Street in San Francisco and he owed his creditors who would clamor for payment. He sold shares in it with himself shareholder by mortgaging Hangover House. Apart from Vida, wife of his distant cousin Erle Halliburton, other large shareholders were four young men from well-off families, two from Maine who were offshore sailors, with the other two also from New England. Those from Down-East were Gordon Torrey, twenty-three, and John R. Potter, twenty-four. George Barstow, III, was from Connecticut and Robert Chase from Massachusetts. Wilfred Crowell, Schwabacher Paper executive in San Francisco, handled the finances. J. Robert Townsend was the attorney.

SEA DRAGON

She leaned dangerously when struck by the blasts of wind. With the storm mounting in fury, our chances of capsizing increased, and I gave the order to let out the sea anchor on some ten fathoms of line, then, fighting like madmen, we clawed at the flapping sails, trying to furl them before they were blown to shreds. Working on the narrow wet foredeck of the junk while she pitched and rolled was dangerous, and, during those careless days of inexperience, we had not learned to tie ourselves on our ship.

E. Allen Petersen in *Hummel Hummel,* a true story of sailing a thirty-six foot Chinese junk Shanghai to California in 1938 to escape the invading Japanese army.

Sea Dragon. Notice dragon eyes on fantail & yin-yang symbol

WELCH

In summer 1938 when John Wenlock Welch, an Australian, showed up in Richard's suite at the Chancellor Hotel in San Francisco, Richard thought he had his man. He had been flooded with letters from people expressing a desire to sign on as captain of his Trans-Pacific voyage. But seeing Welch did it for him. His mind was made up. Halliburton decided to hire Welch at $250 a month. Exuding confidence, with booming voice and master seaman's papers, Welch was the skipper for his junk, the *Sea Dragon*. He had the right stuff. He claimed he was nautical technical advisor in two Hollywood seafaring movies and had sailed the seas for many years. A handsome man, at forty-two he even looked as though he could have been a Captain Bligh or Fletcher Christian shouting commands from the poop deck in some MGM back lot. Even Richard's mother was impressed with him. While visiting in San Francisco she talked to Welch and felt reassured that her boy would be in capable hands. Welch was the masterful sea captain to her. She didn't want Richard to make the voyage and this wasn't the first time she feared for his life but at least with Welch her son had somebody competent.

In fact, John Welch was mainly expert at promoting himself. He did have master's papers and he had sailed many years but he knew nothing about building a Chinese junk or any other boat nor had he competence in making one seaworthy.

Because Richard had experience as an ordinary seaman, he wondered why John Welch was sailing only as second mate on United Fruit banana boats San Francisco to Central America. Why had he not been hired as first mate on some first class ship? Not enough first mate jobs, replied Welch. Richard accepted Welch's explanation.

So the man was hired and together they took passage on *SS President Coolidge* for Hong Kong, where the junk would be built on the docks at

327

Kowloon. Other crew members would follow. Jonathon Root tells us that at the dinner table Welch regaled his fellow *Coolidge* passengers with his tales, some of sea stories and many of lonely females he had seduced. He was quite sure of himself, the passengers found.

Crewman John R. Potter recalled Welch. The Australian held himself apart as captain. During the junk's construction he ate alone at a single table while the others ate at a separate one.

Paul Mooney thought of taking the next ship stateside. Richard persuaded him to stay, promising things would get better, and so they did—until Welch once again returned to his old ways. After their first and aborted voyage, Mooney had the perfect excuse to avoid Welch and the adventure, having broken his ankle, but at that stage of his life he was heavily into drink and maybe he no longer cared. Maybe, too, he stayed on because of his loyalty to Halliburton

In a letter to Wilfred Crowell, Richard complained about Welch. "He flies into an uncontrollable rage if anybody disagrees with him. It's all I can do to keep peace." Welch was "a regular Captain Bligh." He railed at the crewmembers for not doing this or that. They shouted back or scowled into silence.

The *San Francisco News* and Bell Syndicate agreed to pay Richard $6,000 for fifteen "Log of the Sea Dragon" articles. As well, he had subscribers for mail of mimeographed sheets titled "Letters from the Sea Dragon." Richard left the dock and the junk construction and Welch for the quiet of cafés where he could write for stateside readers. He did not tell the *News* and the Syndicate or his subscribers of the huge cost over-runs and the domineering Welch.

Richard spent days at the Honk Kong Hotel lounge. People saw him in the lounge with a tall boy about eighteen, perhaps a crewman. The boy was about the age and appearance of Patrick Kelly, the Portuguese-American mess boy on the aborted voyage, who had never been in the United States. They could be seen sipping grenadine and soda, Richard with a silence curious for somebody normally so animated. The boy gazed at his drink. Outside the hotel, they walked the streets of Hong Kong, Richard probably delaying return to Kowloon and his problems over construction and management.

The *SS President Pierce* tied up near *Sea Dragon* on January 26, 1939. Her captain, Charles Jokstad, was master of the ship on which Halliburton had stowed away, Surabaya to Singapore in 1922. Born in Norway, Jokstad had met Richard as a lively, outgoing youth who charmed his way into friendship. The captain had given young Halliburton free passage, for those were the years when Richard was chipper and spry, finding friends wherever he passed. That day in Hong Kong, Richard invited Jokstad to look at the *Sea Dragon* and Jokstad's reaction was described by Jonathon

·Root, author of *The Magnificent Myth*.

Jokstad had been at sea since he was nine and at twenty-five became ship's captain in the American Merchant Marine. He knew his ships. They must have talked of old times as the captain and the adventurer strolled from one pier to the next. Richard had been quite the freeloader, one who went on to write books and become famous. They climbed aboard the *Sea Dragon*, where Welch was supervising Chinese who caulked the deck.

Jokstad looked long and hard at Welch, Root tells us. He had no seamanly greeting for Welch, no questions for him. He walked past him. Then Jokstad began his inspection.

Jokstad studied the junk, which was a mix of designs, Wenchow and Ningpo, but mostly Wenchow. Bow to stern, *Sea Dragon* ran seventy-five feet with a poop deck unsafely high at twelve feet above the main deck. In Halliburton's letters home, the main mast was described as sixty-five feet tall. Jokstad looked at the mast, then at the shrouds holding it in place. Rising far above them, the mast was supported by lines lashed to flimsy pad-eyes at deck level. When the sail was hoisted, the mast would exert tremendous stress on its fore, aft, and beam shrouds. Jokstad told Richard they would let go in the first strong wind. On the poop deck, he looked at the tiller, took it between his hands and rocked it back and forth. It had at least an inch of play. In heavy seas a five-ton wave would snap it like a pretzel. They climbed down into the main cabin. In the engine compartment he examined the diesel and kicked the supports with his toe. They were not rubber-cushioned motor mounts but leg screws tapped directly into the hull ribs.

He explained to Halliburton that in heavy seas the one hundred horsepower diesel would rock in the same violent motion as the hull, and would easily tear loose the leg screws. As for the ship herself, her water line was too high; she would bounce like a bathtub duckie. She needed at least ten tons of ballast.

The two said goodbye to one another on the dock. Jokstad turned toward *Pierce*, Halliburton to his fate. Jokstad walked away and took with him much of Halliburton's good humor but Richard still needed—desperately needed—to get to San Francisco in his junk. His creditors were waiting for him.

What's *Sea Dragon*'s course to San Francisco? Jokstad asked before he left. Richard told him. The 28th parallel. Too far north, Jokstad said. Gale force winds and if that was not enough, there would be a heavy, following sea, making helm control difficult. Better go south, to latitude 22. That course would have put the junk even later into San Francisco. No, it will work out, thought Richard.

Jonathon Root says that after *Sea Dragon* disappeared at sea, Jokstad said,

"I had the awful feeling, the day I inspected the junk, that I would never see that young man again, and I urged him not to attempt the voyage. It is my guess that the rudder snapped off in a heavy following sea, the ship broached-to in the trough, the masts went out and she broke up, probably in minutes."

Richard did get a Lloyd's of London insurance surveyor to inspect the junk. The surveyor passed the craft but with caveats, and Halliburton insured *Sea Dragon* for $10,000, not enough to pay off his creditors but apparently the maximum he could get. The Lloyd's man noted the high poop deck and the overly wide canvas sails and cautioned that they alone called for "the utmost vigilance at sea." The rounded hull was for rivers and not hard-over sailing. Too far and it would not right itself.

MONEY & DELAY

In Hong Kong, construction of *Sea Dragon* began at the Kowloon docks as Japanese troops swarmed through China, forcing refugees into the British colony. Halliburton wrote his parents that the war was "hardly noticed here" and that things were normal. When they read his letter they wanted to believe it but understood he was only trying to ease their fears. He did not tell them about his nagging worries. Time was running out, Richard was not at all sure the Japanese would be hospitable if they spotted the junk in the South China Sea. Not only Japanese but pirates were a threat. He wrote his parents "in near-by waters, pirates are a very real and constant menace." The junk was stocked with shotguns and rifles against any boarding attempt. The main thing, though, was the Japanese.

The curtain was drawing closed on the decades between two world wars. Richard, the indefatigable optimist, looked at the Chinese refugees briefly safe from Japanese bayonets. He had come of age in the Roaring Twenties, had dreamed bigger dreams in the Thirties, and did not foresee that he and the modern world were being hurled headlong toward their fates.

The junk was built in Kowloon, near Hong Kong, while Japanese forces conquered Manchuria, preparing to march on Hong Kong against the under-manned British garrison protecting the city and *Sea Dragon*'s shipyard. After the Japanese invaded China, five hundred thousand people fled to Hong Kong and, starving, sick, brought typhoid, collapsing on sidewalks with dysentery and cholera. Halliburton saw streams of exhausted refugees from the provinces dying by thousands. His eyes couldn't avoid them on his daily trips to coordinate the boat's construction. The ragged parents with their unshod children foretold things to come. Seeing all this, Halliburton anxiously turned to the work at hand. Despite disaster gathering over the world's continents, he had mustered a crew and boat builders for his next big challenge.

331

British naval officers at the Hong Kong Hotel thought the *Sea Dragon* expedition was folly. They were amused by it and the hotel itself was an emblem of their confidence. In 1941, as the Japanese 21st, 23rd and 38th Regiments marched toward Hong Kong, the Union Jack still flew on the hotel's roof, declaring it invincible, despite the far inferior numbers of British and Canadian troops. A six-story Victorian building, its Roman arches announced its self-assured European presence. Each of its front-facing rooms had a veranda for guests to leisurely sit and peer down on the street below. Chinese passers-by could look up to the veranda balustrades and see potted flowers behind them. They peered wonderingly at English gentlemen officers as the hotel guests gazed down at them. With its concert piano, marble-topped tables and oak furniture, the hotel bespoke Anglo-Saxon privilege amidst all the Asian colonials. Halliburton frequented the hotel to dine and dance. Over dinner, one British navy lieutenant warned him that the wooden ship was too frail for the fierce seas of the winter monsoons. As related by Jonathon Root, an officer said a Japanese destroyer would "blow that ruddy junk galley west" as soon as they spotted her mainsail in the Formosa Straits.

Halliburton couldn't quit. He badly needed money and felt intense stress and pressure. To say he felt troubled is to understate his situation. In January, when the junk was christened, Richard's nerves flared his skin into an eczema that rioted over his body, especially around the nose, cheeks, and forehead. He was in bed at the Kowloon Hotel while a bottle of rice wine was broken against her bow. A doctor told him what he already knew. The *Sea Dragon* project was causing it.

He had not reckoned on a different cultural attitude toward getting things done. This was not a place for an efficiency expert standing with a stopwatch to time each task. The workmen brought their wives to watch them work and would not have listened to the expert's advice. Compounding the slow construction was the lack of power tools. Adzes, saws, and augers were all hand-operated. Richard thought that if he stood watching them as they went about their tasks they would work faster. He had no effect. He wrote home, "I've been through so many ship-building battles, and been so plagued by the superlative perversity of Chinese carpenters, that I'm a mental wreck." In a mimeographed letter to his stateside subscribers he wrote of the "clash of temperaments" and that each of the crewmembers, including himself, had "at least once" decided "to leave this blankety-blank expedition and take the next boat home."

Halliburton became frustrated with the workers' primitive drill, operated by a string, which in an hour drilled a hole in a plank. *Sea Dragon* engineer Henry Von Fehren showed them an electric drill that could do it in seconds and at this they were amazed. They gathered around to watch him. But they refused to use the device, for "it would end their livelihood quicker than the sawmill."

His plans projected $2,500 for construction but his wealthy contractor Fat Kau charged $5000, helping Richard understand how the man became rich. That fee was before the unrelenting cost over-runs. Like Welch, Fat Kau was not the man for the job, though a ship builder. Welch had no shipbuilding experience and Fat Kau had never been to sea. He simply served their whimsy without nay-saying it as not seaworthy.

To speed up construction, Halliburton wanted the boards cut at a mill, but the Chinese workmen would agree only if Richard paid them for the days they otherwise would have spent hand-cutting the wood. Once they laid the hull keel, they stopped working and, despite urging, refused to go on until tradition was followed. They had a ritual party for the laying of the keel and later had a local priest officially "open the eyes" of the vessel.

One day his workers went on strike and he could not understand why as he had paid their wages, had tried to avoid causing grievances. Then he learned that he had failed to give them a party. As it turned out, he had failed to give any party, a distinct affront because two were expected, one at start and one at finish. (The work was far from done.) This meant a shindig for fifty men and their wives. So, on the deck they had a party with rice wine and baskets of food and plenty of music and finally some opium. Richard watched them smoke the drug and saw that, with the wine and the opium, they were having a very pleasant evening.

His funds were shrinking fast. His principal shareholders included himself and four of his crew from well-to-do families, George Barstow, Robert Chase, John Potter, and Gordon Torrey. Richard had thousands of American youth who wanted to ship with him but he needed volunteers with money.

He had mortgaged Hangover House for the voyage and had driven to the ranch of Erle Halliburton, founder of Halliburton Corporation and a distant cousin. Erle said no but his wife Vida gave $2,500 and his daughter Zola put Richard in touch with a friend, John R. Potter, who became a crewman and bought shares in the corporation. Richard had gotten money but was still worried because of cost over-runs.

Halliburton moved his captain and crew out of the Kowloon Hotel and onto the junk. The better-off, including two Dartmouth crewman, Potter and Torrey, couldn't stand Welch and paid for their own rooms at the Kowloon Hotel rather than spend any more time at the pier than necessary.

Back in San Francisco, expedition administrator Wilfred Crowell wrote Halliburton that he could not raise any more money for the *Sea Dragon* expedition and, if by February 1939 she was not at Treasure Island in San Francisco Bay, the fair might give her berth to somebody else. More pressure was on Richard.

On January 27, 1939, and posted from Canton, he wrote that his contractor for *Sea Dragon*, Fat Kau, went with him on the junk's trial cruise. With Fat Kau went the Chinaman's four wives as well as other guests and the ship's carpenters. Although he had built many ships and had never been to sea, Fat Kau had not even been on a day's shakedown cruise. *Sea Dragon* did not prove herself. Their first time on a Chinese junk, Halliburton's crew were green and out in open water some of them as well as Chinese workers became seasick. Richard wrote that "the seas were high (the best way to test joints and caulks) and nearly everyone aboard became seasick. Fat Kau vowed never to get on a ship that was in water again."

Richard was committed. It had to work. It just had to. He drew from his experiences to justify going ahead. After all, things had always worked out in the past, even through the thinnest of scrapes. He would make it work. In an article printed by the Bell Syndicate he expressed his optimism: "First of all, contrary to general belief, junks are among the most seaworthy of ships. For 4000 years China has been building these strange craft, and after forty centuries of trial and error has learned to build them so that they handle remarkably well in all kinds of weather." He continued, "and while the early Mediterranean sailors were hugging the coasts, and using the stars for guidance, the Chinese were sailing up and down the high seas, steering by the compass, one of the many great inventions China has given the world." He reminded his readers of *Hummel-Hummel*, a thirty-six foot junk sailed from Shanghai to San Pedro, California in 1938. With his wife and two White Russians, E. Allen Petersen, an osteopathic surgeon, fled Shanghai in the junk as Japanese forces advanced on that city. Unable to gain passage on a commercial liner, they bought a German-registered junk with that name and made history with the voyage in the small craft.[*]

After all, Richard told himself, it had only been a shakedown cruise. They had probed the junk's weak spots and where it wanted Richard could give. The rounded bottom drew too little water. Richard added ten thousand tons of ballast, which is to say cement inside its hull. The sails were hard to handle so the rigging was changed. The hull had sprouted leaks that could threaten the bilge pump's drainage capacity, so they were re-caulked. Halliburton sent home a clipping of the newspaper article he had written. It described the shakedown, saying that "the ship was being subjected to every possible strain" and that "Captain Welch put her through her paces violently." Richard noted the repairs to be made and concluded that although they were "minor details" they "might prove of vital importance" when at sea.

---

[*] In German, a hummel is a bumblebee and *hummel hummel* is a German onomatopoetic word, imitating the sound of a bee and equivalent to the English *buzz buzz*.

RICHARD WITH THE JAPANESE ARMY IN CHINA

Japanese Imperial Troops were fighting the Chinese army very close to Hong Kong. Not only that, but *Sea Dragon* had to sail in the waters near Japan and Nippon war ships patrolled those waters. Worried about safe passage, he did not want to be boarded and arrested with his crew, nor did he want to be torpedoed. Halliburton traveled to Japan to talk. He asked the Japanese government to assure him safe passage. He returned to China with a guarantee on paper but feared that a destroyer with a Rising Sun flapping from the yardarm would not bother to board to inspect his papers before its guns blasted the junk to bits.

By this time in his life, he reveals a different awareness than the youth seeking a royal road to romance and this is reflected in "The Log of the Sea Dragon." For readers he wrote, "In Tokyo one sees little evidence that Japan is engaged in a great war for the subjugation and annexation of the most populous country on the globe. Half a million Japanese soldiers have been killed, or invalided, in China, but in Tokyo soldiers are little seen and less talked about." He said that the government regulates what the Japanese "think and spend, and they seem to obey without criticism." Here is no gilding of the lily. He writes in a new style. The real-politik message is his even if Mooney did some word-smithing. In describing the alliance of Japan with Germany and Italy he warns Americans that they should not take the "alliance very lightly, and wishfully think that it has no real foundation other then the momentary politics of those three countries." Instead, "in Japan you soon learn otherwise."

He made one comment that should have been warning enough for the United States, had a high official read it: "The average Japanese fully believes that when Italy and Germany go to war with France and England, Japan will seize Hong Kong, Singapore, and Australia, and take the Philippines and French Indo-China in stride. The Japanese have a fixed belief that they can accomplish all this, because France and England will be fighting for their lives in faraway Europe—and because Russia can't fight, and America won't."

At Canton, eighty-five miles inland from Hong Kong, he saw only Japanese troops. Canton had no Chinese army to defend it, for it had no army left. Before he arrived, Canton had a few die-hard troops defending it but they fell back against Japanese artillery and assaults. Not only were Chinese soldiers absent but so was the entire Canton population. With the troops gone, the civilians fled because they knew what occurred at Nanking. Several months earlier, in December of 1937, Japanese troops overran the Chinese army and the civilian population was whole-scale massacred with beheadings and rapes. The Cantonese did not stay to experience what befell Nanking.

In one of his mimeographed letters he wrote this. "On Monday Canton had been one of the busiest cities in the world . . . but over one-million civilians left. On Wednesday, only a few homeless dogs and blind beggars remained. In the midst of the chaos, the Chinese began dynamiting their own ammunition dumps. When the Japanese at last occupied Canton, they came into possession of a ghost town. For weeks before the final capture, Japanese air planes had methodically bombed, trying to destroy the railroad stations and freight yards. Over 10,000 civilians were slaughtered. Whole blocks of buildings were leveled."

Richard stood watching Japanese soldiers as they passed. "Along the main avenue, columns of Japanese soldiers marched up and down. They looked sturdy, well fed, and cheerful, if shockingly dirty. Their uniforms were caked with mud, their boots and puttees in shreds, their faces unshaven. . . . The Japanese hoped that when the bombing and strafing stopped, people would return." Halliburton writes, "Naturally the invaders are indignant at this passive, but stubborn, resistance." He explains, "Tokyo had counted on a rich income from taxes and trade in this former center of commerce. So far the only reward, in return for the huge expenditure of money and material, has been ashes and hatred." As for the Cantonese coming back, he says, "When Japan is forced to retreat, Canton will enjoy a miraculous repopulation."

To get to Canton he had no railroad or riverboat as the Japanese Imperial army had blocked all transportation so to defend the city from Chinese attack. Instead, he had to hitch a ride on an American navy gunboat patrolling the Pearl River to tell the Japanese that American forces could not be scared away. Gunboats remained as a stubborn presence because in December 1937 the American gunboat *Panay* was sunk with its crew and civilians on the Yangtze near Nanking by Japanese planes. Because of this unprovoked attack, US government thinking was not to back down, to stay in China's rivers to discourage increased Japanese aggression. December 7, 1941 revealed the thinking was wrong.

ABORTED

In the afternoon on February 4, 1939 *Sea Dragon* was underway and soon ran into foul weather. They had a fine farewell before leaving harbor. As a good luck ritual Chinese workmen lit firecrackers, hoisting them up the mast as they popped. Tied up at dock, Captain Jokstad had *President Pierce* sound her bass ship horn as *Sea Dragon* passed while passengers lined the rail to wave at the junk's crew. With the diesel running, Welch steered the junk through her channel and around sampans and, once beyond the channel, had crewmen hoist the foresail. With sailing room, he ordered the mainsail up and turned off the diesel. The junk lurched forward as the mizzen sail luffed and filled. All went well through that day and the night and they made good speed at six knots. With daybreak, they were roughly two hundred miles off the southern tip of Formosa, now Taiwan.

In the morning the bow held steady toward the Strait of Formosa, with the plan to sail to the 28th parallel by Japan, then easterly to Midway Island also at the 28th, alone and remote in the far Pacific where they would take on replenishments. Richard was concerned that he was sailing close to Japan and did not want to meet a patrol ship. At noon the junk still followed a northeasterly bearing when the sky blackened and swells replaced the rolling sea, washing over the rails with the junk sometimes heeling almost fifty degrees. Welch, Halliburton, and the crew quickly discovered that she still heeled easily, far too easily, and they worried about her righting moment. Could she return if she went far over and what was the point of no return? Nobody knew how to calculate this during ship construction.

Richard described the second day. His stateside followers read, "At noon on the second day, with incredible suddenness, the sun departed." He explained, "We were awakened by a blast right between the eyes." He tells them that "black clouds raced overhead, the wind swept down, the waves rose. Pitching and rolling, our decks awash, we held to our course . . . everything not fastened down began to be flung about the ship. With the downpours . . . we had to wear our oilskins. At six o' clock on the second afternoon we caught sight of a lighthouse on the coast of China. At six o' clock next morning the same lighthouse was still in the same place. We had not gained an inch. Unfortunately, our oil skins were made in China, so that before long the oil washed off and the rained seeped through."

The mizzen sail was ripped away along with the radio antenna while diesel fumes combined with seasickness to nauseate the crew. Welch throttled the engine wide-open to maintain steerageway as a man on each side of the tiller leaned heavily on the block and tackle to steady it while the seas banged the rudder one way, then another.

Rounding the southern tip of Formosa, the junk climbed tall seas and leaned before high winds, rain jabbing the crews' faces. The Strait of Formosa was not a good idea after all. In search of better weather, *Sea Dragon* came about easterly to make for the seas south of Formosa, then, northerly to the upper tip of the island. They also hoped to catch a current that would boost their speed by a knot or two and send them to less evil weather. On their new heading, they did not find things better. The sea mounted, the wind roared, and the rain drenched. Apparently no thought had gone into a container insulating the engine and routing a good exhaust system because the fumes continued to sicken the crew.

Welch ordered the mainsail reefed and first mate Potter tackled the job. Junk sails are stiffened with battens and are notably easy to reef. John Potter found nothing easy about it. He got a hernia from struggling with the mainsail. A hernia typically occurs from lifting a heavy object and reefing a junk rig should involve no lifting. More likely, in fierce wind and falling from a sixty-five foot mast, the sail heavy with water dropped below the boom, straining Potter as he and other crewmen tried to reef it back in place.

Holding in his intestinal wall, he staggered below and a shipmate lashed him to his bunk. On the crest of a huge wave, the junk dropped as if falling off a cliff and probably at this point Mooney fell down a hatchway, breaking his ankle according to the last dispatched mimeograph to subscribers, dated February 16th from Hong Kong.

Landlubbers and offshore sailors, the crew had their first taste of what deep water was like. Some must have signed themselves with the cross.

Potter was especially sick. Halliburton had a choice. After all, Potter had signed on for the full voyage, knowing he would have to take his lumps. With a rupture, Potter became feverish and probably had an inguinal hernia, the most common type among men, with it becoming trapped outside the abdomen, thereby strangulating, or losing blood supply and blocking food passage. Richard didn't know that Potter risked tissue necrosis and could die. He only knew the man was sick and in great pain. He had Welch bring *Sea Dragon* about on a southwesterly heading for Hong Kong.

There were other matters. Several hull seams were leaking and the bilge pump was working hard to drain water. The hull righted slowly. What would it do in a knockdown wind? In brief, *Sea Dragon* needed improvements.

Richard explained it differently to his subscribers back in the states. "We swung the tiller with a mighty swing, spun the ship about and set course back to China." Heroic words, these. On a more humble note he wrote, "I burned an extra stick of thanksgiving-incense before the shrine of our good-luck god, and asked him to speed us on our way to the Golden Gate. But I just wasted my incense. The god didn't listen to one word I said . . . we're back in Hong Kong."

The month after they got back, in early March 1939 during a bombing raid on Shenzhen, a few bombs fell accidentally on Hong Kong, destroying a bridge and a train station. The Japanese apologized to the British of course and not until 1941 did they invade the colony.

BACK AT KOWLOON

To get Potter to the hospital, Halliburton gave up valuable days before the monsoons. About midnight February 9, 1939, Welch guided *Sea Dragon* past the channel markers into the harbor at Hong Kong and almost foundered it on riprap while trying to find the channel.

Promptly on tying up at Kowloon, an ambulance took John Potter to the hospital. With a seriously injured ankle, Mooney followed him and it was put in a cast, after which Paul wobbled on crutches.

When Halliburton visited him at the hospital, Potter said he would not return to the junk even if he were well. It was not just about the boat, said Potter. He not only did not like Welch but he did not trust the man.

In the hospital Paul Mooney certainly held equal misgivings but he did return to the junk. He was disgusted and thought seriously about taking the next liner stateside. The voyage would be comfortable, a luxury, and he could nurse his ankle while letting the months of strain and worry slip away on clean sheets in a comfortable stateroom bed. He thought about it but in the end his loyalty to Richard prevailed.

Eighteen-year old Patrick Kelly, the mess boy, made up his mind. He had enough and left. In a letter home, Richard wrote his parents "Patrick Kelly lay in his bunk, half-dead from seasickness."

Gordon Torrey claimed appendicitis and checked himself into the hospital and out of the crew. He despised Welch and thought Halliburton very different from the adventurous, fun-loving man of the books he read when a boy. It was over for Torrey.

Potter said *Sea Dragon* had too many design and handling problems. The tiller was an eight inch by eight-inch wooden shaft about ten feet long. Maneuvering was extremely clumsy, needing two double blocks with three-quarter inch lines on each side to move the tiller port or starboard. The junk's portholes had to be boarded up because they rolled under water when the hull leaned hard. The junk couldn't sail windward without making leeway as well as headway. As for Welch, not only was he a martinet but also a lousy sailor, nor did he know much about navigation.

Potter gave Richard five hundred dollars and wished him luck. Years later he wished he had tried harder to talk Halliburton out of the voyage.

YOU KNOW HOW MUCH I LOVE YOU

After returning John Potter to Hong Kong, Richard spent almost a month with *Sea Dragon* in dock undergoing repairs and adjustments. She had proved herself, thought Richard, and now he knew how to make her better. Despite ten tons of concrete as ballast, she still had rolled too much. Then add a fin keel, said Welch, so Richard had an eighteen-foot fin keel installed on her bottom to inhibit the rolling. Welch did not tell him that a fin keel was too narrow and not for a big, heavy, sea-going sailing vessel like the cumbersome *Sea Dragon*, nor could he because he did not know. Maximum sail is determined by righting-potential and Welch's fin keel idea was not a mid-ocean design for a Chinese junk. It would not track well in rough seas and bad weather could snap it off the hull. Richard agreed to install the keel and turned to other repairs. Leaky seams were caulked once again. The damaged mizzen and main sails were replaced along with blocks and tackle. Tanks were re-supplied with diesel fuel. Two thousand gallons of fresh water re-filled the barrels.

He also needed to replace the crewmen who refused to return to the junk. Costs were mounting and time was running out. He was pushing the edge of monsoon season. He had cost over-run after cost over-run and here was another. He cabled his publisher and friends, begging more money. Bobbs-Merrill sent him $500. One of his crew, Barstow, also a shareholder, put up another $1,500 on top of his original $4,000. Clearly, they would not get to the World's Fair in time for its grand opening. Crowell had warned him that should he arrive late, Richard might not have a berth at Treasure Island when he sailed into San Francisco Bay.

Halliburton felt a desperate need to control his affairs and the more problems he encountered the more desperate his need. Jonathon Root writes that Halliburton then received a letter from his San Francisco attorney saying that he had been named as co-respondent in a divorce case.

A Los Angeles physician was suing his wife for divorce on the grounds of infidelity. Over the years she had written letters to Richard.

He had to wait until celebrations of Chinese New Year—Brown Earth Rabbit Year—were over. The last day was on February 19, 1939. As in the West, the Chinese New Year meant turning over a new leaf. In Hong Kong and at Kowloon, line after line of glowing lanterns were carried in street parades while a dragon snaked down the street with young, happy men inside it. Families had reunions. Old friends were met. Dinners and feasts were held. Houses were cleaned. Stores closed shop and stayed shut until the first week of the New Year. Presents were given. Debts were paid off.

Debts. While his Chinese workers enjoyed themselves, *Sea Dragon* sat at the pier, no work being done on it. Richard sipped grenadine and soda at the Hong Kong Hotel. He wrote nervous letters to San Francisco. This was not the Richard Halliburton of public image, nor was he anybody Richard himself had known—until then. His skin still was rashed with eczema. He watched anxiously as the Chinese workmen leisurely repaired the ship. With Chinese New Year and his search for a crew, it took almost a month to get underway again.

Finally New Year's celebrations were over and workmen resumed repairs to *Sea Dragon*. By the time he finally sailed, Halliburton was two months behind schedule.

To compensate for his loss of crew, Richard hired three Chinese seamen and a Chinese boatswain. Two semi-professional seamen, Ben Flagg and George Petrich, jumped ship to join Halliburton's crew, one from Captain Ahlin's *Coolidge*, the other from Captain Jokstad's *Pierce*.

Halliburton wrote his parents, "Now we'll have March, April, May for our crossing—better than January, February, March." He told them that he still thought he had "a swell idea and that everything is coming out as dreamed." He would be happy to reach California and be rid of "all these burdens and quarrelling seamen." He ended by telling them, "You know how much I love you."

As an old man, John R. Potter recalled that despite the intense stress on him, Richard kept his composure and treated everybody gentlemanly. This was the same man that Gordon Torrey saw as cool and detached, without youthful enthusiasm. In 1986, John R. Potter had different memories of Richard Halliburton than had Gordon Torrey. * He saw a considerate, kind

---

* Although he already had taken Welch's measure, Gordon Torrey went on the initial voyage and found that the junk lurched and wallowed and hove beam-to. Except for Welch and a couple of others, none of the crew was an ocean seaman. After the aborted voyage, Gordon Torrey complained of appendicitis, committed himself to the hospital, and said he was out. He tried to persuade two other Dartmouth men, Chase and Barstow, to leave but they

man, who turned back to Hong Kong so that Potter could be operated on in hospital for his hernia. "I had, and still have, a tremendous respect and admiration for a truly remarkable man." Potter "had recurring and agonizing thoughts, ranging from remorse to guilt . . . for failing to dissuade Dick from making this perilous sea voyage." Potter said that Richard had been given "mostly erroneous advice," presumably by Welch. Potter never saw Halliburton angry, or heard him complain.

Potter recalled that Richard left out the "I"—I want this, I did that. Halliburton's speech typically began with a present participle such as "walking down the street." Potter regarded this as an indicator of Richard as self-effacing. He was also impressed with Halliburton's ability to find something unusual and curious about ordinary things.

---

elected to stay. Torrey had a different take on Halliburton than Potter, who liked Richard.

When a boy, Torrey read Halliburton's books and expected the youthful zest he found in them. Still very young, he had been excited to ship-out with the ultimate adventurer. He anticipated meeting somebody fun-loving, carefree, humorous. On arriving in Hong Kong he found another man. This Richard was driven, grim. He was not fun to be around and Torrey did not understand that Richard was tied in knots with worry. With the strange language, odd smells, and daily news of the advancing Nippon army it was not as Torrey expected. He took a ship back to the states.

Torrey said Richard could have still sailed his junk with family passengers in San Francisco Bay at the Golden Gate International Exposition and without huge risk. *Sea Dragon* could have been hoisted aboard a ship, freighted to Treasure Island, and still enjoy a commercial success. Potter disagreed. He said that carrying the junk on a freighter would have "negated the purpose and meaning of the venture." On his part Torrey believed that the decision to sail her should not have been left to the "whimsy and commercial aspirations of one person." This presumes the others had no free will and were puppets of Halliburton. As for Welch, Torrey shared Potter's opinion of the man and could not understand why Richard had confidence in him.

In a 1987 letter to Michael Blankenship, Torrey recalled those days in Hong Kong. He said the hundred horsepower diesel needed room, which meant that some traditional bulkheads had to be omitted. Not knowing better, Welch did not nay-say Halliburton and also omitted bulkheads to accommodate Richard's living space. He did not argue against the low spoon bow, the type of a Soochow river junk. It was fine for calm, Yangtze river waters but in hard seas the spoon bow would act just like that—a spoon—scooping water as it came over, shattering the skylight, flooding the lower deck, and killing the diesel.

FINAL VOYAGE

Pan-American Airways clipper planes flying across the Pacific were instructed last night to watch for Richard Halliburton and his thirteen companions on the junk Sea Dragon, *unheard from since last Friday morning.* April 1, 1939, *Pittsburgh Press**

Sea Dragon Ship's Company

Lost at Sea on Final Voyage

1. Richard Halliburton.
2. John Wenlock Welch. Captain. Australian. Second mate for United Fruit ships.
3. Paul Mooney. Seaman. Halliburton's companion.
4. George E. Barstow. First mate. Student at Juilliard School of Music, put up $4000 for shares in the corporation, then an additional $1500. Torrey and Barstow landed in Japan Nov 3, 1938. Richard told them to stay in Japan till the first of December.
5. Robert Hill Chase. First mate. Dartmouth senior whose family contributed to the expedition corporation.
6. Henry von Fehren. Engineer. Originally from Germany.
7. Velman E. Fitch. Seaman. Dropped out of the University of Minnesota to see the world.
8. Ben Flagg. First mate. Recent Bowdoin graduate. Missed his ship in Hong Kong and signed on after *Sea Dragon's* aborted voyage.
9. Ralph Granrud. Seaman. Journalist.
10. George Petrich. *Sea Dragon* radioman. Radio operator for Matson Lines and radio operator on a Coast Guard ship on station to monitor Amelia Earhart's Pacific flight.
11. James Sligh. Cook. Wife and two children in Los Angeles. "He has cooked on the ships of a dozen nations."
12. Sun Fook. Boatswain.
13. Kiao Chu. Seaman.
14. Wang Ching-huo. Seaman.
15. Liu Ahsu. Mess boy.
16. Two white Siamese kittens
17. Two Chow puppies

Quit after Aborted Voyage

18. Richard L. Davis, Seaman or engineer. He neither quit nor did he go on the first one. In Halliburton's reports from China, Davis was picked up after the aborted voyage and agreed to go as far as Honolulu. He probably bowed out before the last voyage as Halliburton was uncertain whether he would stop there and, indeed, at sea wired his parents that he would not.
19. Patrick Kelly. Mess boy. Portuguese-American citizen born in Canton, who had never been to America.
20. John R. Potter. First mate. Dartmouth graduate, Maine offshore sailor, and friend of Zola Halliburton, Erle's daughter.
21. Gordon E. Torrey. First mate. Dartmouth graduate and Maine offshore sailor. Torrey and Barstow landed in Japan Nov 3, 1938. Richard told them to stay in Japan till the first of December.

---

* The *Pittsburgh Press* number is unlikely as thirteen is unlucky in nautical tradition. I chose to include it because the *Press* and different newspapers have varying numbers, with the exact number uncertain. Based on the best evidence available from several sources, my list provides what I found.

ONCE MORE INTO THE SEA

After the aborted voyage, Richard tried again on March 4, 1939. The *Sea Dragon* crew waved back at Chinese on shore. The junk must have presented a splendid sight to crowds gathered on the dock. When *Sea Dragon* slipped her moorings at the Kowloon pier, Welch started the diesel and she followed the channel buoys out into the bay. She looked carefree to the sampans floating in the harbor, the liners at dock. A fisherman's family waved at her as they stood on their sampan bobbing in the shadow of a giant British battleship anchored next it. *Sea Dragon's* crew stood topside as her diesel chugged them seaward, her wake gently rocking small boats. A liner sounded her horn in salute to *Sea Dragon* and it echoed across the bay. Sailors stood on the deck of a British frigate and pointed at the junk. Down in the harbor, on other piers, people waved at her and she was a proud sight with her lacquered dragons painted across the transom. Aboard *Sea Dragon*, her crew felt this is it. They were on their way. Some of them might have felt trepidation after all the delays and re-designs but they were committed. In their minds, at least, they had passed the point of no return. Soon they would be out into open water, her wake trailing back in the direction of Hong Kong.

Up on Victoria Peak, perhaps an Englishman and his wife looked down at the busy harbor, noticed the ships and wooden fishing boats, and maybe they saw *Sea Dragon*, tiny, faint in the distance, but if they did they thought nothing of it, for it was merely one craft among many. The crew were a few lives among millions. Back in Kowloon, men, women, and children huddled, refugees from the Japanese Imperial Army. Few of them got up to look at the junk's departure. They were begging for food.

The crew turned away from the stern. Clear of the channels, out in open water, John Welch had Von Fehren shut down the diesel then barked orders to raise the mainsail and watched crewmen hoist it. It luffed as it

346

spread, then snapped smartly into fully billowed canvas. *Sea Dragon* took the wind in her teeth, lurched to her starboard and lifted ahead, her bow knifing through the water. The foresail up, Welch ordered the scarlet mizzen sail raised, watching it flutter then snap out, filled with wind. The breeze felt good and the clouds proclaimed fair weather, at least for the day. As the breeze stiffened, the sails stretched and *Sea Dragon* came about, lurching to port, then her bow straightened ahead with her hull cutting toward the South China Sea.

Maybe George Barstow, a bachelor, thought of the adventure to come and what he would tell his grandchildren one day. We can be sure that Richard thought this would make great material for his next book. He had come through many scrapes and this would be just one more. Halliburton regarded himself as adventurous but not a daredevil. He believed he had taken all necessary precautions. Maybe Welch had other problems but he was a good ship's master, thought Richard. Yes, they were finally on their way. For a few days out, they had sunshine and gentle swells.

Back in Kowloon he had sent Wesley and Nelle, "one more, one last goodbye letter." Without his usual opening, "Dear," it began instead with "Mother and Dad," almost formal. "We sail again in a few hours, far more seaworthy than before. The delay has been heart-breaking, but worth it in added safety. Our crew is far more expert now . . . all our leaks have been plugged and the hull tarred. Our fin keel will keep us from rolling, so we'll be dry and comfortable and even keeled. I'm sorry we have to leave Potter and Torrey behind in the hospital. We have food and water for three months and oil for twenty days running. So we seem to be as prepared as it's possible to be. My spirits have sprung back again, now we are getting away from Hong Kong and its troubles. I'm going to enjoy the trip, and be happy I've gone to such effort to make it. I'm in perfect health, if somewhat weary. Wilfred Crowell writes me there's a big barge anchored in the small ship basin at the Fair and on it a big sign, 'Reserved anchorage for Halliburton's *Sea Dragon*.' So we must hurry and get there. So good bye again. I'll radio you every few days, so you can enjoy and follow the voyage with me. Think of it as wonderful sport, not as something hazardous and foolish. I embrace you all, and will give my sweet mother an extra hug on her birthday." He signed the letter with an "R."

He begins without a "dear" and ends with an initial. He is on edge.

Over the years, his mother must have pulled the letter out of a drawer to read it again and again. Although expressing the need to hurry, it was so hopeful.

HALSEY'S TYPHOON

For an idea of what Halliburton and crew encountered, Halsey's Typhoon offers an example. On December 17, 1944 Admiral William "Bull" Halsey's Task Force 38 met a typhoon that claimed many lives and sank ships. Looking through windows of pilothouses, helmsmen saw water in the air, air in the water. They could not tell where sea ended and sky began. Piles of sea drove horizontally against wheelhouse windows. Wind roared through the rigging. Flags hauled down, only a tiny battle ensign flapped raggedly in the storm. Beaten by the typhoon, some ships were locked in irons, the vessels helpless in the eye of the storm and could not come about to a new direction. Ships could not see one another and a captain's mind was fraught with only one idea—keep to the weather. The bows of small ships, destroyer escorts, plowed into mountains of sea that came crashing down on the wheelhouse.

On aircraft carriers, fighter planes down in the hangar bays tore free of lashings and were hurled into other planes, rupturing fuel tanks and igniting fires. The light carrier *Monterey* was set ablaze at 0911 with fire so intense despite seas washing over the flight deck that it spread below and she quickly lost steerage. On *Monterey* eighteen planes were destroyed or thrown overboard by wind. Another sixteen were almost destroyed. Her ventilation system was badly damaged.

Lieutenant Gerald Ford—one day a US President, then a young officer on *Monterey*—was almost swept overboard. He volunteered to lead a damage control team below. In the bowels of the ship all night, Ford and his men braved stifling smoke and intense heat to put out fires. He had been assigned as athletic officer, assistant navigator and gunnery officer and this, he might have joked years later, was not in his job description.

USS Langley rolled through seventy degrees. A plane broke loose in *San Jacinto*'s hangar and crashed into several other planes. On *Cape Esperance* the

348

flight deck erupted in flames. In heaving seas, the damage control team risked their own lives to put it out and they did. *Kwajalein* rolled so far to port that when she righted, her catwalks came back washing with green water. Flat on the flight deck, crewmen crawled inch by inch to three aircraft torn loose and the men tried to push them from the flight deck before they could do more damage. The men worked and struggled against the storm, expecting any moment to be washed overboard but an hour later they had jettisoned the planes into the ocean.

The destroyer *USS Hull* could not manage the wind and seas. Her helmsman tried hard rudder, engine reversals, everything, but she was locked in irons in huge troughs of ocean. Northerly wind roared over her port beam and swept everything from the deck, whaleboat, depth charges, and rolled her fifty degrees leeward then four hours later it rolled her again at seventy degrees to the lee. Joe Jambor, Chief Electrician's Mate, reported to Chief Quartermaster Archie DeRyckere in the wheelhouse that the hatches were blown stem to stern and water was surging in everywhere. A one hundred ten knot gust kept her horizontal long enough for the sea to flood the pilothouse, then rush down her stacks, drowning the engine, filling the compartments below decks. In very short order she was gone. Eighteen officers and two hundred forty-six men were either trapped in her hull or were swept away by the waves.

Around 1500 on Monday, December 18, 1944, the sky revealed tiny patches of blue. That evening crewmen could glimpse stars in fleeting snatches of sky and the wind dropped to sixty knots. The eye of the storm had passed. The fleet was scattered over the Pacific and only slowly did the ships rejoin one another.

Ninety-three men were rescued including a deck hand swept off the flight deck of *Anzio* by a green sea. Seven hundred seventy-eight sailors were lost or killed while another eighty were injured. One hundred forty-six aircraft were badly damaged or swept overboard. A cruiser, five aircraft carriers, and three destroyers were seriously damaged and out of action.

WISH YOU WERE HERE INSTEAD OF ME

Early on, Sea *Dragon* transmitted messages the weather in its mercy allowed. The crew was blithely ignorant of what was to come. On March 5, 1939 the radio message to Richard's parents expressed his usual optimism and effort at easing their worries,

> RADIO JUNK SEA DRAGON VIA SAN FRANCISCO SAILED
> AGAIN TODAY SOUNDER SHIP BETTER CREW FINE
> WEATHER RADIO SEA DRAGON SAN FRANCISCO POSTAL
> TELEGRAPH HURRYING HOME LOVE

It continued that way, deep into open water and far into the Pacific as reflected in a March 13th message,

> RADIO JUNK SEA DRAGON VIA SAN FRANCISCO
> 1200 MILES AT SEA ALLS WELL

On March 19, 1939, Dale E. Collins, chief mate of the liner *SS President Coolidge* received another message from Welch. "All well," it said. On board the junk, the crew was enjoying fair breeze, scudding clouds, and warm sun. The good weather did not last.

The next message to Richard's parents, also on March 19th suggests either a falling wind or a gathering storm is slowing the junk's progress. Richard is half the distance to Midway Island and behind schedule so after replenishment at Midway, the junk will not pay a port call to Honolulu after all.

> RADIO JUNK SEA DRAGON VIA SAN FRANCISCO

HALFWAY MIDWAY   ARRIVING APRIL FIFTH   SKIPPING
HONOLULU   WRITE CARE PANAMERICAN MIDWAY
AIRMAIL   LOVE

Skipping Honolulu. The San Francisco International Exposition and his
creditors were on Richard's mind because *Sea Dragon* was not making the
progress he had planned on.

Clouds closed in the sky and on March 21ˢᵗ the sky turned grey and the
waves changed from chops to swells. Washing on to *Sea Dragon*, they piled
over her rails. On March 23ʳᵈ she was making five knots as she rocked
through growing waves. That day on *Coolidge* Collins read another radio
transmission from Welch. It read,

FROM 0200 TO 1030 GCT HAD S'LY GALE   HEAVY RAIN
SQUALLS   HIGH SEAS   BAROMETER 29.46   RAN WITH
DOUBLE-REEFED FORESAIL   1100 GCT WIND CHANGED
TO WEST   FORCE SIX   BAROMETER 29.54 RISING
TRUE COURSE 100   SPEED 5.5 KNOTS
POSITION 1200 GCT 31-10N 155 155-00E   ALL WELL
WHEN CLOSER MAY WE AVAIL OURSELVES OF YOUR
DIRECTION FINDER   REGARDS WELCH

After hearing the junk's message, Collins greeted *Sea Dragon* and
suggested the two vessels rendezvous, given good weather. He promised
fresh fruit and vegetables.

On March 22ⁿᵈ a new message was sent from Welch to *Coolidge* and with
a different tone, again asking for navigation assistance.

SOUTHERLY GALE   HEAVY RAIN SQUALLS   HIGH SEA
BAROMETER 29.46   RISING   TRUE COURSE 100   SPEED 5.5
KNOTS   POSITION 1200 GCT 31.1 NORTH 155.00 EAST
ALL WELL WHEN CLOSER MAY WE AVAIL OURSELVES OF
YOUR DIRECTION FINDER   REGARDS WELCH

Welch again asked to use a direction finder because celestial navigation
was impossible with cloudy skies both day and night.

As the United States currently defines its categories on the Beaufort
scale, a force 6 or 7 wind causes a small craft advisory. At 6, the wind
speed is twenty-five to thirty miles per hour. A sailor sees large waves with
foamy crests and spray. At force 7, sea heaps up and foam begins to streak.
On land, trees are swaying. This is considered a moderate gale or a near

gale. A force 8 is the threshold for a fresh gale, with 9 a strong gale as small trees are blown over. Its wind speed is forty-seven to fifty-four miles per hour.

From 10 through 12, say your prayers if you are in a sailing yacht or junk. At 10, waves are very high with curling crests and large patches of foam. The sea turns white from crests. Waves tumble down on a ship, tons of water smashing onto it. On land, mature trees are uprooted and fall on house roofs. 11 is a violent storm, with exceptionally high waves and foam seemingly everywhere, driven by the wind. Spindrift fills the air so that a helmsman can barely see ten feet ahead. On land, the shingles of house roofs are torn off. This is a violent storm. The wind speed of force 11 is sixty-four to seventy-two miles per hour.

Blowing at greater than seventy-three miles per hour, force 12 is a typhoon. (Called a hurricane in the United States.) A helmsman struggles to keep the bow into the weather. He sees waves towering over him. That is, if he can see, for he finds nothing but white and foam everywhere, nothing but walls of water-laden air. On land, windows shatter and walls collapse on mobile homes, barns, and sheds.

Sea Dragon's weather quickly changed from force 6 to 12. Welch reefed sails and cast a sea anchor to hold the bow steady against the current. Unwittingly, they sailed toward the eye of the typhoon.

Collins was on a luxury liner; Welch, on a junk. By the time *Coolidge* battened down for the approaching typhoon, the seas had built into forty-foot crests promising more evil. *Coolidge* was six hundred fifty-four feet long, and cost $8 million to build. The twenty-two thousand ton liner had made twenty-one knots during its shakedown cruise but in that weather Captain K.A. Ahlin slowed the ship to under six knots and even then she plowed into troughs, her bow buried under tons of water. Her screws churned air as the hull pitched and rolled between towering waves. The ship's crew lashed all objects potentially projectile.[*]

Leaving the *Coolidge* dining hall and the first class smoking room, frightened gentlemen and ladies retired to their staterooms but were still flung about. Many were injured after being slammed like rag dolls against bulkheads. Over half became seasick. They had planned on an easy passage to Japan, a route kept open by the U.S. Department of Commerce

---

[*] Two years later American diplomatic relations with Japan ceased, and *Coolidge* dropped anchor in Hong Kong's harbor to take aboard United States citizens fearful of the Japanese Imperial Army at the city's doorstep. On December 7, 1941, the emperor's troops attacked the city's British garrison. The Imperial Navy attacked Pearl Harbor on the same date when Admiral Nagumo's task force of first-line aircraft carriers launched two waves of Zeroes, Vals and Kates to destroy the ships on Battleship Row and the planes at Hickam and Wheeler airfields. On that date other Japanese forces struck the Philippines, Singapore and Simla. The American public only remembers Pearl Harbor but Asia remembers it all.

despite the Nippon invasion of Manchuria.

Coolidge had also carried Halliburton from San Francisco to Hong Kong and its crew knew him, his skipper, John Welch, as well as Henry Von Fehren, the engineer, and the young men Gordon Barstow and Gordon Torrey.*

Either the night before or on Friday morning March 24th, Collins received his last radio transmission from Sea *Dragon.*

CAPTAIN JOHN WELCH OF THE SEA DRAGON TO LINER
PRESIDENT COOLIDGE   SOUTHERLY GALES   RAIN
SQUALLS   LEE RAIL UNDER WATER   WET BUNKS
HARDTACK   BULLY BEEF   HAVING WONDERFUL TIME
WISH YOU WERE HERE INSTEAD OF ME

Weathering mountainous seas, the junk was moving into her doom. Then deep in the typhoon, radio contact with *Sea Dragon* was lost.

Coolidge had only a fifty-watt radio in ship-to-shore with land operators of Mackay Radio and Telegraph.   Although not much, fifty watts was standard for those times, and in electrical storms its super-heterodyne vacuum tubes failed to transmit clearly.   Pan American Clipper pilots could route around the bad weather and in contact with Mackay radio operators on Guam they were told that the Guam receivers picked up words from *Sea Dragon* garbled by static.   Because of electrical storms it is possible that the junk continued transmitting unheard by anybody but this was not likely as the force of the typhoon probably sank her before that.

As for *Coolidge*, the ocean liner was "experiencing very high seas" with water "fifty feet high."   The liner bobbed and tossed like a tin can.   Chief mate Collins noted that *Sea Dragon* was experiencing similar weather for "the storm covered a huge area according to weather reports."   By his estimate, *President Coolidge* was no more than four hundred miles from the junk on March 24th.   On the 25th they should have passed within a few miles of *Sea Dragon*, and Captain, K. A. Ahlin, who took his first command in 1894, set lookouts on that day.   He ordered two men for every one normally assigned and told them to watch very carefully.   Collins reported that they "never sighted as much as a stick floating."

---

* Four years before, to beef up the Philippine army against the Japanese threat, *Coolidge* carried General Douglas Macarthur and aide, Major Dwight D. Eisenhower, for the General's new assignment as de facto Commander in Chief of Philippine Armed Forces, an arrangement between Presidents Quezon and Roosevelt.   In May 1942 it would carry Macarthur and Quezon to San Francisco after the Japanese roundly defeated them at Corregidor, then with prodding bayonets gathered the surrendered troops, American and Filipino, for the infamous Bataan Death.

Lost at Sea, the headlines proclaimed. This was big news. Another famous adventurer had disappeared. The year before, Amelia Earhart with her navigator Fred Noonan had ditched a Lockheed Vega somewhere in the Pacific and was lost to everything but history. Before *Sea Dragon's* disappearance, across the continent, San Francisco to New York, families had huddled in living rooms, bent to their radio sets to hear of the junk's nine thousand mile progress toward the San Francisco World's Fair, opening in spring of that year.

On March 29, 1939, the *Evening Independent* of St Petersburg, Florida headlined a report from San Francisco, "Richard Halliburton Is Feared Lost at Sea." It went on, "S.W. Fenton, marine superintendent of the Mackay Radio Company here, expressed fear today for the safety of Richard Halliburton, author, and ten other men aboard the Chinese junk *Sea Dragon*, en route from Hong Kong to San Francisco and unheard from since last Friday." The paper explained that the Mackay Company had scheduled regular radio transmissions with the junk but had lost contact Friday morning about when a typhoon hit. The junk was two thousand four hundred miles from Hong Kong bound for Midway Island. The article explains, "The *Sea Dragon* was scheduled to reach Midway Island April 5."

Also on March 29th in Dubuque, Iowa, *The Telegraph-Herald* stated that the "75 foot craft, with its crew of ten Americans and four Chinese, was approximately one thousand miles west of Midway," and that "all ships, meanwhile, have been asked to keep a watch for the craft."[*]

---

[*] Even for *Coolidge*, time was running short as war clouds gathered. After the attack on Pearl Harbor, the United States Navy made the ship a troop carrier, stripping her plush interior and painting her hull a haze gray. The *USS President Coolidge* met her end on October 26, 1942 when Japanese mines sank her in Espiritu Santo harbor.

Today she lies on the bottom of the harbor as a tourist attraction for divers. Swimming among reef fish, barracuda, lion fish, and moray eels they explore holds and decks to discover her military side with helmets, guns, cannons, Jeeps, and trucks as well as her luxury liner side with chandeliers, mosaic tile, and a lovely porcelain figure of a woman riding a unicorn. War has forgotten her. A coral reef and the fish have claimed her.

SEARCHING THE SEA

On April 4, 1939 Richard's parents petitioned the Navy Department to search for their son. The search for *Sea Dragon* began officially on the 21st of May 1939 when the heavy cruiser *USS Astoria* commanded by Captain Richmond K. Turner was ordered to hoist anchor out of Guam to look for the junk and her crew. Two months after the disappearance she arrived on station. To find Halliburton and crew, the cruiser began a boxed search of every quadrant of one hundred fifty-two thousand square miles in the coordinates where radio contact had been lost. Ship's company learned that a celebrated author was missing. His name was Richard Halliburton. Officers and men knew him through his books they read when boys.*

Just before dawn each day *Astoria* launched four floatplanes from its catapults, both port and starboard. The four Curtiss SOC-1 Sea Gull's were shot from launch rails, two planes off the port, two starboard. The pilot and radioman-gunner peered down on the sea, lulled by the endless drone of the radial engine, noticing their shadow skimming over the waves. The pilots followed prepared grids and criss-crossed the sea one square at a time. The grids, though, were imposed, a bit of human reason on an indifferent, mindless ocean. Sunlight streaming into the cockpit, warming it, the men slid open the canopy to let wind rush in and to better see any specks on the water.

The radioman-gunner sometimes lifted binoculars if he spotted something and told the pilot to circle lower for a closer look. Under the wings, waves rippled in their shadow, each forever changing, reaching in a chain to Calcutta, Cairo, Naples, Sierra Leone, Hong Kong, San Francisco.

---

* A few years later *Astoria* herself would be lost, sunk by nightlong salvos from a battle line of Japanese cruisers at Savo Island. As for Turner, promoted to admiral, he had his 1961 obituary in *Time* magazine after he choked to death on a piece of chicken.

Each said nothing about the fate of *Sea Dragon*. Each day they returned, taxied on to a floating sled, and were hoisted aboard the cruiser, again no luck. Another coordinates box had been checked off the quadrant list but nothing was found. Eight men in the four planes searched daily. Hour after hour they peered down at vast expanses of ocean reaching from horizon to horizon. Lookouts from *Astoria* were posted on the bow and in the crow's nest as she boxed the ocean. The search was called off on May 28 th.

By June 8, 1939 in San Pedro, California, Navy headquarters CINCPACFLT, Commander in Chief Pacific Fleet, came to an official position after a formal board of inquiry. Halliburton had been lost at sea.

At first, both Navy and Coast Guard had been leery of his disappearance, regarding it as potentially a stunt for publicity. He had faked disappearance before. Newspapers once reported him missing after swimming the Hellespont between Europe and Asia; yet he turned up safe and sound. CINCPACFLT finally concluded it was no stunt and he was dead.* Case closed.

---

* When he was reported missing at sea some did think it a publicity stunt. Living that year in Boot Leg Canyon near Halliburton's Hangover House, Tennessee Williams wrote that he believed it a hoax.

THE END

His parents never believed it a stunt and slowly gave up hope until, finally, on October 5, 1939, the Chancery Court in Memphis, Tennessee declared Richard Halliburton officially dead. Wesley and Nelle requested the judgment because they had waited long enough. They wanted it over so the healing could begin but for the world a wound was opened when, the month before, World War II began with Hitler's invasion of Poland.

At first, his parents could only rent Hangover House, Richard's eccentric Laguna Beach, California home. Finally, in 1941 they sold it for $7,500 to the only bidder, a Marine Corps aviator, Wallace T. Scott. Halliburton had built it for $36,000 in 1937, an expense they had warned him against. He had even taken out a mortgage against it in order to help finance the Chinese junk expedition. Today the house is worth millions.

At age twenty-six, he had earned $70,000 a year from sales of his book *The Royal Road to Romance*. His parents found his estate to consist of four modest life insurance policies and about $9,000 in royalties from publisher Bobbs-Merrill. They learned Paul Mooney was a policy beneficiary but he was lost at sea so the proceeds went to Richard's estate.

They needed the insurance policies to pay off his debts but had also asked the chancery court to pronounce Richard dead because it would mean closure for them. He was gone and declared so in public record. They could get on with their lives, holding memories of their son while the world slowly forgot him.

In 1945, a wooden keel with several ribs washed up on shore at Pacific Beach, California. Richard's mother, Nelle, was contacted where she was vacationing in Tucson Arizona and she could not be persuaded it was all that remained of *Sea Dragon*. Not that she hadn't accepted his death but that she wanted a better explanation than derelict wood.

She lifted the phone in March 1939 and heard the news about Richard's disappearance at sea. She thanked the caller, hung up and told Wesley that their son was gone. Wesley bluffed, "They'll make it," adding "You can't sink a junk." To himself, he whispered "Goodbye, son. It's all over now."

In a sense, Richard's end was fitting. A settled life seems impossible given his conflicting temperament. He could not continually endure a measured pace despite writing of his need for it. Ambivalence marked him in middle age and he was split. Against a desire for peace and rest was the call of more adventure. The horizon had become a habit and he built Hangover House to see it as he looked out a window. Even there, it lured, would not stop enticing.

Years before, in the 1920s, the Princeton Alumni Bulletin declared, "Dick Halliburton is going to be like any other mortal with a home, wife, and kids."

Years later, in the 1960s, Wesley Halliburton told James Cortese, "Richard was a meteor." He "blazed across the heavens" and then "was gone."

I do not want to die in bed. Richard Halliburton

EPILOGUE

Nelle got through another decade and a half after that. She heard the news of the attack on Pearl Harbor. She listened to the announcement of FDR's death. She welcomed VE Day and then VJ Day, after the atomic bombing of Hiroshima and Nagasaki.* She watched television—Milton Berle, Ed Sullivan, Jackie Gleason, Lewis and Martin. She read that Harry Truman had sent American troops into Korea. As a Democrat, she voted for Adlai Stevenson rather than Eisenhower. All those mornings, all those evenings with Richard's pictures on the walls and tables. She looked at them and at Wesley Junior, also gone long ago. On June 19, 1955 she died.

On August 21, 1910, Wesley senior had written to himself, "I am 40 years young today. Passing from the 30s into the 40s is like passing from the teens into the 20s. I hope I may live 40 more years." He had more than his wish. On October 23, 1960, the *Nashville Tennessean* reported that Wesley lived alone and that "from time to time, he sallies forth into the world, following the footsteps of his son. Last winter he went to Machu Picchu." Maybe he emulated his son as a kind of tribute.

In a statement to the press in 1939, Wesley said, "The world is not as beautiful as when Richard wandered it. The destruction of the old world, in this coming war, the world he loved most, would have made him desperately unhappy."

Without wife, without children or grandchildren, Wesley died in 1965, just as the Civil Rights movement appeared in public consciousness. He had admitted to a friend that he was very lonely and very tired. He didn't think much of Elvis Presley and—and though they were both celebrated Memphians—he resented any comparison of the hip-swinger to his son.

One evening in the late 1950s James Cortese sat with Wesley in the old

---

* VE: Victory in Europe; VJ: Victory over Japan.

359

man's study. They sipped Jack Daniels and gazed at the shadows growing on the walls. Wesley picked up a picture of Richard taken all those long years before in front of the Taj Mahal. His son wears a turbine on his head, his arms akimbo, his feet spread as if he could straddle the world. The old man pointed at the picture and said, "Doesn't he look spunky!," and then added, "His life might be compared to a Greek tragedy, blessed by the gods with youth, enthusiasm, talent, the spark that brings renown and glory, but destined to fly too high and die."

Wesley donated $400,000 to a Memphis college for a Gothic bell tower in his son's name. On Oct 19, 1962, the day the Cuban Missile Crisis erupted, *The Sou'wester,* announced that Halliburton Tower had been dedicated at Southwestern College in Memphis—later to become Rhodes. The school paper explained that at the dedication Halliburton's Princeton classmate, James Penfield Seiberling, remembered him as a person with "strengths of mind and spirit" akin to genius but despite that "he was still a very human person" because "for him life was something more than breathing, eating, drinking and sleeping, over and over again. Rather, it was a precious adventure of the mind and spirit to be experienced to the full." President of Seiberling Rubber, Penfield died in 1982. Mike, the sometime dreamer, as Richard described, him, was also there. Long before, in a 1941 interview with a reporter for *The Kansas City Star,* he recalled Richard. Mike said that Halliburton often visited the Hockaday's in their home "when lecture tours or travels brought him through Kansas City." He added that Richard "was here at Christmas time before his last trip." Mike died in 1993, age ninety-four, retired as vice president of an investment firm. As for the Gothic bell tower, it has a plaque with these words: "To Richard Halliburton. Traveler—Author—Lecturer. Born 1900—Lost at Sea 1939."

"When you saw him on the lecture platform," Hockaday said, "you saw a colorful fellow, dressed up for the part and something of a poser. He felt that was a necessary part of his build-up. When you saw him out of that role, as my wife and I did, you found an infinitely simpler and entirely charming gentleman."

Hockaday said, "He loved people. I remember the first time I introduced him to my wife. In five minutes he was sitting on the floor beside the fireplace, talking to her and eagerly discovering what sort of person she is, it was if she had had known him always. He was the same way with our boys, Dick Hockaday and Byron Spencer Hockaday." Mike recalled his friend as somebody far from the public persona while the public knew just the man who did what they could only read about.

At first, people did not let go of him easily. As late as 1941 they still speculated on what happened to both Richard Halliburton and Amelia Earhart. Some thought she had been captured by the Japanese on some remote island and the same had happened to Richard. But there was evidence for what happened to Halliburton: Welch's messages to *Coolidge* and *Coolidge*'s report to the press. There was none for Amelia, although she appeared on the public scene long after Richard and disappeared before he did.

The mind loves mystery and the pieces could not be fitted together for Earhart. She remained in public memory while he faded. That is not to say it happened in a brief span. Over the years, *The Royal Road to Romance* and other books by Richard Halliburton were still checked out of libraries until new generations came along and the books gradually began collecting dust on shelves.

For all his fame and success he was a modest man. He told his mother that if the public remembered him at all it would be for two things. He lectured at ladies' tea parties and he once claimed to have dived into a reflecting pool at the Taj Mahal that was three inches deep.

Even that has been forgotten.

Richard Halliburton life mask
Courtesy Rhodes College

Headstone at family plot
Forest Hill Cemetery, Memphis

Historic Marker
Brownsville, Tennessee

Halliburton Tower
Rhodes College

Halliburton columns with headstones, including Mary G. Hutchison

Moye Stephens, 24, Richard, 30, in LA, about to embark on global flight

Moye & Richard dressed for cold, with Flying Carpet

Pancho Barnes as shown
on 1926 pilot's license

Elly Beinhorn

In French-style Kepis, Persian officers
look on as Moye repairs Elly's Klemm

Elly Beinhorn German postage

Richard & Moye by Flying Carpet, 1932

Lady Sylvia Brook (White Ranee), center, surrounded by daughters Valerie (left) and Elizabeth (right), Richard, (left) & Moye (right)

John Welch in Hong Kong

Richard & Sea Dragon

Richard nursemaids boy
at Chichen Itza

With little girl in Borneo

Tramping through Vosges to Alps   Ophelia, Otto, & Richard
Both photos by Mike Hockaday

366

Richard's Lawrenceville
class ode

Richard at Lawrenceville

Richard in his 30s, as celebrity
Courtesy Rhodes College

MISCELLANY

(1) *The Eagle*, Reading, Pennsylvania, January 27, 1935, a column titled, "As Seen by Her," by Lilly Marsh. Richard Halliburton "is very nice looking. He has all of his hair—a nice grade of wavy auburn—and his swimming and mountain climbing and what not have certainly not done his figure any harm. He speaks with a pleasant if unidentifiable accent, and has the kind of charm that mows down audiences all in a minute. In all honesty, it is only fair to admit, that he could probably speak on the dreariest, dullest subject in the world, and still hold the attention of his listeners. He is very attractive. He has a great deal of personality, and I suppose it would be asking a little too much to require of him a sense of humor, also. We can't have supermen walking the earth. (There is besides the possibility that a lecture tour would knock every ounce of humour of even a super man. Maybe he has one.)"

(2) Video of John Booth Interviewed by Stan Welsh, March 6, 1994. Rhodes College archives.

In the video, John Booth wears a bow tie, with grey suit, and a Band-Aid on the bridge of his nose. In the background, palm leaves wave in the breeze. Booth is seated outdoors, probably a backyard. He tells the camera that he is a retired Unitarian minister and that he made films. Booth also toured as a professional musician. He played in Rio de Janeiro. He became travelogue filmmaker and speaker because of Richard Halliburton and he and Halliburton exchanged letters over the years. Booth saw seven or eight Halliburton lectures and found they were mainly duplicates of one another. In his early career Halliburton used glass slides in his lectures.

The influence of Richard Halliburton on John Booth was enormous. Booth traveled the world. He went to Rio de Janeiro, to the Rajong River in Sarawak. He lived in jungle long houses. He traveled in Indonesia. He met Anthony Brooke in Singapore in the late 1950s. Brooke's uncle was the last reigning White Rajah of Sarawak. The nephew said his uncle could not run the government because of war ravages and that the British took it over.

He met Richard when he was a student at Cleveland Heights High in

Cleveland, Ohio. Halliburton was there for a lecture on *The Royal Road to Romance.* Booth did not interview Richard at this time. When Halliburton walked to the lectern, girls shrieked as they later did with Frank Sinatra. He had charisma, recalled Booth, and was an "extra handsome young man." Richard was introduced by the school principal. Halliburton talked about climbing the Matterhorn. His punch line was Mike Hockaday spitting.

After Ohio, John Booth's family moved to Hamilton, Ontario, Canada. Halliburton lectured at Eaton auditorium in Toronto in the fall of 1932 or 1933. The boy sent Halliburton a note asking for a meeting. Before that, he had sent Richard a photograph of himself atop a totem pole in British Columbia, waving to the totem gods.

He went back stage to meet Halliburton and found eight or ten people in line. When he finally got to speak with Richard he identified himself as the one who had sent the photograph. Richard said he remembered it and asked him to stand aside. When done with the greeting line, Halliburton invited John Booth to dine. Sitting at a restaurant table, Richard glanced through the letter Booth had sent him and the photograph fell out, leading Booth to conclude Halliburton hadn't seen the picture after all. They talked one hour.

Once, when Halliburton was in Detroit, he called a stagehand to say he was John Booth, a friend of Halliburton, and wanted Richard to call him. The stagehand said, Who? John Booth repeated his name. The stagehand thought he was a wacko claiming to be John Wilkes Booth. John did not get to visit Richard because Halliburton did not receive the message. Next day, he saw Halliburton at the Cadillac Hotel in Detroit. On seeing him, Richard laughed. He explained that Booth called at the same time Richard was discussing John Wilkes Booth.

Planning the *Sea Dragon* voyage, Richard said to Booth that he would have an auto manufacturer, Buick, sponsor him. Buick would have a regular weekly radio program on the progress of the junk. Richard added that this would be a big help because the expedition was very expensive. Later, Booth found Halliburton glum. Richard told him it was off with Buick. Richard and the Buick people were making good progress at a meeting table when somebody said, "junk." Even though the junk was a Chinese boat, as they thought about it, they did not like the association of their product with the word "junk." The project was nixed because of a word.

Booth was in Panama in 1936 in a hotel on the Atlantic side. He asked a hotel clerk if the man remembered Halliburton. The clerk said that at first they were all derisive. Richard had to come back to this hotel for the first half of his trip. His helpers brought him in blistered, haggard, dead tired. He could barely walk and could not sleep. He was a thin man and not athletically built. After that, they praised Richard Halliburton to the skies.

Booth said Halliburton's critics were off base. Richard told him that he tried to give his audience a bouquet of roses. "I give them the roses with the thorns cut off."

(3) Seventy-four years after she said goodbye to Richard and Moye, in 2003, Elly Beinhorn sat in a German retirement home for an interview with a journalist. On March 30th of that year a photograph shows her on her ninety-sixth birthday, a petite, well-coiffed lady who recalled for the journalist her flight into Africa, across other continents and over oceans and that she had no radio and could rely only on compass, experience, and the seat of her pants, the sensation most trusted by pilots of her era.

Bernd, her son, a German orthopedist, was there to assist. He prodded his mother's aging mind by pointing out an airplane in a photograph as a Heinkel. She said it was not because she only flew Klemms. He did not correct her.

As the journalist interviewed the ninety-six year old lady, she recalled so many names, names unknown or forgotten today. Professor Eberan-Eberhorst, technical director of race car development, Auto Union. Professor Ferdinand Porsche, inventor of Hitler's Volkswagen, or People's Car, and the fancier one, the sleek vehicle that is his namesake. She mentioned many others but had forgotten much. She did not mention Richard Halliburton. Halliburton wrote an introduction to her book, *Flying Girl*. He said that "Elly was an expert mechanic,' and that "cylinders, sparkplugs, and piston rings were just so much knitting to her. She thought nothing of standing an entire day in her overalls, with monkey-wrench and oil can, dismembering engines. But when sundown came, she'd disappear for half an hour and emerge in evening dress, looking so lovely, so fragrant, so feminine, that Stephens and I were enchanted all over again each time."

Elly Beinhorn died on November 28, 2007 at 100 years old in a home for the elderly near Munich, Germany. A German obituary stated that after the funeral service the family received condolences in Ottobrunn, near Munich. It explained that in 1936 she married Bernd Rosemeyer, the most successful Auto Union Grand Prix driver and that she would be buried next him in the Dahlem district of Berlin.

(4) Born February 21, 1906, Moye Stephens retired to Ensenada, Baja California, Mexico, and on December 10, 1995 died in Calistoga, the Napa Valley, California. In his old age, Moye thought about how the course of his future changed. He thought back on those days with Richard, or as test pilot of the Flying Wing, or as a founder of Northrop Aviation. His life came close to many might-have-beens. He might not have given flying lessons to Howard Hughes. He might not have chummed with barnstormers and World War I aces such as Sandy Sandblom, Leo Nomis, Bud Creech, Eddie Bellande, Frank Clarke, Ross Hadley, and Pancho

Barnes. He might not have known movie stars Richard Arlen, Ramón Novarro, Sue Carol, Reginald Denny, Wallace Beery, and Dolores Del Rio—or movie executives Cecil B. DeMille, Victor Fleming, Howard Hawks, and Howard Hughes. He might have lived out his life in Brazil, where he started an aviation business with his young family. He might have crashed and died as a movie stunt pilot. He might have graduated as a lawyer from Stanford University. He might have joined the law office of his father and grandfather. Most of all, he might have gone straight home after classes rather than stopping to admire the planes at Rogers Airport.

Looking back on his life, Moye Stephens thought about events that decided his future, a future he could have foreseen as stable and predictable had he not accepted Halliburton's offer. He did accept it and because of that he had a life far more interesting.

Index

ABOUT THE AUTHOR

A husband and father, John Alt has not traveled the world like Richard Halliburton but he traveled it and knows the vagabond lure of horizons, though modest in comparison. In his life he has manned flight decks of aircraft carriers, swept floors as a janitor, adjusted insurance as an agent, overseen divisions as a manager, and taught English as a professor. Born in Iowa City, he holds a PhD in English, grew up in the San Francisco Bay Area and, apart from travels, has lived in Arizona, Kansas, Virginia, Texas, Georgia, Germany, and The Netherlands. While the outward course of his life took him afar, the inward course kept him near the same place as he circled back on central tenets—he holds no sword of orthodoxy but above all believes in human caring, conscience, kindness, self-control, self-responsibility, and respect for others.

Made in the USA
San Bernardino, CA
21 April 2013